Martin Ravndal Hauge teaches in the Institute of Biblical Studies at the University of Oslo.

JOURNAL FOR THE STUDY OF THE OLD TESTAMENT
SUPPLEMENT SERIES
323

Sheffield Academic Press

The Descent from the Mountain

Narrative Patterns in Exodus 19–40

Martin Ravndal Hauge

Journal for the Study of the Old Testament
Supplement Series 323

Published by Sheffield Academic Press Ltd
Mansion House
19 Kingfield Road
Sheffield S11 9AS
England
www.SheffieldAcademicPress.com

Typeset by Sheffield Academic Press
and
Printed on acid-free paper in Great Britain
by Antony Rowe Ltd, Chippenham, Wiltshire

British Library Cataloguing in Publication Data

A catalogue record for this book is available
from the British Library

ISBN 1-84127-177-2

CONTENTS

Acknowledgments 7
Abbreviations 8
Introduction 11

Chapter 1
THE OUTLINES OF A STORY 21
1. The Encounter Episode 21
2. The Structure of Encounter Episodes 34
3. The Structure of the Three Theophanic Episodes 44
4. The Shape of Exodus 32–34 64

Chapter 2
THE MAIN STORY: THE ENCOUNTER BELOW AND THE NEW THEOPHANIC FIGURES 97
1. The Divine Mountain and the Human-Made Tent 97
2. The Theophanic Movement—Divine and Human 109
3. The Divine Descent and the Participation of the Non-Ascenders 120
4. Conclusions 139

Chapter 3
THE PARALLEL STORY: THE APOTHEOSIS OF MOSES 156
1. The Double Function of Exodus 32–34 156
2. The Apotheosis of Moses 164
3. The Hero Dismissed and Exalted—The Parallels of David and Elijah 174
4. Conclusions 182

Chapter 4
THE COMPOSITIONAL TECHNIQUE OF PARALLELISM 190
1. The Day of Erecting the Dwelling: Leviticus 8–10 190

2. Conclusions 200
3. The Day of Erecting the Dwelling: Numbers 7–9 209
4. Conclusions 238

Chapter 5
THE CYCLICAL CHARACTER OF THE SACRED EVENTS 247
1. Exodus 18 247
2. Numbers 11 and Exodus 18 258
3. Numbers 13–14 278
4. Numbers 13–14 and Exodus 14 296
5. Conclusions 308

Postscript
THE READER AS WHORE AND POTENTIAL SAINT 323

Bibliography 339
Index of References 345
Index of Authors 361

ACKNOWLEDGMENTS

Important parts of this book were conceived and tentatively given shape at Tantur Ecumenical Institute for Theological Studies in Jerusalem, where I stayed as 'scholar in residence' during the spring term of 1996. The kindness of the staff, the fellowship of the Tantur community, and the daily impressions of the gardens turning from winter into spring, are still with me, and I address my thanks to 'Father Tom' Stransky, the rector of Tantur at that time, and Sister Marianora, the head librarian.

My efforts have been sustained by the collegiate spirit of the old testamentlers at the Theological Faculty of the University of Oslo. For representatives of this spirit I name Professor Hans M. Barstad and Research Fellow Kristin Joachimsen. The former for his professional brilliance and his personal wisdom, both aspects indispensable when I was wringing my hands at some impossible obstacle. The latter for shouldering with me some intolerably heavy burdens, and also for sharing much laughter and a common vision.

I am doubly grateful to Sheffield Academic Press, both for accepting my work into the Supplement Series, and for ensuring that it represents the best of what can be provided by this author!

Finally, I am indebted to Dr John Day of Lady Margaret Hall, Oxford. Patiently identifying deficient English and sloppiness, and mercifully suggesting substitutes, he has also made the foggier aspects of my observations, hopefully, a little clearer.

ABBREVIATIONS

AB	Anchor Bible
AnBib	Analecta Biblica
ATD	Das Alte Testament Deutsch
Bib	*Biblica*
BJS	Brown Judaic Studies
BKAT	Biblischer Kommentar: Altes Testament
BZAW	Beihefte zur *ZAW*
CBOTS	Coniectanea Biblica, Old Testament Series
FOTL	The Forms of the Old Testament Literature
FRLANT	Forschungen zur Religion und Literatur des Alten und Neuen Testaments
HAT	Handbuch zum Alten Testament
HUCA	*Hebrew Union College Annual*
ICC	International Critical Commentary
Int	*Interpretation*
JAOS	*Journal of the American Oriental Society*
JBL	*Journal of Biblical Literature*
JQR	*Jewish Quarterly Review*
JR	*Journal of Religion*
JSOTSup	*Journal for the Study of the Old Testament*, Supplement Series
JSSM	Journal of Semitic Studies, Monographs
JTS	*Journal of Theological Studies*
MTS	Marburger Theologische Studien
NCB	New Century Bible
OBO	Orbis Biblicus et Orientalis
Or	*Orientalia*
OTL	Old Testament Library
POS	Pretoria Orienta Series
SANT	Studien zum Alten und Neuen Testament
SBLMS	Studies in Biblical Literature Monograph Series
SB	Sources bibliques
SBS	Stuttgarter Bibelstudien
SJLA	Studies in Judaism in Late Antiquity
SJOT	*Scandinavian Journal of the Old Testament*
TBü	Theologische Bücherei
VT	*Vetus Testamentum*

WBC	Word Biblical Commentary
WMANT	Wissenschaftliche Monographien zum Alten und Neuen Testament
ZAW	*Zeitschrift für die alttestamentliche Wissenschaft*

INTRODUCTION

This study has its origins in an offshoot from an earlier work on the 'Individual Psalms'. Searching for narrative parallels, I found some connections between the I-figure of the Psalms and the roles of Moses and the people in the book of Exodus. Aspects of the Exodus story seemed highly meaningful when read as a narrative application of the motif structure in the Psalms.[1] But gradually, the comparative reading was accompanied by a growing feeling of dissatisfaction. While fruitful for my immediate aims, the very process of comparison made me ignore both the depths as well as the delicacy of the narrative exposition. Such qualities tend to be disregarded when the reading is too forcefully directed by interests imported from the reading of other texts. So I decided to return to the Exodus texts in order to read them for their own sake as a more 'passive' reader, open to a process in which the flow of materials would find its own course.

This story also implies a certain ideal of reading, as well as an acknowledgment that the ancient texts are potentially 'active' also for a modern reader. Negatively, this acknowledgment implies the renunciation of a reading too protected against surprises from the textual reality. Concretely, this refers to the tradition of Pentateuchal criticism with its fateful emphasis on categories of 'original' and 'secondary',[2] which in turn are connected to problems of text production and producers. After the dissolution[3] of the J source and the corresponding

1. M.R. Hauge, *Between Sheol and Temple: Motif Structure and Function in the I-Psalms* (JSOTSup, 178; Sheffield: Sheffield Academic Press, 1995).

2. Cf. H.M. Barstad, 'History and the Hebrew Bible', in L.L. Grabbe (ed.), *Can a 'History of Israel' be Written?* (JSOTSup, 245; Sheffield: Sheffield Academic Press, 1997), pp. 45-46, on a parallel example of 'the strongly genetic approach of classical historicism'.

3. Either in the literal sense as illustrated by R. Rendtorff, *Das überlieferungsgeschichtliche Problem des Pentateuch* (BZAW, 147; Berlin: W. de Gruyter, 1977); or by the demise of J as the classically early pre-exilic source illustrated by R.N. Whybray, *The Making of the Pentateuch: A Methodological Study* (JSOTSup, 53;

demise of the classical phenomenology of criticism, one might have expected a period in which alternative categories would be sought. But rather quickly, the traditional perception of the texts as compilations of older and younger materials has reasserted itself as the basic *datum* for the reading.[4] New terms of analysis might indicate that the categories of classical criticism have been changed. The emphasis on the creative significance of the redactors[5] and the final shape of the composition seems to represent a new situation. The concept of the texts as the result of mechanical 'additions' has been changed into more organic concepts, for example of 'repetition'[6] or an editorial process connected to categories of 'macrostructural' coherency.[7] Even the very effects of the narrative process itself for the shaping of the materials have been introduced as relevant for the discussion.[8] But fundamentally the new terms of analysis[9] reflect the traditional impression of the texts. The

Sheffield: JSOT Press, 1987) and John Van Seters, *The Life of Moses: The Yahwist as Historian in Exodus–Numbers* (Contributions to Biblical Exegesis and Theology, 10; Kampen: Kok Pharos, 1994).

4. Mark S. Smith, *The Pilgrimage Pattern in Exodus* (JSOTSup, 239; Sheffield: Sheffield Academic Press, 1997), pp. 144-79, provides a good illustration of the return to the traditional categories of analysis; pp. 144-76 are dedicated to a presentation of current 'diachronic' approaches, followed by a short presentation on pp. 176-79 of literary readings qualified and criticized as 'synchronic' approaches. This discussion forms the background for a presentation of the Priestly redaction.

5. Cf. especially Thomas B. Dozemann, *God on the Mountain* (SBLMS, 37; Atlanta: Scholars Press, 1989), pp. 9-12. This attitude to the idea of 'redactor' is also demonstrated by Van Seters, *The Life of Moses*, pp. 457-64, reverting to the Yahwist not as an accumulation of traditional materials, but as 'a purposeful composition by a scholar who may rightly be characterized as a theologian'.

6. Dozemann, *God on the Mountain*, pp. 145-55.

7. Helmut Utzschneider, *Das Heiligtum und das Gesetz: Studien zur Bedeutung der sinaitischen Heiligtumstexte (Ex 25–40; Lev 8–9)* (OBO, 77; Freiburg: Universitätsverlag; Göttingen: Vandenhoeck & Ruprecht, 1988), p. 258. In this process of 'reworking', the old texts have been integrated in the new. The integration is expressed not only by the old texts as formally retained, but by a conceptual relationship. The old concepts are taken over by the new texts and '*zugespitzt*' ('reinterpreted') by the application in a new context.

8. Cf. the eulogy to the power of the narrative interest creating 'a world of Narnia' by Thomas L. Thompson, *The Origin Tradition of Ancient Israel*. I. *The Literary Formation of Genesis and Exodus 1–23* (JSOTSup, 55; Sheffield: JSOT Press, 1987), pp. 196-204.

9. E.g. 'die vorpriesterliche Komposition' (KD) and 'die priesterliche Komposition' (KP) (the separation between a 'pre-Priestly' [KD] and a 'Priestly'

composition is still to be understood as a compilation of layers that can be easily isolated and described with regard to their theological interest and background. It is taken for granted that the fragments can be related to each other as parts of some reconstructed literary or theological wholeness.

It must be important that the traditional analysis, based on an impressive wealth of observations, cannot have taken place without a basis in textual reality. An alternative exegete who wishes to do better, is challenged by the tenacity[10] of the traditional positions. According to Erhard Blum the search for some final version ('Die Endredaktion' represents a methodological delusion, possible only when the reader ignores the character of the redactional process.[11] This could be seen as a new version of the classical source-critical contempt for the latest layers of the texts. But also the reader who emphasizes the final shape and composition as basic for a new approach, must acknowledge that Blum's assertion can be related to a number of textual phenomena.

Moreover, the attraction of simplified hermeneutical positions is as easily accessible for the alternative as for the traditional reader. For the latter, the impression of the texts as composite narratives is related to categories of 'early' and 'late' and to a process in which 'redactors' or 'editors' are important. For an alternative reading, however, the composite character of the texts can be as easily related to the 'direction of a controlling genius'.[12] Inconsistencies and narrative gaps can be turned into literary virtues[13] easily seen and transcribed by the sensitive

composition [KP]) according to Erhard Blum, *Studien zur Komposition des Pentateuch* (BZAW, 189; Berlin: W. de Gruyter, 1990). According to Utzschneider, *Das Heiligtum*, p. 258, 'die Wanderungserzählung' and 'die Sinaierzählung' in a 'dtn/dtr' redaction is reworked in the 'Heiligtumstexte' of which the 'Priesterschrift' forms a certain layer. According to Dozemann, *God on the Mountain*, chs. 19–24 of Exodus reflect an original pre-exilic Zion tradition reshaped by a Deuteronomistic redaction in its turn reshaped by a Priestly redaction. A short presentation of the most used labels are provided by Van Seters, *The Life of Moses*, pp. ix-x.

10. Good illustrations of this tenacity are provided by Van Seters, *The Life of Moses*, on the one hand reverting to von Rad's idea of J as a purposeful theologian (p. 464), on the other hand establishing a J source which has 'much in common' (p. 458) with the 'D-Komposition' of Blum, *Studien zur Komposition*.

11. Blum, *Studien zur Komposition*, pp. 380-82.

12. Whybray, *The Making of the Pentateuch*, p. 235.

13. Cf. Meir Sternberg, *The Poetics of Biblical Narrative: Ideological Literature and the Drama of Reading* (Bloomington: Indiana University Press, 1985),

reader.[14] Both as pedantic requirements of proper literary and theological consistency or as modern notions of literary creativity, the reader's expectations will channel the textual impressions into too prescribed courses.

That such positions represent projections of rather simple ideas of textual production can be illustrated by Wilcoxen's attempt in 1968 to describe the contribution of the Pentateuchal 'redactors'.[15] According to Wilcoxen, two considerations were decisive for the efforts of these redactors: the first was the desire to preserve 'older traditional materials in their original wording'; the second was the 'complex patterning of such traditional materials'. The 'patterning process' is due to a setting in religious education. As religious teachers, the redactors were simultaneously reflecting and shaping the world of their contemporaries, and thus adding to the complexity of the stories. The older expressions for the Israelite apprehension of reality were recognized and further elaborated. This resulted in a final Pentateuch more complex than the older narratives. Correspondingly, the readers of the final Pentateuch were also more sophisticated than their predecessors, able to 'discern and appreciate larger and smaller patterns delineated by the succession of narrative' units.[16]

This model implies that the editorial contributions can be seen mainly in the organization of the materials. The narrative structure reflects an 'analogical level of significance'. The analogy refers to categories of function, connected to the religious education through many generations and gradually influencing the narrative structure.[17] The five themes of the Pentateuchal narratives present the making of Israel, corresponding to the five successive stages in the development of a human being.[18]

pp. 186-229, 365-440; for whom the 'gaps' and 'doublets' are regarded as important expressions of a sophisticated literary technique.

14. Illustrated by Robert Alter, *The Art of Biblical Narrative* (New York: Basic Books, 1981) pp. 133-40; cf. Whybray, *The Making of the Pentateuch*, p. 52. On the other hand, Whybray's cautious portrait of his author on pp. 237-42 also seems basically to equate the impact of 'the controlling genius' with influence upon the textual shape.

15. Jay A. Wilcoxen, 'Some Anthropocentric Aspects of Israel's Sacred History', *JR* 48 (1968), pp. 333-50.

16. Wilcoxen, 'Some Anthropocentric Aspects', p. 338.

17. Wilcoxen, 'Some Anthropocentric Aspects', p. 350.

18. Wilcoxen, 'Some Anthropocentric Aspects', p. 347.

By necessity speculative and rather loosely connected to textual evidence, Wilcoxen's ideas on the editorial process present a refreshing alternative. Whether right or wrong, they are at the very least as plausible as the more current suppositions. The assumed sophistication of Wilcoxen's editors and readers underlines the methodological optimism of the traditional scholarly analysis, readily describing the literary, theological and historical dimensions of the ancient texts. The idea of some 'patterning activity' which reflects the collective experiences gathered in through some specific religious activity of many generations implies a most complex editorial process. At the very least, the possibility of such a process should warn against a reading centred around some simplistic image of how the ancient texts were made.

Positively, Wilcoxen's ideas represent a concrete example of categories that add to the traditional scholarly reading without negating or ignoring the mass of observations patiently and diligently acquired. The history of research makes it impossible to ignore the perception of the texts as composite narratives, which most directly is indicated by the overlappings, repetitions and 'contradictions' within them. At one and the same time, the reader is at times awestruck by phenomena that are naturally perceived as signs of 'creative genius', occasionally also humbled by glimpses of a different mental presence equally veiled and attractive. This could be related to some 'patterning activity' or, for example, to the categories of some abstract 'theme'.[19] Above all, the wealth of textual impressions sets out the poverty of analytical categories[20] for a proper transcription of the textual reality.

Introducing a study on the Song of Songs, LaCoque asserts that the interpretation of the Song is the hermeneutical challenge par excellence, more acute than for any other text.[21] At the very outset, the scholarly

19. In the sense of David J.A. Clines, *The Theme of the Pentateuch* (JSOTSup, 10; Sheffield: JSOT Press, 1982), pp. 17-21. By 'theme', Clines refers to a level of reading which transcends 'intention', 'motif', 'topos', 'subject', expressed by a reader's statement on 'what it means that the work is as it is' (p. 21).

20. Norman K. Gottwald, *The Tribes of Yahweh: A Sociology of the Religion of Liberated Israel 1250–1050 B.C.E.* (Maryknoll, NY: Orbis Books, 1979), and Niels Peter Lemche, *Ancient Israel: A New History of Israelite Society* (The Biblical Seminar, 5; Sheffield: JSOT Press, 1988), imply radically new models of reading. It must be significant that their contributions are not primarily based on textual, but on historical and sociological arguments.

21. André Lacocque, *Romance She Wrote: A Hermeneutical Essay on Song of Songs* (Harrisburg, PA: Trinity Press International, 1998), p. 6.

reader has to relate to two sharply opposed interpretations of 'allegorical/spiritual' or 'scientific/mundane' character.[22] But if acutely experienced in connection with the Song, the poverty of hermeneutical models could represent a similar and far more serious challenge with regard to the Pentateuch. Ultimately, the two challenges must be connected. The development of a modern tradition of scholarly reading has had the Pentateuch as a pivotal text. When the application of this tradition upon the Song leads to such a strange division of sharply opposed readings, this cannot but reflect problems inherent also in the other applications, however well hidden.[23]

The Song of Songs provokes two mutually exclusive types of reading, both professing to reflect the textual reality. In contrast to readings split between 'allegorical/spiritual' and 'scientific/mundane', the alternatives for reading the Pentateuch seem strangely undramatic. On the other hand, this could reflect the fact that the established scholarly reading in this case has presented a rather lopsided orientation towards special aspects of the textual reality. Hidden due to the seemingly simple texture of the narratives in the Pentateuch, the 'mundane' character of the scholarly approach is revealed when related to the exhuberant poetry of the Song.

Moreover, LaCocque's claims that a 'naturalist' reading of the Song of Songs must leave room also for its spiritual dimensions, can also be transferred to the Pentateuch. According to LaCocque (influenced by Ricoeur), it is arrogant for a modern reader to ignore more than 20 centuries of mystical interpretation.[24] This is equally relevant for the Pentateuch, the reception history of which does not start with Wellhausen but also includes Midrashic and New Testament readings. It would be rather difficult to maintain that the religious significance of the Pentateuch for the communities of faith is mirrored by modern scholarly interpretations. One can easily envisage a situation in which the current emphasis on reception history and the reader's contribution to textual meaning will lead to a split between 'mundane' and 'spiritual' readings as radical as the alternative readings of the Song of

22. Lacocque, *Romance She Wrote*, p. 3.

23. The connection between the two sets of reading is stressed if we accept Lacocque's assertions on the intertextual dimension of the Song. Its meaning is given by the intertextual relationships to central 'provider-texts' within the Biblical tradition, Lacocque, *Romance She Wrote*, p. 37.

24. Lacocque, *Romance She Wrote*, p. 4.

Songs. Such a split would be equally tragic for both perceptions of textual reality.[25]

Accordingly, what follows represents a search for textual data that might contribute to an alternative model of reading. As to the practical character of this search, I cannot do better than refer to the term 'close reading'. Too vague for any theoretical definition, its practical implications are according to my notions demonstrated by the studies of Exodus by Brichto,[26] Moberly,[27] and Childs (when he writes in the special mode of 'Old Testament context').[28] These scholars represent different methodological standpoints; they have different views on the character of the texts and the literary processes which shaped them, and refer to different categories of analysis. But more importantly, they have in common[29] a basic discipline of reading that both accepts the co-existence of seemingly disparate elements in the text and strives to absorb these elements in the order indicated by the textual organization.[30]

The pitfalls of 'close reading' are obvious.[31] I have added to them by some of my own, the most important made visible by the subtitle *Narrative Patterns in Exodus 19–40*. The emphasis on *narrative*[32] could

25. The parallel of the Song also suggests that the problems involved can not be solved by 'multidimensional exegesis', as suggested by Louis C. Jonker, *Exclusivity and Variety: Perspectives on Multidimensional Exegesis* (Contributions to Bibilical Exegesis and Theology, 19; Kampen: Kok Pharos, 1996).

26. Herbert Chanan Brichto, 'The Worship of the Golden Calf: A literary Analysis of a Fable on Idolatry', *HUCA* 54 (1983), pp. 1-44.

27. R.W.L. Moberly, *At the Mountain of God: Story and Theology in Exodus 32–34* (JSOTSup, 22; Sheffield: JSOT Press, 1983).

28. Brevard S. Childs, *The Book of Exodus: A Critical, Theological Commentary* (Philadelphia: Westminster Press, 1974).

29. It can hardly be coincidental that Smith (*The Pilgrimage Pattern*, pp. 176-79) too singles out Brichto and more particularly Moberly as representatives of a special and questionable type of approach. This could reflect both some common character as well as the inherent significance of their approach.

30. The perception of such qualities as important also for the reading of the Pentateuch owes much to the influence of Clines (*The Theme of the Pentateuch*) and Whybray (*The Making of the Pentateuch*).

31. J. Barton, *Reading the Old Testament: Method in Biblical Study* (London: Darton, Longman & Todd, 1996), pp. 140-79, under the heading 'New Criticism'.

32. Cf. the significance attached to this category Moberly, *At the Mountain of God*, pp. 34-38.

imply potential interference from a self-professed 'close reader'.[33] In my case, the term does not refer to any specific theories of narrative, but to the simple fact that chs. 19–40 of Exodus represent a composition of stories.[34] The materials can be described as different *traditions* or literary *genres*, some of them even satisfying the requirements of *Gattungen*. But whatever the character of the concrete literary sub-unit, it is linked to other sub-units by the narrative frame, presenting a set of events taking place within a certain space at a particular time. Also the solemn proclamation of the divine will form part of the narrative development, presented as events following upon and preceding other events.[35]

Moreover, the categories of event, time and space are applied in stories related to other accounts and thus presented according to literary requirements—'literary' being understood in a broad sense as referring to other interests than the mere presentation of events which preceded or followed each other. This implies modes of presentation that transcend the character of events as they normally are experienced in everyday life. But while the narrative frame could contain rather subtle effects, the basic mode of reading is connected to the narrative form which presents a linear relationship of consecutive events.

This makes 'story'—connected to 'episode'[36] made up by a series of 'events', with 'situation' and 'scene' for certain steps in the narrative

33. Illustrated by the potential implications of the term 'story'; cf. Smith, *The Pilgrimage Pattern*, pp. 21-22.

34. Cf. the definition of L. Stone, 'The Revival of Narrative: Reflections on a New Old History', *Past and Present* 85 (1979), p. 3: 'Narrative is taken to mean the organization of material in a chronologically sequential order and the focusing of the content into a single coherent story, albeit with sub-plots'.

35. Smith (*The Pilgrimage Pattern*, p. 21) argues that the category of story does not 'account for the profound relationship between story and laws and priestly instructional literature in a book like Exodus'. If right, Smith's contention could indicate a serious flaw in my approach. On the other hand, the amalgamation of the categories of Torah and narrative represents the established hermeneutical positions; the Sinai texts read, for example, as expression for different modes of 'covenantal' religion. Methodologically, my emphasis on narrative categories aims at a simplification of the issues, in order to avoid the fateful attraction of the established conventional wisdoms. If fruitful, the description of the narrative development could provide a setting for a better understanding of the theological implications of Torah.

36. Brichto, 'The Worship of the Golden Calf', pp. 2-3.

development—a key term for the practical delimitation of the sub-units which make up the composition, as well as for the relationship of these sub-units.[37]

The emphasis on narrative *patterns* could also imply a reading of interference. In contrast to the studies of Brichto and Moberly on Exodus 32–34,[38] chs. 19–40 represent a large corpus for a process of 'close reading', which at times must manifest itself in a mode typical of a redactio-critical study. But the category of patterns within a corpus reflects the belief that a better reading of single stories or special passages must reflect the setting in a wider narrative frame. The implications of this frame can be linked to narrative movement perceived as 'patterns' or 'structures'. 'Composition' is linked to these terms, conveying the literary space in which the narrative movements take place. These terms are important for my analysis, both with regard to larger compositional units as well as to single stories. They reflect the belief that when reading ancient texts, even the closest of non-interfering, receptive readings will not fathom the flow of the narrative without some perception of directions and levels—the reading being very much a search for indications of narrative direction.

Finally, my concentration on Exodus 19–40 represents a problematical decision.[39] The materials within these chapters could be related to many centres of gravity. The introductory itinerary in Exod. 19.1-2 refers to Exod. 15.22-23, 27-16.1 and 17.1, the arrival at Sinai the continuation of earlier events within a larger story centred round the same actors, their interaction even comparable to what took place at Sinai.[40] And if the wilderness stories set before ch. 19 have some

37. As a matter of convenience, I have used the term 'author' when the shape of the story is related to some literary process. This term does not imply any profession on the character of the processes which resulted in the present shape.

38. Brichto, 'The Worship of the Golden Calf'; Moberly, *At the Mountain of God.*

39. This is illustrated by the significance of the pilgrimage for Smith (*The Pilgrimage Pattern*), compared to 'the encounter episode' in this study. At least to some degree, the parallelism—and difference—of the two concepts could reflect the delimitations of the materials and the corresponding change of focus. With regard to the book of Exodus as a whole, the concept of pilgrimage represents a natural centre of gravity for the organization of the materials. Similarly, the focus on chs. 19–40 entails that the encounter on the mountain emerges as the central episode.

40. Cf. Blum, *Studien zur Komposition*, pp. 162-63, on the extension of the Sinai category to the wilderness stories.

bearing on the Sinai event, a relevant concern might be mirrored by the repetition of the wilderness stories set after Numbers 10.

In the same way, the story of Exodus 19–40 is not concluded in ch. 40, but is continued in Leviticus 1. Also, if 'Sinai-stories' are found as a narrative nucleus, the entity of Exodus 19 to Num. 10.10 forms a natural corpus. Or, given the significance of the separation into books demonstrated by Olson's work on Numbers,[41] the book of Exodus should form the natural literary unit.[42] And as a Moses-biography, the books from Exodus to Deuteronomy could also represent the meaningful unit, in continuation of the Genesis stories.

The ever-widening list of possibilities demonstrates that the reader has to start somewhere, at the risk of distorting the story. Originally, Exodus 32–34 provided the starting point in my case. The contextual setting of this story indicated chs. 19–40 as a special literary unit, in its turn serving as a sub-unit within a larger story. Whatever corpus is chosen, the problem of contextual relationships remains and even gradually emerges as the major riddle for the reader. It seems to me that the character of these texts is such that a reading is turned into a process where stages are determined by the constantly changing perception of contextual relationships.

I am afraid that my own literary mode also will reflect the problems when such a process is communicated to other readers. Repetitions and the effects of parallelism are the most visible expression for contextual references, and have led me willy-nilly to a discourse of a rather circular character. Aside from the obvious repetition of certain basic insights, this has made it difficult to find the proper place for the presentation of textual data. The result will, I fear, at times burden the reader with data that anticipate later discussion, at other times cause irritation as a postponement of data that could have been useful in an earlier context. While such effects are regrettable, they have been unavoidable as parts of the effort to trace the narrative movement.

41. Dennis T. Olson, *The Death of the Old and the Birth of the New: The Framework of the Book of Numbers and the Pentateuch* (BJS, 71; Chico, CA: Scholars Press, 1985).

42. Smith, *The Pilgrimage Pattern*.

Chapter 1

The Outlines of a Story

1. *The Encounter Episode*

From the very beginning of Exodus 19, the reader is impressed by the mountain imagery in the Sinai stories.[1] The motif forms part of an established scene dedicated to YHWH communing with Moses on the mountain. Repeated over and over again, the successive mountain scenes mark the steps of the story development. The significance of such a nucleus scene is underlined by similar effects outside the context of Sinai. The plagues of Egypt are presented as a series of stereotyped situations with the same set of actors again and again acting out their roles. Correspondingly, the people's complaint in the desert and the divine response form the event structure of the journey stories. Traditionally, such repetitions have served as the starting point for questions of editorial origin and development. But as a mode of repetition, they can also be related to more organic categories of literary technique.[2] In any case, the very application of narrative stereotypes repeated within different sets of stories underlines the significance of the mountain imagery for the first part of the Sinai stories.

This is also reflected by the present separation of the books of

1. Cf. especially Dozemann, *God on the Mountain*, pp. 12-17, on the significance of the mountain setting for these stories, 'the symbolic role of the mountain' making it both 'a structuring device within the narrative' and a channel for theological discourse concerning divine cultic presence' (p. 14).

2. Alter, *The Art of Biblical Narrative*, pp. 88-113, and especially Dozemann, *God on the Mountain*, pp. 145-56. While demonstrating the potentialities of treating the repetitions of Exod. 19–24 as a literary device, Dozemann greatly limits them by concentrating on two modes of repetition: '*mimesis* in which repetition is rooted in similarity, and *ungrounded doubling* in which repetition arises from difference' (p. 149). Abstracted from modern literature, these categories represent far too simple alternatives; c.f., e.g., Sternberg, *The Poetics of Biblical Narrative*, pp. 365-440.

Exodus and Leviticus. According to Lev. 1.1, the divine speaker is calling Moses 'from the tent'. This contrasts the call 'from the mountain' in Exod. 19.3. The two 'superscriptions' of 19.3 and Lev. 1.1 present Exodus 19–40 as a set of stories linked by the repeated mountain scene. This set of stories is concluded by the divine movement from mountain to tent in ch. 40. Within this framework, chs. 19–40 represent a story of sacred localities, dedicated to the divine movement from mountain to tent.

With regard to traditio-critical categories, the mountain imagery has usually been seen as part of some comprehensive thematic complex, related to, for example, the 'Sinai/Horeb', 'Moses', 'Torah', 'Covenant' or 'Theophany'[3] traditions. But the 'divine mountain' can also be seen as a specific theme in its own right, marking the pivotal point for the traditio-historical and redactional process. Booij finds that a Midianite 'Mountain of God' tradition associated with sacrifices represents the original tradition. This has later been added to by traditions of theophanic descending and of Torah, in a process of 'Sinaitization' centred around the Moses figure.[4] A similar, but more complicated model, is presented by Dozemann.[5] The pre-exilic Mountain of God tradition, centred around the theophany concept, was presented as an account of arrival at an unnamed cosmic mountain, cultic preparations followed by theophany as thunderstorm (Exod. 19.16-17) and a sacrificial ritual at the base of the mountain (Exod. 24.4ab-5). Corresponding to the 'Zion-Sabaoth theology of the pre-exilic Jerusalem cult', the divine presence in a thunderstorm on the cosmic mountain was described as static and permanent. This tradition was expanded by a Deuteronomistic redaction adding the Deuteronomic legislation to the event, the theophany being an occasion for covenant and the promulgation of law. By this expansion, the arrival of Israel is connected to the divine 'Proposal of Covenant', theophany to the promulgation of law, and the sacrifical ritual is transformed into a 'Covenant-Closing Ceremony'. And the 'Zion-Sabaoth theology' is qualified 'with a vision of the impermanent auditory presence of God', corresponding to Mount Horeb. In the Priestly elaborations, theophany became an experience of the impermanent

3. Van Seters, *The Life of Moses*, p. 254.

4. T. Booij, 'Mountain and Theophany in the Sinai Narrative', *Bib* 65 (1984), pp. 1-26.

5. *God on the Mountain*; cf. the critical remarks of Van Seters, *The Life of Moses*, pp. 266-67.

presence of God as fire on the mountain, now identified as Mount Sinai. The Deuteronomistic 'Covenant-Closing Ceremony' was reframed into a 'Sanctification Ceremony' in ch. 24, culminating in the Priestly legislation of chs. 25–31.[6]

With the traditio-critical problems involved, the very description of the mountain scene implies some confessional position regarding the nature and thus the origin of the scene. The writing of the ancient authors obviously was determined by very different concerns compared to the categories of organization applied by modern readers. This is demonstrated by the seemingly haphazard compilation of the very names of the mountain.[7] And when related to the theme of 'divine presence', the different versions of the mountain scene present a seemingly unworried mixture of various expressions for the immanent presence and theophanic manifestations. The mixture probably reflects a historical development of different traditions and theological understanding. But its present application can just as well reflect the unworried compilation of different expressions for the 'same', each motif referring to an established set of connotations experienced by the authors as fundamentally identical.[8]

Whatever the background of the language, it must be important that human actors are included in the scenes of the sacred mountain. The imagery is not limited to a presentation of a special mountain or to representations of theophanic presence, but entails a scene of divine and human togetherness. In the scholarly discussion, certain aspects of the imagery are stressed, while the mountain as the locus for a scene of encounter with divine and human interaction tends to be disregarded. In these stories, the divine presence is set together with the human presence in a series of events.[9] Consistent with the mountain imagery, the

6. *God on the Mountain*, pp. 197-99.

7. Booij, 'Mountain and Theophany', pp. 1-26.

8. Cf. the discussion on the theophany language in Van Seters, *The Life of Moses*, pp. 254-70, who concludes that the J materials represent a special transformation of the traditional language and clichés of the theophany tradition in the hymns and prophetic literature.

9. Both aspects are reflected by the idea of a pilgrimage paradigm, seen as constituting the pattern for the Priestly redaction of Exodus by Smith, *The Pilgrimage Pattern*, pp. 264-65, 287. But the significance of this idea for the mountain scenes is greatly reduced when the materials centred round the mountain imagery (chs. 19–20 and 24 according to p. 244, and chs. 32–34 according to p. 248) are seen as pre-Priestly. Related to inherited materials, the pilgrimage pattern would

special character of this relationship is indicated by corresponding categories of locality. The actors—most often the human in 'ascent'—are described in movement relative to each other. The mountain serves as the focal point of this movement, with a function as the place of meeting.

For the composition of Exodus 19–40 as a whole, the situation of Moses communing with God on the mountain is important and must be vital to its meaning. This situation links chs. 19–24 and 25–40, which, in their present form, are organized in a structure of repeated encounters. In spite of the collapse of the classical source-critical positions, the separation of chs. 19–24 from the Priestly materials in 25–31, 35–40 still represents the obvious scholarly position.[10] But whatever the literary origin of the stories, the elaboration of the mountain motifs in ch. 24 presents ch. 25 as the continuation of the preceding chapters, while the divine instructions of chs. 25–31 according to 31.18 and 32.7-19 form part of the encounter introduced in ch. 24. Thus, for a reading interested in traditio-critical models and for a reading that stresses the final shape of the materials, the mountain episode is important for the perception of how the materials have been organized. To the former it can be seen as a structuring device which has permitted a constant

accordingly represent a superficial imposition upon materials centred round different ideas. A further reduction of the relevance of this pattern for the Sinai texts is indicated by the assumed setting in normal, institutionalized religous behaviour (pp. 52-141). It would be impossible to refuse any linkage between 'pilgrimage' as a literary theme and sociological categories of religious behaviour. But the linkage should not bind the potentialities of the literary theme too solidly to the ground. On the contrary, the transposition of 'everybody' into a literary reality of heroic proportions, in order that the latter should transform the former, might reflect the very character of a book like Exodus; c.f., e.g., P.L. Travers, *What the Bee Knows: Reflections of Myth, Symbol and Story* (London: Arkana, 1993), pp. 11-18.

10. Cf. the very title of Utzschneider, *Das Heiligtum.* For Blum (*Studien zur Komposition*, p. 302) the Priestly contributions in Exod. 25–40 represent a 'Klammer' (bracket) related to the older materials. Thomas L. Thompson (*The Origin Tradition*, p. 40 and esp. pp. 196-98) represents an approach based on 'literary' categories, asserting the autonomy of exegesis apart from historical and archaeological considerations. But in spite of such assertions, 'the origin tradition' is delimitated to Genesis–Exodus 23 (p. 64). And even with an interest on 'the canonical Sinai Complex', Dozemann (*God on the Mountain*) can 'probe the theology of divine presence' shaped by the process of redaction in chs. 19–24, categorically asserted as a 'core story' presenting 'the central event' (p. 2).

expansion of materials around a nucleus tradition,[11] and to the latter as a prime indication of compositional coherence.

The significance of the scene for the composition corresponds to its connotational impact. According to Exodus 3–4 and Deut. 34.1-6, the biography of Moses is marked both at the beginning and the end by a mountain scene: vv. 1 and 12 of Exodus 3 identify the location of the introductory scene with the mountain of the Sinai stories: Deut. 34.1 refers to a different mountain. But also the latter episode has the characteristics of a scene of encounter. The mountain scene seems to represent a vital expression for the character of the Moses biography. The literary quality of the two stories that introduce and conclude the life of Moses as the servant of God, the details of which are both singular and highly emotive, points to the significance of the mountain imagery. Together, the two texts make a strong impression of an extraordinary relationship between God and Moses. Set into this framework, the introductory description of the people settling down 'in front of the mountain' in Exod. 19.2 must signal the extraordinary character of the situation.

Exodus 3–4 and Deuteronomy 34 also suggest that the connotational impact of the mountain scene is not dependent on a connection with some type of Torah or covenant situation.[12] This does not necessarily imply that such a connection is 'secondary' and should be disregarded as to material significance or seen as a later elaboration. The instruction of Torah represents one expression of the extraordinary meeting, and within the composition of Exodus 19–40 obviously a vital one. But the situation of encounter also entails other matters of communion. The impression of extraordinary relationship between God and man on the place apart represents a constant.

The connotational significance of the mountain scene is demonstrated by 1 Kings 19. The basic motifs are not bound to the Moses biography,

11. Dozemann, *God on the Mountain*, p. 14, and also Childs, *Book of Exodus*, p. 354.

12. Cf. also the emphasis on the theophany motif as the 'original basis and content' of the Sinai tradition according to E.W. Nicholson, *Exodus and Sinai in History and Tradition* (Oxford: Basil Blackwell, 1973), p. 77; and in detail Booij, 'Mountain and Theophany'; Dozemann, *God on the Mountain*. Van Seters (*The Life of Moses*, pp. 462-63) seems to relate the motif to the decisive significance of the prophetic role for the Moses description, in addition to the royal aspects of the king as recipient of the law.

but can be freely shaped in singular applications. It is certainly possible to assert that 1 Kings 19 is literarily dependent on Moses traditions, reflecting an effort to depict Elijah as 'the second Moses'.[13] If so, the elaboration of the common materials in 1 Kings 19 indicates a process not of copy and repetition, but of sophisticated re-shaping.[14] The form of the journey and mountain motifs in 1 Kings 19 suggests that the story represents a parallel application of established literary themes.

Seen together with, in particular, the episode of Exod. 33.12-23, the 1 Kings version is important for our understanding of the mountain scene. In both texts, the stereotyped literary motifs are connected with categories that indicate that the mountain imagery and the extraordinary meeting refers to a special background. The presentation of the theophanic experience seems to reflect some general theological interest not confined to the extraordinary biographies of Moses and Elijah.[15]

This is added to by the connection of the mountain imagery and temple categories.[16] Given the function of temple motifs as the traditional expression for the 'reality apart', it is even possible to regard the encounter scenes with Moses as individual applications of a typical situation usually connected with temple categories. With such a background, Moses could represent the ideal religious figure, while the mountain scene provides the framework of the ultimate religious experience.[17]

13. E.g. Jörg Jeremias, *Theophanie: Die Geschichte einer alttestamentlichen Gattung* (WMANT, 10; Neukirchen–Vluyn: Neukirchener Verlag, 1965), p. 112; George W. Coats, *Moses: Heroic Man, Man of God* (JSOTSup, 57; Sheffield: JSOT Press, 1988), p. 206. Any connection between the two texts is denied by Erik Aurelius, *Der Fürbitter Israels: Eine Studie zum Mosebild im Alten Testament* (CBOTS, 27; Stockholm: Almquist & Wiksell, 1988), p. 104.

14. The special character of 1 Kgs 19 is stressed, for example, by the studies of Leah Bronner, *The Stories of Elijah and Elisha as Polemics against Baal Worship* (POS, 6; Leiden: E.J. Brill, 1968); Russell Gregory and Alan J. Hauser, *From Carmel to Horeb; Elijah in Crisis* (Bible and Literature Series, 19; Sheffield: Almond Press, 1990).

15. Besides Dozemann, *God on the Mountain*, cf. esp. Dieter Eichhorn, *Gott als Fels, Burg und Zuflucht: Eine Untersuchung zum Gebet des Mittlers in den Psalmen* (Europäische Hochschulschriften, 23.4; Frankfurt: Peter Lang, 1972), p. 86; Hauge, *Between Sheol and Temple*, pp. 101-108.

16. Besides the references in the preceding note, cf. Sigmund Mowinckel's classic *Le décalogue* (Etudes d'histoire et de philosophie religieuse, 16; Paris: Alcan, 1927); and Dozemann, *God on the Mountain*, pp. 29-35.

17. Hauge, *Between Sheol and Temple.*

The connotational significance of this situation is also reflected in the biographies of Genesis 12–50. The repeated application of encounter episodes in these stories is comparable to the function of the mountain episode in Exodus 19–40. The traditio-historical relationship between the Genesis stories—often connected with some named sacred locality—and the mountain episodes in the Moses biography constitute a classic riddle.[18] But the Genesis stories stress the biographical, or rather hagiographical, significance of the encounter as an established theme of the extraordinary biography. Set into this pattern, the Moses biography continues the hagiographical descriptions of Genesis, the imagery of the divine mountain being an expression of a new stage of extraordinary meeting.[19]

The established character of the theme is illustrated by the freedom of literary application. It provides the framework for singular scenes such as the burning bush, Moses with the shining face bringing down the divine tablets or even buried by the divine hands, or Jacob wrestling with God, while Abraham receives the divine guest in the shape of three ordinary travellers.

The extraordinary character of the situation is reflected by the categories of locus. The separation from normal reality is expressed by the movement of the hero from one place to another. In the applications of Gen. 12.1 and 22.2, this aspect is underlined by the evocative motif of the hero setting out towards a locus known only to God. The Mountain of God motif presents this aspect of locality with special emphasis by the application of wilderness motifs. The mountain is situated 'beyond the wilderness' (Exod. 3.1). When Jethro goes to Moses, he goes 'to the wilderness' 'there' where Moses has camped near the Mountain of God. (18.5). Correspondingly, the sacred 'there'[20] in front of the mountain' in 19.2 is prepared for by repeated references to the

18. E.g. R.W.L. Moberly, *The Old Testament of the Old Testament: Patriarchal Narratives and Mosaic Yahwism* (Overtures to Biblical Theology; Minneapolis: Fortress Press, 1992).

19. A comparable reference to the patriarchs as relevant for the Exodus stories is represented by Smith, *The Pilgrimage Pattern*, pp. 138-41. On the other hand, Moberly, *The Old Testament of the Old Testament*, pp. 99-104, sharply separates between Patriarchal and Mosaic religion, the concept of the holy mountain being a distinctive feature of the latter (pp. 8-11).

20. Cf. the corresponding applications of *šām* in 20.21 and repeated in 1 Kgs 19.9.

wilderness. Above all, the idea of the sacred mountain in the wilderness as the place apart is expressed by the journey motifs, the human movement towards the special place expanded into a special story cycle.

The ideas of locus and human movement are central also to the story of 1 Kings 19. Elijah's journey encompasses a number of stations. The motif of 'leaving the servants behind' (19.3)[21] reflects the separation between normal and the extraordinary reality. The hero moves from the north, to Beer-sheba, to the desert, to the cave and to the ultimate standing at the opening of the cave. The significance of each station is expressed by some corresponding events. Each episode is marked by the prophet's movement and arrival, the staying at one station leading to a journey to the next. The spatial categories are connected to successive divine actors. Corresponding to the movement from station to station, the prophet is related to the 'Angel', the 'Word of YHWH' and ultimately 'YHWH'. The development seems to indicate a hierarchy of heavenly representatives, depicting a corresponding succession of levels of extraordinary experience.[22] Such an effect is enhanced by the description of four theophanic manifestations in vv. 11-13. The stereotyped character of the description of these manifestations and the repeated negations until the fourth and decisive expression of the theophanic reality clearly describe a narrative movement towards a climax of extraordinary experience.

Three main aspects seem to be reflected by the applications of the encounter situation. The concept of some extraordinary encounter of the divine and human actors is basic. Second, the human actor represents the extraordinary biography—as expressed by Moses, Elijah and the Patriarchs. Third, this separation between ordinary and extraordinary is expressed by motifs of locality, which relate the separate locus to the extraordinary meeting of the divine and human.

The motifs seem to imply a basic understanding of the dual character

21. Cf. also Gen. 22.4-5.

22. Cf. below for the three levels of Exod. 24.4-18, with the events separated between those 'under the mountain', the ascent by chosen representatives to the event of *visio Dei*, and finally the special ascent of Moses. Connected with categories of verticality, with 'ascension' as a central motif, the three stations related to classes of humanity can be compared to the three stations of Elijah related to the one human actor. More importantly, the difference of three divine representatives related to different stations is comparable to the development of the divine actor in the story cycles of Exodus–Numbers.

of reality. The separation between divine and human actors must represent the prime aspect of this duality. But more importantly, the idea of locus and movement towards the locus indicate some basic separation between the ordinary and extraordinary within the human reality. The idea of movement implies that the duality can be overcome—at least confined to the special locus and the special human actor. Such ideas are naturally referred to as a conceptual background of the temple ideology and categories of sacred and profane. On the other hand, such a background would set out the versatility and freedom of exposition when these ideas are given literary shape.

The repeated application of this episode in Exodus 19–40, with its emotive and connotative wealth spilling over into the context, must be important for the composition as a whole. Repeated as a sort of narrative refrain, the episode helps to define the meaning of the story. Besides other aspects of literary development, the very application of the scene could indicate some basic coherence for the Sinai stories.

The People as Actors in the Encounter Episode

The applications of the encounter episode outside Exodus 19–40 underline the special character of the Sinai stories. In addition to Moses as the natural hero of the extraordinary encounter, the presence of the people refers to a second set of human actors. In Exodus 3–4, Deuteronomy 34 and 1 Kings 19, the extraordinary character of the encounter is reflected by the splendid isolation of God and man on the mountain Also the patriarchal episodes are related to God and the lone human figure. In some stories (e.g. Gen. 22; 35.1-5), other participants can be included. But here too, the encounter proper and the divine address are related to the central human figure. Against this background, the inclusion of the people must reflect the special character of the encounter scene in Exodus 19–40 and thus—given the function of this scene—also indicate vital aspects of the compositional interest.

In the Sinai stories too, Moses is retained as the hero of the encounter. But the elaboration of his role reflects the significance of the people. The divine messages are usually addressed to the people, while the different types of response from the people make new ascents necessary. While Moses conforms to the established role, the narrative development indicates God and people as the main actors. Moses is depicted as the go-between, running up and down the mountain.

The categories of locality underline the significance of this role allocation. From the start in Exodus 19, the events of Sinai unfold as a series of contacts between the spatial levels of 'mountain' and 'under the mountain'. The divine manifestations take place 'above', while the people are confined to the space 'below'. This is the more remarkable as the people in the preceding events have enacted the role proper to the hero of the encounter drama. The people have re-enacted the journey of Moses fleeing from Egypt and ending at the divine mountain. Similar to the miraculous journey of Elijah, Israel has been wonderfully fed and sustained on the journey. With the pilgrimage ended by the people being brought to the divine 'me' (19.4), the position of the people before Sinai is comparable to that of the prophet of 1 Kgs 19.8-9.[23] This is underlined by the first divine message in Exod. 19.4-6.[24] The extraordinary position of Israel as, potentially, the holy and priestly people, different from other peoples, corresponds to the exalted character of the actors brought to the locus of encounter.

But instead, the narrative reality is immediately split between 'above' and 'below', the people being very much part of the reality below. A corresponding split takes place between the two sets of human actors. The solemnly repetitive introduction of Exod. 19.1-2, which relates the people to the important location, is juxtaposed to the ascent of Moses in v. 3. The peculiar relationship of the events in v. 3a and bβ—the ascent prior to what is read as the divine invitation to ascent—is traditionally explained as due to different sources. In their present shape, vv. 2-3 describe a relationship of juxtaposition. The people's 'settling down in front of the mountain' is contrasted with the initial movement of Moses 'ascending unto God'. The motif contrast corresponds with the sentence construction. The introductory *ûmōšeh* in v. 3 puts the emphasis on the act of Moses juxtaposed to the former situation. With the people settled, 'Moses, however, ascended'.[25]

23. Cf. the parallel repetitive technique connected to the use of *šām* in Exod. 19.1b, 2 and more elaborately in 1 Kgs 19.8-9a. Introductory narrative sentences end with the presentation of the name of the locality, followed by sentences which repeat shortly the preceding description connected to *šām*.

24. To Blum (*Studien zur Komposition*), p. 47, 19.4-6 are important as a concentrated definition of 'die ideale Gottesbeziehung' (the ideal relationship to God) expounded in the composition chs. 19–34. Concretely, the priestly status of the people is expressed by 24.4-8 (pp. 51-52). Cf. also E.W. Nicholson 'The Covenant Ritual in Exodus XXIV 3-8', *VT* 32 (1982), pp. 74-86.

25. A second effect of the relationship of human ascent and divine calling in v. 3 is that the special invitation of v. 20 is stressed, highlighting the theophanic

While Israel, guided by Moses, has represented the human actor of the sacred story so far, the arrival at Sinai fundamentally changes the roles. Moses is the hero of close encounter, while the people are confined to a lower level of reality. On the other hand, the narrative tension established by the earlier stories is continued. At Sinai too, the people of Israel remain the central human actors of the drama. But the established relationships of the earlier story cycles have been disturbed. This is also reflected by the presentation of the divine actor. The divine presence is now confined to the mountain. In the events so far (summarized at 18.8-11 in a sort of conclusion) YHWH has been wonderfully active. But in the Sinai context, he is confined to the mountain top. With God and people set in their different locations in the 'above' and 'below', Moses' role as mediator is given a corresponding visualization by his constantly ascending and descending the mountain.

The spatial duality is usually simply expressed. God is met on the mountain, while the people stay below. YHWH seems related to the mountain as some permanent divine presence. Exodus 19.18-20 and 34.5 (cf. also the implications of the motifs 24.16) suggest a more complicated relationship. Here, a divine movement from a higher 'above' takes place relative to the mountain. For this three-levelled model, the human movement of ascent from below corresponds to a divine descent from above. According to this visualization, the mountain seems to represent the middle between high and low as a place of meeting for the divine and human beings.

The relationship between the two-levelled and three-levelled visualizations could have traditio-historical implications.[26] In the present shape of the Sinai stories, the scenery points to the juxtaposition of mountain and below the mountain as the high and the low of the

event on the third day as the central event. According to vv. 3 and 8, Moses is active in the two first encounter episodes, while the divine calling of Moses 'to the top of the mountain' reflects the climactic character of the third episode.

26. Dozemann, *God on the Mountain*; contrast Van Seters, *The Life of Moses*, pp. 266-67. Temple concepts provide a similar set of seemingly conflicting ideas, YHWH being seen as both dwelling in and coming to the temple. Thus, in Ps. 24 the qualification of the divine character of the mountain in v. 3 is set in a context which includes the divine 'coming' of vv. 7-10. A corresponding connection of divine mountain and the divine movement—here described as 'passing through'—is found in 1 Kgs 19.8 and 11. The consistency of the motifs must indicate that both ideas represent aspects of the mountain/temple concepts.

narrative reality. Moses ascends to God, the people stay below. YHWH and Moses in interaction are localized to the mountain. The people alone or in interaction with Moses are localized 'under the mountain'. The significant divine manifestations are confined to the mountain. Again and again Moses has to descend to tell the people below what has been decided on their behalf up there, again ascending to tell the mountain-dweller what goes on among the people below.

This imagery is so basic for the presentation of the materials that it is easily disregarded. But its significance is stressed by the context which presents alternative models for the description of divine and human in interaction. The preceding events of exodus and journey demonstrate a narrative reality with the divine actor able to influence human events directly. The imagery of Exod. 13.21-22 and 14.19-20 in particular, with YHWH going in front of and at the end of the human train, presents a situation of close relationship. This makes a puzzling contrast to the scenery of the Sinai stories.[27]

Correspondingly, Moses can enact his role without any change of location in the earlier stories. His function in chs. 5–17 is very much the same as in chs. 19–40. A divine message is given to him and the mediator brings the message to the addressee. The pattern of events in 6.1-8, for example, followed by the presentation of the message in v. 9 corresponds to the pattern of the Sinai stories. Obviously, the people have not been present in the original scene, listening in, but must wait for the proper presentation. But this is not given any narrative expression comparable to the encounter scenes in in the Sinai stories. Some Egypt stories refer to a special situation of intimate communication, comparable to the encounters on the mountain. The dialogues of Exod. 5.22-23 and vv. 10-12, 28-30 of ch. 6 reflect situations apart. Moreover, according to 6.12 and 30 Moses is speaking 'in front of YHWH', just as in 5.22 he 'returned to YHWH'. Such motifs suggest situations that are basically identical with the mountain scenes. But the identity makes the

27. The difference is underlined by the important observation of Blum (*Studien zur Komposition*, pp. 162-63) that not only 18.5, together with vv. 13-26, but also 17.6-7 and further 15.25-26 and 16.4-5, 28-29, reflect an interest in linking wilderness and Sinai stories. For some reason, the categories of Sinai have been extended to the wilderness situation, the mountain imagery of 17.6 and 18.5 even suggesting some identification of events, which in the narrative structure are separated as earlier and later.

differences between these stories and the elaborate scenery of the Sinai stories stand out.[28]

Somehow, with the people brought 'to me'—visualized by the divine mountain—the story enters a new phase, different from the earlier stages. The new nearness marks a new separation, the narrative reality split into high and low, the people emphatically representing the reality below. This is underlined by the motifs of prohibited or limited ascent.[29] Brought 'to me', the people face a God changed from the wonderful saviour and protector into the reluctant killer of Exod. 19.21-24. Confined to the mountain, the divine presence brings death to the trespassers, and the care for the people brought 'to me' can only express itself as worry that they should come too near.

The significance of this elaboration is underlined by the traditional versions of the encounter situation. The stories with Moses or Elijah as the lone human figure reflect the extraordinary character of the encounter. Compared to the traditional hero, the people brought 'to me' and settled 'below the mountain' in ch. 19 cuts an absurd figure.

It is possible that the role allocation reflects aspects of the traditional situation. In 1 Kings 19, Elijah is the sole human actor in pilgrimage and encounter. In the wilderness and Sinai stories in Exodus, his role is shared between two sets of actors, the encounter scene being given to Moses, while the motifs of journey and sacred feeding are related to the children of Israel. The impressive story of Elijah's encounter reflects both the extraordinary character of the encounter as well as the stature of the human actor. But this is combined with a peculiar presentation of Elijah as a 'negative' hero.[30] The elaboration of Moses' negativity in Exodus 3–4[31] indicates a corresponding combination of heroic and

28. Related to traditio-historical categories, this development can be easily attributed to the special character of the Sinai tradition. But even with such a background, the editorial use of the traditions remains questionable. This is illustrated by the narrative development of 1 Kgs 19 moving towards the encounter as the climactic event.

29. Exod. 19.12-13, 21-25, added to by the scene of Exod. 20.18-21; 24.1-2; 34.2-3.

30. E.g. Eckhard von Nordheim, 'Ein Prophet kündigt sein Amt auf (Elia am Horeb)', *Bib* 59 (1978), pp. 153-73; Alan J. Hauser, 'Yahweh versus Death—The Real Struggle in 1 Kings 17–19', in Gregory and Hauser, *From Carmel to Horeb*, pp. 62-63.

31. Usually related to prophetic categories (e.g. Childs, *Book of Exodus*), pp. 54-56 on a basic prophetic 'call narrative' greatly expanded.

utterly human aspects. The juxtaposition of the ascending Moses and the people below in Exodus 19 could represent aspects of the traditional role split between two sets of human actors. But even with such a background, the elaboration of the scenery in ch. 19 creates an absurd tension between the connotations of the people brought 'to me' and the actual situation of the people stuck below the mountain.

2. *The Structure of Encounter Episodes*[32]

The pattern of successive encounter episodes seems to represent the most direct indication of the formal structure of Exodus 19–40. A preliminary and rough idea of how the the encounter scene with the mountain for locus is applied in the materials[33] can be illustrated by Exod. 19.2-8a, 8b-15, 16-25 and 24.1-11 interwoven with the following episode 24.12–32.29, 32.30–33.6 and 34.1-35. Within these seven episodes, the encounter of Exod. 24.9-11 stands out due to the increase in the number of human actors, with priests and the seventy elders added to Moses. Also, the episode of 24.9-11 is interwoven (v. 14) with the following mountain episode introduced in v. 12 and concluded 32.12 with Moses and to some extent also Joshua as human actors. But introduced by two special invitations (vv. 1-2 and 12), ch. 24 seems to refer to two encounter episodes.

These episodes are presented as a series of events centred around three basic situations: (1) preparatory events related to Moses and the people are followed (2) by the ascent and the encounter proper which in turn (3) are followed by the descent and a new scene with Moses set among the people. As parts of the larger story, the episodes are overlapping. The concluding events of the former encounter introduce the encounter that follows.

If the emphasis is put on the encounter proper as a narrative centre of gravity, perhaps 19.3-6, 8b-13, 20-24; 24.10-11; 24.15–31.18; 32.31–33.5; 34.4-28 could better indicate how the mountain episode is set in the narrative flow. But the effect of overlapping episodes, however

32. Due to the tentative character of this chapter, a number of textual phenomena are merely touched upon in this context and discussed more in detail in Chapters 2 and 3.

33. With the mountain as a structuring device, Dozemann (*God on the Mountain*, p. 14) finds the materials of the 'Sinai Complex' organized into the following scenes: Exod. 19.1-8a; 19.8b-19; 19.20–20.20; 20.21–24.11; 24.12–32.35; 34.1-35.

frustrating for a satisfactory delimitation, must be important for the compositional mode.

So far, I have only discussed the episodes that are connected with the mountain imagery. But also other episodes refer to the categories of encounter. Centred around events of theophany and dialogue between YHWH and Moses, the section 33.7–34.3 reflects the characteristics of the encounter episode, but has the Tent of Meeting outside the camp for locus. Similarly, 34.34-35 presents the aftermath of the preceding encounter. But these verses can also be seen as a separate reference to a special set of encounter scenes related to a locus 'inside' and thus probably to the tent of ch. 33.[34] Further, the basic events of encounter are also reflected in 20.1–24.8. The divine speech of 20.1-17 as well as the scene of 20.18-21 continue the events of ch. 19. But with the divine speech disturbed by the people in addition to the movement of Moses towards a special locus of encounter (20.21), the basic event pattern is applied for a sub-episode initiated by the people's interruption.

Set in such a context, the two scenes of 40.1-33 and vv. 34-38 also connote encounter. Compared to the other episodes, the two concluding scenes seem related, the one completing the other. The first is centred around Moses as the human actor, the divine message addressed towards and responded to by Moses. The second scene has no explicit divine message and relates the theophanic event to the people, with the Tent of Meeting for locus.

Finally, Exod. 35.1–39.43 also represents a singular application of certain elements of the event pattern. Describing the mediation of Moses and the response of the people, this passage reflects the third situation of the encounter episode. The divine message which is mediated refers to the encounter episode introduced in 24.12. In this way, 35.1–39.43 could have a function as the positive contrast to the fateful descent of ch. 32, the proper mediation and the people's willing response contrasting with the production of the Golden Calf and the destruction of the divine tablets. But it can also hardly be coincidental that the introduction in 35.1 does not represent any formal rupture with the preceding encounter situation of 34.34-35. Comparable to the dialogue of 33.12–34.3 set after the description of the tent and the theophanic manifestation in vv. 7-11, 35.1 could also continue the encounter

34. E.g. Moberly, *At the Mountain of God*, p. 106; Van Seters, *The Life of Moses*, p. 360.

situation of 34.34-35 as the concrete expression for mediation and response.

Tentatively, it is possible to discern a composition centered around approximately 12 separate applications of the encounter episode. The materials make it impossible to find passages that qualify as sharply delimitated units and sub-units. But more importantly, all of Exodus 19–40 can be regarded as a series of encounter episodes. The composition represents the repeated application of the encounter episode as a literary format. The three situations of introductory events leading to the encounter proper followed by concluding events of response are basic for the episode. At the same time, the difference of application shows that the episode can be shaped differently. In ch. 19, the basic events of the pattern are applied in a rather stereotyped way.[35] With the scene established, the later examples seem to represent more fluid types of application.

The stereotypical character of the literary format invites one to efforts of abstraction and systematization. Related to traditio-historical categories, the three situations of the encounter could reflect some Sinai tradition as a nucleus, ultimately referring to cultic events labelled, for example, preparatory rites, theophany, concluding sacrificial rites.[36] The categories of chs. 24 and 40, for instance, explicitly refer the theophanic experience to a setting of ritual connotations. But the impression of a free or fluid application of established literary themes[37] warns against any easy systematization, especially when mixed with criteria of analysis that separate between 'original' and 'later' layers. Aspects of compositional linearity greatly complicate any precise delimitation of nucleus phenomena. This is illustrated by chs. 19 and 24. In these texts, the third situation of mediation and response clearly has a double function—on the one hand concluding a prior encounter episode, on the other hand introducing the next encounter.

The aspects of linearity could encourage the reader to efforts of

35. Cf. Blum (*Studien zur Komposition*) on the significance of 19.3-8 as 'ein spezifischer Baustein der KD-Überlieferung' (p. 98), with a function as the introductory 'Signaltext' (p. 92), important for the composition of chs. 19–34 (pp. 51-52).

36. Dozemann, *God on the Mountain*, pp. 34-35, 118-20.

37. Cf. also the discussion on the function of the cultic categories in the Sinai stories as 'referential' or 'evocative' in Moberly, *At the Mountain of God*, pp. 136-40.

systematization according to theological interests. The Golden Calf episode of ch. 32 represents the natural example for the expression of such an interest. Greatly disturbing the narrative flow, this episode must be vital for the compositional development. Related to an original context of the Yahwist[38] or to later stages of composition,[39] the story must refer to important theological interests connected with the people's right and wrong response. But in this case also, the complex character of the textual shape warns against an over-simplified systematization, especially when based upon the abstractions of modern theological ideas.

The Four Scenes of Visio Dei

Turning now to the actual application of the encounter episodes, the relationship of stereotypes and more singular elaborations could provide important suggestions of the narrative development. The inclusion of the people alongside Moses at the encounter must be important. However sublime the divine actor and the chosen ascender, the series of extraordinary proceedings is profoundly influenced by the events taking place among the people, settled below the mountain. The significance of the people as actors is stressed by the final encounter episode in ch. 40. The theophanic manifestation is now related to the people (40.36-38). The importance of such a relationship is underlined by the earlier encounter episodes given to Moses as the central human figure. The inclusion of the people, and the corresponding exclusion of Moses suggested by v. 35 (cf. Chapter 2.2), must in the final episode be important as an indication of the narrative movement of the earlier episodes.

The final encounter in 40.34-38, with the people as the human actors,

38. Contrasting 'the ideal end' presented by ch. 24 and perhaps even the original conclusion to the Sinai narrative sequence, see Durham, *Exodus*, p. 416. Moberly (*At the Mountain of God*, p. 188) even refers the theology of Exod. 32–34—presenting Yahweh as gracious and merciful as the basis of the covenant—to the relationship of the 'Mosaic and Davidic covenants'.

39. According to Dozemann (*God on the Mountain*, p. 14) the scenes of the 'Sinai Complex' reflect a structure of Proposal of Covenant, Theophany, Decalogue, Book of the Covenant, Tabernacle, Covenant Renewal. To Peter J. Kearney, 'Creation and Liturgy: The P Redaction of Ex 25–40', *ZAW 89* (1977), pp. 375-87, the shape of Exod. 25–40 reflects a theological structure of creation (chs. 25–31 with a seven-speech structure paralleling the seven days of Gen. 1–2), fall (chs. 32–33) and restoration (chs. 34–40). This was fashioned in order to incorporate the JE traditions in 32.1–34.28, which reflect a structure of 'fall-restoration' (pp. 384-85).

can be related to three other scenes. According to 20.18-21, 24.17 and 33.8-10,[40] the people experience the divine manifestation. In all cases, the extraordinary experience is described by motifs of 'seeing'.

The significance of the *visio* motif in these contexts is demonstrated by 20.18aα—even repeated in 18.b according to the Massoretic vocalization. The formal awkwardness of the motif connected with phenomena which rather were 'heard',[41] is witnessed by the text-critical apparatus and later commentators. Moreover, the use of this motif is stressed by the parallel scene of worry in 19.20-25, given to the fright of YHWH that the people should 'tear down to YHWH to see' (v. 21).[42] The location of this passage, set after the description of the grand theophany 'on the third day', must reflect the importance of this encounter. As the theme of the divine message on the third day (19.20-25), and echoed by the people as their reaction to the same events (20.18-21), the act of 'seeing' related to the motif of 'nearness' must be a central expression for the episode. This is stressed by the connection of seeing and death, which is reflected in both passages. Added to by the parallel descriptions in 24.17, 33.8-10 and 40.36-38, 'seeing' related to the people is obviously the important motif for some extraordinary experience.

This is also reflected by the connotational impact of the *visio* motif. The application of the motif in these scenes corresponds to its traditional usage for the description of some special experience of the divine presence, illustrated by such texts as Isaiah 6 and Psalm 42.[43] That its connotational value is retained and even enhanced in the Sinai stories, is indicated by Exod. 33.18-23. The special elaboration on the experience of *visio Dei* clearly refers to extraordinary events. Repeated five times (vv. 18, 20, 23), Moses' 'seeing' represents the central motif of intimate relationship. Corresponding to the scenes of 19.20-25 and 20.18-21, the special seeing implies the threat of death. Also in 24.10-11, the extraordinary experience by the people's representatives is described by the motif of *visio Dei*, here also with elements that reflect the threatening implications of seeing (v. 11a). Set in the context of

40. Cf. also Lev. 9.23-24, together with the contrast episode in 10.1-2 and Num. 9.15-23, with similar scenes.

41. Cf. also the people seeing the divine speaking in v. 22.

42. Cf. also v. 24, in both cases somehow connected with 'the priests', while the motif of seeing is reserved for the people.

43. E.g. Hauge, *Between Sheol and Temple*, p. 84.

33.18-21 and 24.10-11, the motif of *visio Dei* relates the people to some sublime experience of divine reality.

These passages also illustrate the special character of the motif when the people are presented as the visionaries. Moses alone, or together with a select group specially invited to a situation of extraordinary ascent, represents the proper figure of the *visio* scene. The people as the sublime visionaries must imply a strong effect of opposed connotations. This is reflected by the divine worry of 19.20-25 and the people's fright of 20.18-21, the two sets of voices unanimously demonstrating the absurdity of the people as visionaries.

Given this background, the *visio Dei* motif in 20.18-21 and 40.36-38 must have a special significance. This is also indicated by the location of these passages in the composition. The first *visio* scene refers to the climactic episode on the third day in the introductory ch. 19, while the fourth is set as the concluding event in ch. 40.

This is added to by the theophany motifs. In all the four scenes of *visio*, the description of the people is connected to a description[44] of the theophanic manifestation. The immediate connection between theophanic event and the people's seeing is illustrated by the short form in 19.11b. But in the four special scenes, the two motifs of *visio* and theophany are elaborated as expressions for special and successive events. In the first scene in 20.18, the seeing is related to the theophanic manifestation and refers to the description of 19.16-20. In 24.17 the 'consuming glory of YHWH ' is the object of the people's seeing, introduced by the description of the 'cloud' covering the mountain and the 'dwelling glory' vv. 15-17. In 33.8-10 too, the people's experience is related to a theophanic description, expressed by the descent of the 'cloud column' and its 'standing' at the door of the Tent of Meeting. Further, in 40.34-38 the experience of 'the eyes' is related to the 'cloud' covering the Tent of Meeting and the 'glory' filling the 'Dwelling', in addition to the cloud manifesting as fire in the night (v. 38).

The connection of theophany and the people's *visio* points to the special character of the events. Besides these passages, the only comparable theophanic description in Exodus 19–40 is represented by 34.5-6. In this case, the corresponding human response is expressed by other motifs (v. 8), highlighting the intercession of Moses. But the introductory

44. 'Theophanic description' not according to form-critical criteria (e.g. Jeremias, *Theophanie*), but with the theophanic manifestation presented as a special event of the encounter episode.

presentation of this episode in 33.12-23 is centred around the motif of seeing and thus reflects the usual relationship of theophany and *visio Dei*.[45]

Moreover, the connection of theophany and *visio* is added to by a corresponding connection between the people's *visio* and some special emphasis on motifs of locus. In the first episode, the people's seeing results in Moses 'drawing near' while the people 'stand afar' (20.21). In the second, a select group has 'ascended', while Moses is invited to a special ascent (24.12). The significance of both loci is stressed by v. 2. In the third episode, the description lingers on the location of the tent outside and distant from the camp. Moses is separated from the people by his special 'going out' and returning to the camp, while the people as visionaries are confined to their tents in the camp (33.8-11).

So far the people's *visio* is connected to motifs of locality that present Moses as separate from the people, the separation visualized by motifs which depict Moses moving away from the people to the special locus, while the people are 'seeing' from afar. In order to show that Moses was 'near', the scene even indicates a process of heightened intimacy. He is 'drawing near' in 20.21, 'ascending' higher than the other ascenders in ch. 24, and leaving the camp to meet God 'face to face' in 33.11. But this development is reversed in the fourth episode. Here Moses is related to the special locus represented by the Tent of Meeting. But in this case, the elaboration of the motif is of a negative character. Moses is not able to enter the tent, while the theophanic manifestation is related to the people (40.35-38).

The motif connection of theophany, *visio Dei* and locus is too consistent to be ignored. While chs. 19–40 as a whole can be seen as a series of encounter episodes, the four *visio* scenes of 20.18-21, 24.17, 33.8-10 and 40.36-38 seem to refer to four of these encounters as especially important.

The Visio *Episodes and the Narrative Development*

The application of the *visio* motif represents a remarkable qualification of the people as actors in the story. Besides the 'proper' application of the *visio* in 33.18-23 and 24.10-11, the motif is reserved for the people's relationship to the divine presence. Moreover the awesome character of this relationship is stressed by the motifs of theophany. The

45. Cf. also Lev. 9.23-24 together with the contrast episode 10.1-2 and Num. 9.15-23.

radicality of the motif application corresponds to and sharpens the tension of the introductory scenery of ch. 19. Just as Moses represents the worthy hero of the extraordinary encounter on the mountain, the *visio* should rightly belong to Moses but is related to the people.

The implied tension is increased by the narrative development. In the first three episodes, 20.18-21, 24.17 and 33.8-10, the elaboration of the people as visionaries is linked to the presentation of Moses as the extraordinary figure separated from ordinary humanity. This corresponds to, and subtly develops, the narrative impasse suggested by the scenery of ch. 19. Brought 'to me', the people are introduced as a second set of human actors in the encounter episode, while the incompatibility of divine and human represented by YHWH and the people makes the idea of intimate relationship absurd. The first three *visio* episodes develop this perception of absurdity with regard to the people, underlined by the descriptions of Moses as the truly exceptional hero of intimate encounter. But this development is subtly increased by the application of the *visio* motif related to the people. While seemingly subordinate to the presentation of the exalted status of Moses, the *visio* theme is brought to fruition in the final episode of ch. 40. Here the roles are reversed. The people functioning as visionaries represent the central aspect of the episode, while the earlier emphasis on the exclusivity of Moses underlines his position as excluded from the tent. The elaboration of the locus motifs reflects this development.

In the first scene in 20.18-21, the seeing is connected to the people's fear and their insistence on standing afar, contrasted to Moses coming 'near'. This is stressed by the parallel passage of 19.20-25, which presents the seeing as the result of the people's 'tearing down to YHWH' (v. 21) and adds the motif of forbidden ascent in v. 24.

In the second scene in 24.17, the seeing is simply stated without any other qualifying description of the people. But the elaboration of the scene in ch. 24 implies that the people are related to the theophanic manifestation from afar. The consuming glory is located at the top of the mountain, while the first ascent by the people's leaders followed by the exclusive ascent of Moses have left the people far below. And corresponding to the death motifs and the fear-reaction of the first episode, the glory qualified as 'consuming' refers to the frightening aspect of the divine presence.[46]

46. Cf. Lev. 9.24 together with 10.2.

In the third scene in Exod. 33.8-10 the description lingers on the distance between the people and the locus of theophany outside the camp, visualized by the detailed description of Moses leaving and returning. Thus, the idea of separation between the extraordinary figure and the people perceived as visionaries is retained, as well as the separation between the sacred locus of encounter and the people's place. On the other hand, the locus has now been brought down to the level of the camp, the vertical categories of high and low being substituted by horizontal ones. This must be important for a composition introduced by the mountain imagery of ch. 19 and concluded by the tent as the new place of theophanic manifestation in ch. 40. The significance of the horizontal categories is stressed by the peculiar motif development in 33.10. The symmetry of the people standing at the doors of their tents and the divine cloud standing at the door of the tent, hints at some parallelism between the divine and human actors. Moreover, the positions of the actors reflect the interest in presenting the people as the visionaries in this scene too. While Moses has entered the tent for the encounter apart, YHWH is situated outside at the door. Very inconvenient for intimate communication,[47] the position of YHWH makes possible the people's vision from *their* doors![48] Also, it must be important that the theophanic manifestation is presented as something which happened regularly. This contrasts with the earlier episodes of extraordinary manifestation.

The fourth scene in 40.36-38 concludes this development. Compared to the earlier descriptions, the Tent of Meeting as the new theophanic locus is not separated from the people's locality. The aspect of nearness can also be related to the new tent as produced from the people's gifts, contrasting with the former tent of 33.7, explicitly made by Moses 'on his own'. Moreover, the theophanic manifestation is now directly

47. According to Menahem Haran (*Temples and Temple Service in Ancient Israel: An Inquiry into Biblical Cult Phenomena and the Historical Setting of the Priestly School* [Winona Lake: Eisenbrauns, 1985], p. 266), the peculiar positions reflect that the tent of Moses represents an institutional device for the concentration and sharpening of the prophet's mind in preparation for a revelation from outside. On the other hand, the continuation of the tent situation in 34.34-35 presents a scene better suited for communication, with both actors inside. In this case, the people's seeing is related not to the divine presence, but to the face of Moses.

48. Also the people's response of *hištaḥ^{a}wâ* could mark a new type of theophanic relationship. In chs. 19–40, the motif is found in 24.1 related to the chosen representatives and in 34.8 to Moses, besides the negative 20.5, 23.24 and 34.14.

related to the people as the signal for leaving or staying—thus also the category of communication is included in the people's 'seeing'.[49] The hints of parallelism between the theophanic manifestation and the people in the third scene is continued, the people's movement or non-movement being the reflection of the cloud's ascent or non-ascent. Also, the theophanic manifestation is presented as a permanent fixture of life in the camp. Related to the conceptual implications of the theophany, the idea of a permanent theophanic manifestation must be as astounding as the idea of the people as visionaries. But the final exposition of the cloud motif in vv. 36-38 displays the idea. Day and night, the cloud is there, permanently related to the people's eyes.

Given the stereotyped language with its sparseness of details, the use of motif can hardly be coincidental, but must reflect the narrative development, the central episode of encounter gradually transformed into a new situation. This situation is characterized by the people in the camp as a people on the march and set into a permanent relationship to the theophanic manifestation. The permanent divine presence manifests itself as guidance for the people on the march, as the signal for breaking camp or staying. This implies also that the theophanic manifestation has been transformed. With the book of Exodus concluded by the description of the new situation, the development has important repercussions for our understanding of the stories. The change of the *visio* scenes indicates a composition of linear character, the tension of the situation established in ch. 19 released by ch. 40 as a climax.[50] The climax seems to be characterized by a radical transformation of the encounter situation, introducing a new locus, a new type of actor for the human role, and a new type of divine manifestation.

Also the understanding of the formal structure of chs. 19–40 is brought one step further. The composition as a whole is characterized by the repeated application of the encounter episodes. But the *visio* scenes of 20.18-21, 24.17, 33.8-10 and 40.36-38 point to the four encounter episodes of which they are part, as especially important. This changes the initial impression of the composition as a string of successive episodes. Instead, the *visio* scenes could indicate a structure

49. This aspect is underlined by the 'mouth' and Torah motifs of Num. 9.18-20, 23.

50. While the theophany and *visio* motifs of Lev. 9.23-24 and 10.1-2 and Num. 9.15-23 indicate that also the climax reached in ch. 40 can be climaxed by other stories as the reader moves on.

of superior and subordinate episodes. The pattern of four episodes, for sake of convenience labelled 'theophanic episodes' due to the significance of the theophany motifs, seems to be important for the composition.

3. *The Structure of the Three Theophanic Episodes*

The First Theophanic Episode: Exodus 19.1–24.2 and 24.3-18

The first *visio* scene in Exod. 20.18-21 is centred around the people's reaction when the theophanic manifestation is experienced. The description of the people's fright in v. 18 refers to the theophany presented in 19.16-20. The 'flashback' ignores both the intermittent encounter episode of 19.20-25 as well as the proclamation of the Decalogue in 20.1-17. According to 19.25, Moses descends to proclaim the divine message, after which he and Aaron are supposed to ascend (v. 24). But the divine speaker of 20.1 seems to have forgotten his earlier instruction. Verse 25 leaves Moses on the ground, speaking to the people, while God suddenly starts to speak on his own. Ignored by the people of 20.18, the Decalogue of vv. 1-17 seems to be proclaimed into thin air.[51] Moreover, the implementation of the divine invitation in 19.24 to Moses and Aaron to ascend is disturbed and must be repeated in 24.1-2.

The impression of a peculiar order of events is emphasized by the organization of the scenes in ch. 19, which prepare the reader to expect new scenes given to Moses the mediator and the people's obedient response. The present shape is traditionally seen as the unhappy result of the editors' mixing of older and later materials which disturbs the proper proceedings of mediation and response.[52] The present organization even results in the divine message tacitly ignored—the people's experience according to v. 18 related to the theophanic scene of ch. 19 and not to the words of the Decalogue.[53]

51. Cf. also the lack of addressee in v. 1, compared to the other divine speeches in ch. 19 and 20.22.

52. Contrast Childs (*Book of Exodus*, pp. 349-60) and E.W. Nicholson ('The Decalogue as the Direct Address of God', *VT* 27 [1977], pp. 422-33), the latter understanding the present location of the decalogue as the expression of a theological interest in linking theophany and decalogue.

53. For Nicholson ('The Decalogue', pp. 428-30), 20.22 refers to the preceding decalogue and is a direct expression for the theological interest of the present

While formally disturbing the presentation of the Decalogue, the fear scene of 20.18-21 has a more proper function with regard to the following divine instructions introduced in v. 22 and concluded in 24.2. With the problems of mediation solved, the story introduced in ch. 19 can continue. In such a setting, the narrative of 20.22–24.2 is presented as part of the events on the third day. Also the two introductory encounter episodes in 19.3-8a and 8b-14 are part of this development. Both passages refer to the coming events, preparing for the theophanic episode on the third day. This suggests that 19.1–24.2 should be seen as a special narrative unit centred around the theophanic episode prepared by two introductory encounter episodes.

This impression of formal organization makes it all the more necessary to ponder the function of the fear scene in 20.18-21. Its significance is underlined by the connection with the encounter scene in 19.20-25, which is generally understood as a passage rather clumsily 'inserted'.[54] The two scenes are linked by the conclusion of v. 25, which brings Moses down among the people and thus sets the stage for the interaction of Moses and people in 20.18-21.[55] More importantly, the two scenes are linked by a common 'nearness' theme related to the motifs of *visio Dei* and the people's death. In contrast to the people, Moses and Aaron in the first case and Moses in the second are considered 'worthy' enough to be allowed to come near the special locus. The significance of this theme is demonstrated by the formal setting of 19.20-25 as the very first divine message on the climactic third day. Echoed by the people's reaction in 20.18-21, the two scenes make the people's relationship to the theophanic manifestation the central issue of the climactic events on the third day.

The importance of this issue is underlined by the repeated invitation in 24.1-2. The episode of 20.18-21 has interrupted the implementation of the divine invitation to Moses and Aaron to ascend (19.24).

composition with its emphasis on a direct address from YHWH to the people. On the other hand, the context primarily indicates the connection between v. 22 and the preceding scene. The *visio* motif of v. 22 corresponds to the description of the people's experience in 20.18.

54. E.g. Childs, *Book of Exodus*, pp. 361-64.

55. Cf. the similar arrangement 33.1-6 related to vv. 7-11, here in a form of delicate transition which takes the reader from a mountain scene to a situation in the camp, deftly playing upon the established event structure of encounter followed by descent, mediation and response.

Correspondingly, the invitation—now in extended form—has to be repeated.

It can can hardly be coincidental that the Golden Calf episode provides a corresponding example of solemn proceedings disturbed by the people. Equally problematical when traditio-historical considerations are involved,[56] the Golden Calf makes impossible the implementation of the Tabernacle instructions proclaimed in chs. 25–31, just as the reaction of fear on the part of the people makes the proper ascent of Moses and Aaron impossible.

Both interruptions represent sub-episodes that are set in motion by the initiative of the people, the latter connected to some crisis. This is a stereotyped feature of the wilderness stories. But in the narrative structure of chs. 19–40, such events stand out. While the Golden Calf episode has often been compared to the wilderness stories as a story of 'revolt',[57] 20.18-21 also has a corresponding character.

The parallel function of the two stories could be reflected by the way in which they are introduced, the formal contacts of 20.18 and 32.1 even being possible signs of a referential relationship. While 20.18a represents an expansion of the *visio* motif in participle form and an extended description of what was seen, the sentence *wayyar' hā'ām* in 18.bβ is identical to the introductory sentence in 32.1. And in both cases, the people's seeing results in an appeal introduced by imperatives and addressed to a leading figure.

But as parallel 'revolts', the two stories also have in common a peculiar effect as expression for events that are related to the people below the mountain and parallel to events on the mountain. The people's fright in 20.18-19 mirrors the divine concerns conveyed to Moses in the secluded scene of 19.21-24—both parties worry about the mortal threat of too close an encounter. The people's wish for a concrete representation of the divine guide in 32.1 is not prepared for by any events below the mountain, but is strangely parallel to the divine wish for a dwelling made from the people's gifts in chs. 25–31.

56. E.g. Childs, *Book of Exodus*, pp. 558-59, contrast Brichto, 'The Worship of the Golden Calf', pp. 8-9.

57. The significance of the people initiating a set of events is illustrated by the discussion of G.W. Coats (*Rebellion in the Wilderness: The Murmuring Motif in the Wilderness Traditions of the Old Testament* [Nashville: Abingdon Press, 1968], pp. 184-91) on the Golden Calf episode as part of the 'murmuring tradition'. See, further Childs, *Book of Exodus*, p. 260, and Van Seters, *The Life of Moses*, p. 290.

However improper and disturbing they may be, the people's reactions correspond to the divine intentions confided to Moses in the parallel scene on the mountain and results in a 'building story' that contrasts with the narrative in chs. 35–40 (cf. Chapter 3).

Further, in both cases the interruption is connected to the position of Moses. In the first incident, the people's fright makes Moses the mediator by popular acclaim. The second results in the calf as a substitute for Moses as the people's leader,[58] while the solution of the crisis makes the position of Moses supreme (34.29-35).

The parallelism of the two revolts underlines the significance of the non-implementation of the divine instruction in 19.24 and thus the common theme of ascent and 'nearness' in 19.20-25 and 20.18-21. This is also reflected by the repeated invitation to a special ascent in 24.1-2. The significance of this invitation is illustrated by the obvious discomfort its location poses for traditio-historical sensibilities.[59] Added to the laws of 20.22–23.33, the invitation changes the scope of the context from some assumed situation of general and solemn law proclamation followed by the equally solemn rites of some covenant ceremony to a narrative structure of events centred around the encounter situation.

The theme of ascent is also reflected by the peculiar[60] element in 19.13b centred around motifs of a special ascent to the mountain. In the context of ch. 19, the ambiguous invitation to the unnamed 'these' of v. 13b must be connected to the corresponding motifs of non-admission and ascent in vv. 21-24, the latter now related to Moses and Aaron. 24.1-2 extends the invitation to an even larger group, but distinguishes between two kinds of ascent. Both the theme of ascent and the formal

58. For the connection between Moses and the Golden Calf in chs. 32–34, see esp. Moberly, *At the Mountain of God*, pp. 108-109.

59. E.g. Nicholson 'The Covenant Ritual'; Childs, *Book of Exodus*, pp. 499-502; Durham, *Exodus*, pp. 340-43.

60. E.g. O. Eissfeldt, *Hexateuch-Synopse: Die Erzählung der fünf Bücher Mose und des Buches Josua mit dem Anfange des Richterbuches in ihre vier Quellen zerlegt und in deutscher Übersetzung dargeboten samt einer in Einleitung und Ammerkungen gegebenenen Begründung* (Darmstadt: Wissenschaftliche Buchgesellschaft, 1962), p. 147, on a narrative sequence in vv. 10, 13b and 14, ascribed to the E source. The perception of its isolated function in the present context is mitigated by Childs, *Book of Exodus*, p. 368 and J.I. Durham, *Exodus* (WBC, 3; Waco, TX: Word Books, 1987), p. 265, transcribing the motifs into a movement towards the mountain and the boundaries imposed.

ambiguities[61] are continued in the story of implementation in 24.11-18. Joshua is somehow added to the special ascent of Moses (vv. 13-14), while Hur suddenly seems added to the group of those engaged in the *visio Dei* (v. 14)

At the very least, these formal peculiarities attest the interest in a theme of 'who may ascend the mountain'. This is expressed by 19.13, vv. 20-25 added to by 20.18-21, 24.1-2 followed by vv. 10-11 and the new invitation to Moses in v. 12 followed by vv. 13-18. The theme of ascent and the corresponding prohibition against the usurped 'nearness' related to certain actors is repeated like some narrative refrain. Also, the uncertainties and ambiguities with regard to the 'who' of those ascending are repeated rather consistently throughout this composition. The reference to the priests in 19.22 and 19.24 may certainly illustrate that different traditions provide the raw materials for the elaboration of the theme. Above all, the consistent ambiguity could reflect a deliberate blurring[62] which makes the reader stop and ponder the issue.

At the very least, the repetitions underline the negative aspects of the unworthy ascent. With regard to the people as actors in the encounter episode, the introductory events on the third day are unambiguous. The divine concern of 19.20-25, echoed by the people's fright of 20.18-21, asserts the people as 'standing far' away. The absurdity of the situation in 20.18-21—the people voluntarily taking a position 'far' from the locus of encounter—underlines the implications of the mountain imagery in ch. 19. The divine and human aspects of being—when the latter is embodied by the people—represent irreconcilable levels of reality. The admission of certain individuals into some sort of hierarchical ascent demonstrates the vast gulf that separates the people from the goal of priestly holiness (19.6). Obviously, the categories of nearness are such that YHWH—not wanting to kill—is helpless when the boundary between divine and human spheres is crossed by the unworthy, and has to react like a killing automaton. This aspect is carried over into the next episode. While the invited can be set in a situation of *visio* without any 'letting go' of the the divine hand (24.11), the people from afar experience the theophanic manifestation as a 'devouring fire' (v. 17).

61. E.g. Durham, *Exodus*, p. 346.

62. E.g. Sternberg, *The Poetics of Biblical Narrative*, pp. 390-93, on forms and functions of deviance.

Summary

Exodus 19.1–24.2, with its aftermath in 24.3-18, seems to represent one set of interlinked events, centred around the theophanic episode introduced in 19.16 and dedicated to a theme of 'who may ascend'. The encounter episodes introduced in vv. 3 and 8b of ch. 19 represent narrative units which are shaped according to the same format as 19.1–24.18, with the encounter proper framed by introductory and concluding events. But related to the theophanic event 'on the third day' (19.11, 16), the two episodes clearly have an introductory and preparatory function with regard to the climactic event. In addition, the two sub-episodes of 19.20b-25 and 20.18-21 form part of the grand theophanic event. Exodus 19.20b-25, centred around Moses, represents by itself an encounter episode parallel to the others. Exodus 20.18-21 is dominated by the reactions of the people. But concluded by the movement of the mediator towards a special locus of divine presence and the divine address to the mediator, this scene also represents the central aspects of the encounter episode.

The significance of a basic narrative format as well as a composition of overarching units is illustrated by the relationship of 19.1–24.2 to the following episode. With the divine instructions of 24.1-2 carried out in 24.9-18, the theophanic episode of 19.1–24.2 as a whole seems to have an introductory and preparatory function with regard to the next scenes. In this way, the function of 19.1–24.2 is comparable to the preparatory function of 19.3-8a and 8b-15, related to the climactic theophanic events on the third day.

The introductory and subordinate function of 19.3–24.2 related to the next theophanic episode could also be reflected by the local categories of the two episodes. According to 19.25, Moses is located among the people during the divine speech of 20.1-17. And with the new location expressed by motifs of distance and nearness in v. 21, the locus of extraordinary relationship in the first episode seems to function on the horizontal axis. Given the significance of the mountain imagery for these stories, the basic location of the human actors below the mountain in the first episode, while the proper ascent is left for the second, could reflect the narrative movement towards the climactic events.

Such a movement seems to be reflected by the motif of the tablets in 24.12. While the former episode resulted in Moses' writing down the divine words (24.4), both the tablets and the writing of the second theophanic episode are divinely procured. The movement towards climactic events is also suggested by the number of days. Surpassing the event on the third day in ch. 19, the divine glory covers the mountain for six days, while Moses, having ascended, has to wait before some final ascent (24.16).

The Second Theophanic Episode: Exodus 24.3–34.35 and Chapters 35–39

The composition of the second theophanic episode represents special problems due to the significance of the Golden Calf episode and its aftermath in chs. 32–34. But the introductory parts correspond to the etablished pattern. The three basic situations of the encounter episodes of the Sinai stories entail preparatory events and ascent, the encounter proper, concluded by the events of descent and mediation. Set together in a composition of successive episodes, the concluding events of one episode prepare for the next. Correspondingly, 24.3-18 has a double function. The passage presents the mediation and implementation of the divine instructions of the former episode and thus functions as the aftermath of the theophanic episode in 19.1–24.2. At the same time, the events correspond to those of ch. 19 and indicate that the two passages are parallel expressions of a basic pattern of preparatory events and theophany.

The ritual categories of 24.3-8 with its altar-building (v. 4), sacrifices and blood rites (vv. 5-6, 8) are comparable to 19.10-15, centred around preparatory rites of sanctification and purification. What in 19.3-15 are distinguished as two encounters, are combined in 24.3-8 as one set of events, although related to two days. The preparatory events of ch. 19 are not directly repeated. In ch. 24 the people's response of commitment (24.3, 7 compared to 19.7-8a) is added to by the motifs of book and covenant and the blood rites. Similarly, the altar-building and sacrifices of ch. 24 continue and add to the purification acts of ch. 19. The repeated application of the basic pattern seems to present effects of both parallelism and continuation.

This is also reflected by the motifs of movement related to the theophanic locus. In ch. 19, the people are led out of the camp on the third day 'to meet God', standing 'at the foot' of the mountain' (v. 17). Such motifs are also found in ch. 24. But here the idea of movement is primarily linked to the select group ascending (24.9). Also in this story, the motif 'at the foot of mountain' is applied, connected now to the altar built beneath the mountain (v. 4). The young men 'sent out' (v. 5) stress the local separation of 'beneath the mountain' and the camp. According to 24.8 the people are related to this new locality, the imagery implicitly retaining the motif of the people moving from the camp corresponding to 19.17. But the explicit imagery of movement is elaborated for the ascent of the chosen group.

The shift from people to the special group as central for this episode is also reflected by the prohibitions of 24.2. According to vv. 12-13 and 23-24 of ch. 19, the accepted ascent is linked to prohibitions of ascent that are addressed to the people (including 'the priests' in v. 24). Also in 24.1-2, the invitation to ascend is linked to negative forms. The prohibited ascent related to the people is retained (v. 2b). But the central prohibition is related to the select group, ordered to worship 'from afar' and not to usurp the 'nearness' allowed to Moses (vv. 1b-2a). The motifs of distance and nearness correspond to the categories of 20.18-21 related to Moses and people.

A basic linkage between the two scenes, one 'beneath the mountain' and the other somewhere up in the mountain,[63] is suggested by the motifs of sacrifice (vv. 4-6, 8), extended[64] by a scene of eating and drinking (v. 11). Such a linkage is also indicated by the formal mode. The introductory *wayyaʿal mōšeh* in 24.9 continues the preceding verses. The singular form followed by verbs in plural forms vv. 10-11, referring to the extended group of ascenders, is comparable to the sentence pattern of vv. 3, 5 and 7. The elaboration of the scenes seems to reflect an enlarged version of the basic motifs. This is also indicated by the parallel scenes of vv. 10-11 and v. 17, in which people and the select group are similarly related to the divine presence by *visio* motifs.

This corresponds to the manner in which the movement motifs are related to Moses. In ch. 19, the people's movement towards the locus is continued by the ascent of Moses, the description of which is intermixed with the corresponding divine movement of descent (vv. 16-20).[65] This pattern is adhered to in the second episode, but in extended

63. The carefully ambiguous mode of combining the scenes is also demonstrated by the elaboration of the two mountain scenes in vv. 9-11 and 12-18. The ascent of Moses alone is explicitly connected to the mountain imagery (vv. 12a, 13b, 15a, 18), while the other ascent is only expressed by the verb 'ascend' (v. 9).

64. Cf. 32.6 and also the episode of 18.12, presented as two scenes of sacrifice by Jethro and of 'eating bread' with Jethro by Aaron and the elders.

65. Cf. also the ascent of Moses followed by a new movement of 'nearness' in 20.21. In 24.12-18 too the expanded description of Moses ascending could separate

form. The implicit movement of the people to the altar beneath the mountain and the special ascent by the people's representatives in 24.9-11 is followed by the ascent of Moses vv. 12-18. In this case too the description of the theophany and the special ascent of Moses is intermixed, comparable to 19.16-20.

The parallel events seem to express the effects of continuation and development. The altar outside the camp introduces a new locality in addition to the camp and mountain of the first episode, just as the new sub-figures represented by the ritual servants of 24.5 and the new sets of ascenders elaborate the established roles of the first episode.

So far the compositional development seems to represent a parallel application of a basic structure of events. The events of preparation, ascent and theophany, followed by the encounter in 24.3–31.18, reflect a structure of events that corresponds to 19.3–24.2. At the same time, the second episode reflects a linear development, continuing and surpassing the first theophanic episode. Compared to the first, the motifs of human movement are important for the second set of preparations. The interrupted ascent of the first set is now actualized, elaborated in 24.9-18 as two scenes related to two sets of ascenders. While the main encounter of the first episode (20.21–24.2) seems to be set beneath the mountain, the encounter in chs. 25–31 is located at the top of the mountain. The wondrous character of the latter location is underlined by the extended description of the ascent scenes in 24.9-11 followed by a new invitation and a new ascent in vv. 12-18. The divinely written tablets referred to in 24.12 and 31.18—juxtaposed to Moses' writing in 24.4—are a direct expression for this effect of progress, the second episode the culmination of the first.

As part of this development, the ascent and *visio* by the select group in 24.9-11 must have a special significance as an episode of extraordinary encounter extended to a large number of people. The duality of the first episode—expressed by the contrasts of mountain and below the mountain, divine and human—is retained in the second. The concept of human ascent implies the bridging of the contrasts, stressed by the enlarged number of ascenders in the second episode. But the description of 24.4-18 implies that the people of 20.18-21 are now separated into two groups of ascenders and non-ascenders. Moreover, both groups are separated from the super-ascent of Moses accompanied by Joshua. Also

between an initial ascent related to six days of waiting (vv. 13-15) followed by the ascent into the cloud on the seventh day (vv. 16-18).

retained from the first episode are the sinister implications of the encounter. This is referred to in the two juxtaposed *visio* situations of 24.10-11 and 17. In connection with the successful ascent, the wondrous 'seeing' is twice stated (v. 10a and 11b).[66] The peculiar connection of divine beauty and non-violence in vv. 10b-11a stresses the significance of divine violence as the shadow of the *visio Dei*. This corresponds to the more drastic qualification of the divine glory perceived as a 'devouring fire' by the people in v. 17, the implications of which are illustrated in Lev. 9.24 and 10.2.

Comparable to the first theophanic episode, the description of the preparatory events and theophanic manifestation is followed by the presentation of the encounter proper in chs. 25–31. But this development is interrupted by the events of the Golden Calf, while the pattern of encounter followed by mediation of the divine instructions is returned to first in ch. 35. In addition, the Golden Calf episode is followed by the fully-fledged encounter episode of ch. 34. For the traditional approach, this state of affairs is not perceived as especially problematical. The transition from older to later materials is taken for granted, the connectedness of chs. 25–31 and 35–40 as Priestly and thus basically different from the mass of materials in chs. 19–24 and 30–32, represents an obvious fact. But while the character of the materials seems to indicate a compilation of very different literary traditions, the 'insertion' of chs. 32–34 into the assumed Priestly materials of chs. 25–31 and 35–40 could indicate a process not of automatic addition, but of literary relationships that challenge the reader.[67] *In nuce*, some enigmatic mixture is demonstrated by the Tent of Meeting set up in 33.7-11.

So far, it has been seen that 20.18-21 represents a story of 'revolt' parallel to the Golden Calf episode. Moreover, the presence of these passages in their contexts provokes the modern reader to corresponding reactions. The impression of formal rupture caused by 20.18-21 as well as 19.20-25 and 24.1-2 is comparable to the source- and traditio-critical perceptions of chs. 32–34. Formally, the conclusion of 31.18 should indicate that the encounter on the mountain has come to an end, comparable to the conclusion of 34.27-28. Instead, the flash-back to the

66. Cf. the corresponding application of the motif 'standing afar' introducing and concluding 20.18-21.

67. E.g. for Kearney ('Creation and Liturgy') the shape of chs. 25–40 reflects a theological structure of creation (chs. 25–31), fall (chs. 32–33) and restoration (chs. 34–40).

mountain scene in 32.7-14 prolongs the encounter by the divine reaction to the Golden Calf and the intercession of the mediator. The interweaving of the scenes is comparable to the setting of 20.18-21, with a corresponding flash-back to the situation of 19.16-19. In both cases, the narrative mode reflects the relatively independent character of what happens among the people, parallel to the events on the mountain. More importantly, the two 'revolts' seem to have a similar function within the context. Comparable to the interruption of 20.18-21, the mediation of the divine instructions in chs. 25–31 is disrupted by the events set in motion by the people in 32.1-6. In both cases, the interrupted implementation of the divine instruction is postponed to the following episode. The ordered ascent of the first episode is actualized in the second, while the ordered building of the Tabernacle is actualized in the third. Just as the popular appointment of Moses as the mediator in 20.21 introduces a new series of divine instructions, so his new stature according to ch. 34 introduces the new beginning of ch. 35.

The shape of the divine instructions in chs. 25–31 and the story of mediation and response in chs. 35–39 points to the close connection between the two passages.[68] In spite of the richness and complexity of chs. 32–34, the connection between chs. 25–31 and 35–40 presents the overarching linkage. What was divinely ordered on the mountain is minutely carried out by the people in the camp acting under Moses' guidance, the acts of chs. 35–40 mirroring the divine instructions of chs. 25–31. As part of this development, the Golden Calf episode of 32.1-6, followed by the intercession scenes in chs. 32–34, seems to present a negative parallel to the building story in chs. 35–40. The effect of parallelism is emphasized by the descent motifs. By the new descent of Moses in 34.29-33, which contrasts with the negative descent of 32.15-20,[69] the main story is brought back on track.

Set in such a contextual frame, the immediate function of chs. 32–34 is comparable to that of 20.18-21. The relationship between the short form and the extended version corresponds to the heightened significance of the second theophanic episode compared to the first. It reflects the importance of the Golden Calf episode, with 20.18-21 preparing for the second and central episode of the people's 'revolt'. While it will be necessary to return to these questions later, it seems possible at this

68. Completing 'each other as instruction and obedience, as promise and fulfillment' (Durham, *Exodus*, p. 475).

69. This connection is stressed by Moberly, *At the Mountain of God*, p. 106.

stage to propose that 24.3–34.35, added to by the story of mediation and implementation in chs. 35–39, should be read as a second theophanic episode in continuation of 19.1–24.2.

d. *The Third Theophanic Episode: Exodus 35.1–40.38*

Related to the narrative structure of the preceding chapters, the events introduced in ch. 35 correspond to the preparatory events of 19.3-15 and 24.3-18. As in the ch. 24 account, so too 35.1–40.33 presents overlapping events. The divine instructions of the preceding encounter (chs. 25–31) are mediated to the people and responded to, 35.1–40.33 thus concluding the second episode 24.3–34.35. But preparing for the next scene of encounter, 35.1–40.33 have an introductory function with regard to the climactic theophanic event of 40.34-38. This corresponds to the pattern of preparations and theophany established by the two preceding theophanic episodes of 19.1–24.2 and 24.3–34.35.

Referring to ritual categories, the third set of theophanic preparations are comparable to those of the earlier episodes. The events of ch. 19 are centred around the people's purification in addition to references to the spatial categories of theophanic locus. In ch. 24, the preparatory acts refer to altar building and sacrifices in addition to the elaboration of the locus motifs. Chapters 35–40 are devoted to the construction of the tabernacle and the sacred objects (chs. 35–39), followed by the erection and furnishing of the Tabernacle (40.1-30). In addition, the preparatory acts also include rites of sanctification, connected to the offering of incense, sacrifices and the purification of priests (40.27-32).

While the three sets refer to ritual categories and reflect a parallel function of preparation, the motif elaboration suggests a development of linear character. Moreover, the development seems to indicate a movement towards climactic events. The washing of clothes and the sexual abstinence of the first set of preparations are followed by the altar building and the substitute priests performing sacrifices in the second episode. Concluded by the production of the Tabernacle and its implements, the preparatory acts of the three episodes head towards a climax of elaborate complexity and perfection.

This is more clearly seen when these preparation motifs are related to the locus motifs. In the first episode of ch. 19, the preparations are not related to any special locality, but are implicitly connected to the camp. Correspondingly, the ritual preparations refer to personal categories of purity. In the second episode of ch. 24, the basic localities of mountain and camp are extended by the new location 'beneath the mountain', where the altar is built and the young men are presumably sent. The character of the new locality is reflected by the events—the altar building accompanied by sacrifices and rites of 'eating and drinking'. In the third set of preparatory events in chs. 35–39, the character of the preparations correspond to the character of the new locus. With the theophanic locus and the ritual locus of the people of the second episode now identical, due to the divine move from mountain to tent, the preparations of the third episode are related to the tabernacle that is to be built and furnished and finally entered into. The ritual motifs of the preparatory scenes reflect the importance of the locus theme for the composition as a whole. The growing complexity from scene to scene seems to mirror a process of gradual materialization, the change of the divine reality reflected by a corresponding emphasis on concrete material manifestations in the human world beneath the mountain.[70]

Further, in the third episode, the preparatory events are concluded by motifs of movement relative to the sacred locus. In 19.16-20 this implies the difference between the movement of the people and the special ascent of Moses, the description of the latter being intermixed with the theophanic description. A corresponding separation is found in ch. 24, primarily between the ascent of the chosen representatives and the special ascent of Moses. Also in this case, the description of the latter is intermixed with the theophanic description. Further, the concluding episode of ch. 40 reflects the separation of two kinds of human movement related to the sacred locus. The 'coming' to the Tabernacle and the 'coming near' to the altar (40.32) is performed with Moses and the priests as subjects. This corresponds to the common movement by Moses and the people in 19.16 and by Moses and the representatives of the people in 24.9-11. After the movement of Moses and priests in 40.32, v. 35 alludes to some special movement for Moses,[71] also here intermixed with the theophanic description. But in this case, the special movement of the mediator is presented as a non-event. The connection

70. This surely must indicate that the 'Priestly' interests can not be confined to chs. 25–31 and 35–40 and some superficial redaction of the older materials, but is characteristic of the composition as a whole, so far as we are able to ascertain its character.

71. The repeated motif 'enter into the Tent of Meeting' corresponds to the priestly movement of v. 32. The parallelism is comparable to the usage of 'ascend' both for the movement of the select group and of Moses in ch. 24.

with the earlier scenes underlines the importance of this conclusion, the contrast alerting the reader that some important change has taken place.

The character of the human actors could also be important for the narrative development. In the preparations of 19.3-15, the people, together with Moses, are the actors. In the second set of preparations of ch. 24, the people and the group of priestly young men are active in the first sub-episode, while in the second the movement of ascent is related to Moses and the chosen group of priests and the people's elders. In the third set, the introductory and concluding events of chs. 35–39 highlight the people as active in the first sub-episode (cf. Chapter 2.3). The second sub-episode in 40.1-33 is dominated by Moses single-handedly setting up and furnishing the Tabernacle, concluded by rites of purification related to Moses together with Aaron and his sons entering the sacred space.[72]

This development could be related to a theme of hierarchical separation within the people with a special emphasis on the priestly function. The narrative line of young men as priestly substitutes followed by priestly representatives in the special ascent in ch. 24, concluded by the priestly entering in 40.31-32 and even continued in a further theophanic episode in Leviticus 9, could reflect the significance of the priestly function connected to the change of the theophanic locus.

But while this narrative line seems to represent one interest of the narrative development,[73] it is combined with, and subtly altered by, more central interests. Some ambiguity could even be expressed by the references to the priestly actors. The invitation to Aaron to ascend in 19.24 is contrasted with the reference to the priests grouped among the people as non-ascenders. The renewed invitation of 24.1, the priests invited by name (cf. also v. 9), seems to mark great progress for the priestly class. But this impression becomes rather marred when the reader ponders the identity of these priestly actors. Aaron is set together

72. Cf. Chapter 2.2 for the ambiguity surrounding 40.30-32 (parallel to vv. 35-38). On the one hand this passage presents events on the day of sanctification; on the other, it also widens subtly the description into a presentation of what repeatedly took place.

73. Probably connected to the theme of 'transference of the Moses function'; cf. below for the 'lesser judges' of 18.13-26 and the inspired leaders of Num. 11, in addition to the levites of Exod. 32.25-29 and Num. 8, and also the appointment of Joshua in Num. 27.16-23.

with Nadab and Abihu. This choice of representatives is rather strange.[74] If interests connected to the priestly institution had been considered, the two other sons of Aaron 'should' have been selected. Instead, the choice of Nadab and Abihu cannot but allude to Lev. 10.1-2 and the two negative heroes in a story of priestly usurpation ended by the destructive manifestation of 'devouring fire'.[75] Set in such a company, Aaron's position too becomes rather tainted. The reader's attention is drawn to his function as the maker of the Golden Calf and thus to an episode of priestly 'black magic' comparable to the 'strange fire' of Lev. 10.1. Thus, while the three priestly representatives truly partake in the extraordinary situation of *visio Dei* according to Exod. 24.9-11, the impression of this situation is added to and subtly deepened by a contrasting impression.[76]

Moreover, the priestly motifs primarily seem to underline the development of the people as the central actors. In no episode are the priestly representatives related to the special theophanic manifestation. This is reserved for Moses and gradually related to the people by the *visio*-scenes. The elaboration of the movement motifs, separating between an intial movement by an enlarged group followed by the special ascent by Moses, prepares for the last scene in 40.32-38. A first 'entering into the Tent of Meeting' (40.32) is stated for an extended group of Moses and priests. With Moses as subject, a second 'entering into the Tent of Meeting' is referred to, but negatively (v. 35). Instead, the relationship to the theophanic manifestation is reserved for the people (vv. 36-38). Thus, if the elevation of the priests serves to indicate that some aspects of Moses' function have been transferred to priestly substitutes, the people are presented as substitutes for Moses as actors in the extraordinary theophanic relationship.

74. The significance of selection is illustrated by the added names of the Samaritan version, especially when the present shape of the story is related to traditio-historical categories; see, e.g., Childs, *Book of Exodus*, pp. 499-507.

75. The corresponding qualification of the divine manifestation (24.17) in a story introduced in vv. 1 and 9 of ch. 24 by the actors of Lev. 10.1-2 seems to reflect the connection of the two stories.

76. The delicacy of exposition indicates that the identification of some 'anti-Aaron' tendency in such stories (e.g. Childs, *Book of Exodus*, pp. 561-62) as well as an alternative pro-hierarchical 'Priestly' interest represent too simple categories.

Summary
So far, an understanding of Exodus 19–40 as a composition of three successive theophanic episodes seems to represent a not too artificial construction. Centred around events that prepare for the theophany, the human participation seems to represent the central theme of this composition. The narrative development relates the three episodes to each other in a linear order of preparation and climax.

Both the close relationship of the episodes as well as the linear development of successive events is reflected by the double function of the overlapping sub-episodes in 24.3-18 and 35.1–40.33. On the one hand they clearly continue the preceding encounters, presenting the mediation of the divine instructions from above and the people's response. On the other hand, the response results in a new theophany. It is primarily due to chs. 19 and 40 that we are able to discern a relationship of preparatory events and theophany as the basic pattern of each episode. In the first episode, the events begun in 19.3 prepare for the climax on the third day. Conversely, the special form of 40.36-38, turning the story into repeated acts, together with the transition from the book of Exodus to Leviticus, invite the reader to pause[77] after the descripion of the theophanic events and their significance for the people.

The significance of this pattern is illustrated by the comparable narrative nucleus of ritual preparation and divine manifestation in Exodus 12. The repetition of the formula of implementation in vv. 28 and 50 underlines the pattern of divine instructions mediated by Moses (vv. 1-27 and 43-49) responded to by the people (vv. 28 and 50), and followed by the miraculous events (vv. 29-41 repeated in short-form in v. 51). Leviticus 1–9 too reflects such a pattern, with the divine instructions of chs. 1–7 followed by the ritual implementation of the instructions, which prepares for the climax of the theophany in chs. 8–9.[78]

It seems rather natural to assume that such a pattern ultimately could have a background in some cultic practice.[79] Its actual application

77. A relative one due to the continuation of the episode in Lev. 1–7.

78. Cf. also the episode of ch. 10—the theophanic manifestation 'disturbed' by the parallel events set in motion by human initiative—comparable to the episodes of Exod. 20.18-21 and chs. 32–34.

79. E.g. Dozemann, *God on the Mountain*, p. 19, on a pre-Deuteronomistic 'Mountain of God tradition' in chs. 19–24, consisting of an account of purification

indicates that such a background has been transformed into established literary themes. This is demonstrated by the singular character of each episode. Moreover, it is also applied as the literary pattern of the plague stories. The compositional development of these stories is comparable to the development of the encounter episodes of chs. 19–40, with the same effects of repetition and linear development into a climax. And with the divine intervention as a climax, prepared by introductory scenes of divine instructions and response related to Moses and Pharaoh as the central human actors and a concluding scene of response centred around Pharaoh, the event pattern is comparable to the Sinai stories with Moses and people for human actors.

The pattern of preparatory events and climactic event also seems to be reflected by Exodus 19–40 as a whole. As parts of the linear development, the three grand theophanic episodes are related to each other in a corresponding order. The first episode has a subordinate function of preparation with regard to the following story, which in its turn is subordinate to and prepares for the final story.

Such a pattern of three successive episodes even seems to be reflected within each episode. In ch. 19 the climactic event takes place on the third day, prepared for by two encounter episodes connected to two days of introductory events (vv. 3-8a, 8b-15). In ch. 24, the two days of commitment and sacrifice events in vv. 3-8 present one set of preparatory events. The ascent of the chosen group is elaborated into a second scene of special character. Concluded by the theophanic manifestation and the encounter, this structure reflects the pattern of ch. 19.

The story of implementation in chs. 35–40 also presents two sets of preparatory events concluded by the theophany. The mediation of the divine instructions and the people's response as a first set of events is marked by the elaborate conclusion in 39.32-43. This is followed by a new scene. A set of divine instructions addressed only to Moses in 40.1-15 is followed by a new story of implementation in vv. 16-33. Its conclusion in v. 33b is comparable to the conclusion of the people's response in 39.32-43.[80] Greatly expanded compared to the two first

culminating in a theophany on the mountain (19.10ab-11a, 12a, 13b-15a, 16ab-17) and finally a concluding sacrificial ritual at the base of the mountain (24.4ab-5).

80. The connection between the two separate sets of preparation is also indicated by the references to the Priestly creation story in 39.32a, 43 and 40.33b (U. Cassuto, *A Commentary on the Book of Exodus* [trans. I. Abrahams; Jerusalem: Magnes Press, 1967], pp. 477, 483).

episodes, the formal organization of the materials reflects the same pattern of two preparatory episodes climaxed by the theophany of 40.34-38.

The significance of this pattern is underlined by the character of the sub-episodes. The two sub-episodes of 19.3-15 are centred around two encounter–scenes framed by the ascent and descent of Moses. Of the two sub-episodes of 24.3-11, the first is set among the people, the second in a scene of ascent and encounter by the representatives of the people. In 35.1–40.33 both scenes take place within the camp. The gradual change from categories of verticality and events of miraculous character and selected human actors to events set in the camp among the people, can hardly be coincidental. It corresponds to the main compositional development, mirroring the change of divine locus from mountain to Tabernacle and the introduction of the people as theophanic figures.

In this way, the overarching compositional development of three main theophanic episodes, the first preparing for the next until the climax of the third, seems to be reflected by the narrative structure of the single theophanic episode, each consisting of two sets of preparatory events leading up to the theophanic climax.

It can hardly be coincidental that the Elijah encounter of 1 Kings 19 is composed of a comparable pattern of events, related to one human actor. In this case too, the narrative development reflects the linear relationship of successive events. But the prophet's locations (vv. 3-5, 8-9, 11-13) indicate a pattern of three stages. Each stage is introduced by the prophet's movement towards a place and characterized by the address from a different form of divine manifestation, climaxed by the extraordinary theophany which is experienced by the prophet at a final locus. The connection between the three stages is also reflected by the reference to the prophet's movement towards a new place (vv. 7, 11, 15). Given the other points of contact between 1 Kings 19 and Exodus 19–40, it is natural to assume that the common compositional pattern reflects a special structure, on the one hand traditional and highly connotative, on the other malleable for individual narrative development.[81]

The pattern of three grand episodes, each composed of three sub-episodes, underlines the narrative movement towards a climax and thus

81. Cf. Chapter 3.1 for the similar relationship of the three episodes in 32.31–34.35.

the conclusion of ch. 40. Framed by 19.3 and Lev. 1.1, the story as a whole presents how the locus of the theophany was changed from mountain to tabernacle. This change of locus is connected with the change from Moses to the people as the human actor in the encounter. Moreover, the character of the encounter has also been altered. The divine presence is manifested as a permanent theophany, the people correspondingly set in a permanent situation of *visio Dei*. Related to ch. 19, this development indicates that the radical duality of divine and human—with the people as actors—established in the first scenes has been overcome.

The sharp duality of two types of being that is expressed both by the basic scenery of mountain above and camp below, and fleshed out by the parallel divine and human fright for the deadly nearness, which is established in the first theophanic episode, is retained in the second. But in addition, the second episode returns to the ascent that was intimated in the first episode. The invitation to ascend, interrupted by the revolt scene in 20.18-21, is actualized in the second episode. The extension of the group of worthy ascenders in the second episode could reflect the narrative movement towards the climax of ch. 40. Further, the extraordinary character of the extended ascent is demonstrated by the special *visio* scene of 24.9-11.

But this development of the theme of 'ascent' is abruptly dropped. Without any explicit reason stated, the story is changed by the divine decision to dwell among the people, which is announced in chs. 25–31. Instead of the separation between high and low overcome by the special ascent by special people, the divine actor suddenly has decided to descend to the level of the people below. But while the divine decision seems at first rather unexpected, it can be related to the subtle undercurrents indicated by the gradual development of the camp below the mountain as the locus of the significant events. This development is reflected by the elaboration of the *visio* scenes of 20.18-21, 24.17, 33.8-10 and 40.36-38. Similarly, the elaboration of the three sets of preparatory events indicates the gradual abandonment of the mountain imagery and the categories of the extraordinary encounter on the mountain in favour of events taking place below and acted out by the human actors. Moreover, the identification of the priestly ascenders in vv. 1 and 9 of ch. 24 has subtly disturbed the impression of successful ascent. The presence of Nadab and Abihu, the future anti-heroes of Lev. 10.1-2, taints also the presence of Aaron, the future maker of the Golden Calf.

However successful, the ascent does not represent the solution to the problems of encounter presented in ch. 19.

Within this structure, chs. 32–34 have a special and rather complex function. Related to the over-arching development of the three grand theophanic episodes, the story of the Golden Calf incident, with its aftermath, seems to represent an intermission of a special kind. As some subordinate loop of the main circle, it makes the story deviate from the proper development and then returns, presenting events which disturb and then affirm the proper succession of events indicated by the relationship of chs. 25–31 and 35–41. Some 'circular' relationship is also suggested by the parallel tablet scenes of 31.18 and 34.28, the first set of tablets being replaced by the second.[82] Also the contrasting effect of the two descents in 32.19-29 and 34.29-35 emphasizes the parallelism of the introductory and concluding events.[83]

These effects, seen together with the contextual location, indicate that the Golden Calf incident and chs. 35–39 have a contrast relationship as expressions of a negative and positive response to the divine instructions of chs. 25–31. While chs. 35–39 present the proper mediation of the divine instructions and the people's proper response, the Golden Calf incident and its aftermath represent the contrasting episode. Set in motion by the people's initiative in a series of events interwoven with the encounter episode (32.1-6, followed by vv. 7-14), the Golden Calf episode even includes the aspects of contrasting encounter. Such a relationship is also indicated by the concrete motif development. The people's wish for the divine presence 'in front of us', as a substitute for Moses, mirrors the divine intention 'to dwell in the people's midst' revealed in chs. 25–31.[84] Both stories are centred around costly raw materials presented by the people and processed into material containers for two contrasting types of divine presence. The significance of the gift motifs for the building of the Tent of Meeting is demonstrated by the compositional pains taken in 25.1-8 to present the people's gifts

82. Important to Kearney ('Creation and Liturgy', p. 382) as an expression for the Priestly reworking of the older traditions.

83. Moberly, *At the Mountain of God*, p. 106.

84. On this connection between chs. 25–31 and the Golden Calf as an 'antitype', the latter a 'perversion' of the former, cf. esp. Childs, *Book of Exodus*, pp. 542-43, and Moberly, *At the Mountain of God*, p. 47.

as a basic part of the building instructions[85] and by the elaboration of these motifs in 35.5–36.7.

The deviation from the story caused by the Golden Calf incident has been repaired by the intercession of Moses, and ch. 35 can return to the concerns of chs. 25–31. Set between these two passages, the story about the Golden Calf is to be read as the negative image of the proper ending. Unchecked, it would have ruined the successful ending of the Sinai story, but atoned for it primarily underlines the glory of the happy ending. In this context, the violent confrontation in the camp of 32.19-29 has for its ultimate contrast the scene of 39.32-43. Moses' 'seeing' the calf and the people dancing (32.19) corresponds to his 'seeing' the people's works (39.43). And the inspection concluded by Moses' 'blessing' the people contrasts with the terrible way in which 'blessing' is obtained in the negative story (32.29). The Golden Calf produced by the people taking the law into their own hands has been substituted by the people's perfect 'doing' of all 'which YHWH had commanded Moses' (39.42).

But in addition to an effect of negative parallelism as a contrasting story, the Golden Calf episode along with the parallel revolt of 20.18-21 also have a more direct function within the main development indicated by the three theophanic episodes. Related to the main story line, the behaviour of the people in both cases demonstrates the absurdity of a story that operates with the people as human actors in the situation of *visio Dei*, and reaffirms the special position of Moses as the only mediator between high and low. The two stories of revolt continue and sharpen the effect of the introductory scene in ch. 19, the impression of total incompatibility between high and low fleshed out by the people when acting on their own initiative. This prepares for the wondrous character of the events in 40.36-38, with the people engaged in a permanent *visio Dei*.

4. *The Shape of Exodus 32–34*

At this stage of the present reading, it is necessary to probe the question of how chs. 32–34 are related to the context of chs. 19–40. So far, the

85. Illustrated by the source-critical operations of, among others, Klaus Koch, *Die Priesterschrift von Exodus 25 bis zu Leviticus 16: Eine überlieferungs geschichtliche und literarkritische Untersuchung* (FRLANT, 71; Göttingen: Vandenhoeck & Ruprecht, 1959), pp. 7-10 and also Utzschneider, *Das Heiligtum*, pp. 197-200.

relationship of three theophanic episodes climaxed in ch. 40 seems to reflect the overarching development of the story. Set between chs. 25–31 and 35–40, the Golden Calf episode could have a prime function as a non-event, threatening to destroy the orderly progress of the events divinely proclaimed. Nullified by the intercession of Moses, the distortion of the Golden Calf is overcome. Related in such a way to the central story, the function of the Golden Calf episode is prepared for by the parallel revolt story in 20.18-21. But while this could be relevant for certain aspects, both the singular character as well as the emotive force of certain episodes makes it necessary to question how the shape of these chapters fits into what hitherto is perceived as the main compositional development.

The Golden Calf

The introductory episode of 32.1-6 is formally linked to the main story. The Golden Calf incident of vv. 1-6 is followed by the dialogue between God and Moses on the mountain in vv. 7-14.[86] This dialogue adds a new scene to the encounter of chs. 25–31, which seemed to be concluded by 31.18. Framed by scenes of the encounter, the Golden Calf episode represents events below taking place simultaneously with the encounter above. The reader's attention is drawn from the mountain scene of 31.18 to the happenings in the camp, and then back again to the main situation. The linkage between the events is directly expressed by the dialogue between YHWH and Moses, commenting on the behaviour of the people.

Such a connection is also suggested by the formal introduction of the incident. The abrupt change of scenery and the fatal character of the events taking place among the people are not marked by any dramatic literary effects. The narrative style of 31.18 is continued by 32.1 as well as by v. 7. Only the introduction of new actors marks the transition into a new scene. Moreover, the revolt scene of 32.1 continues the mountain scene of the preceding verse, 31.18. Moses' lingering on the mountain results in the people's demand. Also the people's 'seeing' marks a return to the preceding situation. Left in 24.17-18 'seeing' the divine

86. And correspondingly viewed with suspicion as a later addition when source- and traditio-historical criteria are applied. On the other hand, Van Seters (*The Life of Moses*, p. 295) regards vv. 7-8 as part of the 'base narrative' of vv. 1-6, together with vv. 15a*, 17-24, and 30-34. The base narrative is extended by vv. 9-14, influenced by Deut. 9.12-14, and is also attributed to J (p. 312).

glory, connected to the description of Moses entering the cloud and staying on the mountain for forty days and forty nights, the people are reintroduced in 32.1 'seeing' the absence of Moses.

The connection to the preceding episode is also reflected by the other events in ch. 32. Corresponding to the established event structure, the encounter on the mountain is followed by the descent of the mediator. The description of the descent and the meeting with the people in the camp represents a singular version—greatly extended—of the events that normally conclude the encounter. The linkage is emphasized by the reference to Joshua and the tablets. Corresponding to Joshua being left somewhere on the mountain (24.13-14 related to v. 15), he enters the stage again during the descent (vv. 17-18) and is also referred to in the following tent scene (33.11). Correspondingly, the tablets of 31.18—first presented in 24.12 and referred to in the descent scene in 32.15-16—are destroyed together with the Golden Calf (vv. 19-20).[87] The events of encounter and Golden Calf are interwoven as parts of one episode, the wrathful descent of Moses an individual expression of the pattern of events which have been established in the preceding episodes.

On the other hand, the destruction of the tablets also marks the deviation from the established story line. While the descent should introduce a situation of mediation, the following confrontation in the camp is centred around the events of the Golden Calf. Accordingly, the Golden Calf seems to represent an event set up as a contrast to the parallel encounter on the mountain.[88] The latter is ended with the stone

87. Stressed by Kearney, 'Creation and Liturgy', p. 382 as an expression of the P editing of chs. 32–34, with an important literary and structural function for the linkage of JE and P traditions.

88. Some connection of this type, most often between the Golden Calf episode and ch. 24, has usually been stressed as the original. Durham (*Exodus*, pp. 341-42, 347-48), for example, proposes that the 'ideal end' of the Sinai stories presented in ch. 24 is continued by ch. 32 as a contrasting episode; cf. also Aurelius, *Der Fürbitter Israels*, p. 68, on ch. 32 as originally the continuation of 'die Sinaiperikope', prepared for by 24.12-15a, 18b, 31.18. The ambiguous character of the contextual function of chs. 32–34, when related to traditio-critical categories, is illustrated by Kearney, 'Creation and Liturgy', pp. 382-85. The contrasting relationship between the two descents of chs. 32 and 34 are vitally important for P's inclusion of chs. 25–31 and 35–40 according to a theological structure of creation (chs. 25–31), fall (chs. 32–33) and restoration (chs. 34–40). This represents a reworking of an original JE structure in which chs. 32–34 reflected a structure of fall and restoration. Read according to criteria of narrative development, the

tablets wrought by the divine craftsman, the wonderful character of which is underlined by the repetitions in 32.15-16, in contrast to the calf of gold[89] wrought by Aaron the clumsy craftsman.[90]

These indications of parallelism underline the character of the story in 32.1-6. The structure of the events corresponds to the established pattern of the theophanic episodes. The events are set in motion by a set of 'instructions', in this case issued by the people usurping the role of the divine commander. The people's commandment is addressed to Aaron in the role of Moses, in his turn instructing the people, building the altar and performing as the ritual leader. This corresponds to the established role of Moses usurped, however passively, by Aaron.[91] With the main part of the story connected with ritual preparations and climaxed by the sacrificial meal, the events represent an individual version of the established pattern of the theophanic episodes. The form of the proclamation in v. 4b, 'these are your Gods, Israel!', implies the visual impression of the calf. Added to by the 'seeing' of Aaron (v. 5a),

contrasting relationship of the two descents in chs. 32 and 34 is important to Moberly, *At the Mountain of God*, p. 106. And when Childs (*Book of Exodus*, pp. 542-43) questions the function of the Golden Calf in the 'canonical' shape of the composition, it is seen as the perversion of the proper response described in chs. 35–39.

89. The contrast relationship of the two artifacts is emphasized by the parallel scenes of destruction in vv. 19-20. This could also be reflected by the motif contrast of divine stone and human gold, playing upon some established hierarchy of elements illustrated by Isa. 60.17.

90. The ambiguous and much-discussed character of Aaron's metal-work, especially when related to a tool which according to Isa 8.1 was connected with writing, could simply be explained as a description of Aaron, the clumsy craftsman. This would refer both to the parallel scene of wonderful writing in 31.18 as well as to the proper craftsmanship of the wise and inspired craftsmen in 31.1-6; 35.30–36.8. The parallel description of v. 24 could have a similar function, the accidental character of the process illustrated by the contrasting description of the proper process with the craftsmen meticulously 'doing all what YHWH had commanded Moses'.

91. The parallel motifs and structure in 1 Kgs 12.26-33 underline the special character of Exod. 32.1-6. While rejecting the idea that the Golden Calf of Exodus should preserve an ancient Bethel-tradition about the Aaronide priesthood, Van Seters (*The Life of Moses*, p. 311) asserts that 'the role of Aaron is...completely modelled on that of Jeroboam'. But related to the context of Exod. 19–40, the role of the active people and the passive Aaron in the Golden Calf story must be important as negative reflections of the normal role allocation in the encounter episodes.

these elements are comparable to the *visio Dei* of the parallel episodes. Reflecting the scenes of instruction, mediation and implementation and a ritual climax centred around the representation of the divine actor, the story forms *in nuce* a version of a complete theophanic episode.

The elaboration of the sacrificial motifs seems to be of special importance for this linkage. In the former episode, the preparatory scenes are extended by altar building and sacrifices (24.4-11), the sacrifices connected to the blood-rite of v. 8 and to the special meal of v. 11. Corresponding elements are also found in ch. 32. Aside from the references of 32.5-6, the bloody scene of the Levites killing their relations in vv. 25-29 is of special importance. According to v. 29, the murder is presented as a sacrificial act. Comparable to the connection of sacrifices and ascent in ch. 24, the terrible scene of slaughter in 32.25-29 is followed by the ascent of Moses.

The character of the actors in the sacrificial scene could also have some special significance. In ch. 24, the sacrifices are performed by some 'young men', probably reflecting the lack of properly sanctified priests at this stage in the story. In ch. 32, the slaughter of sons and brothers is qualified as 'hand-filling'. The reference to the rite of priestly sanctification implies that through their terrible act the Levites become priests. The metaphorical[92] application of both sacrificial and priestly categories for the slaughter relates this scene to the corresponding scene of priestly substitutes in the sacrificial scene of ch. 24. The 'young men' performing sacrifices followed by the Levites performing such terrible sacrifices of sanctification must be related to the narrative line that is concluded by the proper sanctification of the Aaronite priests.

Moreover, the people's special relationship to the sacrifices in the two stories seems to refer to the same categories. The blood rite of 24.6 and 8—the repetition connecting it both to the sacrificial scene of v. 5

92. The story is usually understood as an ancient tradition which reflects that the Levites originally were considered as priests: e.g. A. Cody, *A History of Old Testament Priesthood* (AnBib, 35; Rome: Pontifical Biblical Institute, 1969), p. 152; A.H.J. Gunneweg, *Leviten und Priester: Hauptlinien der Traditionsbildung und Geschichte des israelitisch-judischen Kultpersonals* (Göttingen: Vandenhoeck & Ruprecht, 1965), pp. 29-37; Van Seters, *The Life of Moses*, pp. 315-18. But the very imagery of sons and brothers as the sacrifices which 'fill the hands' of the priests indicate the metaphorical character of the language. This is underlined by the sacrificial categories of the contrast story in Num. 8 (cf. Chapter 4.3).

and to the concept of covenant (vv. 7-8)—is traditionally seen as a reference to ancient customs, reflecting ancient covenantal practices[93] or—with the ancient character of the covenant concept now in doubt—to old sacrificial practices later reinterpreted.[94] While the ancient character of the rites is rather conjectural, the motifs suggest some connection between the two sacrificial scenes. The implications of the sacrificial blood sprinkled upon the people[95] is comparable to the imagery of the people as the sacrifices that 'fill the hands' of the Levites, the latter the continuation of the former in a situation arising when the people's solemn promises have been broken.

Further, the sanctification of the Levites can be related to the idea of separation within the people demonstrated by the three-levelled relationship to the theophanic manifestation in ch. 24. In contrast to Aaron and the people usurping their roles in the Golden Calf episode, the position of the Levites introduced as 'belonging to YHWH' (v. 26) corresponds to the selection of a special group within the people in ch. 24.

In this way, the descent of the mediator and the confrontation with Aaron and the people in 32.15-30 mirror—sharply distorted—the normal event pattern of the earlier episodes. Contrasting effects dominate the motif development, presenting a negative of the proper procedure. This proper procedure is primarily represented by ch. 24 as well as chs. 35–40. This connection also underlines the corresponding motifs of the Golden Calf episode in 32.1-6. The building of an altar connected with a material representation of the divine presence, linked to sacrificial rites extended into motifs of sacred meal, represents a version of a full theophanic episode, including both the acts of preparation and the impression of the divine presence. The descent and the confrontation in the camp in vv. 15-29 present a set of events comparable to 24.3-18, concluding the theophanic episode and preparing for a new scene of encounter, which duly takes place in 32.31. Corresponding to the double

93. E.g. R. Schmid, *Das Bunderopfer in Israel* (SANT 9; Munich: Kösel, 1964), pp. 118-25.

94. A sacrificial ritual originally concluding the preparatory events of purification and theophany transformed by the deuteronomistic redaction into 'Covenant-Closing Ceremony' according to Dozemann, *God on the Mountain*, pp. 65-66; cf. also Aurelius, *Der Fürbitter Israels*, pp. 70-72; Van Seters, *The Life of Moses*, pp. 286-89.

95. Especially if transcribed as the binding of the people in a blood oath (Childs, *Book of Exodus*, p. 506).

relationship of the contrasted 'theophanic encounters' presented in 24.3-31.18 and 32.7-14 and in 32.1-6, the descent and the events in the camp refer to both preceding 'episodes'; on the one hand the tablets are indeed brought down, but on the other they are destroyed due to the significance of the self-made theophany.

Comparable to the Golden Calf as a mock version of the proper theophanic manifestation, the sanctification of the Levites also represents a special episode whose function should not be related to categories of socio-religious character, but to some contrasting effect. The violence of the Levites' scene corresponds to the wrath of Moses—a singular motif within the Sinai stories—the violence of which results in the destruction of the tablets and the calf. The connection between the two scenes is also reflected by later contrasting stories. The wrathful descent of Moses is balanced by the new scene of descent in 34.29-35, the tablet motif being a direct expression of the parallelism of the scenes. Correspondingly, the violent sanctification of the Levites is followed by the parallel story in Numbers 8 on the sanctification of the Levites. The Levites offered as substitute sacrifices by the people represent the opposite role allocation, the violent story of Exodus 32 being balanced by a contrasting story. The relationship underlines the antithetical[96] and negative function of the Levitical story in Exodus 32, corresponding to the character of events introduced by the Golden Calf.

Exodus 32.30–33.6

Comparable to the narrative structure of chs. 19 and 24, a scene in the camp is followed by the encounter on the mountain in 32.30.[97] This comparison also underlines the special character of this scene as well as the following encounters. According to 32.31a, Moses initiates the dialogue on the mountain. Compared to the usual role allocation of the encounter situation, Moses is consistently depicted as active in chs. 32–34.

For a traditio-historical approach, the new speech introductions in 33.1-5 suggest that different types of material are combined.[98] But

96. Cf. also the constellation of Aaron, the negative priest, and the Levites as substitute priests in the scenes of 32.21-24 and vv. 25-29 balanced by the contrast of Aaron, the elected priest, and Korah, the usurper in Num. 16.

97. With 19.8b-13 as an immediate parallel, due to the introductory return and the mediator's reference to the former camp scene.

98. E.g. Aurelius, *Der Fürbitter Israels*, pp. 100-102 on vv. 12-17 as 'Keimcelle' (the nucleus) which continues the intercession scene 32.30-34; also Childs,

related to the narrative development,[99] the speech introductions do not signal any important change of scene.[100] 33.1-6, read as a continuation of the scene in 32.31-35, presents an encounter episode centred around the three divine statements of 32.33-34, 33.1-3 and 5, each followed by the narrative elements of 32.35, 33.4 and 6. The linkage between the three passages is reflected by the mixture of repetitions[101] and introduction of new materials. The motifs of 32.34a are repeated in enlarged form in 33.1-3a. To this is added the new element of v. 3b, in its turn repeated in enlarged form in v. 5a. Correspondingly, the repeated element is added to by a new statement in v. 5b. The significance of the concluding statement, ordering the removal of the ornaments, is emphasized by the narrative elements in vv. 4 and 6. Repeated three times, the putting down of the ornaments is both an expression of the sorrow of the people (v. 4) and the obedient response to the divine command (v. 6). The *parallelismus membrorum* effect of these verses underline the other repetitions in the passage, inviting one to label them narrative poetry.[102]

The motifs and formal structure of the narrative poetry point to the influence of the encounter episode. In allusive form, the different elements of 32.30–33.6 refer to the three basic situations of ascent, the encounter proper, and the people's response to the divine message. The passage represents an elliptical[103] and allusive version of the encounter

Book of Exodus, p. 587, pointing to the speech introduction in 33.1 as an argument against the suppositions of Cassuto (*Exodus*, p. 425) that the passages represent the connection of epic poetry.

99. The results of an alternative viewpoint when narrative categories are related to traditio-historical interests, are illustrated by Van Seters, *The Life of Moses*, pp. 320-21. Besides the 'unnecessary' repetition in v. 5 allocated to P, the J composition vv. 1-6 is seen to reflect literary considerations, which provide a contrast to ch. 32.

100. 24.1-2 demonstrate that an oracle with a new speech introduction, even if 'secondary' from traditio-historical considerations, can be set in the framework of a larger composition. Especially the three statements of YHWH in 33.19-23, followed by 34.1-3, illustrate that an artful compilation of speech introductions can used for rhetorical effect. While the three speech introductions of 32.33 and 33.1, 5 are not as evidently rhetorical, their very application need not imply lack of internal coherency.

101. For Moberly (*At the Mountain of God*, p. 61) the effect of repetitions for 33.1-6 underlines the connection of 32.30–33.6.

102. Cassuto, *Exodus*, p. 425.

103. Cf. also Van Seters, *The Life of Moses*, p. 321, on the significance of the alternating scenes in vv. 1-6. Without any narrative frame, the scenes referred to are

episode. The foreshortened presentation of the mediation—the divine message to Moses immediately responded to by the people in vv. 4-6—as well as the concluding position of vv. 4-6, points to the significance of the people's response for the elaboration of this encounter. This is also indicated by the mode of repetition and gradual change. The artful composition sets out the divine absence and the people's response. Owing to the people's 'stiff-neckedness' YHWH shall not be in their 'midst', and his absence is responded to by the people removing their ornaments. The latter aspect is emphasized by the temporal qualification 'after Horeb'. The people's 'self-plundering' represents a permanent situation. Prepared for by the repetitive technique, the last addition to the divine message 33.5bβ must also be important. The problem of any direct connection between the divine presence and human stiff-neckedness is so difficult that YHWH himself is unable to provide an immediate solution. With the outcome of the events kept in suspense, these verses must reflect a most dramatic situation of the Sinai story.[104]

In addition to these effects, the delicate composition also prepares the reader for the next scene introduced in v. 7. The allusive references to the situations of encounter and mediation in 33.1-6 are concluded by the narrative refrain of vv. 4 and 6. This leads the reader's attention from the mountain scene (that is, above) in 32.31-34 to the situation below, where the people take the leading role.[105] The speech introductions of 33.1 and 5 refer to Moses and thus to the basic situation of encounter. But by the divine speech related to the response of the people, the scenery is gradually changed from the mountain to the camp in preparation for the next scene in which Moses is set among the people.[106]

comparable to the frequent trips up and down the mountain in ch. 19. According to Brichto ('The Worship of the Golden Calf', p. 22), the verses reflect a 'synoptic-resumptive narrative technique' often found in the Old Testament stories. An incident is presented in two episodic versions, the first brief and synoptic, the second resumptive and expansive (p. 8).

104. E.g. Moberly, *At the Mountain of God*, p. 63, on vv. 7-11 as the turning point in the story of chs. 32–34; also Durham, *Exodus*, pp. 436-37.

105. The emphasis on the people's response could also be reflected by the unusual introduction to the encounter in 32.30. In contrast to earlier encounter episodes, Moses confides to the people what he is about to do, the people included in the following scene.

106. The narrative technique is comparable to the change of scenes from 31.18 to 32.1 to v. 7 as well as the relationship of 19.20-25, followed by 20.1-17, in turn

Exodus 33.7-11

Given the preparation of vv. 4-6, the formal connection provides scant support for the traditio-historical separation of the events introduced in v. 7 from the context.[107] The deft elaboration of the encounter scene in 32.30–33.6 gradually changes the scene from the mountain to the camp. Corresponding to the emphasis on the people as actors in vv. 4 and 6, the introductory sentence construction of v. 7 continues the story, but puts the emphasis on Moses as actor: 'but Moses, on his side'. The style invites the reader to expect some contrast between the actions of the people in v. 6 and the actions of Moses in v. 7, and that the contrasts are related to each other.[108] While the former scene portrays the people 'plundering themselves' for their ornaments, the latter scene has Moses putting up a tent 'all by himself'.[109] The connection between the two scenes is also reflected by effects of style. The narrative poetry of the first scene is continued by the next, most directly illustrated by the repetitions in vv. 8-10. Also the frequentative forms in vv. 8-11 correspond to the temporal reference in v. 6. Just as the people are depicted in a constant situation of 'self-plundering' after Horeb, the description of vv. 8-11 presents a lasting situation.[110] Together, the ornaments of the people and the tent of Moses represent central aspects of some permanent situation.

The riddle is increased by the qualification of Moses' tent as the

followed by the scene in vv. 18-21. Playing upon the established modes of narration, the changes could signal points of special significance.

107. The transition from historical to contextual considerations is rather dramatically illustrated by Childs, *Book of Exodus*, pp. 589-93. According to Van Seters (*The Life of Moses*, p. 321), vv. 7-11 are a digression which had to be included here in preparation for the scene in 34.34-35. The present location is related to v. 6 as a parallel expression for a practice which took place from Horeb onwards. Brichto ('The Worship of the Golden Calf', p. 23) also labels the verses a digression, but with a function as an integral part of the story. For Moberly (*At the Mountain of God*, pp. 171-77), vv. 7-11 are an important part of the narrative context.

108. Cf. the parallel relationship of v. 11bα and β, the new position of the nominal subject and verb in β contrasting Joshua with Moses. A corresponding contrast is expressed by similar means in 19.3, related to v. 2, the ascent by Moses juxtaposed to the settling of the people. Also in this case, phenomena which at first hand should be related to questions of style and function have automatically been referred to a frame of traditio-historical categories.

109. Or 'for himself'. The context indicates that the contrast between Moses and the people is important.

110. This connection is stressed by Van Seters, *The Life of Moses*, p. 321.

'Tent of Meeting'. This draws the reader's attention to the grand Tabernacle still to be built. The contrast relationship of two Tents of Meeting according to 33.7-11 and ch. 40 should not be mitigated as a mechanical combination of two different tent traditions.[111] Whatever the literary prehistory of the two passages, the name of the two tents set in the context of chs. 19–40 must express some referential relationship, as obvious for ancient editors as for modern readers.[112]

The basic connection between the two tent stories is reflected by the event structure in 33.7-11. The tent set up is followed by a description of Moses' movements related to the locus, concluded by the theophanic manifestation related to the people's *visio*. This corresponds to the events of ch. 40, as well as to the established pattern of the theophanic episode.

The parallelism of 33.7-11 and ch. 40 as two construction accounts is reflected by the elaboration of the motifs. For the grand Tabernacle of ch. 40, the contribution of the people is crucial according to the story in chs. 35–39. This is followed by a new scene dedicated to Moses alone erecting the Tabernacle from the elements prepared by the people (40.1-33). The elaborate conclusion in 39.32-43, mirrored by the parallel conclusion in 40.33b, as well as the new set of divine instructions addressed to Moses in 40.1-15, distinguish between the two scenes of tent production in chs. 35–40. Accordingly, the tent building of 33.7 related to Moses on his own represents *in nuce* a version of the scene in ch. 40. Correspondingly, the relationship of two construction scenes in chs. 35–40 must be important for the relationship of the two scenes in 33.4-6 and 7.

111. Usually in the form of vv. 7-11 as an ancient tent tradition independent of the Priestly Tabernacle (Haran, *Temples*, pp. 262-69). For Van Seters (*The Life of Moses*, pp. 341-44), the passage represents J's historiographical reconstruction based on Deut. 5.22-31 combined with the tradition of 2 Sam. 7.6.

112. While separating between different tent traditions related to JE and P, Kearney ('Creation and Liturgy', pp. 383-84) argues that their present shape and location marks the contrast between a negative symbol of divine distance, no cultic objects or servants, and no holiness in juxtaposition to the proper sanctuary. Also for Moberly (*At the Mountain of God*, pp. 171-77), the connection to the context is important. The tent 'outside' the camp is the expression for the denial of YHWH's presence in the people's midst proclaimed vv. 3, 5. Thus, the tent of 33.7-11 represents a substitute for the proper tent to follow, when the divine favour has beeen restored (p. 64). The interim character of Moses' tent is also stressed by Brichto, 'The Worship of the Golden Calf', p. 24, and Cassuto, *Exodus*, p. 429.

The correspondence highlights the differences between the two scenes. First, the divine instructions are crucial for the successful erection of the Tabernacle. This is reflected by the actions of Moses in ch. 40, which mirror the divine instructions of vv. 1-15, the perfect relationship of divine instruction and human implementation being underlined by the monotonous repetition of the compliance formula in 40.16-32 (cf. also 39.32, 42-43). Such elements are conspicuously lacking in 33.7. The contrast to ch. 40 profiles Moses acting 'on his own' in 33.7, not only with regard to the people, but also to the divine initiative. On the other hand, this corresponds to the description of Moses in chs. 32–34. Moses is consistently presented as active also in relationship to the divine protagonist, 'usurping' the acts normally ascribed to the divine initiative.[113] The constant deviation from the pattern which outside Exodus 32–34 represents the established norm, is remarkable. Given the contextual relationship, it is natural to relate it to the comparable deviation caused by the people's initiative in the Golden Calf episode. The parallelism of the two human-made loci dependent on the initiative of the human actors indicates that Moses' setting up of the tent somehow corresponds to the making of the Golden Calf, although divinely accepted.[114]

Second, the parallelism between the events of Exodus 40 and 33.7-11 corresponds to the connection between the scenes of vv. 6 and 7—the former presenting a scene dedicated to the people, the latter to Moses acting on his own as tent-builder. For the Tabernacle, the people's contribution represents the central theme of chs. 35–39, concluded by the blessing in 39.32-43, and followed by the separate scene of Moses as tent-builder. The significance of the two successive scenes of tent construction is underlined by the general pattern of the theophanic

113. In the three encounter scenes, Moses initiates the dialogue (32.31; 33.12; 34.8-9). The violence of the confrontation in camp is related to his wrath, and the killing scene set in motion by his order (in the context of Exod. 19–40, the claim of 'thus says YHWH' in 32.27 'should' have been substantiated by a concrete order). Moses prepares the sacred tablets in 34.1, 4 and is also performing the role of divine writer in vv. 27-28.

114. Kearney's description ('Creation and Liturgy', pp. 383-84) of how P valued Moses' tent as opposed to the proper Tent of Meeting is peculiarly negative. While a number of details marks the tabernacle of ch. 40 as the climactic episode, the tent of Moses is also described as locus of theophanic manifestation, even related to the people's *visio*.

episode. According to this pattern, two sets of preparatory events are concluded by the climactic theophanic manifestation.

This must be important for the reading of 33.6 related to v. 7. The tent scene in v. 7, set after a scene dedicated to the people, corresponds to the structure of the two scenes in chs. 35–39 and 40.1-33. In both cases, the events are concluded with theophany and *visio Dei*. In contrast to the Tabernacle episode, the non-participation of the people and Moses acting on his own represent the important aspect for the first episode of tent making. Moreover, the non-participation of the people in v. 6 refers to the divine instruction of v. 5, the relationship of divine instruction and human response corresponding to the usual pattern. In this way, the encounter of 32.30–33.5 followed by vv. 6 and 7-11 represents a version of the usual compositional pattern of encounter on the mountain mediated and responded to in preparation for the theophanic manifestation. The obedient response of the people in v. 6 and the high-handedness of Moses acting on his own in v. 7 form the preparatory events for the next theophany.

The motifs add to this impression of referential relationships. For the construction of the Tabernacle, the dedication of the people's valuables represents a central theme (Exod. 25.2-8 and 35.4–36.7). The tent and its contents are made from the raw materials brought by the people. In a parallel setting of tent-building, the correspondence between the gifts of the people in Exodus 35–36 and the 'self-plundering' of the ornaments in 33.6 can hardly be coincidental.[115] This is added to by the parallel motifs in the Golden Calf story. The calf made from the people's gold by Aaron, the clumsy craftsman, represents *in nuce* a building story parallel to the building story of Exodus 35–40. Similarly, the people's ear-rings of Exod. 32.1-6 and the people's ornaments in 33.4 and 6 must refer to each other,[116] the reference underlined by the parallel setting in a 'building story'.[117]

115. The connection between the ornaments in Exod. 33.4, 6 and the people's valuables of Exod. 35 is important to Haran, *Temples*, p. 263.

116. Cassuto (*Exodus*, p. 427) and Moberly (*At the Mountain of God*, p. 60) point to the connection of the sorrow situation (v. 4) and the Golden Calf episode. Moberly also refers to Gen. 35.4 as a comparable act of renunciation, the people removing the objects connected with the construction of the calf.

117. Cf. also the parallelism of the ear-rings removed to produce gods 'which can walk in front of us' and the non-use of ornaments as the people's sorrow caused by YHWH refusing to 'walk in your midst' (33.3-4).

The *parallellismus membrorum* effect of Exod. 33.4 and 6 reflects two aspects of the ornament motif. According to v. 4, 'nobody put his ornaments upon himself'. The non-use is connected to the people's sorrow upon hearing the bad news of vv. 1-3. In a setting of idol production, the non-use of the ornaments alludes to a general background of purification[118] and renunciation.[119]

The connotational richness is added to by the referential value of *hitnaṣṣēl* ('self-plunder') in v. 6. The word represents a rather special choice for the non-use of ornaments. Its immediate function can be related to the contrast scene of the Golden Calf. A scene of 'self-plundering' corresponds to the 'tearing' of the ear-rings in Exod. 32.2, 3 and 24, the violence of an act of *prq* being emphasized when related to men 'tearing' the ear-rings from their women and sons and daughters in v. 2.[120] In contrast, the scene of Exod. 33.6 represents an act of similar violence by 'the sons of Israel', but is now directed towards themselves as self-plunder. To the implications of renunciation and purification indicated by the non-use of the ornaments in v. 4 is added the intensity and fervour of the imagery in v. 6.[121]

In addition to this immediate function, it can hardly be coincidental that the use of the piel form of *nṣl* is also used for the plunder of the Egyptians (Exod. 3.22; 12.36).[122] The people's possession of valuables is an important theme for the three contrasted 'building stories'. It must have been a rather wealthy people that could be asked to make the contributions of Exod. 35.4–36.7. Within the narrative frame, the ownership of such valuables by the former slaves is naturally explained by the episode of Exod. 11.2-3 and 12.35-36 prepared by Exod. 3.21-22. The remarkable use of the plunder motif in Exod. 33.6 can be explained as a

118. Comparable to the preparations of Exod. 19.10-15 related to clothes and sexual abstinence. Such a connection is reflected by the list of preparatory acts related to a situation of encounter in Gen. 35.2.

119. In addition to Gen. 35.1-4, the connotational significance of the ornament motifs is illustrated by Isa. 3.18-26. The act of renunciation expressed by *hēsîr* in Gen. 35.2 corresponds to Isa. 3.18 with YHWH for subject. In Isa. 3.26, the sorrow motif is connected to the situation, corresponding to Exod. 33.4.

120. Cf. Chapter 2.3 for the elaboration of these allusions in Exod. 35.4–36.7.

121. The character of such a situation of extreme penitence could be illustrated by Isa. 3.16-26, with the important difference that in the case of the people 'after Horeb' the denuding is self-inflicted

122. This connection is pointed out by Moberly (*At the Mountain of God*, p. 61) and mentioned as a possible allusion by Cassuto (*Exodus*, p. 428).

direct reference to the plunder of the Egyptians, now subtly inverted to an act of self-denuding. An inversion of this character in a story in which the people's gold has been used for the production of the Golden Calf, corresponds to the implicit connotations of riches of Egyptian origin.[123] The 'self-plundering', added to a situation of non-use in v. 4, implies a situation of radical renunciation.

Summary

Formally, the elaboration of Exod. 32.30–33.6 followed by 33.7-11 conforms to the established pattern of Exodus 19–40. The passage as a whole reflects the structure of an introductory encounter episode followed by events of mediation and response, which in their turn form the preparatory events for the human movement towards the sacred locus, concluded by the theophanic manifestation and the *visio Dei* related to the people (vv. 8-10). The delicate composition seems not only to reflect the established pattern of events,[124] but also the formal structure of the three grand theophanic episodes, each set out in two preparatory sub-episodes climaxed by the theophanic event. Such an organization is also reflected by Exod. 32.30–33.11. A separate scene centred around the people as actors (vv. 4-6) is followed by a new scene related to Moses (v. 7) preparing for the presentation of the theophanic encounter.[125] As a short-form of the established pattern, comparable to the Golden Calf episode, the passage is characterized by its contracted and allusive application of the basic events, combined with remarkably complex and subtle referential effects.

The prime—at least the most explicit—function of the allusive effects seems to be indicated by the referential relationship to the

123. Cf. the connotations of 'Egypt' applied in the wilderness stories. In particular Num. 11 and 14 represent comparable examples of the subtlety of 'Egyptian' references (cf. Chapter 5 Sections 2 and 4).

124. The order of events is also reflected by the dialogue started in v. 12, but seemingly disturbed by the interest for Joshua in v. 11b. The return of Moses in 11b—corresponding to the description of his 'out-going' in v. 8—is parallel to the symmetry of Moses ascending and descending in the mountain episodes. The expansion of this element by the reference to Joshua could reflect the interest in stressing the special character of the Moses Tent of Meeting compared to the tent of ch. 40.

125. Cf. also the encounter in Exod. 32.31–33.3, 5, introduced by two scenes referring to Aaron in 32.21-24 and the Levites in 32.25-29.

Golden Calf and to the great Tent of Meeting. Compared to the proper tent building of Exodus 35–40, the Golden Calf incident, set after chs. 25–31, represents the perverted building story as the perverted response to the divine intentions. The perversion is contrasted with the new building story of Exod. 33.7-11. Moses, with Joshua as a sub-figure (v. 11)—both absent during the Golden Calf episode—are related to the tent while the people are presented as inactive. The roles of the first episode are reversed. As a locus of the theophanic manifestation which prepares for the reconciliation of Exodus 34, Moses' tent must somehow counter-effect the first and negative act of wilfulness. The riddle of this juxtaposition is added to by aspects of activity and passivity. The wilfulness of the people in the first episode, contrasted with the example of the mediator staying on the mountain for 40 days and nights, is mirrored by the wilfulness of Moses in the second episode, acting on his own in contrast to the non-participating people responding to the divine instructions with sorrow and violent renunciation.

But while such a function must be important for Moses' tent, the name 'Tent of Meeting' suggests that the tent of Exodus 40 represents the prime referent. This is also suggested by Exod. 33.8-11, which presents a negative image of the final situation in Exod. 40.34-38. In the latter, the theophanic manifestation is 'filling' and 'covering' the tent, with Moses outside and not able to enter, while the people are related to the theophanic manifestation. The situation of Exod. 33.8-10 represents the opposite. While Moses is inside the tent and YHWH is outside, with the two engaged in intimate 'face to face talking' (v. 11), the people watch from afar. In Exodus 40, the theophanic relationship is presented as a permanent situation, the people always facing the divine cloud over the tent. In comparison, the theophanic manifestation of Exod. 33.8-9 seems most impermanent, the divine descent related to the comings and goings of Moses.[126] The parallelism of the divine and human movements can be related to a corresponding parallelism in the last scene of Exodus 40, but here connected to the people as the actors, the movements of the cloud mirrored by the people staying or leaving the camp.[127] The delicate motif elaboration must reflect a deliberate effect of juxtaposition.[128]

126. The description of vv. 8-9 even puts the movements of Moses before the divine descent, corresponding to the consistent portrayal of Moses as taking the initiative in Exod. 32–34.

127. On the other hand, this parallelism of the divine and human movements

The figure of Joshua in Moses' tent (v. 11) also adds to this effect. Joshua as a permanent fixture of the first Tent of Meeting corresponds to the priests as sub-figures in Exodus 40. The priestly connection to the Tabernacle is reflected by the scenes of Exod. 40.30-32, continued by Lev. 9.22–10.2. A Tent of Meeting with the priests as sub-figures and a Tent of Meeting with Joshua as sub-figure represent a rather marked contrast. While the presence of Joshua corresponds to his absence in the Golden Calf episode, the absence of Aaron in the first tent must reflect his negative role as producer of the calf. This could also be related to the allusive references to the priestly sanctification in the bloody scene of Exod. 32.25-29. Together with the Levites as the priests of the *post*-calf camp, the presence of Joshua in Moses' Tent of Meeting underlines the special character of this locus in contrast to the great tent of Exodus 40.

So far, chs. 32–34 of Exodus represent a singular elaboration of the narrative pattern and central motifs of chs. 19–40. The elaboration seems to reflect an interest in the effects of parallelism and juxtaposition. Related to the context, the story of Exodus 32–34 presents a series of parallel phenomena, which seem to represent a basic function as 'substitutes'. The Golden Calf is made as a substitute for Moses and is also presented as substitute 'gods' for YHWH. The Levites are sanctified as substitute priests. Instead of the divine ascent in the people's midst, the divine messenger is presented as the substitute guide. And finally, the story presents a substitute Tent of Meeting, with Joshua instead of Aaron acting as the permanent servant.[129]

The subtleties of composition make any assertions on meaning rather haphazard. But related to the narrative movement towards Exodus 40, the juxtaposition of three 'building stories' connected to the categories

underlines the peculiar symmetry of YHWH and the people standing at the tent doors in Exod. 33.8 and 10.

128. The frequentative forms of the verbs in Exod. 33.8-9 and 40.36-38, in which both tent situations are presented as permanent, underlines the significance of the motif elaboration.

129. This list of parallel phenomena could even be reflected by the naming of the mountain as Horeb in Exod. 33.6. While possibly reflecting an alternative mountain tradition (just as the other phenomena could have a corresponding history prior to their present function), the introduction of a 'substitute' name in this list of substitutes is rather striking. The mountain named as Horeb in v. 6 could indicate a special set of connotations for a place of sorrow and renunciation as expression for an aspect parallel to the connotations of 'Sinai'.

of divine manifestation and locus, must somehow present the first Tent of Meeting as the antidote to the Golden Calf, making possible the final scenes of Exodus 40.

Together with the description of the people in Exod. 33.1-6, vv. 7-11 could have a function as an expression of the negative character of the events, presenting a situation of divine wrath and judgment.[130] The situation certainly must reflect the grave character of the *post*-calf situation. But the motif development indicates a situation of a much more comprehensive character, corresponding to the richness of allusive layers in vv. 4 and 6. This is also reflected by the description of the tent in v. 7b. Although erected by Moses on his own, the tent outside the camp is related to 'every YHWH-seeker' and is reached in this case also by the movement of 'going out', corresponding to the description of Moses (v. 8). Despite its marginalized location outside the camp and far away, Moses' tent was reached by the 'seekers'[131] of the people.

More importantly, in this case the people are also related to the theophanic manifestation in the form of *visio Dei.* Given the significance of this theme for the composition as a whole, the conditions of the *post*-calf camp includes also this basic situation. Compared with earlier experiences of *visio Dei* related to the people (Exod. 20.18-21 and 24.17), the situation of Exod. 33.8-10 even marks an important development. Verse 8 read in isolation reflects the separation between the accepted mediator and the excluded people, corresponding to the earlier episodes. But continued by the emotive description of v. 10, the first impression is overlaid by a second which presents the people as actively participating in the theophanic experience. The cloud standing at the tent door (v. 10a, repeating 9abg) corresponds to the people in the act of 'bowing down', each from 'his tent door'. Also the latter image is prepared by the description of v. 8a. The poignancy and the beauty of the description is comparable to the relationship of vv. 4 and 6, the

130. Kearney, 'Creation and Liturgy', pp. 383-84; Moberly, *At the Mountain of God*, pp. 63-65.

131. When v. 7 is seen as a fragment which reflects a special tent tradition connected with ancient oracular practice (esp. Haran, *Temples*, pp. 262-64), the qualification of YHWH-seeker is naturally related to the ordinary oracular practice, as, for example 'seeking to know the divine will' (Durham, *Exodus*, p. 442). But in a context of *visio Dei*, the significance of the motif could as well be illustrated by Ps. 24.6 related to vv. 7-10. At the very least, the 'YHWH-seeker' is added to the Levites and Joshua as positive contrast figures.

effect of the narrative *parallellismus membrorum* pointing to the importance of the description. In this case, the effects of repetition underline the symmetry of the divine and human positions, comparable both to the symmetry of the divine and human movements in v. 9 as well as to the climax of Exod. 40.36-38, where the movements of the cloud are reflected by the movements of the people.

Continuing the description of the people in vv. 4-6, the situation of vv. 8-10 must represent an important part of the story begun in Exodus 19 and concluded by Exod. 40.34-38. This is also expressed by the categories of 'horizontality'. For a story centred around the divine movement from mountain to camp, the divine descent into a locus below the mountain—however far from the camp—to be reached by Moses as well as every 'YHWH-seeker', represents a significant step.

Exodus 33.12–34.35

The order of Exod. 33.7-11 and the dialogue of 33.12–34.3 is usually seen as a compilation of different traditions. This is primarily due to the frequentative form of vv. 8-11, which changes the perception from singular events to events of repetitive character.[132] But related to the established pattern, a passage centred around the dialogue of the divine and human actors set after a theophanic episode represents the normal order. This is underlined by the pattern of two preparatory scenes concluded by the theophanic manifestation (vv. 4-11) and followed by the dialogue of YHWH and Moses. This corresponds to the established pattern of the great theophanic episodes. The transition from a repeated situation (vv. 8-11) to v. 12 as expression for a singular event, is unusual. But a corresponding relationship is represented by Exod. 40.34-38, followed by Lev. 1.1. Also in this case, a singular episode of theophanic manifestation is gradually extended into a situation repeated throughout the journey. By YHWH calling from the Tent of Meeting in Lev. 1.1,

132. E.g. Durham (*Exodus*, p. 445), on vv. 12-17 as the continuation of the narrative ended in v. 6 which has disturbed by the insertion of the tent tradition of vv. 7-11. For Van Seters (*The Life of Moses*, p. 321), vv. 12-17 continue the intercessory dialogue of vv. 1-3. The digression represented by vv. 7-11 continues the J account of vv. 4 and 6. On the other hand, Moberly (*At the Mountain of God*, p. 66) asserts the tent of vv. 7-11 as the setting for the following dialogue. To Brichto ('The Worship of the Golden Calf', p. 25), who operates with fairly independent 'episodes' in a composition of 'episodic narrative technique', the connection between the 'episodes' does not require any concrete narrative expression.

the story returns to the scene of Exod. 40.34-35. Introduced in this way, the sacrificial instructions of Leviticus 1–7 present what was said during the encounter. Similarly, the frequentative forms in ch. 34.33-35 are followed by the mediation of the divine instructions in ch. 35 and thus flesh out the situation of 34.32 by presenting what was mediated.

It is, of course, possible that these transitions may reflect the compilation of the different types of material. But whatever their literary prehistory, the organization of these materials corresponds. Singular events are deflected into repeated scenes that are followed by speech passages which return to the narrative line. Given the special character of the three repeated scenes, the narrative technique could signal their importance.

But in one respect v. 12 stands out from the normal mode. The dialogue is initiated by the human actor, the divine actor being set in the subordinate position of having to respond. This corresponds to the role allocation in the encounter episodes of Exod. 32.31 and 34.8-9 and must reflect the special character of the events of chs. 32–34. The three encounters all represent scenes of passionate intercession. Corresponding to the wilfulness of the people in Exod. 32.1, Moses is consistently depicted as active in this series of events.

The details of the first part of the dialogue in vv. 12-17 seem rather obscure, which could be due to the delicacy of the issues involved as well as to subtle rhetorical effects.[133] But the discussion is centered around the motif of YHWH 'walking together with the people' and thus represents a direct continuation of the intercession scene in 32.31–33.5, in its turn continued by the intercession in the next encounter (34.8-9). The second part (vv. 18-23) is introduced by the plea of Moses for a special *visio Dei*. While the implications of this plea represents a traditional interpreter's crux,[134] its development through vv. 19-23 to the conclusion in 34.1-3 at the very least indicates its function. The plea for a special encounter in v. 18 results in the divine invitation to ascend and a set of corresponding instructions. The implementation of divine

133. Its possibilities of meaning 'as unlimited as the power of imagination' according to Brichto, 'The Worship of the Golden Calf', p. 28.

134. Especially Childs, *Book of Exodus*, pp. 595-99; Durham, *Exodus*, pp. 450-52; Van Seters, *The Life of Moses*, p. 323; while the connection between vv. 12-17 and 18-23 is asserted by Moberly, *At the Mountain of God*, pp. 66-83, and also Brichto, 'The Worship of the Golden Calf', pp. 27-29.

instructions (v. 4) sets the scene for the next encounter, which is initiated by the ascent of the mediator in vv. 5-28.

Such a series of events corresponds to the established pattern of encounter episodes. In particular the divine speech of Exod. 20.22–24.2, concluded by the invitation to a special ascent by certain people in 24.1-2, provides a passage comparable to the dialogue of 33.12–34.3, concluded by 34.1-3. Related to this pattern, the main difference between the two sets of invitations is the fact that in 33.18 it is Moses himself who asks to be granted a special *visio*. In this case, the invitation to ascend reflects the divine reaction to his plea. On the other hand, the plea certainly presents Moses in a special mode. This is illustrated by the first mountain scene of the Moses biography. The contrast with Moses' original terror at an improper *visio* (3.6) highlights his audacity in 33.18. Moses in an audacious way corresponds to the manner he is consistently presented in Exodus 32–34, actively initiating events that earlier have been related to the divine subject. In this case, his initiative in starting off the dialogue in v. 12 is continued by his pushing[135] for a special vision in v. 18, to which the divine actor grudgingly has to respond.[136]

The connection with the compositional pattern underlines the relationship of the three encounter episodes in Exod. 32.31–33.5, 33.8–34.3, and 34.5-28. The composition of chs. 19–40 represents the relationship of three grand theophanic episodes in a successive development towards a climax. The three encounters of chs. 32–34, interconnected as scenes of intercession and climaxed by the last,[137] represents a parallel

135. E.g. Childs, *Book of Exodus*, p. 596, on a selfish plea for a 'special, individual revelation'.

136. But also, the very combination of an intense situation of intercession and the audacious plea must have a special significance. Thus, the combination of extraordinary encounter and intercession is returned to in the description of the encounter in Exod. 34.5-9. It can hardly be coincidental that Job 42.1-10 presents a comparable combination of passages. A special *visio Dei* surpassing all other religious experiences (vv. 1-6) is followed by an episode dedicated to Job as intercessor (vv. 7-10). Verse 10 clearly reflects that the intercession represents the climactic scene.

137. The significance of this pattern is illustrated by the understanding of the repeated pleas and divine concessions as really 'unnecessary' after the scene of Exod. 32.7-14. See, for example, Aurelius, *Der Fürbitter Israels*, pp. 91-100, and Van Seters, *The Life of Moses*, pp. 313-14 (and p. 18) on the relationship between Exod. 32.11-13 and 32.30-34.

version of the grand compositional movement. Also in this case, the pattern is reflected by a corresponding sub-pattern by the two scenes dedicated to Aaron and the Levites in 32.21-29 and to the people and Moses in 33.4-7, in both cases followed by the encounter proper.[138] The correspondence highlights a number of deviations from the usual application. In the grand episodes, the theophanic manifestation related to the people by the *visio* motif is reserved for the climactic third episode. In the version of the pattern in Exodus 32–34, the second episode entails a scene of theophany and *visio* related to the people (33.8-10). This is added to by a new theophanic experience in the concluding episode (34.5-8)[139] which, moreover, is exclusively reserved for Moses. The exclusivity is reflected both by the prohibitions in Exod. 34.3 as well as the extraordinary character of the event indicated by the discussion in Exod. 33.18-23.

Also the local setting of the encounters in Exodus 32–34 is special. The first and the third episodes (32.31–33.5 and 34.5-28, respectively) have the mountain as their locus, while the middle scene of Exod. 33.8–34.3 relates the theophany to Moses' tent. The camp setting corresponds to the compositional movement towards the divine dwelling in the midst of the people attained in ch. 40. In chs. 32–33 this is reflected by the contrasting loci of the Golden Calf and Moses' Tent of Meeting, both of which are set in the spatial reality below the mountain. The return to the mountain for the climactic episode of chs. 32–34 seems to reverse the gradual transformation of the motifs. The significance of this reversal is underlined by ch. 34 as the very last mountain scene in chs. 19–40.

Finally, the application of the mountain imagery in the last encounter is accompanied by a return to the idea of human ascent that is central for the development of Exodus 19–24.[140] But the dialogue of 33.18-23

138. The one preparatory scene in Exod. 34.4 differs from this pattern. On the other hand, it corresponds to the emphasis on Moses in the last episode. The non-participation of the people followed by Moses acting on his own in Exod. 33.4-7 seems to be continued by the splendid isolation of Moses in the last episode.

139. On the other hand, this development can be related to the organization of the second theophanic episode. According to Exod. 24.8-11 the second preparatory scene is related to the ascent of the select group extended by a special *visio*. This is followed by the special ascent of Moses and the theophanic experience. In this way, the elaboration of the narrative pattern in the second episode is continued by the order of the main scenes in chs. 32–34.

140. Cf. also below in this Chapter for the new understanding of the concept of

and the invitation of 34.1-3 returns to the imagery of chs. 19–24.[141] The encounter is connected to the idea of ascent and to the categories of the extraordinary human actor separated from the rest of humanity. Moreover, the extraordinary experience of *visio Dei* is related to Moses (33.19-23). Hitherto, this motif has been reserved for the people, aside from the application on the select group in 24.9-11. Now it is transferred to Moses. The significance of this transfer is underlined by the connection of improper *visio* and death in 33.18-23. Up till now, death in connection with an improper relationship to the divine presence has been reserved for the people, but in this scene, the threat of death is transferred from the people and related to Moses as the improper visionary.

This development represents a curious twist in the tale. For some reason, the tension of the story has been shifted from the people to Moses as the problematic theophanic figure. Just as the experience of *visio Dei* hitherto has been reserved for the people, so the tension of the story concluded in Exodus 40 has been connected with the people as unfit for any close encounter with divine reality. Prepared for by Exodus 19, the scenes of Exod. 20.18-21 and 32.1-6 demonstrate that an intimate relationship between YHWH and people represents an impossible idea. The ascent extended to a larger group in ch. 24 and the idea of YHWH dwelling among the people in chs. 25–31 reflect the compositional movement towards ch. 40.[142] But this movement is abruptly interrupted by the reintroduction of Moses as the sole human actor in an episode that is qualified as truly extraordinary by the discussion of Exod. 33.18–34.3. The significance of this development is underlined by the transfer of the *visio* motifs—greatly intensified as related to some special divine essence of 'face' and 'glory'—and the corresponding death motifs connected to the improper relationship. This is increased by the change from the Tent of Meeting as the theophanic locus in 33.8-11 to a new mountain scene. Also the deviation from the established pattern by a scene of theophany and *visio Dei* as part of the second episode in 33.8-11 seems to reflect this development.

'ascent' presented in the intercessionary scenes of Exod. 32.30–33.6; 33.12-17; 34.9.

141. Compared to the parallel prohibitions in Exod. 24.2, the absolute character of the prohibitions in 34.3 marks a return to the situation of 19.12-13a, and even adds grazing in front of the mountain as forbidden.

142. Underlined by the development of the ascent motif in chs. 32–34.

According to this version of the pattern, the third episode is elaborated as a super-climax, dedicated to Moses as the truly extraordinary ascender.

This development is also reflected by the following description of the theophanic episode in Exodus 34. Compared to the earlier episodes, Moses alone prepares for the encounter (v. 4), while the people are reintroduced as actors during the ascent (vv. 30-35). The significance of Moses as protagonist in the last mountain episode is retained and elaborated in the description of his descent in Exod. 34.29-35. Centred around Moses, the person with the shining face, the concluding scene of chs. 32–34 underlines the special position of Moses for this part of the composition.

Summary

At this stage of reading, the impression of Exodus 32–34 as a singular version of the compositional pattern represents the immediate observation. Exodus 32.31–33.3 and 5, 33.8–34.3 and 34.5-28 present three successive encounters, interlinked by events that conclude the former and prepare for the following episode. This corresponds to the narrative movement of the three grand theophanic episodes in chs. 19–40. Moreover, as a singular version of this pattern, chs. 32–34 are part of this narrative movement. The peculiar emphasis on Moses as the problematic and sublime theophanic figure in Exod. 33.18–34.35 is linked to his intercession on behalf of the people (33.12-17; 34.8-9) and thus to a central theme of chs. 32–34. The motif of Moses as intercessor is important for all three of the encounter episodes, and also represents the concluding event of the second theophanic episode in 32.7-14. This prepares for the return to the main story line in ch. 35 that was interrupted by the Golden Calf episode.

Formally, this linkage to the main story line is reflected by the contextual setting of 34.29-35. Corresponding to the earlier encounters, the reference to a scene of descent and mediation in v. 32 would naturally be read as a reference to the preceding encounter. But when Exodus 35 presents an immediate continuation by a new scene of mediation in which the divine instructions are concretely cited, vv. 29-35 of ch. 34 function as the introduction to the scene of ch. 35 which presents the divine instructions of chs. 25–31.[143] Moved by the description of

143. The transition from a single event to a repeated situation in vv. 33-35

Moses and people in ch. 34, the reader is able to accept the new character of the people in Exod. 35.20–36.7, willingly and perfectly observing the divine instructions.

This structure of successive events invites a reading of Exodus 32–34 as part of the linear relationship of successive events in chs. 19–40. The mediation and implementation of the divine orders in chs. 25–31 were interrupted by the Golden Calf episode. But by the intercession of Moses in chs. 32–34 the people have been forgiven and the story can continue.

Despite the fact that this indicates the direction of the narrative movement, the reading of chs. 32–34 also implies a set of riddles not solved by the transition from ch. 34 to 35. The shift of tension from the people to Moses as the problematic visionary represents a major riddle, enhanced by the wonderful description of the last descent of Moses. The significance of such a shift between Moses and the people is underlined by the comparable reversal of roles in the final tent scene of ch. 40, in which Moses is excluded from the tent and the people represent the obedient visionaries.

The juxtaposition of the two Tents of Meeting in Exod. 33.7-11 and 40.34-38 represents a comparable and probably related riddle. Apart from the connection indicated by the common name, the descriptions of the two tents and the role allocations of the narrative figures present the one as the negative of the other. Moreover, the significance of Moses' Tent of Meeting for chs. 32–34 as a whole is underlined by the concluding scene of Exod. 34.34-35. The allusive form of the description—Moses 'entering before YHWH to talk with him' and 'leaving'—must refer to the preceding tent scene of Exod. 33.7-11. This implies that the Tent of Meeting theme is not only important for the isolated passage in Exod. 33.7-11, but represents a central aspect of the scenery of chs. 33–34. The connection between Exod. 33.7-11 and 34.34-35 is also indicated by the common frequentative style.[144] The imagery of the people being 'near' and especially the shining face of Moses, with the covering and uncovering his face, are added to that of the tent scene of Exod. 33.7-11.

In this way, the frequentative forms add to the enigma of the two

followed by a scene of talking in ch. 35 corresponds to the relationship of 33.7-11, followed by v. 12, and also to the scene of 40.34-38, followed by Lev. 1.1.

144. The referential relationship between the two scenes is stressed especially by Van Seters, *The Life of Moses*, pp. 321 and 360.

tents. Moses' Tent of Meeting represents a permanent fixture of the camp, parallel to the people's Tent of Meeting. The indications of permanence are increased by the time scale of 33.6, the 'self-plundering' of the people related to the period 'after Horeb'.[145] The sorrowful and repentant people in an everlasting act of renunciation related to the Tent of Meeting far outside the camp, the sight of the mediator going to and fro, the theophanic manifestation seen and adored from afar, represent one image of the 'after Horeb' situation. To this is added Moses' entering and leaving the tent and covering his face, and the people being 'near'.

It is possible that certain aspects of these images supersede each other. Thus, the last tent-scene with Moses 'entering before YHWH' must indicate that the divine presence is contained within the tent, in contrast to the divine position 'at the door of the tent' in the former scene of Exod. 33.9-10. Also the 'nearness' of the people in the last tent-scene differs from the emphasis on distance in Exod. 33.7-11. Given the narrative development, the last image—with its emphasis on the person of Moses as the embodiment of the divine presence for the people, Moses on his side related to the divine presence when hidden in the special tent—is the central expression for the 'after Horeb' situation.

These images are juxtaposed to the final tent-scene of Exod. 40.35-38. Here, the divine presence is related to the Tent of Meeting produced by the people from their gifts, the people engaged in permanent theophanic relationship while Moses is excluded from the tent. Also in this case, the concluding frequentative forms change the presentation of singular acts into a description of a permanent post-Sinai situation. These effects seem to indicate some peculiar double function for the story of Exodus 32–34 related to the context. The immediate function is related to a setting within the story begun in ch. 19 and concluded in ch. 40, providing the high drama in the story plot. But deftly combined with such a function, chs. 32–34 also seem to represent a story somehow parallel to and juxtaposed to the story of chs. 35–40.

The New Ascent

The development of the ascent motif in Exodus 32–34 is an important expression for the linear function of these chapters within the main

145. The connection between vv. 6 and 7 of Exod. 33 is also emphasized by Van Seters, *The Life of Moses*, p. 321.

story. According to 32.1, the people wish for 'gods who shall go before us'. This represents a new issue in the story introduced in ch. 19. But it corresponds to the idea of YHWH 'walking together with the people' in the rest of Exodus 32–34. The idea is expressed by the motifs 'ascend in the midst of' (33.3, 5), 'go' (33.14, 15), 'go with' (v. 16) and 'go in the midst of' (34.9), related to a divine subject and to the people as 'walked with'.

In 32.1 the divine 'going before' the people is connected to the making of gods. In the following stories the motif is connected to some very special divine presence. The stiff-necked people are offered the divine 'angel' who will go 'before' or 'with' them (32.34; 33.2), while the stiff-neckedness of the people makes it impossible for YHWH to 'ascend in the midst of' the people (vv. 3. 5). An 'angel' as the travelling companion on the people's journey has already been introduced as part of the divine instructions of the second theophanic episode, and without causing any drama (23.20-23). But in the context of the Golden Calf, the angel substituting for YHWH himself as the companion on the journey provokes a dramatic reaction. The people show sorrow and put down their ornaments, the significance of which is underlined by the repetition of both the divine refusal and the people's reaction (33.4-6). Somehow the company of God's angel is not experienced as satisfactory, at least not when contrasted with the possibility of YHWH himself going 'with' them.[146] Thus, there is a return to the issue of divine companionship in the following encounters. According to vv. 14-17 Moses pleads for and YHWH consents to 'go himself' in connection with the people's 'ascent'. And the plea for YHWH to 'go in our midst' is repeated in the third encounter in 34.9.

Representing the main issue of the three intercession scenes, the idea of divine companionship on the journey must be important for the story. Moreover, it must express the main issue of the Golden Calf episode. Gods 'who shall go before us' correspond to the divine companionship of the following stories. God's angel shall go 'before' Moses (32.34) and is sent 'before you' (33.2). This is juxtaposed with YHWH

146. The comparable development of the Elijah story in 1 Kgs 19.3-13 indicates that stages of intimate relationship are alluded to. In the Elijah story, the actor is related to three loci of encounter, each connected to a different divine representation (the angel of YHWH, the word of YHWH, finally YHWH himself). The development of the three scenes clearly indicates the narrative movement towards climactic events.

ascending 'in the midst of the people' (33.3, 5). Also, YHWH goes 'himself' in connection with the people's ascent (33.15), goes 'with us' (v. 16) and 'in our midst' (34.9).[147] The parallelism of the motifs corresponds to the contrasting relationship of 32.1-6 and 33.4 and 6 followed by v. 7. The referential relationship is reflected by the scenes of 32.1-3 juxtaposed with 33.3-4. The wish for divine companions on the journey makes the people put forth the golden ear-rings, while the divine refusal to go 'in your midst' makes the people put down their ornaments. In the same way, the 'fun' around the Golden Calf has the people's sorrow as a contrasting scene.

For some reason, the people of 32.1 have raised an issue that becomes central for the story in Exodus 32–34. The people's wish for gods as substitutes for Moses causes the introduction of God's angel as a substitute for YHWH. The parallelism of the people's desire and the divine decision corresponds to the parallelism of Exodus 25–31 and 32.1-6. In some unfathomable way, the YHWH of chs. 25–31 and the people of 32.1 have reached the same[148] conclusion that there is a need for some kind of close and highly materialistic relationship in the divine Tent of Meeting and the people's 'gods' set up as alternatives.[149] The parallelism seems to be continued by the idea of divine companionship on the journey, in this case introduced by the people below and elaborated in the realms above.

The significance of the new issue is underlined by the idea of 'ascent' in the first part of the story. Related to the mountain imagery, *'ālâ* ('ascend') represents the central idea, in addition to other motifs which reflect the idea of human movement as part of the encounter episode. In the first theophanic episode in Exod. 19.3–24.2, the human ascent represents a major issue for the story development, corresponding to the significance of the mountain imagery as the expression of the profound separation of divine and human. This is reflected by the second episode. The invitation of Exod. 24.1-2 and the response in vv. 9-18 present the ascent related to the mountain imagery as the central theme for the theophanic preparations.

147. The connection is pointed out by Moberly (*At the Mountain of God*, p. 48), but related only at a verbal level.

148. Cf. above to the corresponding parallelism of Exod. 19.20-25 and 20.18-21, the divine worries mirrored by the people's fear.

149. Cf. also Childs, *Book of Exodus*, p. 542, and Moberly, *At the Mountain of God*, p. 47, on the connection of Exod. 32.1-6 and 25.1-9.

But in the following encounter on the mountain, the problems of human ascent are abruptly ignored. The divine intention to 'dwell in the midst of' the people is introduced as the new and central issue for the story development, dominating the instructions of Exodus 25–31 as well as the rest of the composition in chs. 35–40. The development of the ascent motifs in Exodus 19–24 seems to be suddenly ignored in favour of a new theme of divine dwelling.[150] That which once seemed to represent the central problem of the story is now changed by the divine intention to dwell among the people.

The wish for a divine companion on the journey, a theme that is introduced in Exod. 32.1, seems to muddy the waters even more by the introduction of a third issue. But while seemingly different, the ideas of 'divine dwelling' and 'divine going' leads to results which are remarkably parallel. They introduce contrasted 'building stories' centred around the people's presentation of gifts which are transformed into receptacles for the divine presence. The people's adoration in Exodus 32 reflects that the Golden Calf is happily accepted as a travelling companion. In addition the dwelling of ch. 40 is obviously constructed for travelling purposes, underlined by the extra kit of Num. 7.3-9. The combination of the two issues of divine dwelling and divine companionship by the Tent of Meeting is visualized by the cloud imagery in Exod. 40.36-38. The theophanic cloud, covering the tent according to Exod. 40.34-35, manifests itself as the signal for the people's departure. The rather forced character of this imagery,[151] compared to the more 'natural' expressions of divine guidance represented, for example, by Exod. 13.21-22 and Num. 10.33, attests to its importance. The Tent of Meeting seems to represent the combination of the divine wish for a dwelling below and the human wish for a divine guide on the journey.

More directly, the significance of the people's wish is also reflected by the elaboration of the motifs that reflect the idea of divine companionship on the journey. According to Exod. 33.1, Moses and the people are ordered to 'ascend from here'. Hitherto, *'ālâ* has been reserved for the extraordinary ascent related to the mountain

150. The abrupt character as well as the significance of this change is illustrated by its tradition and redaction-historical implications, seen as the obvious result of the compilation of chs. 19–24 and Priestly materials.

151. Underlined by the transition to frequentative form in Exod. 40.36-38 as well as the enlarged repetition in Num. 9.15-23.

imagery.[152] Given the established function of the motif in chs. 19–24, its application in Exod. 33.1 to the journey from Sinai to the land of Canaan must be significant. This is underlined by the elaboration of the motif in the extension of the divine order in v. 1. The people who will ascend are qualified as the people 'whom you have made ascend from the land of Egypt'. Moreover, 'ascend' is twice repeated in vv. 3 and 5 with YHWH as subject. The imagery of the ascended people ascending 'from here' is continued by YHWH as not 'ascending in your midst'.

The elaborate repetition of the word, emphasized by the fateful implications of what is discussed on the mountain,[153] must reflect its significance. Moreover, the combination of 'ascent' and 'journey' is also reflected by the repeated references to 'ascent from Egypt' in the context.[154] The people's ascent from Sinai continues the ascent from Egypt.

In this way the issue of YHWH as travelling companion in Exodus 32–34 is underlined by the special application of the ascent motifs. In a context prepared by chs. 19–24, *'ālâ* has an established function as the expression for the extraordinary ascent to the mountain. Accordingly, it becomes necessary to look for some connection between the two sets of application. Aside from the extension 'from here' and the unusual subjects of the ascent, Exod. 33.1a echoes the orders of 19.24a and 24.1a.

The connection between the ascent to the mountain and the ascent of journey is indicated by the conditions of ascent. In Exod. 19.24 and 24.1-2 (cf. also 34.2-3) the order to ascend is related to the prohibited ascent or nearness. According to 19.20-25, underlined by the parallel scene in 20.18-21,[155] the improper ascent results in death. The same implications of death for the unworthy are retained for the new ascent with a divine co-ascender (33.3, 5). The parallelism of the two applications is underlined by the presentation of YHWH in this episode compared to 19.20-25. In both cases, YHWH evidently does not wish to kill the unworthy ascender—his negativity, on the contrary, reflects his

152. Exod. 20.26 and also 34.24 are exceptions, but set in contexts of general instructions. These usages also stress the sacral implications of the word.

153. E.g. Durham (*Exodus*, p. 436) on a doom of absence, comparable to the expulsion from Eden and the separation of Cain from the soil.

154. Exod. 32.1, 4, 7-8, 23. The significance of the word when used for the journey from Egypt is also reflected by 1.10; 12.38; 13.18.

155. Cf. also Exod. 19.12-13 and 24.11 in addition to the divine deliberations in 33.18-23.

wish not to kill. But evidently he has to do so—if brought into a close relationship with the people. In both episodes, the divine wringing of hands is stressed. In 19.21-24 YHWH is rebuked by Moses as unnecessarily worrying, but still repeats the prohibitions and their motivation. Similarly, the statement on his non-ascent and its motivation is repeated in Exod. 33.3 and 5, the latter verse extended by the divine perplexity about how to solve the dilemma. The two scenes illustrate the connotational connection of the motif usage, both types of ascent having the identical implications. To 'ascend to YHWH' implies the same as 'ascending from here' with YHWH as co-ascender.

The motif application even suggests some subtle chiastic connection. In Exodus 19–24, the people's ascent into the divine space is refused. According to Exod. 33.1-5, YHWH's inability to ascend 'in the midst' of the people is negatively related to the human space. With the death of the people as the given outcome in both cases, both types of ascent reflect the impossibility of any close relationship between God and people, in the reality above as in the below.

In this way, the divine 'going before' in Exod. 32.1 presents an issue which introduces a new application of the ascent theme. The ascent to the mountain is translated to the horizontal categories of journey. But the extraordinary character of the ascent as expression for the movement into divine space is retained. With YHWH as co-ascender, the people's journey as the new form of ascent has the same character as the traditional movement.

The new application of the ascension motif bridges the issues of extraordinary ascent and divine dwelling. When introduced in ch. 25, the idea of divine dwelling among the people seems to interrupt the development of chs. 19–24. But chs. 32–34 relate the seemingly disparate motifs of human ascent and divine dwelling among the people. On the one hand, the idea of the human ascent is retained, although shifted from the mountain imagery to the idea of journey. The death motifs of Exod. 33.3 and 5 demonstrate that the new ascent also refers to events of the same extraordinary character as the mountain ascent. On the other hand, the divine going 'before' or 'with' or 'in the midst' of the people retains the idea of intimate togetherness in the reality below. The ultimate combination of the two themes of dwelling and companionship on the journey is expressed by the conclusion of Exod. 40.34-38—the cloud over the tent being the signal for the people's departure.

All this means that the elaboration of the theme of divine companionship on the journey in Exodus 32–34 is important for the conceptual coherence of the story contained in chs. 19–40. The idea of a new ascent does not 'explain' the abrupt transition from mountain to tent in ch. 25, and probably never was intended to do so in a story dedicated to the wondrous event of divine movement from above to the human world below. But the new type of ascent adds to the understanding of the implications of the divine movement, the categories of extraordinary relationship retained also for the intimacy of YHWH and the people as travelling companions in the world below the mountain.

This development also makes it possible to return to the special application of the narrative pattern in Exodus 32–34. Here, the events of theophany and *visio* related to the people is presented in the second encounter and related to the Tent of Meeting. This is followed by a new theophanic event and *visio* related to Moses, moreover to a Moses in the people's role as the problematical visionary. The significance of these changes is underlined by the change of locus. Corresponding to the compositional movement towards the human space below the mountain, the people's experience is related to the Tent of Meeting. But the Moses experience marks a return to the mountain imagery.

The transference of the motifs of *visio* and mortal threat suggests the parallelism of Moses and people in the two episodes. This is also reflected by Exod. 33.12-17 and 32.18-23. Combined as parts of the same dialogue, the first passage focuses on the issue of divine companionship on the journey, the second on the plea of Moses for a special *visio*. The two situations of special relationship refer to the same motifs of divine presence. The *pānîm* of YHWH—related to the ascent (vv. 14-15) as well as to the special *visio* (vv. 20 and 23)—formally link the two situations of the ascending people having YHWH 'himself' for co-ascender and Moses asking for a vision of the divine 'glory'.[156]

The parallelism indicated by the compilation of the two passages as well as the motif elaboration is underlined by the problem of divine companionship on the journey. The categories of ascent and the introduction of YHWH as co-ascender indicate the extraordinary character of the new relationship between YHWH and people, obtained by the intercession of Moses. Just as clearly the discussion in vv. 18-23

156. The connection suggested by this word is stressed by Moberly, *At the Mountain of God*, pp. 80-82.

demonstrates that to see the divine 'glory' and 'face' represents something very special. While this is refused, the elaborate description of the locus in vv. 21-23 indicates that the vision of the divine 'backside' also represents something exceptional for a person who earlier has been talked to 'face to face' (v. 11).

The motif development seems to reflect stages[157] of intimate relationship. Within the context of Exodus 32–34, the divine condescension of 33.12-17 implies that the people have been elevated into a new type of relationship with a special form of the divine presence, indicated by YHWH 'himself' going 'with' the people. Further, reflecting the contextual connection of vv. 12-17 and 18-23, the upward mobility of the people is related to a corresponding upward movement made by Moses on some hierarchical ladder of visionary experience. Even limited to the divine backside, the new level of extraordinary vision results in some permanent change—Moses' face became infused by divine light. The composition of the two passages in Exod. 33.12-17 and 18-23, together with the special emphasis on the final mountain scene of ch. 34, reflect the parallelism of Moses and people in some common hierarchy of extraordinary relationship to the divine presence. By the divine consent to ascend 'with' the people followed by the elevation of Moses, the role allocation of ch. 19 has been fundamentally changed. Both sets of human actors have moved one step higher on some ladder of intimate relationship. This could also be related to the changed conditions in the camp according to ch. 35.

157. Underlined by the change of locus and divine representation followed by the negated theophanies concluded by a climactic experience in the Elijah story in 1 Kgs 19.3-13.

Chapter 2

The Main Story: The Encounter Below and the New Theophanic Figures

1. *The Divine Mountain and the Human-Made Tent*

At this stage of the reading, the structure of three grand theophanic episodes represents the primary indication of the narrative direction. According to a basic pattern of preparation and theophany, the events of the three grand episodes can be related to the three passages of Exod. 19.1–24.2; 24.3–31.18 and chs. 32–34; 35.1–40.38. This delimitation seems rather artificial when imposed upon the narrative flow. This is amply illustrated by the subtleties of chs. 32–34 when they are related to their wider context. On the one hand interwoven into the second theophanic episode, on the other hand presenting a story which contrasts the third episode, these chapters should not be bound too tightly to any formal structure. But at least for an initial reading, the delimitation of three theophanic episodes is helpful for the perception of the narrative movement. In a pattern of successive events, the one episode overlaps the next. The events of mediation and response that conclude one episode represent the preparatory events for the next episode. This also underlines the linear movement towards a climax.

The pattern of three central episodes is also reflected by a corresponding sub-pattern. Each grand episode entails three sub-episodes in which the third—accentuated by theophanic motifs and the people's *visio Dei*—represents the climax prepared by the two earlier. Also the composition of chs. 32–34 seems to reflect this pattern of three sub-episodes and could, if read in a certain way, be perceived as a theophanic episode in its own right.

The development of preparatory sub-episodes reflects the narrative movement towards ch. 40. The two sets of preparations in ch. 19 refer to the categories of encounter related to the mountain. In ch. 24 the first set of preparations is dedicated to ritual events below the mountain, while the second is related to the mountain by a 'half-way' encounter by the people's representatives. In the third set of 35.1–40.33, both preparatory sub-episodes are set in the camp; the first centred around the people as actors, the second round Moses. The gradual movement from the vertical categories of encounter on the mountain to the horizontal categories of preparatory scenes in the camp must be important. In addition, the gradual increase in the emphasis given to the people must also be considered significant.

As has already been seen, chs. 32–34 both continue and interrupt this development. Centred around three encounters, the first and the third are related to the mountain imagery (32.31–33.5 and 34.4-28), while the second is emphatically set in the camp (33.7-23). On the other hand, the significance of the Golden Calf and Moses' Tent of Meeting in these chapters corresponds to the overarching development that moves towards ch. 40 as the climax of the stories.

The character of the preparatory events could also be indicative of the narrative movement. The preparations of ch. 19 are related to personal categories of purification. This is followed by the events of ch. 24 which introduce a new locality under the mountain, connected with the altar building and sacrifices—the latter account being extended by the visionary meal at which the people's representatives take the active role. This is concluded by the events of chs. 35–40, dedicated to the production of the tent and its implements. The ritual categories and the growing complexity of the preparations seem to reflect a process of gradual materialization, the divine movement from mountain to camp reflected by a corresponding emphasis on concrete material manifestations. The Golden Calf as well as Moses' Tent of Meeting must be related to this development, both reflecting its importance and indicating its profound implications.

Finally, the situations of theophanic experience related to the people (Exod. 20.18-21; 24.17; 33.8-10; 40.34-38) must also be mentioned at this point. At the start of the present reading, the four *visio* scenes made it possible both to discern central aspects of the narrative movement as well as the composition of three grand episodes. Also, they are important expressions for what the story is all about. The series of events concluded in ch. 40, especially when followed by the sacrificial instructions and their implementation in Leviticus 1–10, reflect the importance of ritual and material categories. But connected to the motifs of *visio Dei* and theophanic locus, the emphasis on ritual perfection reflects the significance of the category of extraordinary encounter and theophanic experience. Together with the development of the ascent theme in chs. 32–34, the theme of *visio Dei* links chs. 19–24 and 35–40 as parts of one story.

The essential plot of this story is reflected by the contrasts of Exod. 19.3 and Lev. 1.1. The events in between present how it came about that the divine calling from the mountain has been changed to the Tent of Meeting. The change of localities is connected with the significance of the human actors for the development of the plot. The locus of the divine dwelling is also the place of extraordinary encounter, and this means that the human actors are as important as the divine for the actualization of encounter. These two aspects of locus are deftly reflected by the double qualification of 'Dwelling' and 'Tent of Meeting' (40.34-35). In the present story of changed locus, the plot even allocates the central role to the human actors. The tension of the story is connected with the ability of the human actors to participate. This is expressed by the people as the second—ultimately the central—set of actors. The traditional conditions of encounter are illustrated by the story of chs. 19–24, in its turn underlined by the encounter episodes of chs. 3–4 and 1 Kings 19. The divine mountain is ascended by the extraordinary human actor, leaving the rest of humanity far below. The introduction of the people for such a lofty role presents an absurd situation. The impossibility of any intimate relationship between YHWH and the people is illustrated by the 'revolt' scenes in 20.18-21 and 32.1-6, and is reflected by the narrative development in chs. 19–24 which unfolds aspects of the encounter in its traditional mode. The holy mountain represents the divine reality. Related to this reality, ordinary people and beasts can be lumped together as trespassers (Exod. 19.13; 34.3). Even YHWH has to express the tension of the plot by manifestations rather unseemly for a divine actor. Reproved by Moses for worrying unnecessarily (19.23) and not knowing what to do (33.5), the divine role also reflects the script of a drama that faces unsurmountable obstacles.

The categories involved demonstrate that a change of locus by itself represents an event of enormous significance. This is greatly added to by thc location of the new place of encounter, which according to 25.8 is set in 'the midst of the people'. The radical character of this location can be illustrated by the traditional language available to the author. The imagery, for example, of 15.17 (cf. also Ps. 68.16-18) could have been naturally extended into a story of YHWH moving from one sacred mountain to a new sacred mountain properly situated in the land.[1] But the change of locus does not refer to a divine movement from one holy place to a comparably holy place. On the contrary, the location in 'the midst of the people' introduces a set of connotational contrasts. Compared to the lofty character of the mountain related to the extraordinary ascender moving into the divine reality, the divine movement into the tent represents a descent into human space. And when the character of human space is qualified by 'the people', the connotations established by the story indicate a divine descent into baseness. The implications of this descent are also underlined by the character of the new locus as a travelling sanctuary, and further elaborated by the new character of the theophanic manifestation as a signalling device (40.36-38). The new locus is emphatically set in the human realm.

The Coherence of the Story and Psalm 24

According to the above reading, it is possible to perceive the present composition of chs. 19–40 as a story of successive events which starts from a beginning, presents obstacles for a successful conclusion, and ultimately brings the reader to an end. Formally, the shape of the materials indicates a meticulous composition that reflects the narrative movement towards the climax of ch. 40.

On the other hand, the perception of the inner coherence of this story is disturbed by the special character of chs. 19–24 and 32–34 in contrast to chs. 25–31 and 35–40. While the classic positions of source-criticism have been changed, the perception of the two parts as two different literary 'blocks' represents the obvious scholarly position. The story of the Tent construction represents interests perceived as 'Priestly'. The mountain imagery is related to chs. 19–24, still bearing the marks of a pre-Priestly origin characterized by different theological interests, labelled by terms such as Covenant or Torah obedience or Mosaic Yahwism.[2] The present composition is the result of a special Priestly

1. The point is illustrated by the discussion of Exod. 15 in Smith, *The Pilgrimage Pattern*, pp. 205-26. Zion represents the original referent of the poem, but in the Priestly redaction this has been changed to Sinai as the central place. The rather complex model (pp. 214-26) ignores the fact that, according to chs. 19–40, the human-made tent has been substituted for the divine Sinai.

2. Cf. the very title of Utzschneider, *Das Heiligtum*; see further, e.g., Nicholson, 'The Covenant Ritual', p. 74; Blum, *Studien zur Komposition*, p. 302; Thompson, *The Origin Tradition*, p. 64; Dozemann, *God on the Mountain*, p. 2.

redaction, adding to[3] or even superseding the older theology by a vision of the divine presence related to ritual categories as the highest form of religiosity.[4] Or, conversely, the Priestly redactors found that the institutional temple practice represented a difficult theological problem. Convinced about the supremacy of the Mosaic influence, they present a new vision of the acceptable temple practice. The restoration of the temple cult can take place only within the framework of some Covenant theology.[5] Whatever the relationship of the two traditions represented by chs. 19–24 and the Priestly materials, their character as expressions for different theological traditions and interests is taken for granted.

Such perceptions cannot be declared null and void by the demonstration of the formal consistencies of the story in its present form. However well turned out, the shape of the text obviously reflects the presence of different types of materials. Also, questions of literary consistency should not be confused with questions of literary origin. The implicit expectation of literary efforts as creations *ex nihilo* represents a modern construct.

Moreover, when we ignore the questions of origin and later elaborations and read chs. 19–40 as a story, the transition from ch. 24 to 25 represents a riddle. The very impression of a meticulous composition for chs. 19–40 as a whole makes this riddle the more prominent, challenging the reader to ponder the question of inner coherence. What in traditio-historical categories represents an obvious seam between different materials is perceived as a tear in the narrative texture. Why is the development of the ascent theme connected with the mountain imagery suddenly changed into a theme of divine dwelling in the reality below?

Formally, Exodus 24 and 25–31 are set together as parts of one episode. Moreover, the formal linkage corresponds to a basic conceptual linkage. The two motif-sets of mountain and tent are linked by a

3. E.g. Smith, *The Pilgrimage Pattern.*

4. E.g. Durham, *Exodus*, pp. 353-54, on Exod. 25–31 as an expression of a further and higher revelation which has been prepared for by the proclamation of the Torah and the people's covenant.

5. E.g. Utzschneider, *Das Heiligtum*, p. 296, linking the main Priestly effort to a period in which the 'fromme, gesetzestreue Gemeinschaft' (the pious, Torah-observant community) had taken the place of the ancient Zion sanctuary as the legitimate expression for the divine presence. The texts reflect an effort of 'eine Aussöhnung der etisch-rechtlichen Traditionen mit dem Heiligtum' (to reconcile the traditions of the Torah and the sanctuary).

common reference to temple categories. Accordingly, a story centred around Moses on the mountain continued by a story of tent construction could reflect a story of conceptual coherence. The connection of mountain and tent as two aspects of one overarching concept could also mean that the question of linkage need not be reduced to some abstract idea[6] or to a more superficial arrangement resulting from the redactional reinterpretation of older materials.[7] The common 'something' that links the two parts could be organic to the very imagery centred around mountain and tent, and thus directly reflected by the materials.

The possibility of such a connection between what to modern readers, especially those of a Protestant Christian heritage, seem to be utterly different theological world-views, can be illustrated by the composition of Ps. 24.3-10. The significance of this text for the composition of Exodus 19–40 is enhanced by the scholarly reading of the psalm. This represents *in nuce* a version of the reading of the Exodus story. Also the psalm is perceived as a compilation of materials that have a different origin. The parallel units of Psalm 15 and Isa. 33.14-16 demonstrate that Ps. 24.3-6 represent forms of fixed character. Read together, the three texts make a classical demonstration of the validity of the form-critical approach. There is a firm foundation for the perception of Ps. 24.3-10 as a 'secondary' compilation of components which reflect different functions and also theological interests.[8]

On the other hand, the present shape of Psalm 24 reflects the author's interest in linking the two blocks in vv. 3-6 and 7-10 as parts of one whole. The parallel questions and answers of the two parts indicate that the linkage does not reflect a process of mechanical compilation, but of meticulous elaboration. This is underlined by the comparison with Psalm 15 and Isa. 33.14-16. Given the formally fixed character of these texts, the present shape of Ps. 24.3-10 reflects the delicacy and care of an accomplished literary hand. The handling has resulted in the parallel questions and the parallel presentation of the divine and human actors.

6. E.g. the concept 'theme' presented by Clines, *The Theme of the Pentateuch*, pp. 17-21; or 'pattern' by Wilcoxen, 'Some Anthropocentric Aspects'.

7. E.g. 'pattern' as presented by Smith, *The Pilgrimage Pattern*; or 'Makrostrukturen' (macrostructure) by Utzschneider, *Das Heiligtum*, pp. 134-35.

8. Klaus Koch, 'Tempeleinlassliturgien und Dekaloge', in R. Rendtorff and K. Koch (eds.), *Studien zur Theologie der alttestamentlichen Überlieferungen: Gerhard von Rad zum 60. Geburtstag* (Neukirchen–Vluyn: Neukirchener Verlag, 1961), pp. 45-60.

The formal elaboration must reflect some basic connection between the two parts.

This is underlined by the temple concept common to both parts. The temple is referred to using different motifs. Verse 3 refers to the holy 'mountain' and 'place', while the arrival of the king of glory in vv. 7 and 9 is related to 'gates' and 'doors'. Comparable to the 'mountain' and 'tent' of Exodus 19–40, the formal difference between 'holy mountain' and 'gates' could seduce the reader into perceiving two sets of imagery, which refer to different sets of connotations. Read in such a way, the composite character of the psalm would represent the prime perception. But in this case, the application of different sets of motifs does not cause the exegete any problems. The connection of mountain and gates as parallel expressions for a common temple concept is generally accepted. The parallel application of temple motifs suggests some kind of connection between the two processions of human and divine actors, both described in a situation of temple arrival, both presented in a special way by the pattern of questions and answers.

For Mowinckel it was a matter of course that the two sets of imagery are linked by their background in cultic practice. In vv. 3-6, the procession is defined as one of pilgrims seeking admittance. The admittance is granted and the procession proceeds triumphantly—at this point of the ritual procedure defined as the procession led by the King of Glory.[9] The categories of ritual function represent a meta-structure which links the seemingly disparate elements.

While rather speculative, the cultic approach illustrates the possibility that a secondary composite could express a basic unity, a unity that, moreover, is concretely reflected by the different elements. If the reading is confined to textual data, the parallel references to the temple in vv. 3-6 and 7-10 indicate a connection of conceptual character. Underlined by the formal elaboration of the two parts, the common temple concept suggests that the movement of ascending by those seeking the divine face and the divine movement of entering are closely related.

The character of such a relationship is suggested by the elaboration of the two motif-sets. The temple as mountain corresponds to the motif of ascent. The imagery implies the pilgrims' movement from a lower to a higher place, concluded by their 'standing'. This imagery is added to and deepened by the parallel qualification 'place of your holiness'.

9. Sigmund Mowinckel, *Salmeboken* (Skriftene 1. Del, Det gamle testamente oversatt av Michelet, Mowinckel og Messel, 4; Oslo: Aschehoug, 1955), p. 66.

Related to the human ascenders, the temple represents the holy space of the divine mountain.

The temple imagery is changed in the second part. In connection with divine arrival, reference is made to the temple's 'gates' and 'doors'. Such references present the temple as a closed construction possessing openings that lead into some inner space. The imagery underlines the confined character of these openings when entered by the divine actor. Contrasted with the temple as the holy mountain, its character of confined gates and doors underscores the human-made character of the temple.[10]

Related to the human arrival, the temple is the divine and holy mountain, belonging to YHWH, high above normal reality and to be reached by the human ascent. In connection with the divine arrival,[11] the temple represents confined, human-made space, that is to be enlarged for the one who enters.

In this way, Psalm 24 seems to reflect a formal structure comparable to that found in Exodus 19–40. The scenes of chs. 19–24 are dominated by mountain imagery, and the human ascent related to the holy space is central for the narrative development. Chapters 25–40 are centred around the tent imagery, all the details of tent construction being related to the divine arrival. However complex and enlarged compared to the psalm, the two portions of Exodus are remarkably parallel to Ps. 24.3-6 and 7-10. The temple as holy mountain and as an artifact container for the divine glory—the first related to the human ascent, the second centered around the divine arrival—is common to the two texts, each aspect the point of gravity for a corresponding set of motifs. While easily seen in the psalm due to its poetic shape, the complexities of the Exodus put heavier demands on the reader. But also in this case, the conceptual connection between the two parts is reflected by two sets of imagery which unfold the two aspects of the temple concept in a story of successive events.

The parallelism of the two texts is added to by the common Torah motifs. The connection between Exodus 19–24 and Psalm 24 as expression of some Torah tradition connected to ritual practice, as well as the

10. Cf. the comparable contrasts in 1 Kgs 8.27.

11. The significance of the parallel arrival is underlined when the choice of verbs for Ps. 24.3 is compared to Ps. 15.1 and Isa. 33.14b. The pilgrims 'ascending' and 'standing' in the first part corresponds to the divine 'coming' in the latter part.

conceptual connection of Sinai and the temple motifs of Psalm 24, represent established insights.[12] But the parallelism is even more striking when the composition of chs. 19–40 as a whole is related to the psalm. Underlined by the lack of comparable Torah motifs in 1 Kings 19, the thematic connection of ascent, Torah, and theophanic manifestation related to temple concepts must reflect a special interest common to Psalm 24 and Exodus 19–40.

In the psalm, the two parts present two parallel events of movement and arrival. The human train arriving from below and a divine arrival from an 'outside' location are related by the common locus. The subtle elaboration of the temple motifs in Ps. 24.3, 7 and 9 suggests that the two movements are aspects of one event. Human actors are entering the divine reality, God is entering human reality. The union of the two movements in a situation of extraordinary meeting is explicitly expressed by the *pānîm* motif in v. 6. Heightened by the transition from YHWH mentioned in the third person into the direct address of the second person in v. 6, the ascent of the mountain is qualified as a search for 'your face'. This corresponds to the theophanic experience in vv. 7-10, alluded to both by the challenges to the gates and doors to widen and the questions about the 'who' of the glorious entering. Concluding the first part and preparing the next, v. 6 relates the human procession to the theophany of vv. 7-10. The two scenes of human and divine arrival are linked as two halves of one event, the two sets of movement leading to a situation of extraordinary *visio*.

The linkage underlines the conceptual coherence of Exodus 19–24 and 25–40. Also the two parts of the story are linked by the common reference to the categories of extraordinary encounter connected to the situation of *visio Dei*. The parallelism of a locus of divine mountain related to the human ascent and the extraordinary *visio* and a huhuman-made locus related to the theophanic manifestation and *visio* is common to the two texts. Thus, the structure of Exodus 19–40 must also reflect a basic idea of the divine and human movement as linked, leading towards the one encounter. The connotational effects could bridge the transition from Exodus 24 to 25. What to a modern reader is perceived as an abrupt transition from one set of imagery to an imagery of different connotational value, really reflects two halves of a conceptual

12. E.g. Mowinckel, *Le décalogue*.

wholeness. The first part dedicated to the human ascent must be completed with a representation of the divine movement towards the encounter.

On the other hand, the comparison with Psalm 24 profiles the linear character of the Exodus story. In the psalm, the divine mountain and huhuman-made tent represent complementary aspects of the locus of extraordinary meeting—the poetic elaboration of their connotational parallelism visualizing the wondrous character of the two trains meeting. In the story, this connection is dissolved. The two aspects of the temple concept are translated into two sets of successive events, centred around mountain and tent as successive localities. The divine mountain represents a first locus, the human-made tent the new locus. Exodus 24 concludes the theme 'who may ascend the mountain?' and anticipates the next part dedicated to the preparations for the divine descent.

But also within a composition dominated by the linear relationship of successive events, the basic identity of the two sets of imagery must add to the connotational impact of the story. Besides the impression of a story of successive events, the subtle perception of the two sets of events as ultimately aspects of one event enriches the reading. Related to the parallelism of Psalm 24, the events of ascent followed by the divine decision to dwell among the people represent an organic extension of the basic concepts. The introduction of Moses' Tent of Meeting in chs. 33–34 indicates that the application of the temple concepts serves interests that cannot be confined to the mere presentation of successive events. The peculiar effect of parallelism by Moses' Tent of Meeting juxtaposed to the people's Tent of Meeting reflects the profoundities of the connotational contents.

If the connotational effects on the one hand bridge the transition from ch. 24 to 25, they also add to the reader's perception of a narrative 'gap' between ch. 24 and 25. Why does the author change the two aspects of one story into successive events? Chapter 24 presents the invitation to a special ascent as actualized, the significance of which is emphasized by the great number of worthy ascenders and the event of extraordinary *visio*. Underlined by the traditio-historical reading of chs. 19–24 as a special entity, ch. 24 can serve as a conclusion of one part of the story. According to the pattern of events illustrated by Psalm 24, the narrative concluded in Exodus 24 begs for a completing story centered around the arrival of the divine actor.

But in contrast to what we could expect, the author seems subtly, but deliberately, to separate what conceptually belongs together. This is indicated by the names of the ascenders in ch. 24 which, moreover, are repeated at 24.1 and 9.[13] Besides Moses, the ascenders who are named are to play the roles of villains in the perverted encounters in Exod. 32.1-6 and Lev. 10.1-2. While Exod. 24.9-11 obviously represents an event of extraordinary character, the intimate *visio* of the divine feet unmarred by the divine violence, the impression of the successful ascent is subtly overshadowed by the events to come. The indication of something not quite right extends the narrative gap between chs. 24 and 25. This story cannot continue in the conventional way.

The Exodus story also reflects the traditional aspects of the concepts. But with the original relationship dissolved and extended into a story of successive events, certain aspects are enlarged in such a way that a traditional presentation is impossible. Above all, the special character of the Exodus version of extraordinary encounter is expressed by the introduction of the people as candidates for the extraordinary relationship. The smooth parallelism of the worthy ascender and the divine enterer in Psalm 24 is comparable to the role of Moses. Such ascenders can be expected to be met by the divine descender. But with the story connected to the people as visionaries, the successful conclusion of the story has been greatly complicated.

On the other hand, this difference also can be seen as the result of malleable concepts greatly stretched and elaborated by their translation into a story. The imagery of Psalm 24 also implies aspects of profound incompatibility.[14] In connection with the human ascent, the temple is qualified as divine mountain and holy space. In connection the divine enterer, the temple is qualified as constricted, human-made space. As the locus of the extraordinary encounter, the temple represents the unnatural place for both participants. And with a peculiar mirror-effect, the reversal of imagery also suggests the locus as the natural place for the participants. YHWH is at home in 'his place' of holiness towards which the human train is ascending, while the temple as constricted

13. The significance of these names is added to by the two other ascenders referred to by name in vv. 13 and 14. Readily explained by traditio-historical assertions, the present shape of the story underlines the identity of certain ascenders. This must refer to their function in the contrast encounters, the extraordinary heroes of one episode being allocated the roles of villain in the next.

14. This aspect is underlined by the extension of the question in Isa. 33.14.

gates and doors refers to categories of the human realm. Each actor is foreign to the other's place, and each is welcomed by an actor at home. The imagery reflects a reality of profoundly dual character. The duality dissolved by the encounter presupposes events of truly miraculous character.

It is of course possible that the composition of Psalm 24 translated into categories of religious practice could reflect a less dramatic character. The genre of Ps. 24.3-6 might refer to a type of religiosity for which the human ascent represented a very practical proposition.[15] And if the psalm has formed part of ritual practice, it is easy to envisage that such a practice could reflect aspects of habitual and even manipulative intercourse with the extraordinary. But the motif contrasts demonstrate that as to connotational and ideological impact, the encounter of divine and human represents the meeting of totally different levels of reality.

As a model on a small scale, Psalm 24 represents a striking parallel to the relationship of the two blocks in Exodus 19–40. At the very least, the psalm presents an illustration of a theological process which has resulted in a remarkably parallel application of common materials. The formal character of Psalm 24 supports the immediate impression of the two parts as 'blocks'. According to the usual criteria of transcribing texts into processes of literary dependency and development, the relationship to Psalm 15 and Isa. 33.14-16 could be described as a process of 'extension' and 'addition', taken further, for example, as 'redactional reinterpretation' and even 'canonical shaping'.[16] Even so, the refined motif and conceptual development of Psalm 24 amply demonstrates that in the right hands, such a process of compilation and elaboration could lead to a singular composition, in which the different elements function as organic parts of a new entity.

Psalm 24 also adds to our perception of the processes that underlie

15. E.g. W. Beyerlin, *Weisheitlich-kultische Heilsordnung: Studien zum 15. Psalm* (Biblisch-Theologische Studien, 9; Neukirschen–Vluyn: Neukirchener Verlag, 1985).

16. The categories of Dozemann (*God on the Mountain*, pp. 197-99) for the description of the dominant redactional layers of Exod. 19–24 could be directly transferred to Ps. 24. The original holy mountain-concept with the idea of a static and permanent divine presence is found v. 3. This is critically reinterpreted in a 'Deuteronomistic' redaction vv. 4-5, and finally added to by the theophany visualized as the impermanent presence in a 'Priestly' vv. 7-10. The whole is introduced by the universal scope of vv. 1-2 of the Priestly redaction.

the composition of Exodus 19–40. The editorial and theological efforts cannot be limited to the materials of Exodus, but have found comparable expressions in other genres. The relationship of 1 Kings 19 to the wilderness and Sinai stories of Exodus indicates a common tradition of narrative elements centred around the situation of encounter on the divine mountain. In comparison with this relationship, the combination of the given materials in Psalm 24 and the Sinai stories reflects processes so similar that it is natural to assume some closer connection to a common milieu of religious reflection and literary activity.

Moreover, the psalm also indicates an important aspect of the character of this activity. The application of the temple motifs—underlined by the parallelism of Psalm 15 and Isa. 33.14-16—reflects their character as malleable for individual shaping. The temple presented in the form of holy mountain and confined doors when linked to the different actors of the drama does not primarily refer to ritual or institutional or architectural reality, but unfolds the conceptual implications of the temple motifs. The connection between Psalm 24 and Exodus 19–40 adds Sinai and Tent of Meeting as parallel images of the basic concept. This is even added to by the contrast relationship of the Golden Calf and the parallelism of Moses' Tent of Meeting in chs. 33–34. Together, the representations of the temple demonstrate the freedom of literary application. This indicates that the concrete motifs do not primarily refer to categories of institutionalized reality, but are better read as parts of a literary context.

2. *The Theophanic Movement—Divine and Human*

Psalm 24 indicates that the two parts, Exodus 19–24 and 25–40, could reflect a connection of profound conceptual coherence. The transition from divine mountain to human-made tent does not reflect a new set of connotational references, but the transposition of complementary aspects into the linear space of the narrative. When the divine and human actors are to be intimately related, the relationship is in Psalm 24 presented by a parallel movement towards the temple. The structure of Exodus 19–40 reflects this basic connection. On the other hand, the way in which the transposition of the imagery is effected in chs. 24–25 profoundly adds to its impact. The parallelism of human ascent and the corresponding divine movement is dissolved and presented as successive events. The way in which this dissolution is effected also indicates that the traditional ascent has been abandoned as meaningful for the successful encounter. Corresponding to the change of locus from mountain to tent, the human movement of ascent is substituted by the movement from above to below.

On the other hand, this elaboration points to the significance of the basic structure represented by Psalm 24. This connection is also reflected by the singular episodes in the Exodus story. All the descriptions of the theophanic event retain the central imagery of human and divine movement, presented as parallel and related to some locality.

In ch. 19 the repeated 'ascent' of the mediator and the corresponding divine movement of 'descent'[17] represent the basic motifs for the theophanic situation. Repeated in all the mountain scenes with Moses as subject, *'ālâ* is the central term for the human movement. In Exod. 19.13, together with vv. 21-24, the basic imagery of theophany and 'ascent' is also retained for the other participants, connected with the prohibition against any usurped ascent (cf. also 34.3). The significance of 'ascend' for the composition as a whole is reflected by the re-application of this term with the people as subjects in chs. 32–34. Also in this case, the basic connection between the divine and human movement is retained by the idea of the new ascent combined with the idea of a divine co-ascender.

In addition to the term 'ascend', the introductory chapter also presents a second motif group which refers to horizontal categories. On the third day, Moses made the people 'go out' from the camp towards God, the people 'placing themselves' below the mountain (19.17). This is followed by a new scene of movement by the people 'standing afar' in contrast to Moses 'approaching' the divine 'darkness' (20.18; 20.21).

Both motif groups are retained in the imagery of ch. 24. In the invitation to the second theophanic event (24.1-2), the 'ascent' of the extended group is connected with the categories of nearness and distance, by the motif 'bowing down from afar' contrasted with Moses' 'approaching'. In the story of implementation, the imagery of vv. 4-8 implicitly relates the people to a locus 'beneath the mountain' to which the young men have been 'sent', followed by the 'ascent' of the extended group (v. 9). This scene is followed by the 'standing up' of Moses and Joshua, while the further movements of Moses are expressed by his 'ascending' related to the mountain, his 'coming' to the cloud,

17. Verses 11, 18, 20; cf. further 33.9 and 34.5.

and the extended 'being' on the mountain (vv. 12-18). The human movement related to the mountain corresponds to the divine movement of 'settling upon' and 'covering' the mountain (vv. 15-16).

The divine 'descent' of 33.7-11 is related to a corresponding human movement which refers to horizontal categories. The locus set 'outside the camp' and 'far from the camp' is reached by 'going out' and the corresponding 'return' to the camp. Also in this case, the mediator's movement towards the locus is extended to other human subjects, every 'YHWH-seeker' 'going out' (v. 7). But when the imagery is related to a concrete situation, the mediator's movement is the central event, his 'going out' and 'entering the tent' are related to the divine movements of 'descending' and 'standing' (v. 9). But also in this case, the imagery retains aspects of the people participating. The mediator's movement is connected to the people's 'standing up', everyone 'placing himself' at his tent door and looking after Moses 'going out' (v. 8). A corresponding imagery is applied to the description of the people during the theophanic manifestation. After the cloud has 'descended' and 'stood itself at the tent door', the people 'stand up' and 'bow down', 'everyone at his tent door' (v. 10).[18] Thus, while the exposition of the scene underlines the position of the people as confined to the camp far from the locus, the delicate details reflect the basic significance of the theophanic movement for the people, as well as the parallelism of the divine and human movements.

The imagery of distance and nearness is also applied to the description of the people's relationship to the 'descending' (34.29) Moses in the final mountain scene. The people's 'approaching' is first negated—in a description comparable to 20.18-21—and then stated as related to two groups of leaders and common people (34.30-32).

The description of the grand theophanic event in ch. 40 presents the final representation of the imagery. Corresponding to 24.16, the theophanic manifestation is 'settling' and 'covering', now with the cloud for subject and related to the tent. In addition, the divine glory 'fills' the sanctuary (40.34-35). For the human movement, 'enter into the tent', corresponding to the expression of 33.8-9, is used twice.[19] Continued by

18. The significance of the terms in vv. 7-10 is underlined by the corresponding descriptions of the separate encounters of Moses in 33.21 and 34.2, 8.

19. Cf. also Lev. 9.23. In this case, the parallelism between the two sets of human actors is expressed by the double blessing by Aaron (v. 22) and by Moses and Aaron (v. 23), followed by the theophanic manifestation. The connection

the motif 'draw near' related to the altar, 'entering into the tent' is first used for the preparations by Moses and the priests prior to the theophanic manifestation (v. 32), then for the special movement of Moses in v. 35.

In all these descriptions, the human movement relative to the locus is consistently related to two scenes. One scene is dedicated to the movement of the people. In 24.9-11 and 40.32, this scene is related to special groups. This is followed by a second scene dedicated to the movement of the mediator, the description of which is mixed with the description of the theophanic movement. This pattern is underlined by the different motifs and the different scenery of each episode.

The consistency of the basic pattern underlines the special character of the last application in ch. 40. Formally, it reflects the established events. The 'entering' of Moses in v. 35aα is presented as a second scene of movement set after the preparatory 'entering' by Moses and the priests in v. 32. The parallelism of the two scenes is indicated by the formulaic 'enter into the Tent of Meeting'. Also in this case, the 'entering' of Moses is framed by the theophanic description in vv. 34 and 35aβ-b, corresponding to the descriptions of the earlier theophanic episodes. The meticulous elaboration of these scenes, compared to the established pattern, highlights the change of the second scene. The theophanic movement of the mediator is negated, Moses not being able to enter the tent filled by the divine glory.

The significance of the new version of the mediator's movement is underlined by the extension of the theophanic episode in vv. 36-38. A new version of the parallel divine and human movements is added to the preceding description.[20] The divine movement is related to the locus of the tent and now described by the verb *'lh* (niphal).[21] And directly

between the human and divine acts is reflected by the parallelism of Moses and Aaron 'going out' from the tent and the divine fire 'going out' from the divine face. The theophanic manifestation is also in this case related to the people's *visio* (vv. 23.b, 24b).

20. Probably also in this case as a singular version of established components. The introduction of the people in vv. 36-38, set after two scenes dedicated to the movement of a select group and the mediator's movement, corresponds to the *visio* scenes of 24.17 related to vv. 9-16 and of Lev. 9.23b, 24b related to vv. 22-23a. Also the parallelism of the divine and people's movements related to the tent doors in Exod. 33.10 is comparable to the final scene.

21. Given the subtleties of the motif elaboration, it can hardly be coincidental that the idea of 'asent' has been transferred from the human actors to describe the

related to the divine 'ascending' or 'non-ascending', the people 'break camp' or do 'not break camp' (*nāsa'*). The significance of the final imagery is underlined by the frequentative forms and the concluding reference to 'all their camp-breakings' in v. 38. Differently from the theophanic manifestation of v. 34, the final set of parallel divine and human movements is presented as permanent.

In this final transformation of the encounter situation, the given relationship of the mediator and the people is reversed. The non-entering of Moses is juxtaposed to the people's relationship with the theophanic manifestation. Comparable to 2 Chron. 7.2 (cf. also 1 Kgs 8.11 and 2 Chron. 5.14), Moses not being able to enter the tent could be read quite undramatically as an ornamentation of the awesome character of the divine nearness. But with a parallel 'enter into the Tent of Meeting' permitted as a matter of course in the preceding episode in v. 32 (cf. also the parallel episode Lev. 9.23), Moses' inability in the following episode seems more serious.[22]

The significance of Moses' inability to enter is also indicated by the meticulous elaboration of the motifs in v. 36. In v. 35, the divine presence is described by the cloud related to the 'tent of meeting' (v. 35a) and the glory related to the 'dwelling' (v. 35b), which repeats the application of the motifs in v. 34.[23] While the introductory infinitive construction binds v. 36 tightly to the preceding verse, only the cloud motif is retained in this verse. But with the cloud related to the 'dwelling' in vv. 36 and 38, the two images of cloud-covered tent and glory-filled dwelling in vv. 34-35 is combined into one image and carried over into the next scene. The delicate elaboration of the motifs links the singular event of theophanic manifestation in v. 34 to the permanent manifestation in vv. 36-38. Accordingly, the two sets of human actors are

movements of the cloud. The significance of the stereotyped application of the verb in vv. 36-37 is illustrated by the parallel description in Num. 9.15-23, where vv. 18, 19, 20, 21 and 22 use different expressions for the cloud's non-ascendancy.

22. Cf. Childs, *Book of Exodus*, p. 638, on Moses' inability to enter the tent as an expression for his older role replaced by a new priestly role which he shares with Aaron. Also for Milgrom (*Leviticus 1–16*, pp. 134-39) and Smith (*The Pilgrimage Pattern*, p. 185) the motif is important as an expression of a new situation. But according to Cassuto (*Exodus*, p. 484), Moses waiting for the proper invitation to enter, given in Lev. 1.1, is comparable to the scene of 24.16; cf. also Durham, *Exodus*, pp. 500-501.

23. The parallelism is stressed by the usual assumption of a traditio-historical background in Priestly elaboration; e.g. Childs, *Book of Exodus*, p. 508.

juxtaposed by their different relationship to the one theophanic manifestation. The significance of this juxtaposition is prepared for by the imagery of the earlier episodes. It has been established that the extraordinary ascent of the mediator has the prohibited ascent for its shadow. This forms the negative to the final imagery given to Moses excluded from the tent and the people alone related to the *visio Dei.*

This effect is enhanced by the concluding motifs of movement in vv. 36-38, expressed by the repeated *nāsa'* related to the people. The emphasis on the people 'breaking camp' in the final scene contrasts with the introductory scene 19.2-3, with a corresponding emphasis on the people 'settling down'.[24] Here, the 'settling down' is contrasted with the ascent of Moses. The final scene reverses the first. The people settling down juxtaposed to the ascent of Moses is transformed into a scene given to the people breaking camp, juxtaposed to the the 'non-entering' of Moses.[25]

Also this scene retains and elaborates the basic idea of the divine and human movement. According to the established imagery, the two movements from above and below are parallel, related to a common locus. The aspect of parallelism is central to the final scene in vv. 36-38. As the signal for departure, the movements of the cloud ascending or not ascending are immediately mirrored by the people breaking camp or not breaking camp.

In this way, the idea of the theophanic movement related to the divine and human actors is transformed by the final application. The connection with the theophanic event is retained, as well as the parallelism of the divine and human movements. But the idea has been related to the people's journey. This is also reflected by the corresponding transformation of the theophanic manifestation. Permanently manifesting, the new form of theophany functions as a signalling device.

This shift to the people's journey as the new expression for the theophanic movement has been prepared for by the transformation of the idea of 'ascent' in chs. 32–34. According to 32.34–33.5 and 33.12-17, the idea of the people's ascent has been shifted from the mountain

24. Num. 9.15-23 illustrates that *ḥānâ* and *nāsa'* represent complementary verbs. The separation between them in the two itineraries of Exod. 19 and 40 can hardly be coincidental, but must reflect contrasted images of the people before and after Sinai, related to the contrasting descriptions of Moses.

25. This reflects the stop of the story implied by vv. 36-38. It will be necessary to return to the relationship of this stop and the continuation of the story in Lev. 1.1.

imagery to the movement towards the Promised Land. This is combined with the idea of a divine co-ascender. The emphasis on the mortal dangers of this co-ascent indicates that the awesome implications of the extraordinary theophanic ascent are retained. This corresponds to the transformation of the theophanic encounter in 40.34-38.

So far, this survey demonstrates the significance of the motifs of theophanic movement. Basically, they correspond to the imagery of Psalm 24.[26] The parallelism of divine and human movements relative to the locus is retained in the Exodus story. It is reflected both by the concrete motif elaboration of each theophanic episode, as well as by the conceptual relationship of chs. 19–24 and 25–40. Compared to Psalm 24, the elaboration of the motifs reflects a process of transformation. Consistent with the mountain imagery, the idea of ascent is important. This is most directly reflected by chs. 19–24. But the idea is greatly added to and finally transformed. In the theophanic episodes, the human movement is related not only to Moses as the obvious ascender, but also to the people.[27] The gradual transformation of these scenes reflects the narrative movement towards the climax of ch. 40.

The Incompatibility of Divine and Human

The motifs of theophanic movement are important for the development of a story centred around a basic perception of reality as profoundly dual. Translated into the spatial layers of 'high' and 'low', 'mountain' and 'below the mountain', divine and human represent different levels of reality, and the intimate relationship between the two levels constitutes the problem of the story. Obviously, the presentation of the encounter as truly actualized represents the central interest. But the way in which the story is brought to a successful end demonstrates the significance of the idea of basic incompatibility. In the shortform of Psalm 24, this is delicately suggested by the juxtaposition of the two sets of temple imagery. In connection with the human ascent, the temple represents the holy mountain. Conversely, the temple is depicted as

26. Cf. also 1 Kgs 19, in which the human movement is transferred to the stages of three loci, connected to a journey through the wilderness to the 'cave' (v. 9), followed by the prophet's 'going out' and 'standing' at the opening of the cave (vv. 11 and 13) related to the divine 'passing through' (v. 11).

27. Apart from the episode in Exod. 33.21–34.8, where Moses is alone. This corresponds to the portrayal of the active Moses and the passive people in the aftermath of the Golden Calf incident.

constricted space when related to the divine enterer. This implies that both the human and divine movements can reach the common locus only by events of truly exceptional character.

The tension between these two aspects of encounter as possible and utterly problematical is greatly heightened in the Exodus story. By the introduction of the people as potential figures of theophanic experience, the dual character of the narrative reality fleshed out by the roles of Moses the mediator and the people below, the categories of the encounter are extended into a situation of absurd character. This is even added to by the encounter qualified as the elite experience of extraordinary *visio*. The hierarchical ladder suggested by ch. 24, with Moses on the summit, the select group half-way up, and the mass of the people well confined below the mountain, would have made a reasonable representation of the issues involved. In contrast, the emphasis on the people as elite visionaries represents a radical application of the concepts.

The separation of the story into two parts, the one centred around the divine mountain, the other around the human-made tent, reflects the heightened tension. This is added to by the introduction of the Golden Calf as an alternative locus. Set between the divine instructions in chs. 25–31 and their implementation in chs. 35–39, the Golden Calf represents the natural implementation when the divine intention to dwell in the people's midst shall be actualized by the people.

The development of the story reflects the problem of how the people of the camp below will be related to the divine reality above. The idea of an extraordinary encounter in the traditional sense is abandoned. The radical character of this abandonment is reflected by the sudden shift from mountain to tent in chs. 24–25. In this story, the divine and human movements do not constitute complementary aspects of the theophanic meeting. The human movement into the divine space above has been dropped. The successful encounter depends on the divine movement into the human world below.

The implications of the shift from mountain to tent is also reflected by the gradual emphasis on the camp as the narrative centre of gravity. Prepared for by the Golden Calf, the tent situations of 33.7-11 and 34.34-35 are especially visible expressions for the narrative movement. According to the first the divine actor, who hitherto has been confined to the mountain, has descended to the level of the camp. The imagery of the latter implies that YHWH is inside the Moses tent.

Also the *visio* scenes of 19.18-21, 24.17 and 33.8-10 together with

34.29-33 and 40.36-38, are important expressions of this development. Repeated like some narrative refrain, the elaboration of the scenes reflects the gradual change. While the people are firmly planted in the region below in all the scenes, the divine manifestation is brought down to the camp. Compared to the parallelism of human ascent and divine entering in Psalm 24, the Exodus story has abandoned the human movement as significant for the extraordinary encounter. The divine movement represents the only force which makes the encounter possible

The indications of absurdity and humour—compassion even—in the description of the people must be important for the reading of this story. It seems natural to connect the description of the people to some theme of sinfulness and 'fall', underlined by the scenes of intercession in chs. 32–34.[28] While ideas of human sin as well as divine grace must be relevant, the categories of encounter and theophany as well as the elite character of the *visio* experience suggest that the story probes far bolder and deeper into the very nature of the religious experience. This is also reflected by the qualification of the people. Compared to the versions of the Golden Calf in Deuteronomy 9–10 and the wilderness generation in Ezekiel 20, the Exodus story is peculiarly temperate in its presentation of the people as unworthy.[29] The two 'revolt' stories in 20.18-21 and 32.1-6 are the explicit expressions of such an interest. But this function underlines the lack of any strong effects of indignation and denunciation. On the contrary, the introductory descriptions in 20.18 and 32.1 provide a setting which makes the events a natural reaction by people facing a difficult situation: the reader is invited to identify with actors who have been given roles for which they have neither asked nor been prepared.

This can also be related to the presentation of the wrathful Moses in the camp. In the parallel version in Deut. 9.16-21 the corresponding scenes reflect the contrasting roles of sinners and suffering intercessor. Compared to this Moses, the figure of Exod. 32.19-29 represents a role of brutal violence. The destruction of the tablets, the wondrous character of which is evoked by the repetitive 31.18 and 32.15-16, is related to

28. E..g. Moberly, *At the Mountain of God*, pp. 68-80; Durham, *Exodus*, pp. 347-48, 418; Kearney, 'Creation and Liturgy'.

29. Especially if one accepts the argument of Van Seters (*The Life of Moses*, pp. 301-10) that Exod. 32.7-10 and 32.19–33.5 reflect the background of Deut. 9–10. In such a case, the shape of Exod. 32.1-6 would represent a deliberate effort to mitigate the harsh condemnation of the people's sinfulness.

his terrible anger. This is continued by the terrible slaughter of the people by the Levites ordered by Moses.[30] Related to the people 'letting their hair down' (v. 25) and 'having fun' (v. 6),[31] the imagery underlines the brutal character of Moses' reaction.

While obviously presenting the Golden Calf as fatally negative, the description seems to be tempered by some basic acceptance of human nature being what it is. This impression is enhanced by the peculiar mirror character of the revolt scenes. In both situations, the people's reaction mirrors the divine concerns of the parallel encounter. The people's fear for their impending death in 20.18 echoes the divine worry in the mountain scene of 19.21-25. The people's wish for a permanent divine presence in 32.1 echoes the divine intention just revealed to Moses on the mountain. The parallelism of the divine and the people's concerns cannot be coincidental, but seems to reflect some basic relationship between the two partners.[32] The description of a people totally unfit for theophanic nearness does not seem to be related to any wrong perception of the situation or to sinful depravity, but—emphatically in the Golden Calf episode—to the improper initiative which interrupts the proper succession of events. If sinful, the sin of the people seems to be presented as something rather normal for ordinary people set in a situation of this kind.

On the other hand, such a basic acceptance of the revolt as normal would also underline the main theme of basic incompatibility. It is obvious that for such actors, the theophanic movement of ascent is impossible. The happy ending of ch. 40 can be obtained only by the divine descent into the camp.

But in its turn this development underlines the transformation of the movement motifs in the concluding scene in 40.36-38. Here the idea of the parallel human movement is returned to, but released from the

30. The character of Moses in this scene is underlined by the post-Sinai stories where YHWH, set in the role of violent destroyer, is mitigated by Moses as intercessor.

31. The events are traditionally transcribed as a shameful orgy (e.g. Moberly, *At the Mountain of God*, p. 46). This is hardly confirmed by the connotational impact of *ṣḥq* and *pr'*. With Isa. 24.5-13 and 28.7-8 or Ezek. 16.15-21, for instance, as examples of the language available for the presentation of sinful feasting, the choice of these verbs in Exod. 32 seems to represent a deliberate effect of ambiguity.

32. Such an effect is also indicated by the *visio* scenes. Repeated like some narrative refrain through the story, these scenes reserve the experience of the theophanic manifestation for the people.

vertical categories of the mountain and transferred to the horizontal categories of journey. This marks the successful end to both parts of the composition. The idea of the new type of ascent in chs. 33–34, with ascent related to the journey and with YHWH as co-ascender, refers to the imagery of chs. 19–24. With the divine co-ascender still representing a presence of awesome threat, the new ascent truly represents the extraordinary character of the traditional theophanic ascent. Related to chs. 35–40, which have seemingly abandoned the significance of the human movement in favour of the divine dwelling among the people, the conclusion of 40.36-38 returns to the parallelism of divine and human movement. Set on the way to the Promised Land, the people are engaged in the process of sacred movement, permanently related to the theophanic manifestation.

In this way, the last twist in the tale returns to the basic parallelism of the divine and human movement in Psalm 24. The ultimate encounter, expressed by the permanent theophany and the corresponding permanent *visio*, is connected to the imagery of God and people moving together. Moreover, in this new alignment the divine movement even seems to have a secondary role compared to the human movement. As the signal for the people's departure, the divine movement is subordinated to the people's journey, presented as a part of the concluding image given to the idea of the journeying people. The converse of the abandonment of the traditional ascent and the emphasis on the divine descent, the conclusion of ch. 40 points to the significance of the human movement made possible by the new *visio*.

Underlined by the exclusion of Moses, the conclusion of the story in ch. 40 must have important theological implications. The elite figure of extraordinary relationship, Moses, like Elijah in 1 Kings 19 or the pure ascenders of Psalm 24, represents the natural human actor. His substitution by the people as the new theophanic figures makes an astounding conclusion.[33] The very introduction of the people as a second set of human actors in the situation of encounter represents an application which stretches the categories of the encounter *in absurdum*. Even

33. The implications of this are missed when the conceptual categories of the story are too directly identified with a setting of ordinary, institutionalized religiosity. To Smith (*The Pilgrimage Pattern*), the Priestly redaction reflects a literary pattern dependent on the normal practice of pilgrimage. Such an understanding is natural to a scholarly generation weaned on the categories of *Sitz im Leben*. But it distorts the perception of the literary effects.

confined to an extension of this character, the story would represent a radical probing of the character of religious experience. But by the remarkable conclusion in ch. 40, excluding the natural ascender and retaining the absurd figures, the story seems to present a new vision of the proper alignment of divine and human. The change of locus corresponds to the change of theophanic actors. Divinely inhabited, the world below has become the locus of the world above. Correspondingly, the theophanic movement of the divine actor is part of the new form of ascent by the inhabitants of the world below.

3. *The Divine Descent and the Participation of the Non-Ascenders*

According to the compositional development, the building story of chs. 35–40 has the divine movement from mountain to tent as the conceptual centre of gravity. For the new form of intimate relationship, the traditional ascent into the world above has been abandoned as meaningful, while only the divine descent into human reality makes the encounter possible. Accordingly, one could have expected a story in which the human participants are presented as totally passive. But on the contrary, the building story is dedicated to a people extremely active. For the aftermath of the Golden Calf incident in chs. 32–34, the idea of a passive people is important. Moses builds the first Tent of Meeting 'on his own', the people contributing by their non-participation (33.4-7). Centred around the intercession of Moses, the story as a whole is characterized by the people as spectators. This is abruptly changed in ch. 35.

Formally, the shift from a passive to an active people corresponds to the development of the theophanic episodes. In the third theophanic episode, both preparatory sub-episodes are set in the camp, the first centred around the people as builders (chs. 35–39), the second around Moses (40.1-33). The local setting continues the development of the earlier preparatory sub-episodes. In ch. 19 both are related to the encounter on the mountain. In ch. 24, the first is set in camp, the second up on the mountain. The connection with the first part of the story is also reflected by the formal relationship. Chapter 35 presents a scene of mediation, while the rest of the story is dedicated to the implementation of the divine instructions. The instructions refer to chs. 25–31. In this way the building story continues the events of the second theophanic encounter introduced in 24.3.

The main difference is expressed by the greatly enlarged role of the people in the last theophanic episode. Also the role of Moses as the mediator (35.1-19; 35.30–36.6) is greatly expanded. Moses inspects what has been produced and blesses the people (39.33-43). Also the presentation of Moses performing the Herculean efforts of putting all the elements together (40.1-33) corresponds to his enlarged role. But formally, the order of preparatory events presented in 35.1–40.33 corresponds to the version of the building account *in nuce* in 33.6-7. The erection of the tent is related to a scene with the people as actors, followed by a second centred around Moses as builder.

In this way the emphasis on the camp as the locus of the third set of preparatory sub-episodes is prepared for by the compositional development. Within such a setting, it is perfectly natural that 40.1 abruptly presents the divine actor as speaking to Moses. According to the order established by the preceding events, a new set of divine instructions should require the proper conditions of enounter, and at the very least be introduced by the mediator's movement towards the special locus. The immediacy of the divine address in 40.1 corresponds to the local setting of the third theophanic episode.

The Royal Role of the People

But while the shape and function of chs. 35–40 reflect their setting within the composition, the genre of temple building account implies a special set of connotational references for the reading of this story.[34] The account of Solomon's temple building is of special importance.[35] The genre presents the temple builder as the embodiment of a paradig-

34. Reading Victor Hurowitz (*I Have Built You an Exalted House: Temple Building in the Bible in Light of Mesopotamian and Northwest Semitic Writings* [JSOTSup, 115; Sheffield: JSOT Press, 1992]) makes one ponder how the impact of interpretative labels could influence scholarly positions. Given the significance of the label 'Priestly' for Pentateuchal criticism in the last hundred years—'Priestly' interests contrasted to other sets of interests perceived as 'non-Priestly'—one could speculate as to what would have happened to scholarly perceptions if Wellhausen had described a source of 'Sacred Architecture' or 'the Temple Builders'.

35. Hurowitz, *I Have Built You*, and also 'The Priestly Account of Building the Tabernacle', *JAOS* 105 (1985), pp. 21-30; further Arvid S. Kapelrud, 'Temple Building, a Task for Gods and Kings', *Or* 32 (1963), pp. 56-62; Baruch Levine, 'The Descriptive Tabernacle Texts of the Pentateuch', *JAOS* 85 (1965), pp. 305-18; Utzschneider, *Das Heiligtum*, pp. 154-67.

matic role connected to royal ideology.[36] The references point immediately to the significance of Moses set in the role of royal temple builder. This corresponds to the address in second person singular form which dominates the instructions in chs. 25–31. The connotational references are also indicated by the 'wise craftsman' motif. Comparable to Solomon and the wise Hiram (1 Kgs 7.13-14), Moses is provided with extraordinarily gifted craftsmen (Exod. 31.1-11).[37]

While the building account of Exodus 35–40 provides a more complex set of actors, it must be important that the story returns to Moses as the supreme builder in 40.1-33. The significance of this return is underlined by the two parallel conclusions of 39.32-43 and 40.33. Also the new set of divine instructions addressed to Moses in 40.1-15 reflects the special character of the scene dedicated to Moses the builder. The process of building is separated into two phases. The first phase is given over to the production of the single elements, the second to Moses on his own erecting and furnishing the tent from the single elements produced by the people. Moses completes the sacred work which prepares for the theophanic manifestation. In this way, the building account returns to the role allocation of the instructions in chs. 25–31 which present Moses as the temple builder. This pattern of events also underlines the connection with the first tent building. According to 33.6-7, the erection of the first Tent of Meeting, accomplished by Moses on his own, is preceded by a scene given over to the people 'plundering' themselves.

The building account proper in 36.8–39.31 is centred around the wise craftsmen as the 'doers'. Moses supplemented by the craftsmen reflect the traditional roles of the genre. So far, the relationship of the divine instructions followed by the two scenes of building corresponds to the

36. Hurowitz, *I Have Built You*, pp. 110, 313. This connection is also important to Utzschneider, *Das Heiligtum*, pp. 154-67. But related to a limited set of texts (pp. 154-59), the connection is found to express a fundamental and polemical contrast between the Jerusalem temple as the 'Eigenkirche' ('privately-owned church') of the Davidic kings and the Sinai sanctuary as 'Eigenkirche Jahwes' ('privately-owned church of YHWH') (pp. 182-83). This results in an impressive set of valuable and sensitive observations related to a rather simplistic model of interpretation based on the contrasts of the traditional cultic practice and a new understanding 'vom Heiligtum als einem Ort und einem Gegenstand des Gesetzes' ('of the sanctuary as a place for observance of the Law and as a place regulated by Law') (p. 182).

37. Hurowitz, *I Have Built You*, pp. 158-59.

relationship of 1 Kgs 6.1-38 with Solomon as the builder, followed by 7.13-45, which present the actions of Hiram the craftsman, and concluded in vv. 46-50 with the return to Solomon as the subject of the process.

The basic adherence to the traditional role allocation of the genre underlines the significance of the people as active in the enterprise. In the Solomon story, the people do not play any active role until the events of sanctification in 1 Kings 8.[38] In the Exodus version, the people are associated with the royal task from the very beginning. The building instructions are introduced by 25.2-8. According to this passage, the raw materials for the production are to be brought as voluntary gifts by the people. The significance of this introduction is demonstrated by the rest of the instructions, which are addressed to the singular 'you'. Also the formal irregularities of vv. 2-8[39] could reflect the interest in the people as active participants.

In the building story, the gift motifs of 25.2-8 are greatly expanded. The exhuberant response of the people to the challenge is elaborated in 35.4–36.7. They bring too many gifts, even disturbing the craftsmen (36.3-7). This description must express an important concern. In more traditional expressions of the genre represented by Numbers 7, 1 Kgs 7.40b-50, or Exod. 39.32-41, the special and costly character of the gifts is the important aspect.[40] Exodus 35.4–36.7 greatly adds to this by a special interest in the inner and emotional state of the givers. References to the heart connected with derivatives of *ndb* represent a sort of narrative refrain. The heart is 'incited' (35.5, 22; cf. also the 'spirit' 35.21), 'inciting' (25.2; 35.29) or 'carrying' (35.20, 26).[41] Given the scarcity of references to emotions and inner disposition in the rest of chs. 19–40—with 33.4 representing an important exception—the

38. Aside from the note on conscripted labour 1 Kgs 5.27, which according to Utzschneider (*Das Heiligtum*, p. 167) contrasts the 'voluntarism' of the people in Exod. 35–36.

39. The oscillation between the plural 'you' and 'they' in vv. 3, 8-10 could even reflect the fact that the introduction of the people motifs has disturbed the dominating you-address of the rest of the instructions; cf. Koch, *Die Priesterschrift*, pp. 7-10, and also Utzschneider, *Das Heiligtum*, pp. 197-200. On the other hand, while seemingly awkward, this introduction corresponds to the oscillation between the different active groups in the building account.

40. Levine, 'The Descriptive Tabernacle Texts'.

41. Cf. Utzschneider, *Das Heiligtum*, pp. 160-63 on the concept of *ndb* connected with 'heart'.

elaboration of the heart motifs in such a vital context must be important.

The connotational impact of this story is illustrated by the corresponding motifs in 1 Chronicles 29.[42] With a similar emphasis on 'hearty' response and exuberant 'willingness' connected with a parallel situation of gifts dedicated to the building of the sanctuary, the texts must reflect a rather close literary relationship.[43] As an extension of the 1 Kings story, 1 Chronicles 28–29 provide an interesting linkage between the Exodus and 1 Kings version. In the latter, the raw materials for the building are provided by the king. In 1 Chronicles 29, this theme is related to David. He is presented as the supreme giver of costly materials (vv. 1-5). But in addition, the king extends an invitation to the leaders of the people to *hitnaddēb* their gifts (vv. 5-8). The 'democratization' of the procurement of raw materials is not extended to the people. Also in 1 Chronicles the people are present, but as on-lookers, delighting in the 'whole-hearted' willingness of the leaders (v. 9). Compared to this scene, Exod. 25.2-8 and 35.5–36.7 mark a further step, both with regard to aspects of 'democratization' as well as to an extended scene of exuberant generosity.

In this way, 1 Chronicles 29 provides a 'missing link' between the situations of temple building in 1 Kings and Exodus.[44] Read together,

42. Cf. the heart motifs in vv. 9, 17, 18 and 19 in addition to the use of *hitnaddēb* in vv. 5, 6, 9, 14 and 17 corresponding to the heart qualified by *nādab* in Exod. 25.2; 35.21 (related to 'spirit'), 29, and *nādîb* in 35.5, 22.

43. Usually the Chronicles story is seen as dependent on the Sinai story; cf. Utzschneider, *Das Heiligtum*, p. 62, and Simon J. DeVries, *1 and 2 Chronicles* (FOTL, 11; Grand Rapids: Eerdmans, 1989), p. 219 on 'Chr H' influenced by P's image of the tabernacle. On the other hand, the Chronicles account seems to represent the 'missing link' between the two versions of the building account in 1 Kings and Exod. 35–40. This tempts one to assert that the Sinai account represents the fusion of the two separate versions in 1 Kgs 6–7 and 1 Chron. 28–29. But the wealth of comparative material provided by Hurowitz (*I Have Built You*, p. 110, even for the gift motifs), indicates that the genre of building account included a variety of traditional themes. The relationship of the Sinai account and the 1 Kings version extended by Chronicles represents a referential frame too simple for any definite assertions with regard to literary dependence.

44. This is underlined by a common theme of 'substitution'. According to 1 Chron. 22.7-13 and 28.2-3, Solomon is designated as the temple builder instead of David. The language of 1 Chron. 22 and 28 has been related to Deut. 3 and Josh. 1, indicating some important parallellism between David/Solomon and Moses/Joshua; cf. Dennis J. McCarthy, 'An Installation Genre', *JBL* 90 (1971), pp. 36-38; Roddy Braun, 'Solomon, the Chosen Temple Builder: The Significance of 1 Chronicles 22,

the three stories illustrate the elaboration of the traditional genre with regard to the procurement of the costly raw-materials. Related to the king's treasury and then to the leaders of the community, the emphasis on the common people's being 'driven by their hearts' as the donors of the costly gifts[45] seems to represent a final elaboration of the traditional theme.

The comparison with the traditional versions indicates that the new step of 'democratization' represented by the Exodus version must reflect a special interest. Comparable to the Chronicles version, anxious to include David in the glorious task of temple building in spite of his bloody hands, the Exodus account presents the people as the princely donors. The connotational clash effected by this presentation points to its significance. Moreover, such a role allocation corresponds to the description of the people in the context of Exodus 19–40. The people as the donors of the costly gifts is comparable to the connotational impact of the people introduced as actors in the encounter situation. In both cases the people are 'inserted' into traditional roles reserved for actors of a special stature. Both as princely donors and as participants in the extraordinary *visio* the people as actors represent an astounding role allocation.

The People as Temple Builders

The role of the people as princely donors is added to by a comparable transfer of the craftsmen's roles. The traditional role of the 'wise craftsman' is reflected in the instructions in Exodus 31. This is adhered to in the part of the building story that is dedicated to the concrete process (36.8b–39.31). But now the craftsmen are presented to the people (35.30-35), parallel to their presentation to Moses the builder in 31.1-11. More importantly, the traditional role allocation is disturbed by the introductory invitation to 'everyone' in 35.4-19. The first part of the invitation 35.4-9 corresponds to 25.2-7. The divine challenge to the people to bring their gifts is mediated by Moses. But to this is added a parallel set of divine commands (vv. 10-19). 'Everyone' is invited to

28, and 29 for the Theology of Chronicles', *JBL* 95 (1976), pp. 586-88. But given the connection of the theme of 'substitution' and temple building, the parallelism of Moses/the people and Solomon/David seems to represent a more visible expression of two strangely parallel versions of the traditional temple building account.

45. The aspect of costliness and financial efforts is underlined by Levine, 'The Descriptive Tabernacle Texts'.

partake in the process of sacred 'action'. Corresponding to the 'everyone incited by his heart' (v. 5), 'everyone wise of heart among you' is invited to take part (v. 10). The addressed 'you' must refer to the assembly of 'the children of Israel' in v. 4.

The parallelism of the two invitations is retained in the story of response. The 'heart-driven' came with their gifts (35.21-24), and the 'wise of heart' took part in the production (vv. 25-26). The introductory *w^e^kol* in vv. 23, (24), 25, 26 indicates the connection of the two sets of actors as part of the 'children of Israel' according to v. 20. The parallelism of 'everyone' 'heart-driven' and 'wise of heart' underlines the transfer of the 'wise craftsman' motif to the common people.[46] In v. 26, the two heart-motifs even are combined, by the qualification of the women 'whose heart carried them in wisdom'.

The fusion of the two types of motifs, and the corresponding identification of the two groups, is also carried over into the passages reserved for the craftsmen. Moses calls upon not only two professional craftsmen, but also 'every man of a wise heart, to whom YHWH has given wisdom in his heart, everyone whose heart carries him' (36.2, cf. also v. 1).

The mixing of the classes is continued in the building account proper which starts in 36.8.[47] But in this case, the transfer is more subtly effected. Aside from the introductory v. 8, the following description is dominated by the sterotyped *wayya'^a^ś* in the third person singular, until the anonymous 'he' in 37.1 is identified as the craftsman Bezalel. But by the introductory v. 8, the anonymous 'he-story' in ch. 36 is framed in a special way. Here the stereotyped verb is in plural form. 'They did' and 'they' are qualified by the element 'everyone of wise heart'. The

46. Utzschneider, *Das Heiligtum*, pp. 163-67, seems to distinguish two groups within the people described as partly 'Freiwilligen' ('volunteers'), partly as 'Kunstfertigen' (craftsmen) whose parallel participation is rather opaquely presented (p. 164). This is stressed by the assumption of a different traditio-historical background for the concepts, the former related to the royal role of the temple building account, the latter to 'Salomos sprichwörtlicher Weisheit' ('Solomon as the proverbial figure of Wisdom') (pp. 165-66). This construction, which ignores the traditional connection between royal temple builder and his 'wise craftsman', seems to reflect Utzschneider's assumption that an anti-royal tendency is important for these texts, given to an ideal of the Second Temple as 'Bürger-Tempel-Gemeinde' ('citizen-temple community') (pp. 295-96).

47. According to Utzschneider, *Das Heiligtum*, p. 88, also v. 4 presupposes the people as included among the wise craftsmen.

combination of a verbal form in the plural, followed by an element referring to 'everyone', corresponds to the style of vv. 21 and 22. Also in the latter case, the combination introduces a description of detailed events. Framed in this way, the 'he'-story in vv. 9-38, followed by the Bezalel-story in chs. 37–38, is presented as the actions of the heart-inspired 'everyone' of the people. The inspired people are the subjects of the sacred process as a whole, the details of which are presented in the following story and thus include the processes attributed to a named craftsman.[48]

This development is concluded in 39.32-43. The sacred process as a whole is ascribed to the 'children of Israel'. This is formally prepared for by an artful combination of different elements, corresponding to the relationship of 36.8 followed by the 'he-story' and the Bezalel-story, but in reverse order. The Bezalel story in 37.1–38.20 is concluded by the accounts of 38.21-31. This is followed by the production of the priestly vestments in 39.1-31. Here, the 'actions' in the third person plural form is attributed to an anonymous 'they'-group. This description is continued by v. 32b. The introductory 'they did' continues the stereotyped forms in the preceding verses. But comparable to the construction in 37.1, the introductory 'they did' is followed by a nominal subject. 'The children of Israel' have done all the sacred actions.

This corresponds to the way in which the people as actors in 35.4–36.7 is continued by the building account proper. Just as the introductory 'they' followed by the 'everyone'-element in 36.8a prepares for the anonymous 'he'-account of the rest of the chapter, which in its turn prepares for the identification of 'he' with Bezalel in ch. 37, so the anonymous 'they' of 39.1-31 prepare for the identification of the craftsmen with the people in v. 32.

The character of this composition could reflect that different types of materials are combined. More importantly, the deft compositional technique seems to have a double function. First and most importantly, the production is related to the people as the subjects of the sacred work.

48. Utzschneider, *Das Heiligtum*, pp. 201-202 asserts that the 'he' of 36.8b-38 refers to the addressed 'you' of the instructions in chs. 25–31. The formal clashes of the 'Du/Sie (Ihr)-Inkohäsion' ('you' and 'they' as temple-builders) in chs. 25–36 and and the 'Sie/Er-Inkohäsion' ('they' and 'he') in chs. 36–39 is seen to reflect the combination of two different concepts of the sanctuary in the Priestly traditions. The understanding of the temple as the dwelling for the Ark has been combined with the concept of 'Volk-Heiligtums-Konzeption' ('citizen-sanctuary') (p. 200).

The inspired craftsmen who perform the highly skilled operations represent the people as builders, their craftsmanship being presented as the concrete details of the effort attributed to the people as a whole. Secondly, the presentation of the details of production connected with special craftsmen underlines that the sacred work truly was done by inspired craftsmanship. With hearts filled with divine wisdom the people performed wonders of inspired miraculous action.

The elaboration of the two aspects corresponds to the description of the gift motifs. In the latter case, the presentation of the people as donors is connected with a scene of princely representatives who dedicate the really costly gifts (35.27-28). But framed by references to the people (vv. 20-26 and 29), this scene also reflects the main theme of the people as donors. This is comparable to the combination of the people and the craftsmen in the building story. In both cases, the composition succeeds in conveying the double impression of the 'democratization' of the roles as transferred to the people, while their connotations of extraordinary perfection are retained. The established imagery of the royal temple builder and the wise craftsman, unmarred by any negative aspects of 'democratization', is transferred to the people, the hearts of whom are not only generous as a prince but filled with wisdom for extraordinary action.

The compositional pains taken for the insertion of the people in the sacred undertaking must reflect the significance of the role allocation. At least some of the implications of the transfer are suggested by the relationship of 1 Chronicles 22 and 28–29 to the traditional account of 1 Kings. In the Chronicler's version, the role of Solomon as the chosen builder is added to by David as a sub-figure, the dedication of the rejected builder preparing for the efforts of the builder. This represents an extension of the building story strangely parallel to the extension represented by the Exodus version.[49] In the latter case, Moses as the addressed 'you' of the divine instructions, underlined by ch. 40 as a separate building story, presents Moses as the 'real' tent builder. His

49. The parallelism can be illustrated by the Chronicler's main object in adding to the 1 Kings version, as it is perceived by McCarthy, 'An Installation Genre', p. 36. The temple is presented as really due to David, while Solomon is 'like the constructor of a pre-fabricated house'. Although this is an interpretation of the Chronicler's account (duly criticized by Braun, 'Solomon, the Chosen Temple Builder', p. 588), McCarthy's description is remarkably apt for the relationship of Exod. 35–39 and 40.

extension by the people as a second set of actors is comparable to the addition of David to Solomon. And while David the idealized king—however bloody his hands—represents a natural extension of the builder's role, the insertion of the people into the Exodus account represents a radical role allocation.

Related to the context of chs. 19–40, the function of this role allocation must be indicated by the similar character of the encounter episode. The insertion of the people as a second set of temple builders corresponds to the elaboration of the people as theophanic figures. In both cases the role of the people implies a connotational clash, the people being invested with the mantle of elite figures. But compared to the final substitution of Moses by the people as theophanic figures, the relationship of Moses and people as temple builders is perfectly harmonious. The transition from ch. 39 to 40 reflects the immediate continuation of their efforts.

The parallelism of the people and Moses as temple builders is underlined by the parallel conclusions of the two building scenes in 39.32a and 40.33. Added to by the formulaic elements in 39.43, the conclusions echo Gen. 2.1-3.[50] The sacred works of Moses and the people are qualified as somehow similar to the divine acts of creation. The subtle references to the categories of creation correspond to the equally subtle connection of Sabbath and tent building. Concluding the instructions in 31.12-17 and introducing the mediation in 35.1-3, the Sabbath instructions are presented as part of the building instructions. The implications of this combination are uncertain.[51] But some direct connection between the two sets of instructions is reflected by the formulaic language. To 'do the work' (*āśâ mᵉlā'kâ*) is a significant term important both for the introduction and conclusion of the building story[52] and for the Sabbath instructions.[53] In the latter case, the term refers both to the divine acts of creation and to human actions. The parallelism is underlined by the relationship of 31.13-16 and 17. The observation of the Sabbath by the cessation from 'doing work' corresponds to the divine

50. Cassuto, *Exodus*, pp. 477, 483.

51. E.g. Kearney, 'Creation and Liturgy', on the significance of the creation theme for the P redaction of chs. 25–40, while Childs, *Book of Exodus*, pp. 541-42, understands Sabbath and tabernacle as two parallel signs. The observance of the one and the building of the other represent two sides of the same reality.

52. Exod. 35.29, 33, 35; 36.1-8; 39.43.

53. Exod. 31.14-15; 35.2.

rest from 'doing work'. The human working week mirrors the six days' creation by the divine worker. Set within such a framework, the temple building marks the concrete representation of the sacred parallelism of divine and human work.[54] The references to the creation story in Exod. 39.32, 43 and 40.33 are parallel expressions for this connection. The actions of Moses and people mirror the divine actions.

The implications of this parallelism are profoundly added to by the blessing scene in 39.43. With its echoes of Gen. 1.31–2.3, Moses' first 'seeing all the work done' and then blessing the people cannot but indicate a rather close relationship between the divine and human roles. Here, Moses embodies the divine role. The reference to YHWH in v. 43ab, as well as the immediate return in ch. 40 to YHWH instructing and Moses obeying, protects the astounding terminology against misunderstanding. But even so, its implications are rather remarkable. As temple builders, Moses and the people perform sacred roles, mirroring the divine acts of creation. By the blessing scene, the sacred character of their undertaking is added to and made more explicit by hierarchical categories. Inspecting the sacred works and blessing the people, Moses enacts the divine role. The significance of this scene is underlined by the corresponding elevation of Moses in ch. 34. Moses, accepted as the sublime visionary of the theophanic 'backside' in ch. 34, corresponds to the elevation of the people as theophanic figures in ch. 40. The building account reflects a comparable parallelism of hierarchical elevation. Moses as the embodiment of divine functions corresponds to the elevation of the people as embodiments of the sacred function of temple building.

The Contextual References of the Building Story

Exodus 33.4-11 as a building story *in nuce* must be important for the composition of chs. 35–40. This is indicated by the parallelism of the two tents, both named 'Tent of Meeting'. The pattern of two scenes given to the people and to Moses is common to both stories. Related to the erection of a Tent of Meeting, the activity of the people in the second story is contrasted with their passivity in the first. Here Moses is doing everything, while the contribution of the people consists in acts of renunciation. The exuberance of the people's response in ch. 35—

54. Cf. Chapter 2.2 for the corresponding parallelism expressed by the motifs of theophanic movement.

important enough when read on its own[55]—is prepared for by the contrast of the earlier episode. Moreover, this linkage underlines the contrast relationship to the Golden Calf episode. The calf produced by Aaron and the people in collusion is contrasted with the Tent of Meeting made by Moses 'by himself', with Joshua as a sub-figure and with the people distantly present. This contrast is harmonized by the final Tent of Meeting produced by the people and erected by Moses, with Aaron and the priests as sub-figures, and finally concluded by the people as the human representatives of the theophanic encounter. Similarly, the people's 'fun' of 32.6, contrasted with their sorrow in 33.6, and concluded by their 'heart-driven' response in ch. 35, present corresponding effects of contrast and harmonization.

The relationship of the Golden Calf, Moses' Tent of Meeting and the final Tent of Meeting is profoundly added to by the parallel 'gift scenes' of the three stories. According to 32.2-4 and ch. 35, the people provide the raw-materials for the sacred production. A corresponding scene, with the sign reversed, is alluded to in 33.6. The non-use of the ornaments reflects the contrast relationship with the Golden Calf episode, while the structure of the events—a scene of non-participation by the people followed by a scene dedicated to Moses the sole builder—contrasts with the building story of chs. 35–40. The parallel scenes indicate a subtle connection between the golden ear-rings, the unused ornaments, and the final abundance of gifts dedicated to the sacred production. This is supplemented by the reference to the Egyptian plunder in 33.6. The peculiar motif of the people 'plundering themselves' (*hitnaṣṣēl*) in 33.6 corresponds to the people 'plundering' (*nṣl* in piel form) the Egyptians in 3.22 and 12.36.[56]

Some reference to the Egyptian plunder is the more natural as the description of the people's gifts in ch. 35 represents a narrative 'gap' that begs to be filled. The golden ear-rings of ch. 32 and the ornaments

55. E.g. Durham, *Exodus*, p. 477, on the 'priestly euphoria' of 'this ecstatic narrative'.

56. Cf. also Cassuto, *Exodus*, p. 428 and Moberly, *At the Mountain of God*, p. 61. For the latter, the reference indicates that after the Golden Calf, the triumphant character of the people 'plundering' others is ended as they are no better off than the Egyptians. Some connection is also indicated by Thomas B. Dozemann, *God at War: Power in the Exodus Tradition* (Oxford: Oxford University Press, 1996), pp. 47-48. On the other hand, 33.1-5 is understood as 'clearly meant' to function as an aetiology for aniconic cultic practice (p. 75).

of ch. 33 might be consistent for a story with runaway slaves as figures. But the people of the final building account are remarkably rich, especially after the two earlier denudements. Even somewhat mitigated by 35.27-28, according to which the really costly gifts are attributed to the leaders, the people's response is rather overwhelming. To a certain degree, this could be related to the requirements of the genre. At this stage of the story, costly raw-materials must somehow be introduced, for if not, there will no story of temple building. But even so, a reasonably good storyteller can be expected to prepare the introduction of elements which are important to the narrative; or—if some 'gap' is needed to lure the reader from the narrative surface to some deeper level of perception—to leave the gap teasingly open.

The reference to the Egyptian plunder in 33.6 can be related to both aspects. It suggests the origin of the people's riches. More importantly, it adds to the connotational depth of the building accounts. The three stories of the Golden Calf, Moses' Tent of Meeting and the grand Tent of Meeting have in common a theme of the people's valuables related to the production of the sacred locus. Also, the theme is connected to categories of gender. Rather subtly presented, this connection is especially perceptible in the last building account. In 35.22, 25-26, 29 and 36.6 the description of the people is marked by the interest in presenting the women as responding together with the men. When the exuberant willingness of the people is described, the parallelism of 'every man' and 'every woman', equally heart-driven, is a distinctive feature.

This is quite remarkable within a story of sacred production. Within the context of Exodus, references to female actors stand out and can be expected to reflect some specific interest. According to 35.20-22, the women even are related to the 'congregation' of the people. 'Every woman' as well as 'every man' represent the response of the 'congregation of the sons of Israel' (cf. also v. 4). The parallelism of men and women as equally important is even shifted in favour of the women by vv. 25-26. As we have seen, the description of the people as part of wise craftsmanship is essential to the composition of chs. 35–39. But the only visualization of the people concretely producing something is found in the scene of the spinning women in 35.25-26. The 'heart-wise' women represent the people as active in sacred craftsmanship.

At this stage of the story the women are obviously important for the sacred production. This interest underlines the significance of the more allusive references in 32.2-3. A comparable scene of costly raw materials necessary for the sacred production is connected with a situation of male actors related to women—the latter together with their children.[57] The elaboration of the two parallel scenes seems to indicate an effect of juxtaposition. In chs. 35–36, the repeated application of *ndb* connected with the heart motifs implies a situation of voluntary and 'heart-driven' response, men and women responding in perfect harmony. The parallel gift scene in 32.2-3 presents a contrast situation. The verb *prq* (piel and hithpael) implies acts of brutal and violent force. This is underlined by the constellation of actors. In v. 2, the violence of the verb is enhanced by the image of men 'tearing' the ear-rings from 'your wives and your sons and your daughters'. The image is continued by the hithpael form of v. 3. All the people are depicted in a situation of 'self-tearing from their ears'. The violence of this dedication[58] presents the contrast to the scene of ch. 35, where women together with men are 'heart-driven' towards a sublime effort of voluntary dedication.

The violence of the Golden Calf dedication is carried over into the next situation of sacred building in 33.6. In this story, the people's ornaments are negatively related to the erection of the Tent of Meeting by Moses. According to 33.6, the 'sons of Israel' 'plundered themselves' for their ornaments. This image is prepared for by the parallel (v. 4) given over to the sorrow-reaction of the people, none 'putting his ornaments upon himself'. While the implications of violence are common to the two scenes of 32.2-3 and 33.6, the contrast effect is evident. The denudement of the first scene serves the production of the Golden Calf. The second scene of denudement represents the non-use of the ornaments in the sacred building, which is performed by Moses acting 'on his own' (v. 7).

The delicate contrast-effects even seem to include a reference to the male–female motifs of Exod. 32.2 and 35.21-29. In 33.4 the people's sorrowful non-use of their ornaments is expressed by special constructions. The plural forms referring to the people are specified by a construction with *'iš* for subject. This corresponds to 35.21-29. Here the plural forms referring to the people as a whole are followed by constructions given both to a female as well as a masculine form

57. Cf. also Utzschneider, *Das Heiligtum*, p. 86.

58. Underlined by the hostile character of the introductory scene in v. 1, the people 'assembling against' Aaron; cf. Moberly, *At the Mountain of God*, p. 46.

'everyone'.[59] Moreover, the image of the people represented by the 'man not putting his ornaments upon himself' evokes the image of 32.2 as a contrast, given to the men tearing the golden rings from the ears of their women and children. In its turn, this contrast effect underlines the masculine character of 33.6, the self-plundering attributed to the 'sons of Israel'.[60]

However subtly, the three descriptions seem to indicate a gradual and meticulously elaborated transformation of the gift scenes. The violence of the first is continued by a contrast scene of self-inflicted violence, the contrast added to by the sorrow motif and connotations of renunciation. In the last scene the contrast is transformed into the 'heart-driven' dedication of both men and women.

The significance of the three scenes is added to by the referential effect of 33.6, when the men's renunciation is described as an act of 'self-plundering' (*hitnaṣṣēl*). The special verb relates the act to the plunder of the Egyptians (3.22 and 12.36, in addition to 11.2-3). This connection is underlined by the description of the Egypt scenes. In 3.22 the address to the plural 'you' is specified by the singular 'woman' asking her female neighbour for valuables which 'you' shall 'put upon your sons and daughters'. The imagery corresponds especially with the scene of 32.2, while the emphasis on female actors also can be compared to ch. 35. In addition, the sentence construction with a plural address specified by a singular 'everyone' is comparable to 33.4 and especially 35.20-29.

Both the stylistic effects as well as the reference to women are reflected in the second version of the Egyptian plunder in 11.2-3. The order addressed to the plural collective is specified by the parallel male and female version of 'everyone': 'they shall ask, man from his neighbour and woman from her neighbouress' (v. 2b). The rather elaborate reference to 'everyone' corresponds to the elaboration of the dedication scene in ch. 35. In the third scene 12.36, the people, referred to by verbs in masculine plural form, are the subjects of plunder.

The motif connection and the effects of style can hardly be coincidental. A common theme of 'personal valuables' related to the singular

59. Cf. especially 'every man' (vv. 21, 23) balanced by references to 'every woman' (v. 25) and combined as 'every man and woman' (v. 29).

60. The parallelism of 33.4 and 6 also underlines the special character of the two visualizations of the dedication in 32.2-3, the first presenting the men tearing the gold from women and children, the second the 'self-tearing' of the men.

members of the people, together with the emphasis on women in certain versions, link the scenes. This is also indicated by the peculiar collusion of violence and emotional categories. The connotations of 'plunder' in 3.22 and 12.36 clash with the image of the people attracting the 'favour' of the Egyptians. The motif of 'favour' is repeated in all three applications, which in 12.36 seems rather strange for a situation set after vv. 30-33.[61] A corresponding collusion is also represented by the three Sinai applications. The violence of the men towards the women and children in 32.2 and towards themselves in acts of 'self-tearing' in 32.3 is continued by the self-inflicted violence of 33.6, while the latter is balanced by the sorrowful response of v. 4. The emotional categories, as total devotion and voluntary dedication, dominate the last scene, attributed to men and women as equally heart-driven.

While the meaning and its implications remain rather obscure, the very application of comparable motifs together with the parallel effects of style must indicate the referential relationship of interconnected scenes. Parallel to the three references to the plunder in Egypt, the story of plundering is continued by the three episodes of sacred production. A scene of violent plunder for the production of the Golden Calf is contrasted by a scene of self-plunder, the duality of the two dissolved into the joyful scene of voluntary dedication by the plunderers and the plundered in the final episode.

The parallelism of the two sets of three scenes points to the Egyptian origin of the people's gifts. A theme of 'Egyptian influence' also corresponds to the description of the people in the wilderness stories. Particularly dramatic in the post-Sinai stories of Numbers 11 and 13–14, Egypt represents the point of attraction for the apostate people. Comparable to the contrast of the Golden Calf and the Tent of Meeting, the return to Egypt contrasts with the people's movement of sacred journey. The production of the Golden Calf from Egyptian riches and a process of renunciative self-plundering valid for the period 'after Horeb' (33.6) seems a natural extension of the theme of 'Egyptian influence' in the journey stories. The post-Sinai events of revolt and divine retribution could even represent the concrete expression of how a permanent situation of self-plundering 'after Horeb' was actualized.

In this way, the traditional imagery of the royal temple-builder

61. Exod. 3.21-22, 11.2-3 and 12.35-36 represent 'a planned theological insertion' which reinterprets the death of the Egyptian firstborn as an instance of holy war, according to Dozemann, *God at War*, p. 47.

providing the raw materials for the sacred process, supplemented by the scene of princely voluntarism in 1 Chronicles 29, is reapplied and profoundly added to in the Exodus version. The 'insertion' of the people as central figures in the story of sacred building corresponds to the role allocation of chs. 19–24. Comparable to the 'insertion' of the people as theophanic figures parallel to Moses, the people as princely donors and wise craftsmen represents an astounding role allocation, the strange character of which is underlined by the established connotations of encounter and temple building.

The impression of some process of profound 'democratization' is underlined by the role of the women in ch. 35. At this stage of the story, the image of the people serves for a representation of human lowness. But this image is underlined even more markedly by 35.25-26. The role of women performing the traditional 'task for gods and kings'[62] cannot but add to the impression of the people as rather strange embodiments of sacred roles.

Related to the rest of the story, the heart-driven people providing the raw materials for the new locus underlines the new character of the encounter set in a reality of base ordinariness. The subtle references to the Egyptian origin of the raw materials add to the depth of this description. As contrasts of 'black' and 'white' magic, the Golden Calf and the Tent of Meeting are processed from the raw materials of Egypt. When the people act on their own initiative, the Egyptian riches turn into the Golden Calf. When meticulously shaped 'just as YHWH had commanded Moses' (e.g. 39.42-43), the materials are made into the container of the divine presence.[63]

While too elusive for any definite transcription, the presence of allusive effects, equally subtle and rich, can be illustrated by two related texts. The Elijah story of 1 Kings 19 and the Chronicler's elaboration of

62. Cf. Kapelrud, 'Temple Building'.

63. The dual character of the people's gifts could be reflected by Aaron's headdress related to the 'guilt' of the people in 28.38. The marked juxtaposition of the concepts of 'guilt' and 'holiness' for the people's dedications reflect a connotational tension which can be compared to the implications of the Egyptian riches. It is even possible to find an allusive reference to this idea in the concluding statement on the Golden Calf episode in 32.35. Related to 28.38, the overloaded construction in 32.35 could represent an ironic twist. The implications of the people's gifts, laden with guilt and to be 'carried' by Aaron, are reversed by the people being punished for their own and Aaron's actions.

the temple building account have important sets of elements in common with Exodus 19–40. They also seem to share perceptions of more abstract character. 1 Chronicles 22.7-9 and 28.3 emphatically present David the warrior as totally unacceptable in the role of temple builder, due to all the blood he has spilled. But even so, he is included in the building process, his inclusion being underlined by the 1 Kings version given over to Solomon as the builder. Comparable to the people of Exodus 35, David dedicates his riches to the sanctuary. When completing the dedication by collecting the gifts from the nobles (ch. 29), he is even comparable to Moses. His elevated role is greatly added to by ch. 28. The shape of the sacred building is revealed to David in a way that combines the two impressions of Moses seeing the shape of the tent (Exod. 25.9, 40) and receiving the stone tablets. The shape of the sanctuary 'had happened in the spirit with him' (1 Chron. 28.12), everything written down 'by the hand of YHWH' (v. 19).[64] The perception of David the warrior too bloody for the sacred role of temple builder is combined with his function as the divinely illuminated architect. Concluded by the gift scene of whole-hearted dedication, the Chronicler's presentation of David reflects a collusion of roles comparable to the presentation of the people in the Exodus story.

A different but related aspect is illustrated by the description of the theophanic manifestation in 1 Kings 19. In the Exodus story, the Golden Calf and the Tent of Meeting are closely linked as contrasting episodes. As expressions of black and white magic, the two episodes represent the negative and positive expression of the people as temple builders. Set immediately after the divine instructions of chs. 25–31, the Golden Calf presents the type of implementation that can be expected by the people left to their own devices. The contrast of the successful implementation refers to extraordinary events.

A formally different but comparable perception seems to be expressed by the imagery of 1 Kings 19. The prophet's movement towards the encounter is reflected by three successive loci where the prophet is related to a special divine manifestation. The third represents the climax of theophanic manifestation. The structure of the events is comparable to the formal structure of three theophanic episodes in Exodus 19–40. In the latter the actualization of the third episode is disturbed by the episode of the Golden Calf. A comparable pattern is also found in

64. The connection between the texts is underlined by the terminological references; cf. DeVries, *1 and 2 Chronicles*, pp. 219-21.

1 Kings 19. The climactic third scene is 'disturbed' by three negative manifestations. While 'wind', 'trembling', and 'fire' form part of the theophanic event, the presence of YHWH 'in' these manifestations is emphatically negated (vv. 11-12).[65]

The composition reflects both the connection and the difference between the final manifestations. According to v. 11, the 'word of YHWH' orders the prophet to 'go out' and 'stand himself' before YHWH. The next element 'behold! YHWH is crossing' could be part of the divine order. But followed by the three negative and the one positive manifestation in v. 12 and in the narrative v. 13, it seems part of the theophanic description. This is also indicated by the introductory 'behold!' (*w^ehinneh*) in v. 11. Followed by a reference to the divine subject it corresponds to the stereotyped presentations of the divine representatives in the two preceding encounter scenes (vv. 5b and 9b). But in v. 11, the reference to the divine presence is not followed by the element 'he said' (*wayyō'mer*) corresponding to the preceding encounters. Instead, the introductory sentences are followed by the description of the negated manifestations. First, in v. 12b the positive manifestation is presented. Then the prophet responds to the order of v. 11, 'going out' and 'taking his stand' (v. 13).[66] And now the story returns to the stereotyped style of encounter established in vv. 5b and 9b, and alluded to in v. 11. The divine manifestation is introduced by the elements 'behold!', followed by a nominal reference to the 'voice', and continued by the narrative 'he said'.

The meticulous character of this description underlines its significance. By the 'insertion' of the negative manifestations, the climactic scene is expanded. The connotational value of 'fire' and 'wind' in particular as traditional expressions of divine presence adds to the impact of this expansion.[67] According to their significance, the prophet ordered to move could be expected to react to the tremendous events. But he

65. E.g. Jeremias, *Theophanie*, pp. 112-15, on 'Begleiterscheinungen' ('accompanying manifestations') which on the other hand have a polemical function.

66. The separation of the divine order and the prophet's implementation is illustrated by the rather free transcription of the scene by Simon J. DeVries, *1 Kings* (WBC, 12; Waco, TX: Word Books), p. 236: the tumult has frightened Elijah back into his cave, while the gentle breeze draws him out.

67. Cf. also the subtle parallelism of the three negative manifestations and the three positive manifestations of divine messenger, word of YHWH, and YHWH.

does not obey until the proper moment, patiently waiting while the impressive non-YHWH manifestations take place.

Compared to the material categories of sacred production in the Exodus story, the phenomena of 'wind', 'trembling' and 'fire' refer to supernatural categories of divine presence. Yet in spite of this difference, the two stories are remarkably similar in their understanding of the character of the divine presence when related to human experience. Also the calf of Exodus 32 represents a hagiograhical cliché, comparable to the traditional impact of the 'non-YHWH' manifestations of 1 Kings 19. The two stories seem to share a parallel perception. In both cases, the theophanic manifestation is closely connected to phenomena of substitute character. As the tremendous companions in the divine 'crossing' in 1 Kings 19 or as the human-made substitute in Exodus 32,[68] the non-YHWH phenomena are part of the extraordinary experience. Turned into a mock version by the people, or as supernatural phenomena ignored by the prophet, the non-YHWH phenomena represent real or potential substitutes. As events which manifest before the actualization of the real event, they even seem to represent the normal and natural situation.[69] With substitute phenomena for its shadow, the divine presence experienced by the human actors represents the truly miraculous situation.

4. *Conclusions*

The connotational richness of the story, so subtly presented, makes it impossible to set forth any well-ordered series of conclusions. But at the very least, the narrative consistency of Exodus 19–24 and the story of tent building must be underlined. The divine mountain as the locus of extraordinary encounter is substituted by the human-made tent. Correspondingly, the idea of the parallel movement of divine descent and human ascent is substituted by the divine descent into the human

68. The connection between the two texts is underlined by the comparable scene in Lev. 9.23b–10.2. Here the theophanic manifestation of fire is followed by the human-made 'strange fire', comparable to the relationship of Calf and Tent. On the other hand, the shadow scene is also according to 10.2a (cf. the parallel 9.24a) related to the theophanic manifestation of 'consuming fire'.

69. While Lev. 10.1-2 is set after the actual event in 9.23a-24, the peculiar parallelism of the two events reflects a correspondingly close connection between divine manifestation and the substitute event.

world as the sole means of encounter. Permanently settled in the world below, the theophanic presence is related to a new version of divine and human co-movement. Connected to the horizontal categories of the human reality, the human ascent and the divine co-ascent is represented by the people's journey. This development is connected with the juxtaposition of Moses and the people in a delicate process of role transfer. Moses as the traditional ascender is substituted by the people engaged in permanent theophanic *visio.*

Corresponding to the development of the main story, chs. 25–40 are dedicated to the reception of the divine descender. While the traditional idea of the human ascent has been abandoned for the people as actors, their efforts as temple-builders are necessary for the successful implementation of the divine descent.

The description of the people in chs. 35–39 corresponds to the categories of the first part of the story. The introduction of the people as a second set of theophanic actors in addition to Moses is continued by a corresponding 'insertion' in the building account. Supplementing Moses as temple builder, the people have been allocated a role that 'usurps' the traditional royal role. Both as theophanic actors and as temple builders, the people represent strange figures for the roles they have been asigned. This is also reflected by the development of the story, dedicated to the problems of actualization of the roles. For the first part, the tension of the story is connected with how the people ever can be part of the extraordinary encounter. For the second part, the divine intention to dwell among the people is profoundly disturbed by the Golden Calf episode. The tension of the first part is released by the divine wish to dwell in the world below the mountain and the corresponding abandonment of the traditional idea of human ascent. The effects of the Golden Calf are countered by the intercession of Moses followed by the successful production of locus.

The New Character of the World Below

The story development seems to reflect a profound shift in the description of human reality. Some traditional emphasis on human activity as essential for the experience of encounter has been abandoned in favour of a new emphasis on the divine actor as active. Related to the divine force descending from above, the imagery of the non-ascending people engaged in a permanent *visio Dei* could present a new ideal of passive receptivity. Such an ideal seems to be suggested by the first tent story in

Exod. 33.4-11. Engaged in a situation of sorrowful non-use of their ornaments, completed by the process of 'self-plundering', the people's passivity is related to a building account dedicated to Moses' erecting the tent 'on his own'. This image is completed by the situation of the people adoring the theophanic manifestation from afar. The significance of these images is underlined by their character of permanency, the whole period 'after Horeb' being qualified as a situation of permanent renunciation (v. 6).

This impression is balanced by chs. 35–39 as the first part of the final building story. Human activity is emphatically presented as possible and even necessary for the miracle of encounter to take place. If 'passivity' seems an apt term for the basic character of the human role with the people as actors, it is qualified by the emphasis on whole-hearted dedication and sacred doing. This aspect of a passivity profoundly active is underlined by the return to the encounter categories in the final episode of ch. 40. The idea of the human movement—transformed into the imagery of the long journey through the wilderness—is presented as the paramount aspect of the new encounter, the people truly engaged in the sacred movement of ascent guided by the divine co-ascender. This imagery represents the final qualification of the new situation according to chs. 19–40. Its significance is underlined by the parallel conclusion in Num. 9.15-23.

Illustrated by the parallel descriptions of the people as allocated the sacred roles of ascender and temple builder, the term of 'democratization' seems to encompass certain aspects of this development. The aspects described by such a term should not be reduced to institutional or religio-sociological categories, but are connected with a profound reinterpretation of the religious reality. This seems to imply a new perception of the alignment of divine and human when the two levels of being are intimately related in the situation of encounter. The substitution of Moses by the people as theophanic actors represents a radical expression of the new perception.

Also the presentation of the theophanic presence seems to imply some radical change. The subtle transition from vv. 34-35 to 36-38 in ch. 40 indicates that YHWH is as fully present at the new location as at Sinai. But even combined with the implications of theophanic presence, its manifestation as some signalling device represents a remarkable change. Corresponding to the 'democratization' of the visisionary role and the new form of extraordinary ascent, the theophanic manifestation seems peculiarly reduced in its new role of supporting the human movement. Compared to the introductory imagery of mountain above and camp below, the development of the story suggests the world below as the sole expression of reality. The new character of the human world as the permanent locus of the divine reality is indicated by the imagery of the people in the camp and on the journey related to a permanent theophanic manifestation.

The term 'secularization' could indicate one aspect of the profound change when the divine actor moves from the mountain to the camp as a signalling device in support of the people's movement. This term could also be related to the change of theophanic actors. The shift from figures like Moses or Elijah and the pure ascenders of Psalm 24 to the ascending people plodding from camp to camp seems to substitute the challenge of the soaring mountain with categories of a rather mundane character. But conversely, the perception of the world below as the locus of the world above could as well indicate that the narrative development implies a most radical process of 'sanctification'.

This development also implies that the original duality has been transferred to the world below. The scenery of Exodus 19 relates the basic contrasts to vertical categories. Confined to mountain and camp, divine and human are separated as 'high' and 'low', with a corresponding separation in the human realm between the extraordinary ascender and the non-ascenders. Some basic character of duality is retained in the second part of the story, but now as an expression of the potentialities of the world below. Above all, this character is reflected by the contrasts of the Golden Calf and the Tent of Meeting.[70]

The connection between the two contrasted episodes of sacred production is underlined by their relationship to the same set of actors and even to the same type of raw-materials. The same people are active in the contrasting processes of white and black magic. The people 'assembled against' the passive Aaron, succumbing to their will according to 32.1, is contrasted with the people of ch. 35 perfectly obedient to the divine will mediated by Moses. The one set of actors are depicted in a scene of men brutally violent, contrasting with another scene in which men and women together are 'heart-driven' in a sublime effort. The juxtaposed acts related to the same people set in parallel

70. 'Holy' and 'profane' could represent natural terms for the description of the duality. But related to sets of images which seem to reflect categories of profound ontological character, these terms would render only certain aspects of the contrasts.

scenes of sacred production reflect the sharp contrasts of the world below. The one situation of sacred production entails the sharply opposed potentialities of calf or tent production. When serving the divine initiative mediated by Moses, the people produce the perfect receptacle for the divine presence. When set in motion by their own initiative, the same people start a process in which their riches are perverted into the abomination of the calf.

The aftermath of the Golden Calf episode seems to continue and sharpen the perception of duality transferred to the world below. The calf of Aaron and the people is juxtaposed to the tent of Moses and Joshua. The violence of Moses crushing the Golden Calf corresponds to the violent way in which it was produced, and is continued by the terrible scene of the pro-YHWH Levites set against brother and neighbour.[71] The impression of the people split into sets of opposites is profiled by the idealized image of the people in chs. 35–39.

The contrasts of Golden Calf and the Tent of Meeting relate the perception of duality to what could be transcribed as right and wrong 'sacramentalism'. These categories are linked to the people as the performers of sacred action, both by the people contrasted to themselves in different situations, or by the people split into sharply opposed fractions.

It must be important that this perception of duality is tempered by the narrative movement. The sharp contrasts of the people as calf-producers and sacred temple builders form part of a more comprehensive story climaxed by the theophanic episode and the people's journey. This setting reflects a composition dedicated to the miracle of encounter truly taking place in the world below and with the people for theophanic actors.

The Aspects of 'Materialization'

Terms like 'democratization', 'secularization' and 'sanctification' indicate certain aspects of the narrative movement. Important aspects invite the label 'materialization'. This is expressed by the mass of concrete details given over to the elaborate presentation of the raw materials and their proper transformation by sacred craftsmanship in Exodus 25–31 and 35–40. Such an interest corresponds to the very genre of the temple

71. Cf. also the 'YHWH-seeker' able to 'go out' to Moses' Tent of Meeting, while the people are presented as confined to the camp (33.7-8).

building account, the dedication of the royal temple builder being expressed by the costliness of the raw materials[72] and the 'wisdom' of the craftsman. The traditional connotations of some process of sacred 'materialization' is added to in the Sinai stories. Introduced by Exodus 19–24, the character of the new locus is set out by the divine mountain as the original locus. Set against this background, the human-made tent as the receptacle of divine presence indicates a remarkable change to some form of 'sacramentalism'. The divine movement from the mountain makes necessary some material basis for the permanent theophanic presence.

This effect is enhanced by the introduction of the people as the builders, the princely dedication and the inspired craftmanship being transferred to ordinary people. The divine presence is not only made dependent on the successful production of material artifacts, but is related to actors emphatically qualified as irregular for such a sacred process. Whatever the implications of this description, the collusion—if not collision—of high and low is most remarkable.

These aspects underline the significance of the Golden Calf episode as a negative story of materialization. As stories of white and black magic, related to the contrasts of human and divine initiative, one would have expected that the most costly materials and the most worthy craftsman would be related to the successful production, while the ordinariness of the common people would be reserved for the failure. But instead we find that gold, the most costly of materials, is only used for the wrong kind of materialization, corresponding to Aaron as the craftsman.[73] This imagery stands in contrast to the women of 35.26, 'whose heart carried them in wisdom' spinning goats' hair. While this contrast is combined with the delight in costly materials also in the positive story (vv. 22-24, 27-28), the inclusion of the women as the concrete example of the people as wise craftsmen is astounding. These implications of some profound 'materialism' as essential for the actualization of the divine presence are deepened by the connotations of Egyptian origin for the people's riches.

The implications of the motif elaboration can be illustrated by the workshop scene of the Mesopotamian 'Mouth-Washing' ritual, as pre-

72. Levine, 'The Descriptive Tabernacle Texts', p. 309.

73. The choice of Aaron is underlined by Deut. 9.12-21, attributing the calf to the people.

sented by Thorkild Jacobsen.[74] When the craftsmen have finished their job and the statue is ready for consecration, the workshop is cleaned and ritually prepared. A representative of each class of craftsmen who have worked on the statue stands forth and has his hands ritually cut off by the officiating priest. This is followed by the craftsman's oath: 'The god Gushkinbanda, Ea of the goldsmiths, verily made it. I did not make it!' Similar oaths by the other classes attribute the deed to other gods of magical transformation, for instance 'Nin-ildu, Ea of the carpenters'. The significance of these acts is stressed by the finished statue being consistently referred to as a 'plank', that is, as unworked wood. And in the following ritual, the 'plank' is moved step by step towards its beginnings. It is taken from the workshop and set up as the tree standing in the forest, later to the waters which gave it life, until the birth of the god incarnate is ritually performed. Set in this context, the significance of the introductory rite in the workshop is clear. 'The fact that the statue is the work of human hands is ritually denied and thus magically made non-existent, nullified'.[75]

Compared to such a process, the building account in Exodus seems to reflect the opposite tendency. Here the truly magical process of materialization is emphatically related to human hands, their aspects of ordinariness underlined by the elaboration of the sacred process. Aaron's description of how the calf emerged by itself, according to 32.24, would qualify as a story of real magic according to Mesopotamian standards.[76] But according to the standards of the Exodus account, the ordinariness of the human world below represents the reality in which a truly magical process can take place. Such a perception also corresponds to the final transformation of the theophanic encounter in ch. 40. The new parallelism of divine and human movement, the extraordinary ascent of the divine mountain transformed into the plodding categories of journey, corresponds to the character of a truly magical process of materialization presented in the building story.

74. 'The Graven Image', in Patrick D. Miller Jr, Paul D. Hanson, S. Dean McBride (eds.), *Ancient Israelite Religion: Essays in Honor of Frank Moore Cross* (Philadelphia: Fortress Press, 1987), pp. 15-32 (23-24).

75. Jacobsen, 'The Graven Image', p. 24.

76. E.g. Samuel E. Loewenstamm, 'The Making and Destruction of the Golden Calf', *Bib* 48 (1967), pp. 481-90.

The Aspects of 'Individualism'

The aspects outlined above are connected to categories of individualism and inner disposition in the building story.[77] The 'everyone'-constructions (25.2; 35.5, 10, 21-29; 36.1-2) reflect the fact that the people are represented by 'everyone' or 'every man' and 'every woman'. Also, the sentences imply that this 'everyone' is characterized by the heart as 'inciting' and 'willing' or 'wise'. The repetitive applications of these forms must reflect the significance attached to this qualification, with the response of the people defined both as coming from individual representatives and from these individuals as 'heartily' motivated.

It must be important that the parallel building account of Exod. 33.7-11 is introduced by a comparable description of the people. Given the scarcity of emotional references in these stories, the sorrow motif in v. 4 must be important, especially when underlined by the parallelism of v. 6 with 'self-plundering' as a complementary motif. Followed by the building story related to Moses' Tent of Meeting in vv. 7-11, the motif structure represents a version *in nuce* of Exodus 35–40, with the people's sorrow and self-plundering parallel to the exhuberant dedication by the heart-incited. The parallel motifs must reflect some basic referential connection. This is underlined by the relationship to the Golden Calf episode. However subtle the relationship of the three building accounts,[78] the people in the contrasted situations of sorrow and renunciation and of perfect and willing response is juxtaposed to Exodus 32.

77. Usually ignored, but important to Utzschneider, *Das Heiligtum*, pp. 160-67, for the character of the new 'Bürger-Tempel-Gemeinde' ('citizen-temple community'). Related to the 'Makrostruktur-Ebene' ('macrostructural level') of the older Sinai texts, the theme of the 'Freiwilligen' ('volunteers') as well as the whole project of temple building is subordinated to a general Torah-theme. The project of temple building is part of the Sinai commitment, and the temple is legitimate only as an 'Ort des Gesetzes' ('place for observance of the Law') (p. 296).

78. Ezek. 43.7-11 reflects a structure comparable to the three building scenes of Exodus; cf. M.R. Hauge, 'On the Sacred Spot: The Concept of the Proper Localization before God', *SJOT 1* (1990), pp. 49-55. Centred around the concepts of temple and divine dwelling in the people's midst, the passage distinguishes between three stages of temple relationship. The first was a period of abominable temple practices (vv. 7-8), followed by the prophet's 'proclamation' of the house which results in the people's shame over their iniquities and the measuring of the temple (v. 10, cf. also the purification motifs in v. 9). This is followed by the presentation of the shape of the temple and all its rules which are to be observed and 'done' by the people (v. 11).

It is possible that the description of the people in ch. 35 implies some separation within the people—the positive character tacitly excluding those not incited by their hearts.[79] On the other hand, one would expect more explicit expressions for such an interest if it were important for the story of chs. 35–39.[80] While the 'hearty' character of the participants is repeated like a refrain, there are no indications of any contrasting group. On the contrary, the meticulous description is dominated by the wish to present the people as a whole being perfectly attuned to the divine will. The transition from plural to singular forms in Exod. 25.2 as well as 35.4, 21 and 22 reflects an immediate transition from the people as a whole to the singular everyone as representative of the people. The significance of the style is underlined by corresponding effects in the story of building. Also in this case, the transition from plural to singular forms includes the people in the sacred production. The composition of Exodus 35–39 demonstrates the interest in including the people participating, both with regard to the presentation of the raw materials and to the production of the sacred implements. This image of a people totally dedicated to the sacred undertaking corresponds to the repetitive use of the formula of compliance in vv. 32 and 42-43 of ch. 39.[81] Comparable to the repetitive presentation of the people as totally committed in 35.4–36.7, the formula underlines the people 'doing' the perfect materialization of the divine will. This is climaxed by the blessing scene in 39.32-43, according to which the 'children of Israel' are presented as the subjects of production and accordingly blessed.

The emphasis on the people as perfect 'doers' underlines the significance of the people as 'everyone'. On the one hand, the people as a whole are engaged; on the other hand, this entity is represented by the single man and woman driven by their heart.

Hitherto, the narrative development has been related to the human

79. The qualification of 'everyone' entails a separation within the people between the 'Freiwilligen' ('volunteers') and the rest of the people, according to Utzschneider, *Das Heiligtum*, pp. 167, 295-97.

80. This is underlined by the explicit separation between different groupings in the post-Sinai stories.

81. Cf. also vv. 1, 5, 7, 21, 26, 29, 31. Seen together with the transition from the anonymous 'they' of vv. 1-31 to their identification as 'the children of Israel' in v. 32, the application of the compliance formula in ch. 39 also connects the people with the process of sacred craftsmanship.

actors in each situation responding as an entity, 'the people'.[82] The change to categories of individualism connected with the inner disposition of each individual—the people as a whole perceived as 'everyone heart-incited'—must reflect a new situation within the narrative development. Moreover, hitherto the role of the people has primarily been related to the demonstration of the human reality as a negative contrast to divine presence, the lowness of the people below making any idea of ultimate encounter utterly problematical. As the positive complement, the story of chs. 35–39 demonstrates the circumstances under which the miracle of encounter can take place with the people as theophanic figures.

The description of these special circumstances can be related to different traditions.[83] The possible confluence of traditions makes it necessary to stress the special character of Exodus 19–40. The perception of duality transferred to the human reality could be important for the emphasis on the people being represented by individual members. The description of the heart-driven 'everyone' in ch. 35 contrasts with the violent scenes of the Golden Calf episode and its aftermath, which are characterized by individuals and groups juxtaposed to each other. In this respect, Exodus 35–39, concluded by 40.36-38 and underlined by the expanded version in Num. 9.15-23, presents an idyll of a united people perfectly attuned to the divine will.[84]

Also, it must be important for the perception of this idyll of perfect obedience that it is not directly connected with a general theme of Torah obedience.[85] Rather strangely within the context of Sinai as the

82. E.g. Exod. 19.8 and 24.3, 7. On the other hand, the categories of individualism and inner disposition in 35.4-7 underlines the significance of the elements 'together' (19.8) and 'with one voice' (24.3), the latter further emphasized by the repeated commitment in 24.7. However delicate, these qualifications of the people's response could prepare for the narrative development climaxed in the latter part of the Sinai stories.

83. E.g. Utzschneider (*Das Heiligtum*, pp. 162-63) refers to a theological description of the law-observant ('eine Anthropologie des Gesetzestreuen'), close to the application of the heart motifs in Deut. 30.11-14 and also to Neh. 2.17 and 7.5. The concepts of the 'new heart' provided by a divine miracle in Deut. 30.6; Jer. 24.7-10; 31.27-34 or Ezek. 11.17-21; 36.22-32; Ps. 51.12 represent applications parallel to the narrative development of the Sinai stories.

84. In its turn contrasted by the post-Sinai episodes.

85. This is reflected by the traditional separation between Exod. 19–24 and later materials perceived as 'Priestly'; contrast the preceding references to Utzschneider.

place of law-giving, the new disposition of the people is not an expression of perfect observance of divine commandments comparable to the set of Exodus 20–23.[86] On the contrary, the earlier 'covenant scenes' with the people responding perfectly 'together' (19.8) and 'with one voice (24.3) led to the disaster of the Golden Calf.[87] Given this background, it can hardly be coincidental that the last mediation of the divine commandments (34.32) within the context of chs. 19–40 is not followed by any scene of popular commitment.[88] The new character of the people according to chs. 35–39 is related not to a general Torah commitment, but to the building of the tent according to the divine plan revealed to Moses. Correspondingly, the final scenes of Exod. 40.36-38 and Num. 9.15-23 relate the perfect obedience to the situation of breaking camp or staying.

This corresponds to the function of the building account as part of the main story. Centred around the categories of encounter and the problem of the people as participants in the theophanic event, the story of the tent presents the actualization of the divine movement from above to a dwelling in the world below. The comparison with Psalm 24 underlines the special character of the Sinai story. In the psalm, the Torah motifs are organically connected with the motifs of ascent. The ascent to the holy mountain is actualized by human actors of pure hands and hearts. In comparison, the Sinai story breaks up the parallelism of divine and human movement as well as the parallelism of holy mountain and human-made temple. Compared with Psalm 24, the aspects of Torah commitment are also changed. Distorted by the Golden Calf episode, the Torah commitment of the people (Exod. 19.8; 24.3) seems to have a negative function, illustrating the incompatibility of the people.

This cannot mean that the process of temple building is separated from the category of Torah. Within the narrative structure, the divine instructions of Exodus 25–31 are presented as parallel to the divine

86. Underlined by the immediate connection of heart and Torah obedience in Deut. 30.6-8; Jer. 31.31-34; Ezek. 11.19-20; 36.26-27.

87. Cf. also the Ten Commandments of Exod. 20.1-17, ignored by the people of v. 18, and according to 34.28 written down on the tablets.

88. This could also be reflected by the character of the commandments in ch. 34. A traditio-historical puzzle (cf. Childs, *Book of Exodus*, pp. 604-609; Van Seters, *The Life of Moses*, pp. 326-33), the set of divine instructions in vv. 11-26 is oriented towards the situation of the people having arrived in the land (vv. 11-16, 21-26).

instructions of the preceding theophanic episodes, just as the mediation by Moses and the response of the people correspond to the established pattern. Such a connection can also be illustrated by the compilation of building instructions and Sabbath observance (31.12-17; 35.1-3). The parallelism of YHWH 'acting' as creator and human 'acting' is connected to the tent as the sublime expression of human 'acting'.

In contrast to the earlier failures, the last episode represents the successful implementation of the divine will. For this set of commandments, the people are able to respond. As temple builders and those engaged in the journey through the wilderness,[89] the people are perfectly attuned to the divine will. The imagery of the divine commandments written on the tablets (34.28), and according to 40.20 put in the ark and thus brought along on the journey, seems a fitting representation of the new situation. Comparable to the permanent 'self-plundering after Horeb' (33.6), the more comprehensive implementation of the divine will must be left to future stages of the people's journey. At some stage, the ark will be have to be opened.

The Function of the Temple Concept

The development of the story in Exodus 19–40 raises the question of the function of the temple concept. The traditional separation between chs. 19–24 and 25–31 and 35–40 has rested on the axiom of a close relationship between the Priestly materials and the cultic practice of Jerusalem.[90] While there has been some disagreement over the exact

89. This is underlined by the parallel and greatly extended version of Exod. 40.36-38 in Num. 9.15-23. Here, the movements of the cloud are qualified by the formulaic expressions 'according to the mouth of YHWH' in vv. 18, 20, 23 and 'the observance of YHWH' which the people 'observe' in vv. 19, 23. This qualification indicates that the observation of the movements of the cloud is the expression for Torah commitment.

90. The influence of such modes of interpretation is illustrated by two contributions which assert that the Priestly materials reflect a critical understanding of traditional temple practice. According to T.E. Fretheim, 'The Priestly Document: Anti-Temple?', *VT* 18 (1968), pp. 313-29, the Priestly tent did not serve as a model for a permanent temple, but represented the advocacy of a return to the theocratic age prior to kingship and temple, with the people related to a movable sanctuary. According to Utzschneider, *Das Heiligtum*, pp. 296-97, the whole project of temple building in the Priestly Sinai-texts is subordinated to the general Torah-theme. The new 'Bürger-Tempel-Gemeinde' ('citizen-temple community') reflects an anti-royal

relationship between the ideological fervour and the concrete practice of the details of the imagery, the tent theme has been understood to reflect a massive Priestly interest in temple and temple ritual which has been added to the original interest(s) represented by the older materials.

The reading of 'the main story' in chs. 19–40 indicates that the 'Priestly' materials are firmly embedded in the narrative development. The introduction of the tent imagery and the genre of building account does not imply some conceptually new interest, but continues the story started in ch. 19. While the first part of the story is centred around the imagery of encounter on the mountain, the imagery of the tent represents the complementary half, both expressions of the basic temple concept. This connection is reflected *in nuce* by the structure of Ps. 24.3-10. The parallelism of divine mountain related to the human ascent and the human-made tent related to the theophanic manifestation in the psalm is reflected by the development of the locus theme in Exodus 19–40. Compared to the parallelism of the psalm, the Exodus exposition of two successive loci as well as the transformation of the ascent motif represents a radical reinterpretation of the traditional imagery.

The elaboration of the locus theme in the two texts reflects the special character of the temple concepts. This is also illustrated by parallel applications in texts that represent different literary traditions. In Psalm 68, the enigmatic expression 'Sinai (is) in the sanctuary' (v. 18b) has been the object of much discussion. Read in its literal sense, the expression is comparable to the imagery of Exod. 40.34-38. The latter refers to the preceding theophanic manifestations and underlines the connection between the final theophany and the earlier scenes. YHWH manifesting himself on the mountain is identical with the YHWH of the tent. As repository for the divine presence, the Tent of Meeting retains the basic character of the mountain. The contraction of two different loci is comparable to the poetic localization of 'Sinai' to 'the sanctuary' in Ps. 68.18. This is underlined by the context. The mountain chosen by YHWH for his dwelling (v. 17) is contrasted with the mountain of Bashan qualified as the 'Mountain of God' (v. 16). The two motif sets of Ps. 68.16-18 and Exod. 40.34-38 seem to represent singular elaborations of some basic imagery. In the latter, tent and divine mountain are successive loci, but with essentially the same character. This corresponds to the poetic image of the mountain Sinai 'in' the temple, the

and anti-traditional ideal of the Second Temple period. In both cases, the argument presupposes an immediate connection between text and institutional reality.

implications of which are supplemented by a second mountain motif of Bashan as a contrasted divine mountain. With Bashan as a competing locus, the implications of the imagery can even be extended to the contrast of Golden Calf in the Sinai story.

A comparable application of the temple motifs is represented by the description of the sanctification of Solomon's temple in 1 Kgs 8.3-11. Centred around the ark (vv. 3-4aα, 5-9), the 'expansions'[91] in v. 4 add the Tent of Meeting and all its implements to be introduced into the building already completed in all respects by Solomon and his wise craftsman. The imagery of a completed sanctuary put into a completed sanctuary is strangely parallel to Ps. 68.18, the poetic visualization of the divine mountain contained within the sanctuary being rather heavy-handedly translated into prose. But the parallelism is stressed by the corresponding imagery of Exod. 40.34-38, which relates the mountain manifestation to the new locus.

Also, the connection of a first scene of building related to one group of actors followed by a scene of perfecting preparations by a new and superior lot of actors in 1 Kings, is comparable to the two series of temple building in Exodus 35–39 followed by ch. 40. Comparable to the activity of Moses putting together and furnishing the tent in ch. 40, the activity of the priests in 1 Kings is also followed by the theophanic manifestation of cloud and glory. The parallelism of the two accounts is stressed by the 'contrived' character of both accounts. According to Exodus 39–40, everything is perfectly finished by the people and concluded by the inspection and blessing of Moses. Then, Moses puts everything together on his own in an effort of truly Herculean proportions. In the 1 Kings account, the priests introduce a complete sanctuary with all its implements into a sanctuary already perfectly equipped with all that was necessary for its sacred functions.

But however contrived, the 1 Kings description with a sanctuary introduced into a sanctuary corresponds to the connection of Sinai and

91. E.g. DeVries, *1 Kings*, pp. 122-23, on the original *hieros logos* added to by the post-exilic theocracts interested in stressing the exclusive priestly prerogatives (vv. 3-4), while the expansions in vv. 10-11 'anxiously offer' the surrogate cloud for the original theophanic 'glory'. On the other hand, Haran (*Temples and Temple Service*, pp. 141-42) asserts a 'non-priestly' identity for these sections. To Hurowitz (*I Have Built You*, pp. 262-66), the Priestly expansions reflect a 'continuity motif', comparable to the Mesopotamian rite of 'the former brick' by which a brick from the original temple is used as a foundation for the new.

sanctuary in Ps. 68.18a. Together the two texts seems to represent parallel versions of the temple imagery which forms the basis for the Exodus elaboration of mountain and tent.

Held together, these texts together with Psalm 24 demonstrate the malleable character of the temple concepts. While probably firmly embedded in an origin of institutional character, they represent a language that vastly transcends the confinements of institutional practice. The description in 1 Kings invites a most literal reading of the account of what took place when the temple of Solomon was dedicated. But such a reading leads to a rather absurd set of images, the servants of the Solomonic temple constantly stumbling over the old sanctuary. If not attributing the 'expansions' to priestly fanaticism ignoring everything but its prerogatives, the reader of 1 Kgs 8.3-4 will have to undertake some mental operation comparable to the requirements posed by the contracted imagery of Ps. 68.16-18 where Sinai is located 'in' the temple and is glowered at by Bashan the divine mountain!

The need for some leaps of imagination even for the reading of such a simple text as 1 Kings 8—underlined by the mental sprightliness required for the reading of Psalm 68—is important for the appreciation of the literary character of Exodus 19–40. Both the mountain and the tent imagery can be assumed to represent independent and established traditions.[92] Correspondingly, the building account of Exodus 35–40 prepared for by chs. 25–31, represents a traditional genre of ancient Near Eastern literature. Both as expressions for definite genres as well as 'traditions', the law collections and Moses as recipient of divine laws must also reflect a complicated literary prehistory. The present combination, with the different character of the materials retained while united by a common conceptual framework and by a common function as parts of the narrative development, must reflect the flexible and adaptable character of the main concepts.

To me, it seems natural to assume that the application of the temple concept and its central images of divine mountain and human-made tent in Exodus 19–40 reflects an established language of 'transferred' character. At this stage of reading, it is impossible to describe the precise character of this language. Terms like 'metaphors' or 'similes' could be equally possible for some approximate idea of the function of the texts. Above all, the elements of the story refer to themselves, the

92. E.g. on the one hand Dozemann, *God on the Mountain*; on the other, Fretheim, 'The Priestly Document'.

reader correspondingly referred to the 'literary' reality established by the story. The very imagery of the divine mountain invites one to a reading that corresponds to this character.[93] Added to by the tent motifs and the transformation of the motifs of divine and human movement, the imagery of the story vastly transcends categories of institutional reality or the socio-religious problems of the Second Temple period.

This is underlined by the subtle juxtaposition of the three events of 'temple building', when the grand Tent of Meeting of ch. 40 is related to Moses' Tent of Meeting set against the people's Golden Calf. The versatility of imagination required to relate the three sanctuaries to each other and to the basic counter-motif of divine mountain indicates that the motifs are part of some 'transferred' language, as opposed to a 'literal' language illustrated by the usual assertions of 'Priestly' and institutional interests.[94] Basically, the main story seems to ponder profoundly the possibility of any intimate relationship of divine and human and the conditions for any intimate relationship. The query is represented by the contrasts of mountain above and camp below which represent the fundamental problem of divine and human incompatibility. This is overcome by the idea of the tent in the camp. In their turn, the implications of this solution are represented by the new contrasts of the Golden Calf and Tent of Meeting. Ultimately, the new relationship of divine and human is expressed the concept of journey as the new ascent with a divine co-ascender.

This description might represent an approximation of the theological concern of the story. But as a definitive statement on how the story should be properly read, it is instantly called into question when the story of Exodus 19–40 is continued by the sacrificial laws of Leviticus 1–7. Any appeal for the total dismissal of the traditional understanding of 'Priestly' interests would be as stifling as the automatic identification of the textual interest with some hypothetical socio-religious problems of the post-exilic situation. The traditional Jewish readings referred to in Milgrom's *Leviticus*, or Cassuto's *Exodus,* as well as Christian

93. E.g. Dozemann (*God on the Mountain*, esp. pp. 12-17) for whom the categories of 'symbol' and 'metaphor' are important for the concepts of Sinai/ Horeb and Zion. But connected with a special model of traditio-historical development and with Zion as an 'archetype' (pp. 152-53), the reach and applicability of these 'symbols' seem rather limited.

94. But it must be reasonable to assume that also as 'transferred', the temple concepts must reflect a basic connection with the concrete institutional practice.

readings since Wellhausen, demonstrate the story as meaningful to readers who presuppose a rather close relationship to institutional practice.

Also in this respect Psalm 24 provides an interesting parallel. This text could be taken as an indication of language both grounded in concrete ritual practice as well as malleable for 'metaphorical' applications. The language could be as relevant for some conventional ritual practice of institutional character as for types of *exercitia spiritualia* of more exclusive character.[95] To me, the character of Exodus 19–40 indicates that the latter provide the more suitable framework for the perception of the subtleties of composition. On the other hand, the impression that some process of profound religious 'democratization' is represented within these chapters would put to shame any interpretation of too elitist a character.

95. Cf. the parallel and as tentative discussion on the character of the language in the Individual Psalms by Hauge, *Between Sheol and Temple*, pp. 187-97, 258-62.

Chapter 3

THE PARALLEL STORY: THE APOTHEOSIS OF MOSES

1. *The Double Function of Exodus 32–34*

The impact of the composition is greatly added to by the complex function of Exodus 32–34. Set in the structure of the three theophanic episodes (Exod. 19.3–24.2; 24.3–34.35; 35.1–40.38), the events of the Golden Calf are part of the second episode. This connection is indicated by the reference to the mountain scene in Exod. 32.7, which continues the story concluded in Exod. 31.18. Parallel to and contrasting with the encounter on the mountain, the Golden Calf distorts the established pattern of events. Compared to the earlier scenes, the descent of Moses and the mediation in the camp are turned into a set of negative events. But the mediation of the divine instructions in ch. 35 returns to the story line concluded in 31.18. Seemingly ignoring the events of Exodus 32–34, the divine instructions of Exodus 25–31 are mediated and implemented by the people. Accordingly, Exodus 32–34 seem to have a function as an 'intermission'. The Golden Calf and its aftermath are presented as a 'non-event'. Distorting and threatening to destroy the proper succession of the events, the consequences of the event are nullified by the intercession of Moses.

As a description of events that should not have happened, events that, once complete, serve to postpone the actualization of the proper events, the story of the Golden Calf is comparable to Numbers 14. This episode interrupts the people's journey to the land. The people will turn circles in the wilderness for forty years until the journey to the land can be resumed. In both cases, the story separates 'proper' events which are related to the divine intention and a set of events set in motion by the people and which have to run their course until their effects are nullified.

In the Numbers story, the time span and the change of actors makes a distinctive separation between the proper events and the intermittent happenings. In the Exodus story, the transition from the intermittent events of chs. 32–34 to the proper story line is rather imperceptible.[1] The mediation of ch. 35 can be read as a direct continuation of the scene in 34.34-35, the encounter in the tent concretely mediated to the people.

The immediate connection of the intermittent and proper events in the Exodus story is comparable to the presentation of the theophanic manifestation in 1 Kgs 19.11-13. As traditional manifestations of the divine presence, the negated phenomena represent alternative situations for the prophet to implement the introductory order of v. 11. If the prophet had responded to the 'wind' or to the 'fire', the events of encounter would have unfolded in a different order. But in this case, the prophet is not disturbed by the non-theophanic manifestations, but waits with his response until the fourth manifestation of the 'fine-grained silence'. The story of the Golden Calf seems to explore the alternative line of events. In this case, the human actors are not able to wait for the return of Moses and thus for the proper actualization of the divine dwelling in their midst, but initiate an alternative line of events according to their own perception of the crisis. The empty space of the absent Moses is filled by a substitute. But after the successful intervention of Moses, the story concluded in 31.18 is back on track.

But in addition to a function of intermittent non-events, the Golden Calf and its aftermath also have a vital function as part of the linear development. Having experienced the violent scenes of Exodus 32, the harsh divine words and the people's sorrow in 33.1-6, and the concluding scene in 34.29-35, the reader can accept that the people of the earlier parts of the story have been changed into the exhuberantly and meticulously obedient people of chs. 35–39, which ultimately can even be set in a situation of permanent *visio Dei.* Also the development of the central themes of ascent and locus reflects the crucial significance of Exodus 32–34 for the connection of chs. 19–24 and 35–40. Bridging the two parts of the composition, the Golden Calf and its aftermath are part of the line of events which lead to the climax of the story.

In this way, the events of Exodus 32–34 seem to function both as intermittent events and as part of the linear development of successive events. Both aspects can be related to the setting of these chapters

1. Illustrated by the traditional understanding of Exod. 35 as a return to Priestly traditions, the composition of which reflects the editorial interest in a smooth transition.

within a 'main story'. But in addition, more subtle effects enhance the perception of the Golden Calf and its aftermath as a special story within a story.

Such a function could already be indicated by the formal character of these chapters. Introduced by the events of the Golden Calf, the three encounter episodes of Exod. 32.30–34.28 reflect the established structure of two preparatory sub-episodes climaxed by a third event centred around the theophanic manifestation. Accordingly, Exodus 32–34 can also be read as a special fourth theophanic episode, parallel to Exod. 19.3–24.2, a second episode now delimited to 24.3–31.18, and 35.1–40.38.

Some special character for these events is also suggested by Exodus 34 as the last mountain scene. Due to the significance of the mountain as the original locus, the last application of the mountain scene in chs. 19–40 must be important. This is also reflected by the mediation scene which concludes the episode (v. 32). Compared to similar statements in 19.6, 25 and 24.3, 7, the formula 'all the words which YHWH had spoken with him on the mountain Sinai' suggests a concluding event.[2] Above all, the extraordinary description of the descent in Exod. 34.29-35 underlines the significance of the last mountain episode. Compared to the earlier descriptions, the elaboration of the scene and the singular emphasis on the appearance of the descender leaves the reader in no doubt that the story has passed some watershed.

Finally, the juxtaposition of two tents both named 'Tent of Meeting' highlights the special position of chs. 32–34 within the composition as a whole. The parallelism implied by the common name is elaborated by Exod. 33.7-11, prepared for by vv. 1-6. As a short version of the temple building account, the description of Moses' Tent of Meeting presents a story which contrasts with the grand building account of Exodus 35–40. As has already been seen, the parallelism of the Golden Calf and the tent of Exod. 33.7-11 is important. But the presentation of calf and tent as contrasts is combined with the peculiar juxtaposition of the two different tents. Its significance is stressed by the function of the tent theme for the composition as a whole. Together, the sacred mountain and the grand Tent of Meeting as successive loci link the story of Exodus 19–40.

2. This could also be reflected by the use of *ṣiwwâ* for the mediator's function in v. 32. Aside from 27.20 in a divine instruction addressed to Moses, this verb is reserved for the divine subject in Exod. 19–40.

Due to the usual understanding of Exod. 33.7-11 as a redactional insertion (and badly placed at that!), it is easy to disregard the significance of the Tent of Meeting theme for Exodus 32–34. But it is also referred to in the concluding Exod. 34.34-35. The allusive character of this reference even suggests that the tent is a given part of the scenery.[3] In this way, the important passage Exod. 33.12–34.35 is framed by the imagery of the Tent of Meeting. Moreover, as a contrast to the Golden Calf, the tent motif is negatively prepared for by the first part of the story. As two juxtaposed loci of encounter in the world below the mountain, the relationship of the Golden Calf and Moses' Tent of Meeting in Exodus 32–34 corresponds to the relationship of the divine mountain and the grand Tent of Meeting for the composition as a whole.

However subtle the meaning, the very presence of deliberate effects of parallelism is underlined by the frequentative forms of Exod. 33.7-11, 34.34-35 and 40.32, 36-38. In all cases, the series of singular, successive events is subtly altered by a gradual transition from the narrative imperfect consecutive forms into other verbal forms, of which infinitives introduced by *b*^{e} or *k*^{e} are of special importance. The stylistic effects both connect the repeated acts to the singular events of the narrative and widen the imagery into new situations. The meticulous elaboration of the scenes demonstrates the significance of these passages.[4] And also, the parallelism of the stylistic effects together with the common Tent of Meeting motifs seem to signal the referential relationship of these passages.

The connection between these tent descriptions indicates that all refer to permanent situations. Introduced by vv. 1-6, the frequentative forms of Exod. 33.7-11[5] are related to the general situation 'after Horeb': the

3. Van Seters, *The Life of Moses*, p. 327.

4. This is also illustrated by the impression of these texts as disturbing the narrative flow: Childs, *Book of Exodus*, p. 609, on Exod. 34.34-35 as a 'literary break'; Van Seters, *The Life of Moses*, p. 321, on Exod. 33.6-11 as a 'digression'; or Haran, *Temples*, pp. 262-69, on Exod. 33.5-11 as an E-tradition; Blum, *Studien zur Komposition*, pp. 312-13, on Exod. 40.36-38 as the result of the present separation between Exodus and Leviticus into books. The discussion also reflects the perception of some referential relationship between the passages. The traditional assumption of Priestly influence in Exod. 34.34-35 entails some connection with 40.36-38, while Childs (*Book of Exodus*, pp. 617-19) and Van Seters (*The Life of Moses*, p. 360) stress the referential connection between 33.7-11 and 34.34-35.

5. Cf. also Van Seters, *The Life of Moses*, p. 321, on the connection of these verses. On the other hand, Moberly (*At the Mountain of God*, pp. 64-65 and 171-77)

people in a permanent situation of ‘self-plundering’, the Tent of Meeting as the theophanic locus outside the camp and related to Moses’ comings and goings experienced by the people inside the camp, concluded by the impression of the shining face of Moses as the person being ‘talked to’ in the tent; all these images represent part of a permanent post-Horeb situation.

This must have repercussions for our understanding of the function of Exodus 32–34. As we have seen, the story of the Golden Calf and its aftermath can be perceived both as an intermittent ‘non-story’ and as part of the linear development. But leading to the presentation of a permanent post-Horeb situation centred around Moses’ Tent of Meeting, the story also represents a ‘loop’ within the story line as a relatively independent episode.

The implications of this function is indicated by the contrasting relationship with the building account of Exodus 35–40. The referential effects of the frequentatives of Exod. 33.7-11, 34.34-35 and 40.36-38, correspond to the juxtaposition of Moses’ Tent of Meeting and the grand Tent of Meeting as well as to the contrasting effects of the two building accounts. The explicit time reference ‘after Horeb’ in Exod. 33.6 corresponds to the references to what happened ‘on all their journeyings’ in Exod. 40.36, 38. Accordingly, Moses’ Tent of Meeting and the final Tent of Meeting are presented as parts of the permanent wilderness situation after the departure from the divine mountain. This implies that the end of the Golden Calf story should be read as some sort of conclusion to the Sinai story, parallel to the conclusion of Exodus 40.[6]

Very subtly, apart from the bluntness of the name ‘Tent of Meeting’, the composition encourages the reader to make a prolonged stop after the last mountain event to contemplate Exodus 19–34 as an alternative version of what took place at Sinai. Probably not for a first reading, the grand compositional design of Exodus 19–40 must primarily invite one to a perception of the main story climaxed in Exodus 40. As we have seen, the elaboration of the tent scenes in Exod. 33.7-11, 34.34-35 and

argues that the frequentative forms of Exod. 33.7-11 are expressions for the ‘impermanence of the arrangement’ (p. 172). But in the case of Exod. 40.36-37 the corresponding imperfect forms can hardly refer to an impermanent arrangement.

6. Such an interest might even be reflected by ‘Horeb’ as the name of the divine mountain in Exod. 33.6. In a ‘Sinai’-context, the alternative name implicitly alludes to the connotational parallel ‘after Sinai’.

40.34-38 can be related to the development of the *visio* scenes of such a 'main story', delicately reflecting the gradual stages of the divine movement from mountain above to camp below, as well as the inclusion of the people as theophanic figures. But for a second reading of deeper pondering, the motif elaboration cannot but reflect deliberate effects of parallelism and juxtaposition.

With regard to traditio-historical categories, the parallelism of the two permanent tents in their contextual settings is easily explained as the expression of different editorial voices, the older traditions of chs. 32–34 being given a new function in a Priestly setting.[7] But while the different materials probably have a many-tongued past, the delicacy of the literary effects excludes the possibility that the present composition has such a crude process of compilation as its prime cause. The perception of a main story of which certain elements also function as parts of a parallel story could even convey the impression of different voices to some subtle connection of overtones and undertones.

A connection of this character is also indicated by the contrast effect of the two sets of imagery in Exod. 33.7-11, concluded by 34.34-35 and 40.35-36. The descriptions indicate a peculiar relationship of the one tent scene negatively mirrored by the other. The image of the Tent of Meeting set up by Moses 'by himself' outside the camp is elaborated by Moses inside the tent, the divine cloud standing outside. This imagery is reversed in the corresponding scene given over to the Tent of Meeting. Here the divine manifestation in the forms of cloud and glory is related to the tent as 'covering' and 'filling' the inside, while Moses is set on the outside and not able to enter (40.35). The effect of juxtaposition is increased by two sets of sub-figures which imply special connotational references. According to Exod. 33.11, Joshua is permanently related to the Tent of Meeting outside the camp. The significance of this relationship is stressed by the later stature of Joshua as Moses' successor (Num. 27.15-23). According to Exod. 40.32[8] the ritual entering of the Tent of Meeting following the rites of purification is performed by Moses together with Aaron and his sons. The people of the future are related to two sets of tents and two types of Moses substitutes.

The effect of juxtaposition is underlined by the two sets of theophanic figures. The human movement towards the encounter repre-

7. Cf. especially Kearney, 'Creation and Liturgy', pp. 383-84.

8. Formally, the infinitives of v. 32 correspond to the frequentative forms of vv. 36-38 and thus link the two scenes as expressions of the permanent situation.

sents a fixture of the theophanic situation. Given this background, the contrasting images of Moses' 'coming to the Tent of Meeting' in Exod. 33.8-9 and 'not coming to the Tent of Meeting' in 40.35 can hardly be coincidental. In the final scene, Moses is not able to enter the tent. By the subtle linkage between the singular event of theophanic manifestation in v. 34 and the frequentative forms in vv. 36-38, the two sets of human actors are juxtaposed in a contrasting relationship with the theophanic manifestation. Moses is excluded from the tent, while the people are related to the *visio Dei.* This contrasts with the imagery of Exod. 33.8-11. Here Moses is inside[9] the tent and the cloud outside, while the people are watching from afar. Moreover, the elaboration of the motifs of theophanic movement reflects the parallelism of the two scenes. In the former, Moses' 'coming' is related to the cloud descending. This corresponds to the motif elaboration of Exod. 40.35-38. The 'non-coming' of Moses in connection with the theophanic manifestation is continued by the imagery of the people's breaking camp or not breaking camp in accordance with the ascending or non-ascending of the cloud.

The effect of juxtaposition[10] is increased by the presentation of the people in Exod. 33.6, depicted in a permanent state of 'self-plundering of their ornaments after Horeb'. Related to the erection of the tent by Moses 'on his own', the negative participation—seen together with the sorrow motif of v. 4 which resonates with the 'fun' motifs of Exod. 32.6, 19, 25—contrasts with the role of the people as temple builders in Exodus 35–40.

In this way, we end up with two sets of images which are both presented as descriptions of the post-Sinai situation. The two sets of imagery represent contrasting situations, with Moses and people in reversed roles. The effect is underlined by the unexpectedness of this reversal. Hitherto, Moses has acted as the sublime human figure in the encounter episodes. The rearrangement of the basic roles in the final scene, the people set in the place of Moses as the new human heroes of

9. The 'inside' position is also implied in Exod. 34.34-35.

10. The absolute character of this mitigated by the parallelism of the divine and the people's standing at the tent door in Exod. 33.9-10, comparable to the scene of 40.36-38. The linear relationship of the tent scenes could also be reflected by the final scene of ch. 34 which implies that the divine presence is contained within Moses' tent.

the extraordinary theophanic relationship, represents a rather strange conclusion.

The unexpectedness of the final scene is underlined by the narrative development. It is difficult to reconcile a final scene of exclusion to the description of Moses in the building account of Exodus 35–40. Moreover, the lasting character of Moses as the extraordinary mediator is underlined by the continuation of the story in Lev. 1.1. Here he is depicted in his usual position of listening mediator, although probably outside the tent.[11] The reader is even expecting a concrete scene of Moses being admitted into the tent. According to Exod. 25.22 a special revelatory locus inside the tent is reserved for Moses.

That the final scene of Exod. 40.35-38 underlines certain aspects of the post-Sinai situation, at the cost of other aspects, can also be illustrated by Num. 9.15-23. Given the close relationship of this passage and Exod. 40.36-38, the former must have some bearing on the reading of the latter. The Numbers version repeats and greatly expands the *visio Dei* motifs, adding new details to the description of the people set in a direct relationship to the theophanic manifestation and the people's perfect observation of the divine will. Related to the position of Moses, the repeated application of the element *'al pî YHWH* in vv. 18a, 20b, 23a and 23b is especially important. In the final application, the element *b^eyad mōšeh* is added. Corresponding to Exod. 40.36-38, the description puts the emphasis on the people set in a theophanic relationship and perfectly obedient to the divine 'mouth'. But the final application, which relates the divine mouth to the 'hand of Moses', has repercussions for the formulaic language. The emphasis on the people as theophanic actors is balanced by the concluding reference to the preeminence of Moses. The mediation of Moses is also included in the new situation. The elaboration seems to strike a careful balance between the new situation of popular *visio* and a permanent hierarchical relationship of Moses set between God and people. In comparison, Exod. 40.36-38, given over to the people as the new theophanic actors in contrast to the excluded Moses, presents a rather one-sided version. Related both to the parallel conclusion of Num. 9.15-23 and to the narrative development of Exodus 19–40, the implications of a new and elevated position for the people in Exod. 40.35-38 must somehow include or presuppose some reference to the lasting significance of Moses.

11. Milgrom, *Leviticus 1–16*, p. 138.

The questions raised by the special character of the final scene accentuates the questions concerning the function of Exodus 32–34 within the composition. The referential effects point to the parallelism of the two tents. The first Tent of Meeting, related to Moses as the all-important figure, is presented as a permanent institution. This implies the co-existence of this tent and the grand Tent of Meeting, likewise a permanent post-Sinai institution but related to the people as the theophanic figures. The juxtaposition implies that Exodus 34 functions as a concluding episode, somehow parallel to the climax of Exodus 40.

2. *The Apotheosis of Moses*

The relationship of the two tent situations in Exodus 33–34 and 40 underlines the enigmatic character of Moses' position in the story of Exodus 19–40. Dismissed as the theophanic figure in ch. 40, Moses is the all-important figure in the earlier tent scenes. The latter aspect is greatly elaborated in chs. 32–34. As we have seen, the peculiar compilation of vv. 12-17 and 18-23 of ch. 33 reflects a special interest in the position of Moses. A scene of intercession is suddenly changed by the plea of Moses for a special *visio*. Connected with the invitation to an extraordinary ascent (Exod. 34.1-3), the change implies a peculiar role allocation. Hitherto, the *visio* theme has been reserved for the people, as well as the mortal implications of the improper relationship. The problematical character of the special ascent related to the people has been mitigated by the reinterpretation of the ascent in Exod. 32.34–33.5, which relates the theophanic movement of ascent to the idea of the people's journey with YHWH as co-ascender. According to Exod. 33.12-17, YHWH has condescended to accompany the people 'himself'. But with the problems of the people as ascenders happily solved, the following verses (vv. 18-23) suddenly reintroduce these problems in their original form. And now Moses represents the problematical theophanic figure.

The role transfer is strangely parallel to the concluding role allocation in ch. 40. Corresponding to the people set in the place of Moses as theophanic figures, the Moses of ch. 33 suddenly embodies the role of the problematical visionary set above his normal station. Somehow, the drama of Exodus 32–34 with Moses as central actor is parallel to the development of the people as narrative figures in Exodus 19–40.

On the other hand, the roles are not completely identical, but reflect the different stature of the actors. In Exodus 33, the role of Moses as the problematical visionary is connected with his function as mediator. Verses 18-23 conclude the intercession in vv. 12-17. And when the special encounter is actualized, it is exploited for a last urgent intercession (Exod. 34.8-9). Also, the issues discussed in vv. 18-23 indicate that this encounter vastly transcends the *visio* of the people. Related to the same categories of ascent, *visio* and mortal danger—and even reduced from the divine front to the divine back—the *visio* of Moses refers to experiences of a higher order. The parallelism and the differences seem to imply the mediator and the people in a parallel movement of upward mobility. The people are set in the position formerly held by Moses, while Moses is elevated one step further on some hierarchical ladder of extraordinary *visio*.

The special character of the elevation of Moses is underlined by the description of the last descent from the mountain in Exod. 34.29-35. The tablets are important for this scene. Introduced by the instructions in Exod. 34.1 and Moses' response in v. 4, and concluded by vv. 27-28, the last mountain episode is framed by the tablets as a central motif. This corresponds to the second theophanic episode which is also framed by references to the tablets (Exod. 24.12 and 31.18). The parallelism of the two episodes is reflected by the juxtaposition of the descent scenes. The tablets brought down from the mountain (34.29a) provide the positive contrast to the former descent of ch. 32, which was concluded with the tragic destruction of the tablets.[12]

The parallelism of the two scenes underlines their difference. The tablets are important as an indication that all has ended well, and the proper story can continue in Exodus 35. But even with such a central function in the final descent, the tablets are outshone by the miracle of Moses' face. The description of the former descent lingers on the wondrous character of the divine tablets, according to Exod. 32.15-16 which repeats and enlarges 31.18. Comparable effects of repetition are also used in ch. 34. But in this case the tablets are only referred to as the preliminary to the detailed description of the truly remarkable feature of the last descent (v. 29a). The repetitions in vv. 29, 30 and 35 linger on the impression of Moses' face. These effects are underlined by the detailed scenes in vv. 30-31 and 33-35.

The singular concentration upon the face of Moses is increased by the

12. Cf. especially Moberly, *At the Mountain of God*, p. 106, on the contrast of the two descents.

pānîm ('face') motifs of the context. Their application is comparable to the tablets as some narrative framework for this episode. The last mountain episode is introduced by the discussion on the divine face seen by Moses (33.18-23). This corresponds to the emphasis on the face of Moses seen by the people in the concluding scene (34.29-35). The parallelism seems to indicate a basic connection between the two types of seeing as well as the two 'faces'.[13] This is also indicated by the parallel 'cover' motifs in Exod. 33.22-23 and 34.33-35. Moses' face covered by the divine hand to be protected from the glory of the divine face corresponds to the veil covering Moses' face from the people. The parallelism between the two faces is also underlined by the categories of the concluding encounter scene. Differently from the tent scene of 33.7-11, YHWH is now implicitly related to the inside of the tent (34.34-35). In this situation, and in contrast to the earlier *visio* scenes related to the people, the face of Moses is the sole visible expression of the extraordinary experience.

The significance of this description can be reflected by the shift of the *visio* scene from the third to the second encounter in this episode. The basic pattern of two sub-episodes climaxed by the third theophanic episode is also reflected by the three encounters of Exod. 32.30–34.28. But while the *visio* scene is usually part of the climactic third set of events, in this application of the pattern set it is found in the second encounter (cf. Chapter 1.4 on 33.8-10). The discussion in 33.18-23, which points to the experience of *visio Dei* as the central issue also of the climactic third episode, even underlines that the traditional *visio* scene is 'missing' in the third episode. Conversely, the impression of something lacking is balanced by the detailed description of the people seeing the face of Moses. Added to by the parallel *pānîm* motifs of Exod. 33.18-23 and 34.29-35, the composition subtly indicates that the experience of Moses' face substitutes the traditional experience of *visio*. While the theophanic manifestation and the people's usual *visio* have been shifted to the second encounter of 33.8-10, the climactic third episode is concluded by a new form of extraordinary *visio* by the people.

Such a development is also reflected by the scene when the people meet the descending Moses. In vv. 30-32, the motifs of 'seeing' and 'fear' connected with distance and nearness describe the people's

13. Moberly, *At the Mountain of God*, p. 106; further Brichto, 'The Worship of the Golden Calf', pp. 42-44; Van Seters, *The Life of Moses*, p. 360; Blum, *Studien zur Komposition*, pp. 71-72.

reaction. This reflects a situation comparable to the people's reaction to the theophanic experience in Exod. 20.18-21.[14] The visual impression of the face of Moses has the same effect as the theophanic presence. Also, the separation of the people and a special group composed of Aaron and leaders in Exod. 34.31-32 is comparable to the situation of 24.9-11 as well as the confrontation in the camp related to Aaron (32.21-24) and the people (vv. 25-30). The references to the theophanic situation underline the motifs of 'nearness'. While the people in the second episode are 'seeing' from afar (33.7-11),[15] they are able to 'come near' in the final episode. And now, after the initial fear, the people can stand being 'talked to'.

The subtle elaboration of the established scenes indicates that in the story cycle of 32.30–34.35 too, the third episode represents a climax of 'theophanic' experience. The categories of *visio Dei* have been shifted from the traditional imagery of theophany to a transformed version with Moses as the embodiment of the divine presence.

It must be important for our perception of this rather radical development that it is not stated directly, but is implied by effects of ambiguous allusions. The significance of the special motifs are hinted at by the delicate elaboration of situations which refer to established scenes of the narrative pattern. Just as Moses is initially ignorant of his new stature, so the ambiguous description makes it difficult for the reader to be absolutely certain of what it is all about.

Above all, this is illustrated by the description of the divine light emanating from the face of Moses. The importance of this extraordinary manifestation is indicated by the stereotyped refrain in vv. 29, 30 and 35. But the 'horned' character of the divine light makes the reader's visualization of the scene rather uncertain. Scholarly discussion of the imagery tends to be polarized into seeing a reference to *either* 'horns' *or* 'light', with the latter usually being preferred in contrast to the older speculations on the implications of a 'horned' Moses.[16] But while 'light' certainly seems basic for the imagery of ch. 34 and also can be attested

14. Childs, *Book of Exodus*, p. 618.

15. Cf. also Exod. 20.18-21 and 24.1-2.

16. M. Haran, 'The Shining of Moses' Face: A Case Study in Biblical and Ancient Near Eastern Iconography', in W. Boyd Barrick and John R. Spencer (eds.), *In the Shelter of Elyon: Essays on Ancient Palestinian Life and Literature in Honor of G.W. Ahlström* (JSOTSup, 31; Sheffield: JSOT Press, 1984), pp. 159-73; Van Seters, *The Life of Moses*, pp. 359-60.

by the use of the noun in Hab. 3.4, for example, the linguistic material makes 'horn' rather unavoidable as the prime connotation.

The description seems to comprise both aspects. The splendour of the divine light emanating from the face of Moses is combined with the character of his skin as somehow 'horned'. The latter aspect is underlined by the context. Given the words accessible to the author for the description of light-phenomena, the choice of the unusual *qrn* for a verb can hardly be understood as anything but a deliberate allusion to the other horned being of the context, namely the Golden Calf.[17] Just as an ox conceptually represents an ancient Near Eastern stereotype of a divine being, so any suggestions of horns somehow related to a human figure would refer to iconographical categories. The 'horned' character of the shining skin could simply serve as an indication of the divine character of Moses' presence.[18] Whatever metaphysical questions are involved, the imagery of 'horned light', related to the interplay of divine and human *pānîm* and set in the context of the Golden Calf, invites the reader to a rather radical understanding of Moses as a divine figure. Emanating 'horned light', his bodily manifestations have been completely and permanently changed, forever distancing Moses from normal humankind.

The connection between the Golden Calf and Moses[19] is also

17. Above all Moberly, *At the Mountain of God*, pp. 108-109, but also reflected in a traditio-historical version by Coats, *Moses*, pp. 173-75. According to the latter, the story reflects an original northern tradition, in which the calf was a positive symbol of Moses.

18. More cautiously Moberly, *At the Mountain of God*, p. 109. The ambiguity makes 'the point that Moses was to the people what they wanted the calf to be', stressing Moses as leader and mediator and the calf as a gross parody. For Van Seters (*The Life of Moses*, pp. 359-60), the impression of Moses as 'bearer of divine majesty' is transcribed into the divine presence 'symbolized and attested by the shining face'; while Blum (*Studien zur Komposition*, p. 72) refers to 'dieser Abglanz der Gottesgegenwart' ('a reflection of divine presence'). For Brichto ('The Worship of the Golden Calf', p. 44), the imagery suggests some connection with the divine image concepts of Gen. 1.

19. Cf. Chapter 1.4 on the juxtaposition of the Golden Calf as the alternative locus related to the two versions of the Tent of Meeting. The elaboration of ox and Moses as alternative 'containers' of divine presence adds to the locus theme. The confluence of the two sets of motifs is primarily expressed by the final tent scene in Exod. 34.34-35. The tent is only alluded to, the emphasis of the scene having been shifted to the interaction of Moses and people. Basically, the tent retains its significance as the container of the divine presence, but is now related to Moses who

intimated from the very beginning of the story. According to Exod. 32.1, the 'gods who can go in front of us' clearly are meant as substitutes for the absent Moses.[20] This connection is underlined by the parallelism of the formulaic 'who made us ascend from the land of Egypt' related to Moses (v. 1), and 'who made you ascend from the land of Egypt' related to the calf (vv. 4, 23). The parallelism is even repeated by YHWH in vv. 7-8. The final scene in Exodus 34 represents a comparable combination of divine qualities related to the person of Moses. The imagery of Moses substituted by the 'gods' in the shape of an ox is reversed by the imagery of divine presence 'horned' from the skin of Moses.

The connection between Moses and the ox is also reflected by the application of the tablet motifs. In Exod. 32.19-20 the destruction of tablets and ox are connected in one scene given over to the violent anger of Moses. Parallel to the connection of tablets and ox in this scene, the tablets in 34.39 are set together with Moses' 'horned' face. The connection is underlined by the function of Moses as the divine scribe according to vv. 27-28.[21] The motif structure of Moses as the divine scribe, followed by his carrying the tablets and the motifs of the horned skin, is comparable to the introduction of the story. The making of the Golden Calf in 32.1-6 is juxtaposed to the scene of divine writing

enters and leaves. With regard to the people, the divine presence is emanated by the face of Moses. A similar confluence of motifs and change of emphasis is reflected by the final tent scene in Exod. 40. Also here, the tent is the locus of the divine presence. The scene is similarly expanded by the interest in the human actors. Moses is unable to enter, while the divine manifestation over the tent is related to the journey of the people.

20. Moberly, *At the Mountain of God*, p. 46.

21. The reading of vv. 27-28 has been greatly complicated by the traditional, but questionable, assertion that 'he' of v. 28b does not refer to the 'he' of the preceding half-verse and to the divine command of v. 27, but to a divine subject; e.g. Childs, *Book of Exodus*, p. 616; Moberly, *At the Mountain of God*, pp. 101-105; Durham, *Exodus*, pp. 462-63; Van Seters, *The Life of Moses*, p. 327. For any normal reading, the relationship of vv. 27-28 presents Moses as the writer, implementing the divine command. This also corresponds to the special preparation of the second set of tablets. According to vv. 1 and 4, it is prepared by Moses, while the first set seems wholly produced by divine hands (24.12; 31.18). The ambiguity of Mosaic writing, caused by the relationship to the divine promise of v. 1b, corresponds to the character of these scenes, deliberately blurring the traditional separation of the divine and the human.

in 31.18. The much-discussed 'stylus' of Aaron (32.4), rather unsuitable for metal work, but well applied for perverted 'writing', could reflect the basic connection between tablets and calf.

However ambiguous the meaning, the subtleties of the composition point to the parallelism of Moses and calf and thus to the significance of Moses as a divine representation in the final scene. While the effects of parallelism seem to add one set of ambiguities to another, the very imagery of the Golden Calf as a locus of divine presence underlines the implications of Moses as a bodily container 'horned' by the divine light.

The radical character of this presentation corresponds to the description of Moses in the context. Compared to his role established in the preceding stories, Moses is peculiarly active in Exodus 32–34. Interceding on behalf of the people, he opposes and changes the divine will. The presentation of Moses as active is consistent with the story as a whole. He crushes not only the calf but also the divine tablets. He orders the terrible killing of sons and brothers. He puts up the tent on his own initiative. Compared with the other stories of encounter, the presentation of the successive acts in 33.8-9 even indicates that the encounter is initiated by the human actor departing the camp, and responded to by the divine descent. Moses is the one who initiates the dialogue in all the three encounters, and even dares to ask for a vision of the divine face.

With regard to the character of these scenes established in the preceding stories, Moses not only functions as the all-important human actor, but also usurps aspects of the divine role. The consistency of this description reflects the special character of these events. Comparable to the people usurping the divine role in the initial event of the Golden Calf incident, the aftermath of this incident is centred around Moses as active in situations where human passivity would seem the appropriate position. He is even related to the production of the new set of tablets, now however—and this must reflect the significance of these acts—divinely ordered both to prepare them (34.1) and even to perform the act of writing earlier related to the divine writer (vv. 27-28).

Some strange interest in blurring the separation between the divine and the human seems to be intimated by the very start of the story. The absent Moses is to be substituted by 'gods'. The parallelism is underlined by the formulaic reference to Moses and 'gods' as the authors of the Exodus from Egypt (vv. 1, 4, 7-8, 23). In addition, the application of the formula in 32.11 attributes the Exodus to YHWH, in 33.1 to Moses. The special definition of the Golden Calf, on the one hand made as a substitute for Moses, on the other hand identified with the divine guidance from Egypt, corresponds to the double authorship of the ascent from Egypt. From the very start of the story, the reader is confronted by the enigmatic character of Moses' position. The rest of the story, dedicated to the consistently active Moses who usurps aspects of the divine role, adds to this impression.

Conversely, Moses' plea for a special vision and the divine deliberations on the limits of human tolerance (33.18-23) mark the return to the traditional relationship of divine and human. The impression of Moses as the problematical visionary, striving to be set above his proper station, seems to reverse the image of Moses in the context. But while Moses is cut down to human size in this scene, it prepares for the concluding scene which invests him with the 'horned light'.

The development of Moses as a divine representation, climaxed by the descent scene in Exodus 34, can also be related to the following story. The exhuberant response by the people to Moses' mediation in Exodus 35–39 represents the natural continuation of the scene in 34.31-35. More directly, the blessing scene in 39.42-43 implies a comparable role transfer. The subtle reference to the creation story concluded by the divine blessing connects the tent production with the events of creation. The parallelism with the creator's inspection and blessing implies Moses' enacting a divine role. The application of the formulaic language combined with the allusive vagueness of what it really says, attests to its significance. The effect of some deliberate ambiguity also corresponds to the presentation of Moses' apotheosis in Exodus 34.

For all its delicacy, the development of Exodus 32–34 represents an astounding conclusion. The people's wish for a divine representation, concretely and visually present in the world below, has been actualized by Moses. The chiastic relationship of the two representations of divine being, the ox as the divine substitute for Moses juxtaposed to Moses as the human container 'horned' by the divine light, points to the significance of the events.

The riddle of what this might imply is deepend by the comparable categories of divine substitution in Exod. 32.33–33.5, concluded in the intercession scenes of 33.12-17 and 34.9. After the people have made the calf, YHWH himself will not ascend 'in the people's midst', but will instead send his 'messenger' to go in front of the people.

Accordingly, the people's wish for 'gods' as substitutes for Moses, which also implies the substitution of YHWH, has resulted in a divine representative sent to substitute YHWH. Comparable to YHWH as co-ascender, the divine representative is connected with Moses as the leader of the people's march, going 'in front of' him (32.34) and 'together with' him (33.12). And finally, when the plea of Moses for the presence of the divine 'self' has been accepted, the 'horned light' of Moses represents the visual expression of the divine presence in the people's midst. To this series of substitutes can also be added the divine representations of 'face' versus 'backside' in 33.18-23. While the divine 'face' and 'glory' are too much for a mortal man, Moses can be exposed to a *visio* of the divine backside, the impression of which makes his own face shining unbearably for normal people.

Rather enigmatically, this series of substitutes at the very least illustrates the heights and depths of the ontological references of the language in these stories. Their reach certainly seems wide enough also to encompass the elevation of Moses as a divine representation. This can be compared to the series of divine representations in 1 Kings 19, the 'messenger' followed by the 'word of YHWH', and ultimately 'YHWH' himself with the non-YHWH companions of 'wind', 'trembling' and 'fire'. In this story, the succession of divine figures seems to mark the progress of the prophet's movement towards a climax of theophanic experience. Exodus 32–34 seems to refer to a corresponding perception of divine reality. 'God' is composed of many levels of divine representation. The levels reflect the differentiation of divine being by a scale of relative presence. The stiff-necked people can co-exist with the messenger, but not with YHWH himself. Moses can see the divine back, but not the front. YHWH as 'face' and 'glory' represents the highest representation of the divine reality. But also the other representations 'lower' on the scale manifest the divine reality. While second-best, the experience of the divine back is strong enough to change the bodily essence of Moses forever.

The elevation of Moses implies that also the level of being represented by the human actors is—actually or potentially—part of this scale of divine being. Thus, the differentiation of the divine reality corresponds to the elaboration of Moses and people as narrative figures. Both human, they are presented as parallel figures of upwards mobility on some scale of being.

This also implies that the ontological references are important for the story of Exodus 19–40 as a whole. A corresponding perception is reflected by the compositional structure of theophanic episodes, which separate the 'ordinary' encounter on the mountain and the grand theophanic episode including the experience of *visio Dei.* Above all, these aspects must be vital for the development of the locus theme. The divine movement from the sacred mountain to the human-made tent is an expression of this perception of divine being. The permanent theophanic manifestation over the tent in Exodus 40, as well as the new theophanic mode of a signalling device, reflects the differentiation of 'God' within the story. This corresponds to the narrative development of Moses and the people. At first sharply separated as embodiments of different roles in the encounter episode, the story ends with the people elevated into the role of Moses. The differentiation of divine being corresponds to a similar differentiation of human being. In both cases, the original position can be changed. The elevation of the people in Exodus 40 and the apotheosis of Moses in Exodus 34 represent parallel expressions of such a change.

On the other hand, the perception of potential changes within the scale of divine-human being retains aspects of relativity. This is firmly established by the dialogue of Exod. 33.18–34.3. However exalted the position of Moses, the new relationship between divine and human is the result of an extraordinary divine presence humbly seen from behind. Correspondingly, the final scene of 34.34-35 reflects the established alignment of divine and human. This is continued by the mediation scene of Exodus 35. As before, Moses mediates the divine instructions, and the perfect character of the people's response is expressed by the formula of compliance (e.g. 39.42-43). The perfect compliance of Moses is expressed in the same way (40.16-32). However changed the divine and human actors, the relationship of 'man' related to 'God' is fundamentally the same.

This is also reflected by the hierarchical relationship of Moses and people. The final scene in 40.35-38 excludes Moses from the tent, while the people enact the role of theophanic actor. But the continuation of the scene in Lev. 1.1 returns to the established roles. As before, Moses receives the divine instructions and mediates them to the people.

These aspects reflect the connection between the events of Exodus 32–34 and the rest of the story. Both the conceptual development as well as the narrative movement of successive scenes indicate the basic function of Exodus 32–34 as part of chs. 19–40. On the other hand, they also accentuate the questions of contextual function. The apotheosis of Moses adds to the impression of Exodus 34 as a conclusion somehow parallel and juxtaposed to the conclusion of Exodus 40. As we have seen, the story of chs. 35–40 implies a situation of profound 'democratization'. In contrast, the scenes of ch. 34 indicate an extremely opposite situation of sublimely elite character, likewise presented as permanent. The divine presence hidden within the tent, the people 'after Horeb' are related to a permanent *visio* of Moses' face, intolerably bright.

The contrasts seem to reflect some subtle relationship between two story lines. While chs. 19–40 represent the main story, the apotheosis of Moses indicates that important aspects of this story can be discerned when chs. 19–34 are read as a parallel account which presents an alternative version of Sinai events. The Golden Calf serves as some focal point for the two story lines. As the locus in the story of perverted production, the Golden Calf contrasts with the Tent of Meeting, which is the result of a story of perfect materialization. As the perverted Moses substitute, the Golden Calf contrasts with Moses as the 'horned' container of divine presence. The two tent scenes of Exod. 33.1-11 and 34.34-35 are important for the development of both story lines. A contracted version of the building account, 33.1-11 primarily reflects the connection between the Golden Calf and the grand Tent of Meeting. While alluding to the first tent scene, 34.34-35 is centred around the presentation of Moses as the divine representation. Essential to both story lines, the relationship of the two tent scenes indicates the delicate weaving together of the two strands.

3. *The Hero Dismissed and Exalted—The Parallels of David and Elijah*

Confronting the possibility of a story line that on the one hand is concluded in Exodus 34, and on the other hand is part of the more comprehensive story represented by Exodus 19–40, the reader seeks some assurance that such an organization of narrative materials really is feasible. The effects of juxtaposition, the 'democratization' of ch. 40 opposed to the hierarchical categories of ch. 34, imply a strange combination of what a modern reader would perceive as contradictions. The development of David as active in the building story of 1 Chronicles 28–29 could represent a comparable combination of seemingly different interests. As we have seen, the relationship of David and Solomon is comparable to the relationship of Moses and the people in Exodus 40. Parallel to Moses substituted by the people as the theophanic figures, the old king is substituted by Solomon, both with regard to the royal succession[22] and to the temple building. The latter aspect is underlined by the divine refusal to accept David as temple builder. David wished to build the temple, but is refused due to his bloody hands. Instead, Solomon is designated as the temple builder (1 Chron. 22.7-13 and 28.2-3). The significance of the Chronicles description is underlined by the relationship to 1 Kgs 5.17-19. The elaboration of the divine refusal attributed to the bloody hands of David must express a special concern.[23]

But the emphasis on the spurned king is combined with a description of David as most active participant in the preparations. He mediates the sacred form of the building which 'had happened in the spirit with him' (1 Chron. 28.12), everything written down 'by the hand of YHWH' (v. 19). This corresponds to the description of Moses as the builder of the sanctuary. Moreover, the description of David as the visionary temple builder is added to by 1 Chron. 29.1-19. David dedicates his own gifts to the sacred task and further challenges the nobles to make their contribution. This combines the roles of Moses and the people in Exodus 35–36. Certain aspects indicate the parallelism of the roles of David and people (cf. Chapter 2.3). But the elaboration of David in 1 Chronicles is also relevant for the development of the Moses figure.[24]

As the rejected builder and the divinely illuminated initiator of the sacred efforts, the David figure of 1 Chronicles represents a peculiar collusion of roles. The combination of contradictions is comparable to

22. For the theme of substitution in these chapters cf. also McCarthy ('An Installation Genre', pp. 36-38), and Braun ('Solomon, the Chosen Temple Builder', pp. 586-88), who point to the parallelism of David/Solomon and Moses/Joshua in 1 Chron. 22 and 28.

23. Braun, 'Solomon, the Chosen Temple Builder', pp. 582-86. According to Hurowitz (*I Have Built You*, pp. 164-67), the divine refusal to approve a building project is a traditional Mesopotamian motif. The parallels underline the significance of the David tradition which combines the motif of refusal and the positive portrayal of the king (p. 165).

24. The relevance of the David figure for both sets of human actors in the Sinai stories underlines the parallelism of Moses and people as narrative figures. This is also illustrated by the Elijah figure in 1 Kgs 19. As the lone human actor, Elijah combines the roles of the negative people and the 'positive' mediator in the Sinai stories.

the contrasts of Moses apotheosized and Moses substituted according to Exodus 34 and 40. The significance of this comparison for the Sinai story is underlined by the relationship between the two building accounts of 1 Kings and 1 Chronicles. The latter represents a reworking of the older traditions and thus must reflect a special interest. The character of the new portrayal is comparable to the elaborate contrasting effects of Exodus 34 and 40. For both biographies, the combination of certain contradictions must be important.

But while David related to Solomon and Moses related to the people represent a comparable collusion of contradictions, the elaboration of this collusion differs. Juxtaposed to each other, Exodus 34 and 40 seem shaped to convey an effect of contrasts. In comparison, the relationship of David the rejected and David the idealized builder is presented as unproblematical. Set in the imagery of the father preparing the way for the son, the rejected builder adresses the people on his son's behalf and even admonishes his substitute (28.9-10, 20). The smooth relationship of the two builders corresponds to the relationship of Moses and people according to the building story of Exodus 35–40. Here the efforts of the people are concluded by the inspection and blessing scene in 39.32-43 and perfected by the tremendous effort of Moses setting the stage for the climax. Comparable to David preparing the way for his son, Moses makes possible his substitution by a new set of theophanic actors. But in addition to the paternalistic idyll represented by the two sets of temple builders in these scenes, the juxtaposition of Exodus 34 and 40 seems to elaborate the implications of the events. The contrasts of Moses elevated and excluded underline the two aspects of David as the rejected and idealized temple builder.

The Elijah stories also represent a collusion of contrasts that are comparable to the two sets of imagery in Exodus. The two Elijahs of 1 Kings 18 and 19 represent a peculiarly sharp contrast of human modes.[25] The impressions of strength and confidence juxtaposed to despair and dejection are so marked that they seem to beg for some authoritative traditio- and redactio-historical clearance work, just as in the case of the Exodus texts.[26] According to 1 Kgs 19.1, the two moun-

25. Von Nordheim, 'Ein Prophet kündigt', pp. 153-73; Hauser, 'Yahweh versus Death', pp. 62-63; and Gregory, 'Irony and the Unmasking of Elijah', in Gregory and Hauser, *From Carmel to Horeb*, pp. 91-169 (111-13).

26. E.g. Odil Hannes Steck, *Überlieferung und Zeitgeschichte in den Elia-*

tain episodes are set together in a linear relationship, the events of 1 Kings 18 leading to the next series of events. But in their present combination, the two chapters seem to reflect primarily an effect of juxtaposition. This is also indicated by the parallel mountain setting comparable to the locus theme of the Sinai stories. The Elijah of the mountain of Carmel is juxtaposed to the Elijah of Horeb. The contrasting scenes of victory and of defeat—the first with Ahab as royal protagonist, the second with Jezebel—represent a rather illogical series of events. The actor is totally unable to transfer the exhuberant experience of the divine power in the first episode to the crisis of the second. The parallelism of the two chapters indicates that the description of the prophet in two diametrically opposed modes represents a deliberate effect of contradiction, comparable to the juxtaposition of Exodus 34 and 40.

The collusion of apparent contradictions is continued in the description of the mountain episode in 1 Kings 19, and now with a more direct thematic connection with the Sinai stories. On the one hand, the encounter in vv. 11-13 clearly presents a most extraordinary situation. The delicate elaboration of the scene leaves the impression of unique events related to a hero of special stature, comparable both to the extraordinary *visio Dei* in Exod. 33.18–34.28 and to David as divinely instructed according to 1 Chronicles 28. Also in the case of 1 Kings 19, the impression of human elevation is marred by contradictory effects. According to the dialogue in vv. 13b-18, the role of the prophet in this extraordinary situation—his part so far movingly concluded in v. 13a—consists in bitter complaint (v. 14), which moreover repeats v. 10. The repeated complaint in its turn underlines that the story of the extraordinary encounter is introduced by scenes that present the prophet in a mood of dejection and utter despair.

The divine message in vv. 15-18 responds to Elijah's mood. 'Instead of you' Elisha shall be sanctified as prophet (v. 16). A corresponding event of implementation takes place immediately after the encounter (vv. 19-21). Descending from the mountain, Elijah meets Elisha and throws his mantle over him.

Whatever the 'original' relationship of the two scenes in 1 Kings 19,[27] the present organization of the materials represents an event

Erzählungen (WMANT, 26; Neukirchen–Vluyn: Neukirchener Verlag, 1968); DeVries, *1 Kings*, pp. 206-10.

27. Also in this case, the present relationship of the two scenes is usually under-

structure which corresponds to the encounter episodes of Exodus 19–40. The encounter on the mountain is followed by a scene below in which the divine words are implemented. Moreover, in both cases, the implementation of the instructions results in the hero being substituted by a new actor. What is presented as a single episode in 1 Kings 19 is elaborated in Exodus 19–40 through a number of successive episodes which climax in ch. 40. But the result is the same. A new hero takes the place of the old. Elijah is succeeded by a prophet 'instead of you'. Moses is excluded from the tent, while the theophanic manifestation is related to the people as the new human actors.

Underlined by the differences of plot and scenography, the parallelism of the two stories must be important. They seem to have in common some basic event-structure related to the categories of encounter. The situation of encounter also includes a common theme of 'the substitution of the hero'. This connection is also reflected by the first mountain episode of the Moses biography (Exodus 3–4). In this case, the theme of substitution is introduced by the human hero himself. Moses, declining to be elevated, begs for a substitute (4.13). This request is granted in a special way by an angry YHWH. Moses is not excused, but will be supplemented by Aaron as his 'mouth' (vv. 14-16). That this represents a singular version of a more traditional form of substitution is indicated by the following scene of meeting in Exod. 4.27-28. Comparable to the meeting of the old and the new prophet immediately after the mountain scene in 1 Kgs 19.19-21, the meeting of Moses and Aaron is also related to the divine mountain. In this case the dependence on some given event structure is illustrated by the intermittent scenes in Exod. 4.18-26, which separate the mountain episode and the meeting of the brothers. The forced character of the local setting, according to the present organization of the materials, seems to presuppose that the meeting of the hero and his substitute needs must be related to the sacred locus of encounter.

Compared to the symbiotic relationship of the hero and his 'mouth' in Exodus 4, the 1 Kings 19 story both presents the theme of substitution in a literal sense and provides a narrative context fitting a situation of dramatic character. Consistent with Elisha as the substitute prophet 'in your place', the old prophet is presented in a negative mode. The portrayal of a prophet giving himself up to utter despair is vividly

stood to reflect an editorial combination of different traditions; DeVries, *1 Kings*, pp. 238-39.

detailed by the absurdity of the scene vv. 5-7. The despondent prophet is visited by a heavenly representative in his sleep. Awakened in such an extraordinary way, the prophet accepts the angel's gift as a matter of course and promptly returns to sleep (vv. 5-6).[28] The following journey of 40 days might indicate the prophet in a more positive state, fitting a situation of extraordinary pilgrimage.[29] But the complaints of vv. 10 and 14 suggest that the initial despair is retained for the rest of the story.[30] Related to such a negative hero, the substitution by a new prophet seems to imply aspects of dismissal.[31]

In this way, the story of 1 Kings 19 adds to the contrast of chs. 18 and 19 by a remarkable combination of the prophet extraordinarily elevated in a situation of encounter with the idea of the prophet as the negative hero substituted by a new actor. The Elijah story also presents a new version of substitution and elevation, related to the same actors, in 2 Kgs 2.1-15. A double share of Elijah's spirit is transferred to Elisha as his rightful heir (vv. 9-10, 15).[32] In this case, the substitution is

28. Hauser, 'Yahweh versus Death', p. 65.

29. Hauser, 'Yahweh versus Death', p. 66; Gregory, 'Irony and the Unmasking', pp. 114-15.

30. These effects are underlined by Moses as the peculiarly negative hero in Exod. 3.11–4.13. Elements of refusal are traditional for the vocation story; cf. Coats, *Moses*, pp. 57-58. But in this case, the elaboration of these elements has clearly superseded the confinements of such a tradition and become an expression of a special interest comparable to the negative image of Elijah, especially when resulting in a divine reaction of anger (Exod. 4.14). This is illustrated by the efforts of Childs (*Book of Exodus*, p. 54) to maintain the traditional understanding of the vocation story. Exod. 3.1-12 is seen as 'the basic call narrative'. The repeated objections allow a variety of divergent traditions to be incorporated within the narrative framework, reflecting widely differing concerns related to the gradual development of the tradition over a considerable length of time. In its final shape, the second major portion of the call narrative represents a 'portrayal of resistance' (*Exodus*, p. 73). The parallelism with 1 Kgs 19 indicates that it is not necessary to submit this final shape to any traditio-historical process of repeated addings. The presentation of the hero as negative—connected with ideas of substitution—reflects elements of a given set of literary topics.

31. Von Nordheim, 'Ein Prophet kündigt', p. 167; Hauser, 'Yahweh versus Death', pp. 77-79; Gregory, 'Irony and the Unmasking', p. 117.

32. Mordechai Cogan and Hayim Tadmor, *II Kings: A New Translation with Introduction and Commentary* (AB, 11; Garden City, New York: Doubleday, 1988), p. 32.

directly related to the elevation of the old prophet. When Elisha is able to 'see' Elijah's ascent to heaven (vv. 10 and 12), the prophet's spirit is transferred. For the connection to the Moses story, it must be important that the very idea of a heavenly ascent represents a unique expression of the elevation of a human being, comparable to the apotheosis of Moses according to Exodus 34.

The significance of the motifs that present the transformation of the hero into a new and superior state of being is increased by comparable aspects in the encounter episode of Exodus 3–4. The story presents Moses as elevated to a singular role. But in addition, the relationship of Moses and his substitute is qualified by a rather special terminology. When extended by Aaron as his 'mouth', Moses will be 'God for' him (4.16). The Chronicler's image of David as the divinely illuminated visionary, combined with his bloody hands and the idea of substitution, represents a third and special version of a comparable combination of aspects.

The connection between these stories is also reflected by the continued function of the substituted hero. Moses talks through Aaron as his 'mouth'. The encounter episode of Exod. 40.34-38 presents the people as the new theophanic figures, but is continued in Lev. 1.1 by Moses in his normal function as the mediator. In the same way, Elijah is presented as active in the chapters after 1 Kings 19, while the stories centred around Elisha begin after 2 Kings 2.[33]

The stories seem to reflect a common dependency on certain basic themes.[34] The contrasts of the hero substituted/dismissed and translated are remarkably parallel to the contrasting imagery of Exodus 34 and 40, the former centred around the elevation of Moses, the latter around his substitution by the people. 1 Kings 19 and 2 Kings 2 compare particularly to the two separate Sinai scenes. The aspects of the prophet as the negative and substituted hero dominate the narrative development in 1 Kings 19, while the significance of the prophet's elevation in 2 Kings 2 is underlined by the unique character of the heavenly ascent. But both stories reflect the combination of the prophet as exalted and substituted.

33. Cf. also David, the rejected builder, making the most elaborate preparations for the building according to 1 Chron. 28–29.

34. Cf. also von Nordheim ('Ein Prophet kündigt', pp. 169-70), relating the despair of Elijah in 1 Kgs 19 to Jeremiah's confessions and the Jonah biography, both seen as typical for the perception of the prophetic function.

In 1 Kings 19 this is connected with the negativity of the prophet, in 2 Kings 2 with his impending death.[35]

While the relationship of Exodus 34 and 40 as parallel conclusions remains a riddle, the Elijah stories together with the Moses/Aaron relationship of Exodus 3–4 and the David/Solomon relationship of 1 Chronicles 28–29 at the very least underline the indications that the two tent scenes are related to each other in a special way. The two scenes represent individual versions of a narrative tradition based on the themes of the hero as substituted and exalted. Formally, the connection between the themes as aspects of a comprehensive set of events has been dissolved. The aspects are elaborated in separate scenes that are not directly related. In Exodus 40 the encounter situation is connected with a theme of substitution. Moses excluded and the people enacting the human role in the encounter reflects the role of the original hero substituted by new actors. In contrast, Exodus 34 is centred around the hero translated to some special stature. But while formally separated into independent scenes, the basic connection of the two aspects is retained by the allusive effects of parallelism and juxtaposition.

The portrayal of the hero in the negative mode, comparable to Elijah in 1 Kings 19 or David with the bloody hands, is in Exodus 19–40 mainly reserved for the people as the improbable theophanic actors. Related to the Moses biography as a whole, this aspect is above all[36] central for the first mountain episode in Exodus 3–4. But also the image of Moses in Exod. 33.18-23, asking for and being refused a position above his station, could be related to this aspect.

The categories of the Elijah stories and also Exodus 3–4[37] might point to a prophetic setting for the narrative tradition. But when similar contrasts are elaborated for the relationship of David/Solomon in

35. Both aspects are relevant to the other applications of the theme of substitution in the Moses biography. The transference of the prophet's spirit in 2 Kgs 2 is comparable to the transference of the Moses 'spirit' to the elders according to Num. 11.16-17, 24-30, and of the Moses 'majesty' to Joshua according to Num. 27.12-23. In the latter, the substitution is related to the death of Moses. In the story of Num. 11 this theme is emphatically combined with the hero in a negative mode. Moses' complaining, with a death wish included (vv. 10-15, 21-22) is comparable to the Elijah of 1 Kgs 19. In Exod. 18, the substitution is also connected with a negative scene, but in this case perceived as such by Jethro (vv. 13-14, 17-18).

36. Cf. below on Num. 11.

37. Cf. also the references to the Jeremiah and Jonah biographies by von Nordheim, 'Ein Prophet kündigt', pp. 169-70.

1 Chronicles and Moses/the people in the Sinai stories, it seems more natural to refer to some general hagiographic tradition, of which the common elements represent nucleus topics. Their application within stories so highly singular with regard to plot and actors and scenery demonstrates the malleability and flexibility of this tradition for literary elaboration.

The special character of this hagiographic tradition is also illustrated by the traditional scholarly reading, which in each case has separated the present combination of themes. Based on source-, traditio-, or redactio-critical criteria, each story has undergone the same scholarly treatment. Be it the negativity of Moses and the Aaron motifs in Exodus 3–4, or the tent scenes of chs. 32–34 related to ch. 40, or the collusion of motifs in the Elijah/Elisha stories, or the presentation of David in 1 Chronicles—all these stories are related to ideas of a special literary process. In each case, their present character is seen to be the result of the growth of tradition, where the concerns of later generations have constantly added to, and changed, some core nucleus of tradition. Indeed, the portrayals of David as non-builder in 1 Chronicles and 1 Kings demonstrate the relevance of such assumptions. The relationship of 1 Kings and 1 Chronicles must reflect literary processes that can be transcribed by the categories of 'older' and 'later', related to 'original' materials that have been both added to and changed by later readers/authors. Such a relationship provides a concrete illustration of literary processes that could be as relevant for the other texts. But the relationship of these stories above all indicates the significance of a common pattern, the subtleties of which transcend the traditional methodological categories. This is also underlined by the literary level of the stories which refer to the themes of the hero dismissed and exalted. The singular elaboration of the themes reflects a highly creative process of individual shaping. This is increased by the stature of the figures which are described by the themes of the hagiographic pattern.

4. *Conclusions*

The comparison to the Elijah story and the David story of 1 Chronicles underlines the complex function of Exodus 34. For the hagiographic pattern, the connection between the two aspects of substitution and elevation is important. This corresponds to the function of Exodus 34 as part of the linear development of the main story. As we have seen, the setting of Exodus 32–34 in chs. 19–40 as a whole represents the main indication of its function. Such a function, which implies a basic connection between the scenes, corresponds to the conceptual connection between the aspects of elevation and substitution in the hagiographic pattern. This function is concretely illustrated by the transition from Exodus 34 to 35. The mountain episode followed by scenes of mediation and implementation, the latter concluded in Exodus 40, corresponds to the event structure of 1 Kings 19. While certain events are greatly enlarged in the Sinai story, the imagery of the hero descending from the extraordinary encounter on the mountain to meet a new set of actors designated to take the hero's place is common to the two texts.

The connection of the episodes in Exodus 34 and 40 is also indicated by the parallel aspects of 'upward mobility' for Moses and people. The people as theophanic actors represent the core theme for Exodus 19–40. As we have seen, chs. 33–34 introduce a parallel development of this theme with Moses as the problematical theophanic figure. The parallelism of the people—set in the place of Moses—and Moses—elevated to a new rung of some hierarchical ladder of extraordinary being—is comparable to 2 Kings 5. The combination of the two aspects, on one hand Elijah's spirit transferred to Elisha, on the other Elijah bodily translated into heaven, corresponds to the new stature of the actors according to Exodus 34 and 40.

On the other hand, 1 Kings 19 and 2 Kings 5 underline that the common aspects of elevation and substitution have been elaborated into separate scenes in the Sinai stories. The formal separation of the two scenes is underlined by what seems to represent deliberate effects of juxtaposition. The negative mirror effect of the tent scenes in Exod. 34.29-35 and 33.7-11 compared to 40.34-38 is underlined by the frequentative forms of these descriptions. The post-Sinai situation of Exod. 40.36-38 is juxtaposed to the equally permanent post-Horeb situation of 33.6-11 and 34.34-35. In this way, the 'main story' represented by the linear development of Exodus 19–40 seems to have a parallel story, concluded in ch. 34, as its shadow. Moses excluded from the Tent of Meeting and substituted by the people, and Moses emerging from the Tent of Meeting as bearer of the divine light, represent contrasting descriptions of the post-Sinai reality.

The ambiguities of description seen together with the singular character of the motif development in Exod. 34.29-35 and 40.34-38 do not permit any easy transcription of the theological concerns given such a shape. On the contrary, the deliberate effects of ambiguity seem tailored to avoid any reader's claims of the perfect understanding. The elusive character of the motif elaboration invites one primarily to a process of questioning and pondering, while a process of conceptual analysis aiming at fixed theological positions seems doomed to lose its way among the subtle echoes of the referential effects. Related to conventional categories of consistency and logical development, the two conclusions in Exodus 34 and 40 seem rather defective. Above all, they seem to reverberate with an effect comparable to the poetic *parallelismus membrorum.* However mysteriously, Moses the man and the people's Tent of Meeting are presented as parallel vehicles of the divine presence for the post-Sinai people.

The mountain imagery established in Exodus 19 implies the narrative reality split between 'high' and 'low'. 'God' is related to the loftiness of the mountain, sharply separated from the world below inhabited by the people as the second set of actors, while only Moses is able to bridge the dual realities. The translation of the divine reality into the world below coupled with the people as the new theophanic actors must indicate a most radical change of the perception of reality. The events of Exodus 34 seem to share and even to add to the radical character of this perception. However subtly, the two *visio* episodes of Exodus 34 and 40 have in common the emphasis on phenomena of the reality below the mountain as the locus of divine manifestation.

In both cases the human actors are essential to the divine manifestation in the world below. The building account, with its detailed description of how the raw materials were collected and the divine instructions minutely were implemented by the human actors, stresses the significance of materiality and human 'doing' for the new locus of theophanic manifestation. The 'wordly' character of these categories and the corresponding significance of human actors as vital for the actualization of the divine manifestation, is underlined by the emphasis on the willing hearts and skilled hands of 'everyone'. Providing some sort of material basis for the divine manifestation, the human-made tent seems to imply categories for which 'sacramentalism' or 'magic' are apt terms.

This connection between theophanic presence and human-made reality in the world below is parallel to the connection between the divine and human *pānîm* ('face') in Exodus 33–34. Corresponding to the tent produced by human hands and willing hearts, the human face—

the concrete character of which stressed by the skin motif—is presented as the basis of divine light. And also in this case, the conclusion is prepared by a set of human acts, the divine manifestation of Exodus 34 being the result of an extraordinary series of events initiated by the negative acts of the people followed by a set of acts initiated by Moses.

In both cases, divine reality manifesting in the world below seems to have been somehow embodied in material 'containers'. Moreover, this relationship seems to alter the divine manifestation. According to Exodus 34, 'God', implicitly an invisible presence in the tent, manifests himself through the words of Moses and is seen by the light 'horned' from his face. And in Exodus 40, the sublime *visio* is related to the human-made tent hovered over by the cloud and filled by the nocturnal light. Moreover, 'God' is related to the people's journey, the movements of the cloud being perceived as a signal for departure or non-departure. The imagery even suggests a new alignment of the divine and human roles. In the final transformation of the central motifs in Exod. 40.36-38, the cloud's function as a signal makes the idea of journey the central feature, while the theophanic manifestation is subordinated to the people's movement. The shift of emphasis from the theophanic manifestation per se to events with human actors is comparable to the emphasis on Moses' face as the locus of manifestation in Exodus 34.

Also, the radical character of the imagery is combined in both cases with the retention of established elements. God is still 'talking to' Moses in the tent of Exodus 34, although unseen by the people, and the divine instructions are mediated by Moses as before. In Exodus 40 the manifestations of 'cloud' and 'glory' refer to the original mountain appearances. Basically, the new reality after Sinai is the same as before, however profoundly changed by 'God' translated into the world of the people.

The inner connection between the two perceptions of the new reality below the mountain is underlined by the Golden Calf. As we have seen, the Golden Calf represents the alternative locus both with regard to Moses and to the people's Tent of Meeting. This underlines the parallelism of Moses the man and the Tent of Meeting as containers of divine presence. In contrast to the process of 'sacred materialism', the Golden Calf narrative represents a story in which the categories of materiality and the handling of raw materials are related to a process of 'black magic'. Similar to the parallelism of the two processes of sacred production—with the Egyptian plunder as an implicit common denominator—the parallelism of the ox and the horned character of Moses is a visual expression of the delicate character of the new situation. The transformation of the human reality is truly possible. But the perverted actualization of divine presence represents the normal outcome of the people's activity. Under certain conditions, with 'Moses' as denominator, human action represents a process of sacred magic.

The basic connection between Exodus 34 and 40 is also reflected by the common substitution theme. At first impression, the connection of the themes of substitution/dismissal and elevation in the Elijah stories has been dissolved in Exodus 19–40 by ch. 40 being dedicated to the substitution theme and ch. 34 to the elevation theme. On the other hand, chs. 32–34 also present a series of phenomena set as the substitute for something else. The ox is produced as the substitute for the absent Moses and proclaimed as the substitute of YHWH. In his anger, YHWH will destroy the people with Moses functioning as their substitute. Due to the stiff-neckedness of the people, YHWH cannot mix with the people, but will send the divine messenger as a substitute. Compared to the divine plans of Exodus 25–31, Moses' Tent of Meeting represents a substitute tent. The destroyed tablets are substituted by a new set, moreover with Moses as the substitute divine writer. The horned character of the divine light suggests Moses as the substitute for the people's ox, while the *pānîm* imagery related to the people's *visio* suggests that Moses also functions as the substitute for the divine presence. While the embarassment of riches makes any understanding rather difficult, the constant application and reapplication of concepts of substitution is remarkable. At the very least, this highlights the significance of the final substitution. Similar to the substitution of the divine mountain by the human-made tent and the change of theophanic actors, the radiant face of Moses is presented as the concluding and even permanent expression of the divine presence.

So far—and most tentatively at that!—the *parallellismus membrorum* relationship of Exodus 34 and 40 permits a reading of 'synthetic parallelism'. Corresponding with such effects, the two scenes would refer to a common 'something' which transcends the literal contents of each part. This could also be reflected by the ambiguity and allusive effects of the two conclusions. But while the two conclusions respond to a reading of 'synthetic parallelism', the effects of juxtaposition primarily point to some 'antithetical' function.

The subtle elaboration of the contrasting scenes indicates that the connotational interplay of the two sets of imagery could be rich indeed. But at least the parallelism of Exodus 34 and 40 could have a very practical function for the perception of what the story is all about. The contradictory effect seems to balance the impression of each conclusion read on its own. As we have seen, the main story started in ch. 19 and concluded in ch. 40 represents a radical process of 'democratization'. The twists of the story have resulted in a profane people turned into figures of sacred doing and extraordinary *visio*. Read on its own, such a story could form the basis for substantial theological positions. This is demonstrated by the claim of Num. 16.3. However reduced in significance for the rest of Numbers 16 by the usual traditio-historical operations,[38] the very presence of the claim in v. 3, set by whatever redactional hand into a story of 'hierarchical revolt', demonstrates a concrete interpretation of the past events. The holiness of the people, due to the divine presence 'in their midst', is negatively related to the positions of Moses and Aaron. This claim represents a perfectly logical transcription of the theological implications of the Sinai story, especially when introduced by Exod. 19.6. But such a perception of the process of 'democratization' is put in question when Exodus 40 is balanced by Exodus 34 as a contrast conclusion. The portrayal of Moses radiating the divine light, intolerably bright for ordinary people, presents a counter-ideal of sublime elitist character.

Conversely, if the latter image had represented the sole or the dominant conclusion, the Sinai story itself would have been in vain. The linear development of chs. 19–40 identifies ch. 40 as the central expression for this story, to which is added the subtle shadow effect of ch. 34.

On the other hand, the conclusion of Exodus 40, without any disturbing echoes of parallelism, could invite one to a reading centred around massively cult-institutional interests identified with the function of 'Aaron and his sons'. The possibility of such a reading is demonstrated by the traditional scholarly description of 'Priestly' interests. But balanced by the contrasting Tent of Meeting with Joshua as the sub-figure, prepared by the negative role of Aaron in the Golden Calf episode and the violent sanctification of the Levites as substitute priests, any socio-religious claims based on the priestly role in Exodus 40 is made rather problematical.

38. E.g. B.A. Levine, *Numbers 1–20: A New Translation with Introduction and Commentary* (AB, 4A; New York: Doubleday, 1993), pp. 423-32.

In this way, the parallelism of the conclusions continues and adds to the ambiguous character of each description in Exod. 34.29-35 and 40.34-38. The parallelism implies that any type of reading will be disturbed by the subtle effects of contradictory voices, the reader being prevented from settling too comfortably into any fixed opinion of what the story is all about, and constantly provoked to a process of deeper probing. Such effects would correspond to the elaboration of tent scenes. The Elijah stories together with the David/Solomon relationship of 1 Chronicles indicate the conceptual linkage between the two scenes of Moses exalted and substituted. The translation of this linkage into independent scenes, the aspects of the traditional complex situation changed into seemingly separate themes which, moreover, are set up with an effect of juxtaposition, must reflect special interests.

Fundamentally, the effects of reverberation between the two juxtaposed scenes could reflect a basic understanding of reality as dual in character. That the original duality of 'high' and 'low' has been transferred from the mountain imagery to the 'horizontal' categories of the world below, is indicated by the dramatic events of the Golden Calf episode and its aftermath. The 'building story' of Exod. 32.1-6 contrasts the two tent stories of 33.6-11 and chs. 35–40. The relationship of the calf and the Moses tent represents a pair of starkly opposed contrasts of 'temple building'. But continued by the people's Tent of Meeting, juxtaposed both to the ox and to the Moses tent, the contrasting effect is mitigated by the idyll of the active and perfectly obedient people in the third building story climaxed by Exod. 40.36-38. The idyll is repeated by the enlarged version of the conclusion in Num. 9.15-23. In its turn, this conclusion is marred by a set of contrast images. The description of the perfectly observant people is contrasted with the following camp scenes which present a situation starkly opposite with the people in constant revolt. Accordingly, the narrative development seems related to successive pairs of opposites that are juxtaposed and reconciled in an open-ended story. Such a compositional mode would correspond to the subtle function of Exodus 34, as part of the linear development of chs. 19–40 in addition to its function as a first conclusion of what happened at Sinai.[39]

39. Cf. Chapter 4.1 on the parallel conclusions in Exod. 40.36-38 and Num. 9.15-23, indicating a corresponding relationship between Exod. 19–40 and Lev. 1.1–Num. 9.23 as two parallel cycles of Sinai stories.

But in addition to such aspects, the effects of juxtaposition underlines the 'antithetic' function of the two tent scenes in Exodus 33–34 and 40 as parallel expressions for the post-Sinai situation. This must point to some lasting Dr Jekyll and Mr Hyde effect for the perception of the first and fundamental cycle of Sinai stories in chs. 19–40.

According to this perception, the human situation is described by two juxtaposed images. The first is centred around the apotheosis of Moses, while the people are passively 'outside', in a state of permanent renunciation and related to the divine presence by the *visio* of the radiant face of Moses emerging from the Tent of Meeting. The roles of the human actors are reversed in the second image. Moses is excluded from the Tent of Meeting, while the 'ascending' people is set in a situation of permanent *visio Dei*. And combined with these effects of juxtaposition, the first image confirms and profoundly adds to the main story with its astounding perception of the 'world below' as the locus of theophanic encounter. Underlined by the contrasting images of the awesome theophanic manifestation on the divine mountain and the Golden Calf as the perverse locus, the divine presence is now visible as 'horned light' emanating from a human face and as the signal for the people's departure. The two scenes presented in chs. 34 and 40 share the perception of the Sinai story as a process of profound 'secularization' and 'sanctification'.

Chapter 4

THE COMPOSITIONAL TECHNIQUE OF PARALLELISM

1. *The Day of Erecting the Dwelling: Leviticus 8–10*[1]

The Transition from Exodus to Leviticus

Comparable to the complex function of Exodus 32–34, the transition from Exodus 40 to Leviticus 1 also invites two different readings. On the one hand, the present delimitation into books makes a full stop at 40.38. Accordingly, the theophanic manifestation and the people's permanent *visio Dei* represent the culmination of this series of Sinai stories. On the other hand, the reader accustomed to the organization of the materials in Exodus 19–40 will read Lev. 1.1 as the introduction to a new scene which completes the theophanic event introduced in Exod. 40.34.[2] According to the structure of the theophanic episodes in Exodus 19–40, the divine manifestation is followed by a set of instructions addressed to Moses the mediator. This structure is reflected by the divine instructions of Leviticus 1–7 set after Exodus 40.

Such a connection is also indicated when the instructions in Leviticus 1–7 are followed by the implementation story of chs. 8–10. The structure of the events corresponds to the theophanic episodes in Exodus 19–40. The divine instructions are implemented by two separate sets of ritual preparations. Separated by seven days (Lev. 9.1), the priestly sanctification with Moses officiating (ch. 8) is followed by the first sacrificial performance by the priests (9.1-22). This is climaxed by a special movement of Moses and Aaron into the tent (v. 23a) followed by the theophanic manifestation. The composition reflects the pattern of two preparatory events climaxed by the theophanic manifestation in the theophanic episodes of Exodus 19–40.

1. The term refers to the special construction in Num. 7.1aα.

2. Illustrated by the readings of Cassuto, *Exodus*, p. 484, and Durham, *Exodus*, pp. 500-501.

Due to the common tent motifs, the composition of Exodus 35–40 presents an immediate parallel. In the latter case, a first preparatory scene is dedicated to the people as builders (chs. 35–39), and followed by a second scene centred around Moses (40.1-33) concluded by the theophanic manifestation. While this order of the preparatory scenes is inverted in the Leviticus story, the second scene is in both cases concluded by Moses and Aaron—in Exodus 40 together with his sons—entering the Tent of Meeting. The significance of priestly actors in Leviticus 9 underlines the people's role according to vv. 23b-24. Also in this case, the theophanic manifestation is related to the people's *visio*.

The organization of the materials corresponds to the narrative structure in Exodus 19–40, and represents the same relationship of overlapping events. According to this structure, the divine instructions of Leviticus 1–7 form part of the theophanic episode of Exod. 40.34-38, followed by two sets of response which in their turn prepare for a new climax of theophanic manifestation. As part of this pattern, Leviticus 8–9 represents a fourth theophanic episode.[3] The linear development of Exodus 19–40, in which the preceding theophanic episode prepares the next one, could even invite us to see Lev. 9.23-24 as the climactic event.

But due to the present book delimitation, the reader will stop in Exodus 40 as the climax of the episodes introduced by ch. 19. This corresponds to the parallelism of the two introductions—Exod. 19.3 and Lev. 1.1. The divine calling 'from the mountain' and 'from the Tent of Meeting' separates between two stages of divine address. Accordingly, the materials set between the two passages represent the story of how the locus was changed from mountain to tent. Such a reading, with a corresponding perception of Exodus 40 as a conclusion, is indicated by the special elaboration of 40.36-38 related to the preceding verses. The frequentative forms and the reference to 'all their journeyings' change the character of the events introduced in v. 34. The

3. The formal pattern is also reflected by the divine instructions beginning in ch. 11. Chapter 10 continues the preceding story as its aftermath. This means that the theophanic manifestation in its positive and negative aspects (Lev. 9.23-24 and 10.1-2 respectively) is continued by a set of divine instructions, corresponding to the established pattern. But in the following chapters, this pattern is broken. Chapter 11 does not introduce a new set of preparatory episodes climaxed by the theophanic manifestation, but is followed by complex series of divine instructions.

scope of the story is widened from a singular theophanic manifestation to a general situation valid for the whole of the journey. This is underlined by the repetition of the verses in Num. 9.15-23, which represents an extended version of Exod. 40.36-38.[4] Followed by the description of the departure from Sinai, vv. 15-23 of Num. 9 conclude the Sinai-stories as a whole. This suggests that the short form of this conclusion in Exodus 40 has a corresponding function for chs. 19–40.[5] The repetitive effect of the two conclusions could even indicate a parallel relationship between two story cycles. Accordingly, Exodus 19–40 would present the basic version of what happened at Sinai, while the rest of the materials between Exod. 40.38 and Num. 19.15 presents a parallel version of the Sinai events.[6]

In this way, the composition invites us to two modes of reading. The deliberate character of this invitation is underlined by the relation of Exod. 33.8-11 and 34.34-35 to 40.36-38. By comparable stylistic effects, the three tent passages widen the character of the situation that is described. The singular events are extended into scenes typical of the post-Sinai reality. And after this extension, the story in all cases returns from the aspects of typical and permanent situations to singular events which, within the narrative pattern, represent the natural continuation. In Exod. 33.12, the dialogue between Moses and YHWH continues the preparatory events and the theophanic manifestation of vv. 6-10.

4. Cf. the traditional understanding of Exod. 40.36-38 as dependent on Num. 9.15-23, inserted when the separation between the books of Exodus and Leviticus made necessary a proper conclusion for Exodus. Recently, the significance of the short version has been stressed by Blum (*Die Komposition*, p. 312) and Jacob Milgrom (*Leviticus 1–16: A New Translation with Introduction and Commentary* [AB, 3; New York: Doubleday, 1991], p. 139).

5. The parallel application of *nāsa'* and *ḥānâ* in Num. 9.15-23 underlines the point that only the former is repeatedly used in Exod. 40.36-37, also for the non-departure when the latter word would have been proper. In contrast, the introductory scene in 19.2 repeatedly uses *ḥānâ*. The separation of the word-pair by the introductory and concluding scene corresponds to the reversed juxtapositions of Moses and people in the two scenes and must reflect the character of chs. 19–40 as a narrative entity.

6. Cf. also Milgrom, *Leviticus 1–16*, p. 139, on 40.36-38 as crucial to the understanding of the function of Leviticus. As a 'prolepsis' of Num. 9.15-23, the intervening material in Lev. 1.1–Num. 9.14 is bracketed as one 'giant parenthesis containing the laws given to Israel following the revelation of the Decalogue and Book of the Covenant (Exod 20-24)'.

Exodus 35.1 presents the divine words mediated by Moses, and thus continues the scenes of descent and mediation in 34.29-35. Correspondingly, the divine speech of Lev. 1.1 continues the concluding scene of Exodus 40.

On the one hand, the compositional pattern connects the events of Exodus 40 and Leviticus 1–7 as parts of the third theophanic episode, which prepare for the new episode of chs. 8–9. On the other hand, the separation of the books of Exodus and Leviticus as well as the relationship of Exod. 40.36-38 and Num. 9.15-23 present ch. 40 as the climax of the series of events introduced in ch. 19, while Lev. 1.1 introduce a second cycle of Sinai stories concluded in Numbers 9. The formal signals indicate that the latter represents the immediate reading, while a *lectio continua* is equally legitimate. Further, comparable to the relationship of Exodus 34 and 40, the role of Moses differs according to the two readings. Concluded by 40.36-38, the climax of the events invites the reader to ponder the new situation with the people as the new theophanic figures, in contrast to the exclusion of Moses. Continued by Lev. 1.1, the new situation has not changed the basic role alignment of Moses and people. However visionary and observant the people, the role of Moses the mediator is the same as before.

Chapters 8–9 as a Repetition of Exodus 40

The ambiguity of the transition from Exodus to Leviticus is also reflected by the character of the events. Set after the building account in Exodus 35–40, the sacrificial interest of Leviticus 1–7 could express the continuation of the preceding episodes. When the tent is set up, it is possible to present what should take place in it.[7] But according to traditio-historical readings, the impression of continuation has usually been disturbed by the impression of a more direct relationship between Leviticus 8–9 and the instructions of Exodus 29–30. The elaborate character of both passages, with a common emphasis on priestly sanctification and function, could reflect a special linkage between these passages. In comparison, the short allusions in 40.26-32 represent a rather poor description of how the instructions in chs. 29–30 were implemented. Accordingly, Leviticus 8–9 has usually been seen as the real

7. According to Milgrom, *Leviticus 1–16*, p. 494, Exod. 40.17-33 presents the Tabernacle and its sancta as assembled but not consecrated. The priestly consecration commanded in Exod. 29 cannot take place before Moses has learned the sacrificial procedures of Lev. 1–7.

continuation of the story in Exodus 35–39, which has been interrupted by the insertion of Exodus 40 and Leviticus 1–7.[8]

These readings illustrate the connection between the stories. According to the final shape of the materials, the events of Exodus 40 seem somehow repeated by Leviticus 8–9. Most of the actions of Moses in Exodus 40 are related to the assembling and furnishing of the Tent of Meeting. But the acts alluded to vv. 27, 29 and 31 demonstrate that rites of sacrifice and purification are included.[9] As part of the story of implementation in vv. 16-33, which describe how the divine instructions of vv. 2-15 were carried out, vv. 27, 29 and 31 must refer to the instructions of vv. 9-15. However unsatisfactory these verses may be in comparison to Leviticus 8, they describe the very first ritual acts performed in the new sanctuary and must imply a process of sanctification, with regard to both the sanctuary and the priests. The formula of compliance in vv. 23b, 25b, 27b, 29bβ and 32b, corresponding to vv. 16, 19b and 21b, relates both the burning of incence, the sacrifices and the priestly washing to the parallel acts of vv. 18-33.[10]

In this way, Exod. 40.17-35 and Leviticus 8–9 seem to represent parallel descriptions of the same event. As parallel versions, they stress different aspects. The former is centred around the assembling and furnishing of the sanctuary, while the latter presents the consecration of sanctuary and priests centred around motifs of sacrifice. The Exodus version contains the whole set of events, with a special emphasis on the sanctuary as sacred space. In this version, the sanctification aspects are only alluded to. Contained in embryo, they prepare for the repetition in Leviticus 8–9 dedicated to the priestly aspects.

On the other hand, the introduction of Lev. 1.1 clearly presents the following episodes as taking place after the events of Exodus 40. Corresponding to the pattern of theophanic episodes in chs. 19–40, the divine speech in Leviticus 1–7 takes place after the events of preparation and the theophanic manifestation, and in its turn it prepares for the

8. E.g. Martin Noth, *Leviticus: A Commentary* (trans. J.E. Anderson; OTL; London: SCM Press), pp. 68-69; cf. also Rolf Rendtorff, *Leviticus* (BKAT, 3.1; Neukirchen–Vluyn: Neukirchener Verlag, 1985), pp. 1-7. On the other hand, Koch (*Die Priesterschrift*, pp. 44-45, 67-69) finds P ended in Exod. 40.17, partially represented in vv. 33b, 34-35, and continued in Lev. 1.1. The P story of chs. 8–9 reflects not only the instructions of Exod. 29, but also Lev. 1–7.

9. In spite of the assertions of Milgrom, *Leviticus 1–16*, p. 494, in particular.

10. Cf. also Chapter 4.3 on Num. 7.1.

next theophanic episode climaxed in ch. 9. The relationship of successive episodes is also reflected by Lev. 11.1, according to which the divine instructions are addressed to Moses and Aaron as parallel mediators. While Moses continues his established role as mediator according to 1.1, the sanctification of the priests implies that Aaron too must be present for the new set of instructions in 11.1.

The linear relationship of the events is also reflected by the concrete motifs. Although 'really' descriptions of the same event, the emphasis on the tent and its furnishing in Exodus 40 is not repeated by Leviticus 8, which is centred around the sacrificial procedure of sanctification. The different character of the two sets of preparation corresponds to the two descriptions of the theophanic manifestation. In Exodus 40 the theophanic manifestation is related to categories of locus represented by the Tent of Meeting and linked to the people's journey. In Leviticus 9 it is related to the transformation of the sacrifices as consuming fire.

The different character of the two sets of preparations are comparable to the development of the three sets of preparatory events in Exodus 19–40. Ritual categories are important to the preparatory sub-episodes.[11] As we have seen, the ritual references are not repeated by the successive episodes, but seem to reflect a development towards ritual perfection and complexity. The elements of personal purification in ch. 19 are followed by the altar building and sacrifices performed by substitute priests in ch. 24 and concluded by the erection and sanctification of the perfect structure in ch. 40. By emphasizing sacrificial and priestly aspects, Leviticus 8–9 could complete such a development towards ritual perfection. Prepared for by the 'young men' as priestly substitutes in Exodus 24 and the contrasting story of the Levites as priestly substitutes in ch. 32, the allusions to the priestly entering in 40.31-32 are concluded by Leviticus 9.

Such a development could also be related to the description of the theophanic manifestation in Lev. 9.24 and 10.2. The imagery of the divine glory as consuming fire corresponds to the theophanic manifestation in Exod. 24.17. The fiery aspect of the divine glory related to the people's *visio* is intimated in the latter, while its implications with regard to altar and sacrifices are presented in Leviticus 9.24–10.2. Comparable to this relationship between the second theophanic episode and

11. Exod. 19.10-15, 24.4-8 and chs. 35–40, and also reflected in the Golden Calf episode, the sanctification of the Levites in 32.25-29, and the first Tent story in 33.6-11.

Leviticus 8–10 as a fourth,[12] the cloud motif connects the theophanic imagery of the first and third episodes. While an important aspect of the theophanic manifestation in Exod. 19.16-19 and 20.18-21, the cloud is elaborated as the central motif in 40.34-38.

So far, the materials underline the impression of an ambiguous relationship between the episodes of Exodus 35–40 and Leviticus 8–9. The latter represents a parallel version of the former, unfolding certain aspects only intimated in the first and basic version. On the other hand, Leviticus 8–9 can as well be seen as a fourth theophanic episode, part of the linear development and in continuation of the Exodus episodes.

The Priestly Usurpation in Leviticus 10.1-2

The Nadab and Abihu scene in Lev. 10.1-2 strengthens the impression that effects of parallelism are important for the relationship of Exodus 40 and Leviticus 8–9. In contrast to the events of ch. 9, the scene of 'strange fire' has a function comparable to the relationship of the Golden Calf episode and the building account of Exodus 35–40. In both cases, the proper human preparations and the theophanic manifestation are juxtaposed to a negative scene. After the divine fire has consumed the sacrifices, Nadab and Abihu offer incense and bring 'strange fire' before YHWH. This is responded to by a new manifestation of the divine fire which consumes the usurpers (10.1-2).

The stereotyped description presents a negative short-form of the proper events in ch. 9. The version of the compliance formula 'which he had not commanded them' contrasts with the positive version in 9.7b, 10b and 21b and the versions in vv. 6a and 5a. The effect of juxtaposition is underlined by the parallelism of 9.23a and 10.1. Two sets of two ritual servants are related to sacred space, both performing acts which call forth the divine fire.[13] The mirror effect is also reflected by the sentences that describe the divine response of consuming fire (9.24a and 10.2a). And the 'weeping' of the people (10.6b)[14] and the

12. Cf. also Nadab and Abihu as actors in both episodes.

13. Cf. also the priestly acts defined by *lāqaḥ* concluded by *hiqrîb* (v. 1). This corresponds to the construction in 9.2 and is also reflected in v. 5, aside from the repeated applications of *hiqrîb* in chs. 8–9.

14. The weeping scene as a contrast to 9.24 is underlined by N. Kiuchi, *The Purification Offering in the Priestly Literature: Its Meaning and Function* (JSOTSup, 56; Sheffield: JSOT Press, 1987), p. 71.

'stillness' of Aaron (v. 3b)[15] contrasts with the joyful 'shouting' (*rānan*) of the people in the first scene.

The juxtaposition of proper events and a mock episode is comparable to the Golden calf episode as the mock version of the proper story in Exodus 35–40. While merely stated in short-form and by stereotyped language, the significance of the 'strange fire' episode is demonstrated by its aftermath in the rest of ch. 10. As the conclusion of the story begun in ch. 1, ch. 10 decisively influences the impression of what took place in the fourth theophanic episode. This corresponds to, and even exceeds, the consequences of the Golden Calf episode for the development of the story started in Exodus 19.

The parallelism of the two mock episodes is underlined by their conceptual relationship. Compared to the independent and unconditional manifestation of the first theophanic episodes, the two stories about the building of the tent and the first sacrificial events stress the significance of human activity for the manifestation of theophanic presence. Certain types of 'raw materials' are handled in a certain way, and the character of this process sets the conditions for the divine manifestation. The proper activity, done 'according to what YHWH had commanded', provides the scenery for the miraculous manifestation. The contrasting process of 'black magic'—superficially identical with the proper action—is set in motion by human initiative and leads to the mock manifestation of the Golden Calf or the destructive manifestation of the divine fire in Leviticus 10. The significance of the contrast is deepened by the presence of the same actors performing the 'same' acts in both scenes. The people dedicating their gold to sacred production in Exodus 32 are also the exuberant givers and the heart-driven craftsmen of the positive story. The story of Aaron assisted by 'his sons' in Leviticus 9 is contrasted by events set in motion by two of the priestly sons.

This aspect is underlined by Exod. 24.1 and 9. Included in the group selected for a special ascent climaxed by a scene of extraordinary *visio*, the villains of Leviticus 10 have served as the human heroes of a positive contrast episode. Aside from Moses, the three priestly representatives, Aaron, Nadab and Abihu are the only persons of the select group in Exodus 24 whose presence is stressed by name.[16] The emphasis on these persons as present corresponds to the four actors split into two

15. Milgrom, *Leviticus 1–16*, p. 604.

16. This is underlined by vv. 13 and 14, which indicate that the list could have included other actors.

groups in Lev. 9.23–10.2. Moses and Aaron are the actors in the positive scene, in contrast to Nadab and Abihu in the negative scene.[17] The significance of such a reversal of roles—the heroes of one episode the villains of the next—is also reflected by a corresponding juxtaposition of the roles of Aaron. Among the visionary ascenders and especially related to Moses in the positive scene of Exodus 24,[18] Aaron is alloted a negative role in the following Golden Calf episode. The allusive character of the references does not in any way disturb the impact of the scene in ch. 24 as an extraordinary experience for a select group. But at the same time, the relationship of 24.1 and 9 to the negative episodes of 32.1-6 and Lev. 10.1-2 intimates some subtle connection between the roles of hero and villain in contrasting scenes of extraordinary *visio Dei* and perverted manifestation. Added to by the people as the main culprits of the Golden Calf episode and as the perfect actors of the building story, the contrasted roles seem to reflect the perception of the profoundly dual character of the human reality.

The intimations in Exodus 24 of negative episodes to come also point to the subtle relationship of the Golden Calf and the 'strange fire' in Leviticus 10 as parallel episodes of perverted action. This connection is also reflected by the juxtaposition of the divine fire and the human fire qualified as 'strange' in Lev. 9.24–10.2.[19] For the immediate reading, *zār* could be rendered as 'improper, not suitable' corresponding to the usage in a corresponding context in Num. 17.5 or to the 'strange woman' motif of Prov. 2.16 and 5.3, 20.[20] But the juxtaposition to the divine fire adds depth to the aspect of unsuitability. The juxtaposition is comparable to the idea of a huhuman-made representation of the divine reality in Exodus 32. The 'strange fire' procured by human hands and brought before YHWH represents the huhuman-made mimicry of the real manifestation. Comparable to the Golden Calf, the acts of proper

17. The subtle connection is also reflected by the motifs of 'consuming'. The scene of sacred eating by human actors in 24.11 is followed by the *visio* of the theophanic 'consuming fire' in v. 17. This corresponds to the imagery of the theophanic 'consuming fire' of Lev. 9.24 and 10.2, connected to the problems of priestly eating in 10.12-20, followed by the people's eating in ch. 11.

18. Cf. the grouping of the two sets of actors by the use of the prefix w^e in 24.1 and 9, Aaron related to Moses, and Abihu to Nadab.

19. The traditional discussions on the 'real' implications of the 'strange fire', illustrated by Kiuchi, *The Purification Offering*, pp. 68-69, seem to ignore the simple effect of the juxtaposition of the 'strange fire' set over against the divine fire.

20. Milgrom, *Leviticus 1–16*, pp. 597-98.

preparation are perverted into an act of usurpation, procuring a substitute for the divine manifestation. The connection between the two stories of usurpation could also be reflected by the very application of the word *zār*. The connotational reference to aspects of 'strangeness' is comparable to the subtle references to the Egyptian plunder in the context of the Golden Calf, as well as to significance of 'Egyptianism' in the revolt stories.

On the other hand, the parallelism underlines the special character of the priestly version of black magic. The Golden Calf episode and the proper procedure of Exodus 35–40 are separated as successive events. The mock process is not directly related to the proper process, and is even explained as being due to a critical situation with Moses absent. Mitigated by the intercession scenes and the experience of the radiant Moses in ch. 34, the positive process of proper magic can take place. Compared to the Golden Calf, the priestly abomination of Leviticus 10 represents an intensified version of black magic. Set immediately after the experience following the proper manifestation, by actors who have just participated in the proper preparations, the introduction of the strange fire represents an event of blatant usurpation.

In this way, the episode intensifies the contrast between proper and perverse action. By the actors embodying the roles of Dr Jekyll and Mr Hyde in closely related scenes, aspects of human dualism and inner conflict seem to be implied. The implications of sharpened contrasts are stressed by the divine retribution. Compared to the events of Exodus 19–40, the death of the priests marks the first event in which the deadly force of YHWH is manifested. The terrible sanctification of the Levites in Exodus 32 was instigated by Moses. Now YHWH manifests himself for the first time according to the aspect of his character which is referred to Exod. 19.21-24 and 33.3-5. These passages present the mortal danger of the extraordinary relationship as well as the terrible automatism of the divine response. But above all, these passages reveal the divine reluctance to perform in such a terrible way, corresponding to YHWH's consideration in informing Moses of his evil intentions in the scene of 32.9-10. In comparison, the parallelism of Lev. 9.24 and 10.2 makes a gruesome impression of the divine fire as some mechanical device of 'consuming'. Related to the idyll of Exodus 35–40 and the absence of divine violence in chs. 19–40 as well as in the wilderness events prior to Sinai, the frightening scene of Lev. 10.1-2 presents a new situation. This is underlined by the rest of ch. 10, which is dedicated to the aftermath of the priestly usurpation. As the conclusion of this theophanic episode, the negative aspects dominate the presentation of the new reality in the world below. Followed by descriptions of divine violence towards the people in the post-Sinai wilderness, the dual character of the divine presence in the mode of 'consuming' must introduce a new stage in the story of intimate relationship.

These aspects are given an emotive expression by the people's responses to the two types of divine consuming. The people's 'rejoicing' in 9.24 is followed by their 'weeping' in 10.6. The emotional categories underline the heightening of tension. Given the scarcity of expressions for emotional reactions in the context, the short references must be important indications of the significance of the events. The contrasted responses correspond to the contrasts of 'fun' in Exod. 32.6 and 'sorrow' in 33.4 as the two successive reactions to the Golden Calf episode. But contracted into successive scenes in the Leviticus episode, the immediate transition from one state to a contrast state—with the people weeping as the concluding impression—underlines the dual character of the new reality.

2. *Conclusions*

The relationship between Exodus 40 and Leviticus 1–10 seems to reflect an attempt both to separate and to relate the two episodes. The two stories 'really' present the same event of tent sanctification—the latter the unfolding of acts only alluded to in Exodus 40. At the same time, the organization of the materials suggests a relationship of linear development. The ambiguity implies a delicate effect of parallelism, the second episode 'really' the same as the first, but with the 'sameness' transformed.

It must be important that the dating notes of Num. 7.1, 10 (cf. also vv. 84 and 88) contract the events of Exodus 40 and Leviticus 8–9 resulting in a similar ambiguity. Numbers 7.1 combines the anointing of the altar and the erection of the sanctuary and presents them as one event. The 'day of erecting (*hāqîm*) the dwelling'[21] also comprised the anointing and sanctification of the altar followed by the princely gifts. Introduced in this way, the dating notes in v. 10, followed by vv. 84 and

21. The referential character of the note is reflected by the special term *kallôt*, corresponding to its appliction in Exod. 40.33b and 39.32, in their turn referring to the Creation Story.

88, are immediately perceived as repetitive allusions to the former note. On the other hand, these allusions only refer to the altar. Conversely, this underlines the special form of the presentation of altar and tent as an expression of connected events in v. 1. The application of infinitives for the tent events in the introductory construction is followed by narrative forms for the altar events. The formal arrangement separates two sets of events, corresponding to the altar as the sole motif in the repeated references in vv. 10, 84 and 88. With the second set given to anointing and sanctification of the altar, the separation corresponds to the parallel relationship of Exodus 40 and Leviticus 8–9. The delicate wording of the dating notes in Numbers 7 reflects the ambiguous relationship of the two sets of events. On the one hand they represent successive episodes, on the other they are closely related as 'really' the same as events of 'the day of erecting'.

This must have repercussions for our understanding of the function of Exodus 34 as part of the linear development and as a conclusion parallel to ch. 40. The materials of Exodus 40 and Leviticus 8–9 reflect a comparable organization. Accordingly, it must be possible to conclude that the ambiguous effects of parallelism represent a deliberate compositional mode. Related to the preceding tent-scenes of Exodus 33–34 and 40, the scenery of Leviticus 8–9 represents a third arrangement of the given elements. The three tent scenes are alternately centred around Moses, the people and the priests as the primary human actors. The divine presence is depicted as hidden in the tent and revealed by Moses' face in the first scene, as a cloud covering the tent in the second, and finally as 'outgoing' fiery 'glory' upon the altar.

For the relationship of Exodus 33–34 and 35–40, effects of juxtaposition seem to represent the prime function. The *parallelismus membrorum* represented by Exodus 40 and Leviticus 8–9 seems to consist mainly in 'synthetical' effects of parallel elaborations. The idyll of Exod. 40.36-38, related to the sharp contrasts of Lev. 9.23–10.2, could indicate aspects of 'antithetical' function. But above all, the Leviticus episode seems to continue and deepen the implications of the former. The two stories share the perception of some profound 'sacred materialism'. The meticulous details of sacred building according to the divine instructions in Exodus 25–31 is continued by a corresponding interest in the correct sacrificial procedures in Leviticus 1–7. The building account is concluded by the theophanic manifestation related to a locus of dwelling in Exod. 40.34-36. When the proper lodging is prepared, the story logically moves on to the procurement of food for the divine dweller. Correspondingly, the priestly implementation of the instructions of the preparation of divine food is concluded by a theophanic manifestation of 'consuming'.[22]

According to the imagery, the divine movement into the world below implies a process of profound change. The change from divine mountain to huhuman-made tent is continued by the idea of food procured by human hands and absorbed into the divine essence. The concrete character of this imagery is underlined by the parallel emphasis on priestly eating in Lev. 10.12-20. Rather obscurely,[23] the dialogue between Moses and Aaron at the very least reflects the connection between divine and priestly consuming. This is underlined by the following instructions in ch. 11, which deal with permitted and prohibited food. The contextual development implies a basic parallelism of divine and human consuming. While the priestly eating forms an aspect of the consumption of sacrificial food, ch. 11 refers to a general everyday situation. The parallelism of consuming 'as above so below' is comparable to Exodus 40. Basically, the imagery of the latter implies the divine presence in a tent—a rather grand one—in a camp of tent-dwellers.[24] More concretely, the motif elaboration of vv. 36-38 indicates the parallelism of divine and human movements, the signals of the cloud reflected by the people departing or not departing. The parallelism of divine and human consuming in Leviticus 9–10, followed by the instructions of ch. 11, seems to continue and add to the impression of some process of profound 'materialization' for YHWH sharing in the human reality. Conversely, the implications of these events represent a process of sanctification for the human actors (Lev. 11.44-47).[25]

22. Comparable to the priests mentioned in Exod. 19.22, 24, before the proper sanctification of Aaron and his sons, the story seemingly ignores that sacrifices too have been performed before (e.g. Exod. 24.5). Similar effects of 'anticipation' are important for Exod. 18 (cf. Chapter 5.1).

23. Traditionally disregarded due to the understanding of vv. 12-20 as late additions: e.g. Koch, *Die Priesterschrift*, pp. 72-73 and K. Elliger, *Leviticus* (HAT, 4; Tübingen: J.C.B. Mohr, 1966), p. 136. The connection between the two parts of ch. 10 is stressed by Kiuchi, *The Purification Offering*, pp. 67-68, Milgrom, *Leviticus 1–16*, pp. 635-40.

24. Cf. the elaboration of the tent imagery in Exod. 33.10.

25. The connection between divine food and categories of sin could add to this impression. The eating of the sin-offering represents the central event in the aftermath of the priestly usurpation (Lev. 10.16-20). This underlines the significance of

The aspects of some profound inversion of the divine and human situations are underlined when this story is related to the narrative context. The story of Exodus 19–Leviticus 10 presents how the divine movement from the locus of sacred mountain into a new locus in the world below made necessary the procurement of a proper dwelling and food by the human actors. It cannot be coincidental that this story is set within a more comprehensive story of comparable procurement, related to the same categories of locus and food, but with the roles reversed. The movement from Egypt to Promised Land is made possible by the divine intervention, the people sustained by heavenly food during the journey towards a land which, moreover, is qualified as a place of abundant food. Accordingly, the grand story could be read as a process of exchange, the two sets of actors providing the basic elements of existence for each other.

The connection between Exodus 40 and Leviticus 8–9 can also be related to a common theme of the substitution of Moses. According to Exodus 40, Moses is substituted by the people as theophanic figures. The peculiar parallelism between Leviticus 8 and 9[26] suggests a comparable process related to priestly categories. Leviticus 8 presents Moses in a priestly role. According to ch. 9, this role has been transferred to Aaron and his sons.[27] The parallelism of the roles of Moses and Aaron is visualized by the double blessing scenes of Lev. 9.22-23[28] as well as their togetherness as mediators in Lev. 11.1. Comparable to the relationship of Moses and people in Exodus 40, the function of Moses as priest has been transferred to Aaron.

The connection between the two stories of substitution is reflected by

sacrifices related to categories of sin in the instructions in Lev. 1–7 (underlined by Koch, *Die Priesterschrift*, pp. 101-102 as characteristic of P's understanding of ritual practice). For the divine consumer, this indicates a rather special diet—the consuming of priestly sinners 10.2 a natural extension of the normal type of food offered. In contrast to such a divine diet, the people will eat only pure food.

26. Illustrated by Noth, *Leviticus*, p. 75, and Elliger, *Leviticus*, p. 127. So many elements of ch. 8 are repeated in ch. 9, that the latter is understood as a secondary compilation of different sources.

27. This aspect is important to J.R. Porter, *Leviticus: Commentary* (Cambridge Bible Commentary; Cambridge: Cambridge University Press, 1976), p. 71, understood to reflect the High Priest's annexation of the former religious role of the king.

28. Compared to the two blessings related to Solomon in 1 Kgs 8.14-21 and vv. 54-61 by Milgrom, *Leviticus 1–16*, p. 588, while usually read as a secondary composition: e.g. Elliger, *Leviticus*, p. 130; Koch, *Die Priesterschrift*, p. 71.

the relationship of parallel sub-episodes. Consistent with the categories of building in Exodus 35–40, both Moses and people are presented as builders. The first scene in Exod. 36.8–39.43 is dedicated to the people as builders, the second in 40.1-33 to Moses. This corresponds to the parallelism of Leviticus 8 and 9, the first dedicated to Moses as priest, the second to Aaron and his sons. In both cases, the actions of Moses results in his substitution by a new set of figures.

Also in the Leviticus story, this development is connected to aspects which reflect the exalted character of Moses. In this case, such aspects are suggested by the subtle application of the formula of compliance. Corresponding to the use of this formula as a refrain in the building story (Exod. 39–40), the perfect character of the sacrificial process is indicated when all is done 'according to what YHWH had commanded'.[29] The monotony of the application as well as its importance as a stamp of profound perfection underline the versions that substitute the divine commander with Moses (8.31b; 9.5a; 21.b; 10.5b, 7b, 18b). For the story as a whole, the normal version with the divine commander represents the basic expression for the sacred action. But for the relationship of Moses and the priests, the basic expression can be substituted by versions which attribute the divine function of 'commanding' (*ṣiwwâ*) to Moses.[30] Given the precise character of the formulaic language and its obvious significance for the author as theologically vital, the interplay of the versions must express an important concern, while rather subtly expressed. The substitution of Moses by new sacrificial officials implies a new hierarchical order. Corresponding to Aaron taking over the role of Moses the priest, Moses performs in the divine role.[31]

29. Applied in different versions in Lev. 8.4, 5, 9, 13, 17, 21, 29, 34, 35, 36, in Lev. 9.6, 7, 10, and in 10.1, 11, 13, 15.

30. Cf. the application of the formula in the scene of apotheosis Exod. 34.35, where Moses is the subject of 'commanding' related to the divine 'speaking'.

31. This is also indicated by the peculiar parallelism when Aaron's deed as 'good in the eyes of' is related both to YHWH and Moses in Lev. 10.19-20. Concluding the story, Moses obviously accepts the explanation of Aaron (e.g. Milgrom, *Leviticus 1–16*, p. 627). The priestly transgression is related to what Moses has commanded (v. 18). This 'usurpation' of the divine role is added to by Moses as the judge of what is 'good'. To Milgrom (*Leviticus 1–16*, p. 627) this proves that P acknowledges the superiority of Moses the prophet over Aaron the priest. The language of the compliance formula indicates that much more radical categories are

In this way, the story of Leviticus 8–10 too seems to reflect the aspects of Moses substituted and elevated. The elaboration of the formulaic language has implications comparable to the allusions to the new role of Moses in the scenes of apotheosis in Exod. 34.29-35 and blessing in 39.43 juxtaposed to ch. 40. In both cases, the elevation theme represents an aspect of a main story given to the substitution theme. The subtle implications of some process of apotheosis are common to both stories. While new actors perform in the established roles of Moses, the substituted hero is placed upon a new rung of some hierarchical ladder, taking over aspects of the divine role.

The special connection between the two sets of the main story is also reflected by the elaboration of the two scenes of theophanic manifestation. Concluded by vv. 36-38, the story of Exodus 40 is centred around the people as the human actors, while the cloud represents the significant aspect of theophanic manifestation. Both the divine 'glory' (vv. 34-35) and the priests (vv. 31-32) are present, but only alluded to as sub-figures. Conversely, the 'glory' and the priests are the main actors in the Leviticus story, while the people have the subordinate role. Given these differences, it must be important that the *visio Dei* of the people remains a constant for both scenes. Although formally sub-figures in the Leviticus episode, the people are retained as the visionaries, their rejoicing (Lev. 9.24) and weeping (10.6) the response to the implications of the theophanic manifestation as 'consuming' brought into the camp.

In this way, Leviticus also refers to a main story centred around the people as the important figures. This is underlined by the divine instructions on clean and unclean food in ch. 11. Mediated by Moses and Aaron (v. 1), the instructions are addressed to the people (v. 2). This is also reflected by the consistent address to a plural 'you' throughout the chapter.

Formally, the localization of divine instructions in ch. 11 is consistent with the narrative pattern established in Exodus 19–40. The theophanic manifestation of Lev. 9.23-24 is followed by a complementary negative manifestation of divine consuming. The events that follow in ch. 10 continue this episode as its aftermath and are concluded in v. 20. Followed by a set of divine instructions in ch. 11, the organization of chs. 8–11 reflects the pattern of theophanic episodes, which is set out as

involved. Thus, the episode of ch. 10, concluded by the valuation by Moses of what is 'good', is comparable to the implications of the blessing scene in Exod. 39.43.

preparatory sub-episodes climaxed by the theophanic manifestation followed by divine instructions.

The formal consistency underlines the significance of the conceptual connection between ch. 11 and the preceding materials. Corresponding to chs. 1–7, implemented by 8–9 as preparations for the sacred meal, 9.23–10.2 presents the theophanic manifestation in the mode of consuming. This is added to by the motifs of priestly eating in ch. 10. Continued by the instructions on the people's eating in ch. 11, the composition implies a basic connection between divine consuming, priestly eating and a general practice of proper eating.[32] While the priestly eating represents an immediate extension of the divine consuming, the instructions addressed to 'you' are of general character, referring to a permanent religious practice of proper eating. The shift from the singular ritual situation to an everyday discipline underlines the parallelism of divine and human consuming. This is also reflected by the peculiar symmetry of the two actions. In contrast to the double meal of sacrifices and usurpers consumed by YHWH—the divine food in both cases rather tainted by associations of guilt—the two types of food set before the people are separated into categories of clean and unclean.

The intimations of some profound parallelism 'as above, so below' related to divine and human consuming are underlined by a corresponding parallelism in the motivations which conclude the instructions. The proper human eating is related to the categories of holiness. YHWH is *qādôš* and 'you' are potentially holy (vv. 44a, 45b). The everyday discipline of proper eating is connected to the sacred story. The addressees have 'ascended from Egypt to become holy. For I am holy' (v. 45a). However astounding, the repeated parallelism of divine and human holiness implies that the human actors can share in the divine essence. Prepared for by the imagery of divine and human consuming the concepts are comparable to the parallelism in Exodus between the journeying people and the divine co-ascender. Their radical character is underlined by, and in their turn underline, the idea of Moses being elevated into a divine role. With the priestly function also included, the concepts seem to imply the human figures set upon some hierarchical ladder of divine being, in potential movement from step to step. Moreover, this radical idea of human metamorphosis does not refer to lofty categories of ideological speculation, but to aspects of concrete,

32. The connection is also reflected by the function of 'distinguishing' related to the priests (10.10) and to the people (11.47).

physical and practical reality. According to ch. 11, the holiness of the human eaters is linked to the proper food. In this way, chs. 1–11 of Leviticus continue the story of Exodus 19–40. As 'dweller' and 'consumer', YHWH becomes part of the human reality. Conversely, the divine movement from the mountain implies that the world below is invested in aspects of divine character.

The Compositional Mode

The comparison with the Exodus story also underlines the compositional mode when the story moves from Leviticus 10 to the divine instructions of ch. 11. The transition implies a change of address and a corresponding change of the mode of reading. In the Exodus story, Moses and the people are interlinked as figures taking part in the same series of events. This corresponds to the development of Leviticus 8–10. While the events are centred around Moses and Aaron, together with his sons, the people also take part as more subordinate actors. This is changed by the transition to ch. 11. Set in the narrative frame by Lev. 11.1-2, the instructions addressed to the people and mediated by Moses and Aaron formally continue the preceding story. But the perspective is changed from a singular event to a general and permanent situation of religious discipline. Corresponding to the shift from priests to people as the central figures, the focus is changed from the aspects of divine consuming to the people's food.

The significance of this transition is underlined by the change of the compositional pattern. According to the pattern of theophanic episodes introduced in Exodus 19, the reader expects that the instructions of ch. 11 should also be mediated and implemented in new scenes, which in their turn prepare for the next theophanic episode. But in this case a complex series of new instructions follows after ch. 11. The rupture of the narrative pattern must signal that the composition has entered a new mode. Hitherto, the character of the composition has been expressed by the relationship of successive theophanic episodes. Now the narrative movement from event to event is stopped. The divine address of the last theophanic manifestation is extended into a great series of instructions.

The change in the compositional mode highlights the transition from a story that presents 'the sons of Israel' in the third masculine plural, 'them' (also in the instructions in Lev. 1–7), to a set of instructions addressed in the second masculine plural, 'you'. The very transition from 'them' to 'you' shifts the reading into a more importunate mode.

This is added to by the implications of the address. The general character of the instructions implicitly extends the number of potential embodiments of 'you'. This is comparable to the first theophanic episode introduced in Exodus 19, in which the divine address refers to a situation of general Torah observation.[33] But framed by Exod. 19.21-25 and 24.1-2, the divine address in this case is also orientated towards what will take place in the next theophanic episode. The connection between divine instructions and narrative movement is important for the following episodes. The instructions on the tent building in chs. 25–31 intimate the events of the building story in chs. 35–40. Formally, the sacrificial instructions of Leviticus 1–7 are of a general character, describing the conditions for a permanent sacrificial practice. But implemented by the sanctification of the priests and the first sacrifices, the relationship of instructions and the following scenes of implementation corresponds to the function of Exodus 25–31 related to the building story. This connection between the divine instructions and the narrative movement is abandoned by Leviticus 11. Corresponding to the interruption of the compositional pattern of theophanic episodes, the divine instructions of Leviticus 11 refer to some permanent religious practice of general character.

In this way the transition to 'you' introduced to a discipline of proper eating, and related to categories of holiness, represents an important stage in the compositional development. Sharing the qualification of having 'ascended from Egypt', later generations of readers are also involved in the address. This implies some subtle separation between the narrative situation of the preceding episode and the situation of the instructed 'you'.[34]

Conversely, such a separation underlines the significance of Lev. 11.1-2, which identifies the comprehensive 'you' (including also later generations) with the people of the narrative. This is supplemented with the conceptual connection of the passages. However separated, the story about 'them' and the instructions to 'you' are linked by the concept of eating. The impression of a basic separation between the narrative reality of the story and the reality of 'you' is combined with aspects of substantial connection. The situation of 'you' as everyday eaters is

33. Cf. also Exod. 34.11-26.

34. A comparable interest is reflected by the transition into frequentative forms in the tent scenes in Exod. 33.8-9, 34.34-35 and 40.36-38. In these cases the singular events are extended into a permanent situation for the post-Sinai stage.

linked to the event of divine consuming. The difference between acceptable and non-acceptable food is underlined by the dual character of the divine consuming, as an act of profound parallelism and with implications of terrible threat. The relationship of story and divine address seems to imply that Leviticus 11 should be understood as an application of the story. Formally the continuation of the story, the address outlines the implications of the narrated events. The distance between the narrative reality and the situation of 'you', combined with 'you' involved also in the story, could be important as an indication of how these stories are to be read.[35]

3. *The Day of Erecting the Dwelling: Numbers 7–9*

Numbers 9.15-23

As an extended repetition of Exod. 40.36-38, Num. 9.15-23 seems to indicate the effects of a multi-layered presentation. The parallelism is seemingly easily explained when related to historical categories of tradition or redaction criticism.[36] But related to categories of composition, the echo-effect of the two passages indicates an important linkage. The common motifs and the stereotyped language[37] relate the two passages to each other, the Numbers version being an elaborated version of the short-form in Exodus 40.[38]

But at the same time each passage bears the marks of its function in a special context. Exodus 40.36-38 concludes the description of the theophanic manifestation introduced in v. 34, which presents the climax of a complicated series of events. Verses 36-37 extend the description of v. 34 by relating the cloud to the situation of departure and journey.

35. Cf. Postscript for the similar relationship between the story in Num. 13–14 and its application in the instructions in Num. 15.38-41.

36. E.g. J. de Vaulx, *Les Nombres* (SB; Paris: J. Gabalda, 1972), p. 127, on Numbers as a late layer of Priestly redaction which repeats and adapts the earlier texts, working together different types of imagery and eliminating their concrete nature. For P.J. Budd, *Numbers* (WBC, 5; Waco: Word Books, 1984), p. 102, the parallelism reflects an author 'anxious to take up ideas about the divine presence' from Exod. 40 'to develop a theory of divine guidance in the wilderness'.

37. Cf. especially the infinitive-constructions connected with imperfect-forms, Num. 9.17, 19, 22a and b corresponding to Exod. 40.36.

38. The traditional understanding of Exod. 40.36-38 as dependent on the Numbers version has been reversed by de Vaulx, *Les Nombres*, p. 127; Budd, *Numbers*, p. 102; and Blum, *Studien zur Komposition*, pp. 312-13.

The concluding v. 38 combines the two situations. The return to the theophanic imagery of vv. 34-35 is concluded by a reference to the people by the dependent construction 'before the eyes of the people on all their journey'. Framed in this way, the journey motifs of vv. 36-37 are set in a context given over to the presentation of the divine manifestation.[39]

Also for the Numbers version, the imagery of the cloud is important for the description of the people's journey. But here the concluding statement of v. 23 is centred around the people's journey.[40] In addition, the people's obedience is presented by the categories of Torah. The motif of the divine 'mouth' refers to the formula of vv. 18a and 20b. The final application is added to by the terms 'observe' and 'observance', corresponding to v. 19b. The repetitive effects accentuate the final extension of the formulaic language in v. 23, when the divine 'mouth' is connected with the 'hand of Moses'.

In this way, the common imagery of cloud related to the tent and to the people's journey is differently elaborated by the two versions. For the Exodus version, the substitution of Moses by the people elevated into a permanent theophanic relationship is the important aspect of the wondrous events. The repetitions of the Numbers version give the

39. Cf. also the repetition of parallel sentences given to the motifs of 'cloud over the tent' and 'glory in the dwelling' in vv. 34 and 35. The cloud represents the divine manifestation in vv. 36-38. But set after v. 35, ended by a description of the glory, the application of the cloud motif in v. 36aα corresponds to the rythmic change established in the two first verses. Moreover, the cloud related to the 'dwelling' contracts the two motif types of vv. 34-35 (cf. also the verb 'dwell' with cloud for subject v. 35aβ). The micro-details of shaping must reflect the compositional interest in 'adding' these verses to the context. The delicacy of composition even includes a referential relationship to the introductory 19.2. Compared to the rythmic change of *ḥānâ* and *nāsaʻ* in Num. 9.15-23, Exod. 40.36-38 only applies the latter verb also when the former would be the suitable word. This corresponds to the repeated application of *ḥānâ* in 19.2. In the latter, the imagery of Israel settled is juxtaposed to Moses ascending the mountain, while in Exod. 40 the imagery of Israel breaking camp is juxtaposed to the non-entering of Moses in v. 35.

40. Its significance is reflected by the description of the people's departure in ch. 10. The introductory vv. 11-13 refer both to the imagery of 9.15-23 and to the formulaic language of v. 23. Comparable to the singular events of 9.15 extended into repeated events in vv. 16-23 (corresponding to Exod. 40.34-35 followed by vv. 36-38), Num. 10.11-13 transfers the imagery of a permanent journey situation into the singular event when the people departed from Sinai.

impression of a totally dedicated people, minutely imitating the movements of the cloud. This is emphasized by the additional motifs of divine 'mouth', 'observe' the divine 'observance', and Moses' 'hand'. The journey represents a situation of Torah observance, performed by the children of Israel in perfect obedience to the divine commands mediated by Moses.

The perception of the journey condensed into an image of perfect Torah observance is the more important, as the cycle of singular journey stories, starting in ch. 11, presents a totally different situation. The perfect pilgrims of ch. 9 are juxtaposed by the weaklings of ch. 11. The juxtaposition has usually been related to the linkage of different sets of traditions. In contrast to the Priestly background of Numbers 9, ch. 11 has been related to the Yahwist[41] or to a special 'rebellion in the wilderness' tradition.[42] But whatever the prehistory of the materials, their present compilation represents two starkly opposed images of the journeying people, one presenting its total obedience, the other a negative portrayal of a people in revolt.[43]

Due to the relationship of Exodus 34 and 40, the concluding reference to Moses in Num. 9.23, underlined by 10.13, must also be important. In Exodus 40 the exclusion of Moses underlines the elevation of the people. Also Num. 9.15-22 accentuates the people as permanently related to the theophanic presence. But by the final addition to the formulaic language in v. 23, the position of Moses as the mediator is subtly added to the equation. The referential relationship of Exod. 40.36-38 and Num. 9.15-23 underlines the significance of the final addition in v. 23. The finale of Exodus 40 is repeated by a final chord of perfect harmony. The jarring impression of Moses excluded from the tent is neutralized by the new scene of Numbers 9, on the one hand equally centred around the presentation of the people as related to the theophanic presence, on the other hand subtly extending the formulaic language to also include Moses the mediator positively in the imagery

41. E.g. Van Seters, *The Life of Moses*, pp. 226-29.

42. Coats, *Moses*, pp. 109-13.

43. Cf. especially D.T. Olson, *The Death of the Old and the Birth of the New: The Framework of the Book of Numbers and the Pentateuch* (BJS, 71; Chico, CA: Scholars Press, 1976), pp. 121-23, on 10.36 and 11.1 as expressions for a major break in the first half of the book. For Wilcoxen, 'Some Anthropocentric Aspects', pp. 333-50, comparable contrasts are important for the composition of Exodus–Numbers as a whole.

of 'the day of erecting'. The substantial impact of the minute addition is the more significant as it corresponds to the effect of Exodus 40 balanced by ch. 34 as a parallel conclusion.

In this way Exod. 40.36-38 and Num. 9.15-23 refer to each other as parallel conclusions, while their shape corresponds to their different function. The former represents the conclusion of the story begun in Exodus 19, centred around the divine movement from mountain to tent and the introduction of the people as theophanic figures. The latter concludes the grand cycle of Sinai stories, followed by the departure from Sinai presented in ch. 10 and the cycle of journey stories introduced in ch. 11. The relationship to the Sinai events is reflected by the reference to 'the day of erecting', while the extended references to the journey links with the following cycle of stories. As a description of the journey as whole, Num. 9.15-23 presents a condensed image of the events to come. This linkage is concretely reflected by Num. 10.11-13, which turns the permanent journey situation of Num. 9.15-23 into the singular event of departure from Sinai.

The parallelism of two conclusions in Exod. 40.36-38 and Num. 9.15-23 implies a corresponding relationship between two sets of Sinai stories. Exodus 19–40 represents one set followed by a parallel set introduced in Lev. 1.1 and concluded in Numbers 9.[44] Such effects of parallelism correspond to the ambiguous relationship of Exodus 40 and Leviticus 1–10. As we have seen, the relationship of successive episodes is combined with aspects of repetition. Also the shift of compositional mode by the transition from ch. 10 to 11 could reflect the function of two parallel sets of Sinai stories. The transition to ch. 11, extended by the lengthy series of divine instructions in the rest of Leviticus, marks the rupture of the compositional pattern (cf. Chapter 4.2). On the other hand, chs. 1–10 as a fourth theophanic episode reflect the established pattern. Also when the theophanic manifestation is followed by a set of divine instructions in ch. 11, the pattern is adhered to. Set in this pattern, ch. 11, as well as the rest of the book of Leviticus, is presented as the theophanic speech of 'the day of erecting'. Such a function, with a corresponding emphasis on the 'day of of erecting' as the comprehensive framework for the divine instructions, corresponds to the repetition of Exod. 40.36-38 in Num. 9.15-23. The materials set

44. Cf. also Milgrom, *Leviticus 1–16*, p. 139, on Exod. 40.36-38 and Num. 9.15-23, bracketing the intervening material Lev. 1.1–Num. 9.14.

between present what is demanded of the people in the new situation of permanent theophanic relationship.

The Notes of Dating

The significance of 'the day of erecting', as the recurrent theme for the presentation of what took place at Sinai, is also reflected by the conflicting notes of dating in Numbers. According to 1.1, 18[45] and 10.11, the events of Numbers 1–10 are set in a temporal frame of 20 days between 'the first day in the second month in the second year' and the departure from Sinai on the 'twentieth day in the second month in the second year'. This neat setting is disturbed by 9.1. The Passover instructions are dated to the first month of the second year, their implementation to the fourteenth day (v. 5). Scribal errors aside, this seems quite peculiar[46] for a text set in a narrative structure framed by the notes of dating in 1.1 and 10.11. The latter indicate a narrative structure of linear character which is disturbed by 9.1. The impression of narrative inconsistency is underlined by the introduction of the theme of Passover celebration in Num. 9.1.[47]

The temporal reference of Num. 9.15 adds to this impression. The reader, jerked from events of the second month to the first month, is taken even further back in time to the events of Exodus 40. Although the temporal framework is widened to a permanent situation of 'always' in v. 16, the dating in v. 15 must be important due to the parallelism of vv. 15-23 and Exod. 40.36-38. Related to a narrative framework of 20 days in the second month, the reader has been moved backwards in time to the Passover celebration of the fourteenth day of the first month (Num. 9.1-5), to events which according to Exod. 40.1, 17 happened on the first day (v. 15). Finally, the temporal framework is dissolved into a

45. The dating of Num. 1.1 is important to Olson (*Death of the Old*, pp. 46-48), indicating that the book of Numbers should be read as a compositional unit.

46. 'Maladroite', according to de Vaulx, *Les Nombres*, p. 123, and also Budd, *Numbers*, pp. 96-97. Its significance is dismissed in favour of the dating in 1.1 by Olson, *Death of the Old*, p. 34. Levine, *Numbers 1–20*, p. 295, resolves the discrepancy by seeing 9.1 as a caption older than 1.1.

47. Rather loosely connected to the context as an expression of a 'variety of subjects that were previously unaddressed', according to Levine, *Numbers 1–20*, p. 293. De Vaulx, *Les Nombres*, p. 123, points to Ezra 6.16-26 as a parallel. Here the dedication of the temple and the organization of the priestly and Levitical service is followed by the Passover celebration.

permanent journey situation of 'always', which repeats the essence of the very first 'day of erecting' (vv. 16-23).

The significance of Num. 9.15 is underlined by the notes of dating in Num. 7.1, 10 (cf. also vv. 84 and 88). Formally, these notes are closely related. The element *b^eyôm* is followed by infinitives, followed in turn by narrative forms. In the first reference, Num. 7.1, the infinitive forms refer to the 'erecting' of the sanctuary, while the narrative forms present the anointing and sanctification of the sanctuary and its contents and of the altar and its contents. To these events is added the scene in vv. 2-9 with the leaders presenting their gifts. In the second reference of v. 10 (cf. also vv. 84 and 88), the infinitive refers to the anointing of the altar followed by a second scene of dedication in vv. 11-88.

The connection between the dating notes of Num. 7.1 and 9.15 must be important for the understanding of these materials. The linear development of the events suggested by Num. 1.1 and 10.11 is broken by considerations more important than narrative verisimilitude. The *parallellismus membrorum* effect of 9.15-23, related to Exod. 40.36-38, extols 'the day of erecting' as the central event of Sinai. This effect is extended into the preceding chapters by the dating notes of Num. 7.1 and 9.15. The emphasis on the special day, as well as the seemingly artificial character of its contexual setting, is comparable to the ambiguous relationship of Leviticus 8–9 and Exodus 40. In both cases, the formal framework characterized by the linear development of successive events is combined with contradictory effects which accentuate some substantial connection between the events. Centred around different aspects and thus not directly repeating Exodus 40, Leviticus 8–9 represent a parallel expression for the same events. Correspondingly, Numbers 7–9 leave the confinements of the temporal framework of the context to return to the events of Exodus 40.

According to Num. 7.1, 'the day of erecting' entails not only the erection of the tent, but also the consecration of the altar and the ritual implements. The note condenses the events of Exodus 40 and Leviticus 8–9 into one situation. On the other hand, the delicate wording seems to reflect the ambiguous relationship of Exodus 40 and Leviticus 8–9 according to the composition in its present shape. The transition from infinitive to narrative forms in v. 1 separates two sets of events, underlined by the altar as the sole motif in v. 10. And corresponding to Leviticus 8–9, 'added' to Exodus 40, Numbers 7 extends the events of 'the day of erecting' by a third series of events. Formally, such a connection is also reflected by the narrative forms of v. 2. Without any formal rupture aside from the introduction of a new set of actors, they continue the narrative of v. 1, adding the dedication of the princes to the erection of the tent and the sanctification of the altar. In this way, a third chord is added to the presentation of 'the day of erecting'. The composition as a whole represents a threefold repetition of the central event. To the basic chord of Exodus 40 is added the reverberations of the events in Leviticus 8–10 and Numbers 7–9.

This development underlines the Passover dating in Num. 9.1-5. The important connection between Num. 7.1 and 9.15, extolling the climactic event of Sinai, seems to be disturbed by the description of the Passover celebration. But related to the temporal framework of Numbers 7–8, the Passover celebration continues the preceding events. The third presentation of what happened on 'the day of erecting', expanded into twelve days (7.10-11) and followed by the events of ch. 8, is concluded by the Passover celebration.[48] And when Num. 9.15 leaves the events of the fourteenth day to return to the very first day of the first month, the formal character of Num. 9.15-23 indicates that these verses have a special function compared to the preceding passages. The imperfect consecutive forms of Num. 7.1–9.14 present singular events. The imperfect forms of Num. 9.15-23 extend the events of 'the day of erecting' into a typical situation of 'always', repeated throughout the journey.[49] The special function of Num. 9.15-23, indicated by the formal character, corresponds to the echo effect of this passage with regard to Exod. 40.36-38. As some narrative refrain, Num. 9.15-23 concludes the Sinai stories by a final reference to the central event of Sinai.

In a rather forced way according to categories of narrative verisimilitude, the dating notes of Numbers 7–9 refer to the significance of the events. The linear development of successive episodes represents the basic compositional mode. This is reflected by the relationship of Num. 1.1 and 10.11, which indicates the temporal framework for the events presented in the book of Numbers, when the story proceeds from Sinai

48. The 12 days of altar dedications in Num. 7.10-88, followed by the sanctification of the Levites, just might permit a full Passover celebration on the fourteenth day, although the calendar is rather full. But in that case, any blurring of Levitical sanctification and Passover would be rather appropriate.

49. This is underlined by the stylized character of Num. 7.1-2 and 9.15, the infinitive construction of the former introducing imperfect consecutives, while the latter is followed by imperfects.

to wilderness. But the elaboration of 'the day of erecting' implies that the linear development is combined with other modes of composition which underline what 'really' took place. Concluding the cycle of Sinai stories, the dates of Numbers 7–9 accentuate the erection of the tent and the theophanic manifestation in the camp as the significant event. Parallel to Exodus 35–40 and Leviticus 8–10, Numbers 7–9 present the third version of the central event. Moreover, corresponding to Exod. 40.36-38, the third version also extends the climactic event of Sinai into a permanent journey situation. The people's experience of the theophanic presence, permanently manifesting itself below, represents *in nuce* an expression of what took place after Sinai.

The meticulous elaboration makes the introduction of the Passover important. Related to the temporal framework of Numbers 7–9, the Passover celebration is presented as the final event of Sinai. Moreover, the contextual setting of Num. 9.1-14, concluding the events of chs. 7–8 and followed by the narrative refrain of 9.15-23, indicates that the Passover celebration is presented as part of the climactic events when the sanctuary was erected. As the final event of Sinai concluded by the condensed description of the journey as a permanent experience of the theophanic manifestation, the celebration of the Passover implies that the Sinai events represent a new version of the original sequence of Passover and departure from Egypt.

Numbers 7.1-88

This story is closely related to the two preceding versions of 'the day of erecting'.[50] The people's leaders bringing their valuables as gifts to the sanctuary represent a scene of dedication parallel to the dedication of the raw-materials in Exodus 35–40 and of the sacrificial elements according to Leviticus 1–9.[51] The terminology indicates a special relationship to the latter. In the building account of Exodus, the people's

50. Illustrated by the usual understanding of this chapter as a very late elaboration of the older traditions—'une composition artificielle' according to de Vaulx, *Les Nombres*, pp. 109-10; and a similar view is shared by Budd, *Numbers*, pp. 81-82.

51. A basic connection between the materials is indicated by Levine ('The Descriptive Tabernacle Texts of the Pentateuch', *JAOS* 85 [1965], pp. 307-18; *idem*, *Numbers 1–20*, pp. 259-66) on Exod. 35–40, Lev. 8–9 and Num. 7 as parallel types of archival records.

gifts are qualified as *t^erûmâ*,[52] while *qorbān* is the usual term in Leviticus 1–7.[53] The latter is applied throughout Numbers 7. Also the verbs of dedication[54] correspond to the terminology in Leviticus 1–7.[55] In this way, Numbers 7 also reflects the connection between the *t^erûmâ* dedication in the building account of Exodus and the sacrificial *qorbān* of Leviticus 1-7. The texts present the dedication of the people's gifts in three modes.

The character of the first *qorbān* (Neh. 7.1-9) indicates a special relationship between the first episode and the events of Exodus 40. The gifts of oxen and wagons and the corresponding duties of the Levites refer to the transport of the dissembled sanctuary. The story can be read as the continuation of the Exodus story. The assemblage of the sanctuary in ch. 40 is reversed, corresponding to the impending departure of Numbers 10.

The second type of *qorbān* in Num. 7.10-88 can be related both to the Exodus story and to Leviticus 1–9. All the gifts are connected with sacrificial categories and thus primarily refer to a situation that corresponds to Leviticus 8–9. The sacrificial elements repeated in the stereotyped presentations of the individual offering correspond to the types ordered in Lev. 9.3-4, complemented by the improper offering of incense in Lev. 10.1. On the other hand, the presentation of silver bowls and gold dishes, used as containers for the sacrificial gifts of cereals and incense, is comparable to the scene of Exod. 35.27-28 in which the leaders present valuables to the sanctuary.

The separation of the two sets of connected events in vv. 1-9 and 10-88 of Numbers 7 and the character of the gifts correspond to the order indicated by the notes of dating in vv. 1 and 10, which both combine and separate two sets of events connected with the tent and the altar. This corresponds to the relationship of Exodus 35–40 and Leviticus 8–9 as parallel versions of the same events. Numbers 7 presents a third set of events which is formally different from the first set centred around the erection of the Tent of Meeting and the second set centred around events of sanctification, yet of a strangely parallel and repetitive character.

Common to the three sets is a marked emphasis on material

52. Exod. 25.2-3; 35.5, 21, 24; 36.6.

53. In addition to *t^erûmâ* in Lev. 7.14, 32, 34.

54. *hiqrîb* in Num. 7.2, 3, 10, 11, 12, 18, 19; with a parallel *hēbî'* in Num. 7.3.

55. E.g. Lev. 1.2, 14; *hēbî'*, e.g., Lev. 4.23, 28.

categories. The sacred objects are presented as phenomena of material culture, as finished artifacts or as raw materials for further processing; as a building taken down to be transported by wagons and oxen—with implications of heaviness and size—as costly bowls to be weighed and valued together with sacrificial elements of cereals and incense and lots of animals. This could be related to the literary character of the genre reflected by these materials.[56] But it must be important that aspects of costliness are connected to a common gift theme. In Exodus 35–36, the willingness of the 'heart-driven' people is a central motif. In continuation of this story, the episodes in Numbers 7 also seem to reflect a corresponding interest.[57]

The referential relationship to the earlier stories underlines the significance of the human initiative for the dedication of the gifts in Numbers 7. According to the relationship of divine instructions and the offerings of gifts in Exodus 25–40 and Leviticus 1–10, the human acts represent the implementation of the divine commands and are qualified as acceptable by the formula of compliance. The importance of this relationship is underlined by the negative 'gift scenes' of Exod. 32.2-3, contrasting with Exod. 33.4-6 and Lev. 10.1-2. Characterized by the human initiative, the Golden Calf and the strange fire represent contrasting offerings of 'black magic'. But in Numbers 7, the princes bring their gifts on their own and are divinely responded to in the form of acceptance (v. 4) and by directions on the order of presentation (v. 11). In this case, the divine instruction is a response that puts the stamp of approval upon the human initiative. Compared to the earlier episodes, the offering of Numbers 7 both continues the aspect of exuberant 'willingness' and indicates a new situation in which the human initiative does not profane the sacredness of the new locus.

Numbers 7.89

The episode of the gifts is followed by a scene given over to Moses in the inner sanctum of the tent. The verse is generally seen as an isolated fragment from a tradition also retained in Exod. 25.22, 30.6 and Lev. 16.2,[58] now rather loosely connected with the preceding verses[59] or

56. Cf. the accounting function of the genre, according to Levine, 'Descriptive Tabernacle Texts'.

57. For Budd, *Numbers*, p. 84, the sole objective for the chapter is 'the encouragement of generosity and commitment among the post-exilic laity'.

58. Haran, *Temples and Temple Service*, p. 247; while Levine, *Numbers 1–20*,

introducing the following address to Aaron.[60] The present shape of Numbers 7 is underlined by the relationship to Exodus 40 and Leviticus 8–9. The scene of Num. 7.89, with Moses inside the sacred space and related to 'the voice', represents a scene of extraordinary encounter, comparable to the encounter episodes of the Sinai stories. Moreover, the sequence of the events, the presentation of the gifts in vv. 1-88 concluded by an encounter scene in v. 89, corresponds to the theophanic episodes in Exodus 19–40 and Leviticus 1–10, structured by scenes of human preparation and climaxed by the theophanic manifestation.

In Exod. 40.34-38 and Lev. 9.23-24 the events of human preparation and theophanic climax are directly linked. Compared to the building of the tent which is covered by the divine cloud, and the preparation of the sacrifices consumed by the divine fire, the connection of the gifts given by princes and the divine communication with Moses in the inner sanctum is less visible. But formally, the scene of 7.89 is connected to the preceding events. The introductory infinitive construction *ûbᵉbō' mōšeh* is followed by narrative forms. This corresponds to and continues the constructions of vv. 1, 10, 84 and 88. The introductory *û* continues the infinitive construction 'after its being anointed' which concludes v. 88. Moses' entering the tent for an intimate encounter is presented as an event following upon the preceding events.

Thus, while any direct connection between preparatory events and encounter is rather uncertain, the meticulous character of the composition reflects the wish to connect the scenes. This is also indicated by the order of the scenes. Corresponding to the pattern of the theophanic episodes, Numbers 7 reflects the order of two preparatory sub-episodes followed by the encounter. The two separate scenes in vv. 1-9 and vv. 10-83, concluded by the summary of vv. 84-88,[61] are followed by a third scene of encounter in v. 89. Further, corresponding to the theophanic episodes of Exodus 19–Leviticus 10, the divine manifestation of Numbers 7 is also followed by a set of divine instructions (8.1).

p. 258, relates the 'cryptic' verse on the Tabernacle as an 'oraculum' to Exod. 25.22 and 33.6-11.

59. E.g. de Vaulx, *Les Nombres*, pp. 113-14.

60. Budd, *Numbers*, pp. 85-87.

61. Concluding the details of gift presentation, these verses can be compared to 'the list of totals' in Exod. 38.24-30 which according to Levine ('Descriptive Tabernacle Texts', p. 309) indicates Exod. 35–39 to be a document patterned after archival records.

The comparison to Exodus 40 and Leviticus 9 underlines the position of Moses as the human actor in the encounter of Numbers 7. The motif of 'enter into the Tent of Meeting' is common to all these texts. In Exod. 40.32 it is related to preparatory rites with Moses, Aaron and 'his sons' as actors, and in v. 35 with Moses as actor and negatively related to the theophanic manifestation. In Lev. 9.23 it has Moses and Aaron as subjects, related to preparatory rites and immediately followed by the theophanic manifestation. Also, the motif is reflected in the tent scenes in Exod. 33.8-9 and 34.34-35.

The imagery as well as the explicit reference to 'the day of erecting' underlines the special relationship of the tent scene in Num. 7.89 to that of Exod. 40.34-38. The two parallel sets of preparations result in two diametrically opposed situations. In Exodus 40, the building account is concluded by a scene in which the theophanic presence leads to the contrasts of Moses 'non-entering' and the people's *visio*. In Numbers 7, the people's gifts introduce the opposite scene with Moses, in splendid isolation, entering the inner sanctum for a scene of intimate encounter. Given the function of Exodus 40 as the conclusion of the basic set of Sinai stories, the contrasting scene of Numbers 7 must have an important function for the composition as a whole. As we have seen, the conclusion of Exodus 40, with its emphasis on the people as the theophanic figures at the cost of the 'non-entering' Moses, represents a tantalizing riddle. This effect is added to by the ambiguous relationship between this conclusion and the apotheosis of Moses in Exodus 34. Related to the contrasting effect of Exodus 34 and 40, the tent scene of Num. 7.89 represents an effect of harmonization and reconciliation.

This is also indicated by the details of motif elaboration, which refer both to Exodus 34 and 40. The 'entering' of Moses corresponds to the 'non-entering' of Exodus 40. The situation inside the tent, where YHWH speaks to Moses, corresponds to the imagery of Exod. 33.7-11 and 34.34-35, which depicts Moses inside sacred space and related to the divine speaker. The juxtaposition of the two Exodus scenes is mitigated by the third scene of Num. 7.89. The Exodus scenes are not contradicted or implicitly nullified. Corresponding to the contrasts of Moses' Tent of Meeting in Exodus 33–34 and the people's Tent of Meeting in Exodus 40, the third scene refers to the inner sanctum of the tent.[62] Formally, each scene represents a singular situation, to be read

62. And thus implementing Exod. 25.22 and the reference in Exod. 30.6, hitherto ignored by the narrative development, but at last actualized.

and savoured on its own, while the perception of subtle contradictions arises during a later stage of digestive efforts. To the juxtaposition of Exodus 34 and 40 is added a third scene of theophanic encounter, the tension of the former as contradictory mitigated by the effect of the third.

Such an interest corresponds to the concluding element 'by the hand of Moses' in Num. 9.23. The significance of this element is underlined by the function of Num. 9.15-23 as a narrative refrain, repeating and extending Exod. 40.36-38 for the conclusion of the second set of Sinai stories. The second conclusion remains true to the first, echoing that the people as the theophanic visionaries represent the climactic result of Sinai. But in addition, the subtle extension 'by the hand of Moses' in the final application of the formulaic language relates the pre-eminence of the people to the function of Moses the mediator. Seen together, the tent scene of Num. 7.89 and the narrative refrain of Num. 9.15-23 mirror the tent scene of Exod. 40.35 followed by vv. 36-38. The 'entering' of Moses mitigates his former 'non-entering', while the 'hand of Moses' adds to the perception of the people as theophanic actors.

The meticulous elaboration of referential effects is also reflected by the minutiae of stylistic effects. The introductory infinitive construction *ûbᵉbō' mōšeh* followed by narrative forms is formally consistent with the rest of Numbers 7. But it has also been seen that this type of construction seems to function as an indication of the referential relationship between the scenes in Exod. 34.34, 40.36 and (with *kᵉ*) 33.8, 9. The application of this construction in a similar context dedicated to Moses entering sacred space to communicate with God seems to have the same function, reflecting the connotational connection between these texts.[63] But while the construction in the Exodus scenes is used for the transition from singular to repeated acts, in Num. 7.89 it is followed by narrative forms that present a singular event, corresponding to the preceding infinitive constructions in Numbers 7.

The allusive references of the formulaic language and the central motifs seem to represent an abundance of connotational effects. Given the special relationship between Exodus 35–40, Leviticus 8–9 and Numbers 7, also the threefold transformation of the encounter situation represented by these texts could be important. In Exodus 40, YHWH manifests himself as cloud, corresponding to the imagery of the first

63. Cf. also the parallel relationship to a following speech by YHWH (Lev. 1.1 and Num. 8.1) or Moses (Exod. 33.12; 35.1).

theophanic episode in Exodus 19. The fire manifestation of Leviticus 9 seems to refer to the second theophanic episode of Exodus 24. In Numbers 7, Moses enters the inner sanctum of the tent listening to God manifesting as *the* [64] voice. Apart from the reference to Exod. 40.35, the imagery corresponds to the tent scene of 34.34-35. The interplay of the different divine manifestations of cloud, fire and voice is also connected with a corresponding change of locus. The cloud in Exodus 40 is related to the Tent of Meeting as a building. Related to the sacrifices, the consuming fire of Leviticus 9 implies the altar as the locus of manifestation. The voice of Num. 7.89 is emphatically connected with the space above the ark in the inner sanctum, the significance of the localization being reflected by the meticulous description. Such a pattern of sacred loci represented by Exodus 40, Leviticus 9 and Num. 7.89 is mirrored by the composition of the three scenes in Numbers 7, which are related to the tent (vv. 1-9), the altar (vv. 10-88) and the ark (v. 89).

While such motifs probably were meaningful in an address to the ancient *cognoscenti*, the modern reader is at least left with the impression of a meticulous and highly complex composition. Categories of some hierarchical relationship could also be implied. In Exodus 40 the divine manifestation of signalling cloud is related to the tent as a whole and to the people for human actors. In Leviticus 9, priestly categories[65] are central for the manifestation of sacrificial fire upon the altar. In Numbers 7, Moses alone is related to the inner sanctum, God manifesting himself as 'the voice'.[66] But if the theophanic manifestations of cloud, fire and voice related to the loci of tent, altar and ark and to a hierarchical order of people, priests and Moses, really are appropriate, the parallelism also would underline the significance of the concluding

64. The determined form represents a traditional *crux* (e.g. Budd, *Numbers*, pp. 86-87). But with Exod. 34.34-35 as a close parallel (cf. the ambiguous 'to talk to him' vv. 34aα, 35bβ, corresponding to the first sentence in Num. 7.89), it is possible to assume that the language is of an allusive character. Referring to some divine mode of a special type of encounter, 'the voice' is comparable to 'the cloud' in Exod. 24.15-18, 40.34 (cf. also 33.9), and also 'the mountain' in Exod. 19.2.

65. Cf. also the priestly function of Moses in Lev. 8–9 and the priestly themes of Lev. 10.

66. Cf. the comparable relationship of localities and divine manifestations in 1 Kgs 19, the 'angel' followed by the 'word of YHWH' and 'YHWH', the latter manifesting as *qôl* . The leaps from 'cloud' to 'fire' to 'voice' could also be related to the motif development in the negations of 1 Kgs 19.11-12.

reference to the people in Num. 9.15-23. The ultimate significance of the events of Sinai is expressed by the permanent theophanic manifestation in the camp related to the people engaged in permanent *visio*.

Numbers 8.1-4

This passage continues the scene of Num. 7.89. The divine instructions of v. 1 reflect what was said during the encounter in the inner sanctum. The instructions are followed by a story of implementation. This order corresponds to the usual organization of the materials in Exodus 19–40, where the divine instructions of a scene of encounter initiate a new series of human actions, which prepare for the next encounter. The emphasis on the formula of compliance in the concluding vv. 3-4 corresponds to its application in the last part of the building account in Exodus 39–40 and in the story of priestly sanctification in Leviticus 8–9. The structure of vv. 1-4 represents a short version of the pattern, with divine instructions addressed to Moses, the mediator, and responded to by the human actor.[67] On the other hand, the stereotyped character of the story underlines the special character of v. 4.

The emphasis on the lamp and its correct position is rather obscure.[68] It could reflect effects of symbolism.[69] At the very least, the reference to the outer sanctum continues the local categories of Numbers 7. The reference to the tent, altar and inner sanctum is followed by the outer sanctum. This is also reflected by the character of the actors related to the localities. After the dedication of the gifts associated with the representatives of the people, the story turns to Moses, followed by the presentation of the function of Aaron in 8.1-4, and concluded by the Levitical function in vv. 5-26. Also the aspect of 'sacred materialism' continues the preceding story. Corresponding to Numbers 7, Num. 8.1-4 can be related both to the building account of Exodus 35–40 and the priestly categories of Leviticus 8–10. The emphasis on sacred artifacts and their shape corresponds to the former, while Aaron's being instructed in his priestly duties corresponds to the latter. Just as the gifts

67. This order is reversed in Num. 7 where the divine instructions respond to the human initiative, while Num. 8.1-4, 5-26, and 9.1-5 reflect the normal order.

68. Cf. the discussion in Budd, *Numbers*, p. 86.

69. E.g. de Vaulx, *Les Nombres*, p. 117. Also Exod. 27.20-21 indicates the care of the lamp as *the* priestly duty. The motif connection between the encounter in the inner sanctum of Num. 7.89 followed by the priestly tending of the lamp in the outer sanctum in Num. 8.1-4 is also reflected in Exod. 30.6-8.

of ch. 7 do not repeat the events of the building account and the priestly consecretation, but expand them by a parallel situation, so the care of the lamp in Num. 8.1-4 continues the story of its making in Exod. 37.17-24.

The interest in categories of materiality and sacred workmanship is underlined by the extension of v. 4. A story of instruction and compliance would well be concluded by v. 3, corresponding, for example, to vv. 20 and 22 which conclude the sanctification of the Levites. The extra conclusion of v. 4 marks a digression, lingering on the wondrous character of the lamp, produced in a special way from gold and exactly according to the heavenly vision.

Conversely, the special character of v. 4 underlines the elaborate character of v. 3. 'He did so, Aaron' in v. 3aα is concluded in v.3b by the sentence 'just as *YHWH* had commanded Moses'. This represents an extended form of the formula of compliance. In the parallel stories, the monotonous application of this formula stresses its importance for the qualification of the human activity as sacred action.[70] Changes of the stereotyped form must be significant. Thus, Exod. 39.32, 42, 43 and 40.16 represent comparable extensions in plural or singular form. Added to the formula, the sentence 'they (he) did so' corresponds to the version in Num. 8.3. In all cases, the extended version corresponds to a special application in comprehensive descriptions which present a summary of the task, concluding or introducing the presentations of the single acts. Accordingly, the extended version in v. 3 points to the importance of the act described, the action of Aaron being truly the exact observance of the divine command.[71]

This effect is underlined by the repeated application of the formula in v. 4b. The statement 'just as the vision *YHWH* had made Moses see, so he made the lamp', set after v. 3, echoes the formula of compliance. The perfect compliance of Aaron when setting up the lamp corresponds to the perfect compliance of 'he' who made the lamp. The parallelism of the constructions indicates that Aaron is the subject also of the second expression of perfect action. In this context Moses, who is mentioned in v. 4bα, represents the only alternative candidate for the role of

70. Applied throughout Exod. 39–40 and Lev. 8–9. It is also represented in negated form in Lev. 10.1, and with Moses as subject in Lev. 8.31; 9.5, 21.

71. Cf. the corresponding extensions in 8.20, 22 and 9.5. Climaxed by 9.15, 23, the elaborations of the formulaic language indicate a perfect situation of meticulous obedience.

'he', the perfect metal-worker. But the reference to Moses in the versions of the compliance formula does not imply that Moses is the actor but underlines his function as mediator.[72] The steretyped sentences in vv. 3 and 4, based on the constructions of *k^e^* and *'ᵃšer - kēn*, refer to Moses as the mediator in both cases, while presenting Aaron and 'he' as parallel implementors. Rather ambiguously,[73] the symmetry of the sentences indicates Aaron as the perfect actor in v. 4 as well as in v. 3.[74]

Confronting the possibility of Aaron as a candidate for perfect craftsmanship, the reader is reminded of the Golden Calf episode. Here Aaron really did work in gold and rather poorly so. However ambiguous the delicate wording of the formulaic language, the extension of v. 3 by the 'unnecessary' v. 4 adds a special set of connotations to Aaron as the perfect actor. Moreover, such implications correspond to the elaboration of the stereotyped scenes in Numbers 7. Moses located in the inner sanctum harmonizes the tension left by the theophanic scene of Exodus 40. The divine acceptance of the leaders' initiative in presenting the gifts in Num. 7.1-88 contrasts with the wilful initiative of the people in the Golden Calf episode, as well as their passivity when Moses 'on his own' erected the Tent of Meeting. Accordingly, Aaron presented as the perfect actor also as metal-worker seems to represent a third chord of the harmony which concludes the Sinai stories.

Numbers 8.5-26

The story of the purification of the Levites is closely related to the story of priestly sanctification in Leviticus 8.[75] The character of the events

72. In Exod. 40.19, 21, 23, 25, 27 and 29, the stereotyped formula with the usual reference to Moses as mediator is combined with sentences in third person singular which present Moses as implementing also the divine command. But this represents an irregular combination.

73. Cf. the corresponding technique in Exod. 36–39 where the presentation of the people as sacred craftsmen is connected with passages which refer to named craftsmen. Also in the description of Moses writing the second set of tablets in Exod. 34.28, in contrast to the divine writer of v. 1, an ambiguous 'he' makes different readings possible.

74. Cf. also below in this Chapter for the comparable elaborations of the formulaic language in vv. 20 and 22.

75. Cf. G.B. Gray, *A Critical and Exegetical Commentary on Numbers* (ICC; repr.; Edinburgh: T. & T. Clark, 1965 [1903]), p. 78, who finds within vv. 5-22 an original story designed as a parallel to the consecration of the priests in Lev. 8, later expanded by Aaron motifs and the influence of Num. 3.5-13.

also links the two stories. By the qualification of the Levites as priestly assistants (vv. 19, 22), the priestly sanctification of Leviticus is completed. Such a connection corresponds to a context dedicated to 'the day of erecting', the parallelism[76] of the events in this case having an immediate effect of continuation and completion.

The formal structure of the story corresponds to the preceding episode. The divine instructions addressed to Moses in Num. 8.5-19 is followed by a story of implementation in vv. 20-22 connected with the formula of compliance (vv. 20, 22b). The speech introduction of v. 5, as well as v. 23 and 9.1, could even continue 8.1, all referring to what was said during the encounter of 7.89.[77] An interest of linkage could also be signalled by the application of *zeh*/*zō't* when the separate scenes of Numbers 7–9 are concluded. The summary of Num. 7.84-88 is introduced and concluded by this element (vv. 84 and 88), corresponding to 8.4 and the concluding regulations on the service of the Levites in v. 24. Accordingly, the sacrificial implements, the lamp and the Levites as servants of the tent are set together as sacred objects, completing the events of Exodus 35–40 and Leviticus 8–9.

The relationship to the preceding passages is also reflected by the story of implementation in vv. 20-22. Corresponding to vv. 3-4, the elaboration of the compliance formula (vv. 20 and 22b) stresses the perfect character of the actions. The local categories also link the scenes. Moses' listening to 'the voice' in the inner sanctum followed by Aaron with the lamp in the outer sanctum is followed by the Levites set to fulfil 'the service of the Tent of Meeting' (vv. 15, 19, 22, 24, 26). In this way the story returns to the beginning in ch. 7. The first set of princely gifts is related to the 'service of the Tent of Meeting' and given to the Levites for the transport of the tent (v. 5). Followed by the references to the altar in vv. 10-88 and the other localities, the story of chs. 7–8 reflects the circumambulation of the sacred localities, connected with categories of hierarchical relationship and perfect action.

76. The effect of parallelism is emphasized by the traditional assumptions that the perception that the Levites originally served as priests is also reflected in this story. According to de Vaulx (*Les Nombres*, pp. 118-20), the Aaron motifs as a later tradition have been combined with an older tradition on the consecration of 'prêtres lévites', while Budd (*Numbers*, p. 92) finds a combination of Palestinian and Babylonian traditions of priestly consecration.

77. E.g. the parallel instructions of Exod. 32.33 and 33.1, 5, in a corresponding relationship to the encounter scene in Exod. 32.31-32.

The return to the beginning of the story is also reflected by the position of the people as central actors in Num. 8.5-26. The extended formula of compliance in v. 20 sets the people together with Moses and Aaron as the perfect actors. The repetition in v. 20bβ even mentions 'the children of Israel' alone as the subjects.[78] The elaboration of the formulaic language corresponds to the significance of the people in this story. Repeatedly it is stated that the Levites are taken 'from among the people' (vv. 6, 14, 16, 19). According to Exod. 28.1, for example, the priests also are 'brought near' as the representatives of the people. But the elaboration in Numbers 8 of the role of the people makes this aspect crucial for the understanding of the Levitical function. The Levites will 'fulfil the people's service' at the Tent of Meeting (v. 19). The special relationship of people and Levites is underlined by the sacrificial motifs. The Levites are presented by the people as a 'wave-offering' (vv. 11, 13).

In this way, the people as offering sacrificial 'gifts' are also brought into the presentation of the perfect action in these chapters. In a complementary relationship to the introductory events of Numbers 7, the people's 'offering' of the Levites continues and supplements the dedications offered by the people's leaders. Corresponding to the relationship of Exodus 35–40 and Leviticus 1–10 that presents the building of the sanctuary completed by the sacrifical rites, the gifts related to the tent as a building and to the altar in Numbers 7 are perfected by the sacrifice of the Levites. By this act, the people form a part of the hierarchical relationship of Moses, Aaron and his sons, and the Levites. This relationship is underlined by the versions of the compliance formula in vv. 20 and 22, which present the four groups as parallel subjects for the perfect action.

The relationship of the Levites' story to Leviticus 8–9 underlines important aspects of the relationship of Leviticus 8–9 to Exodus 35–40. Just as the Leviticus version completes the latter, so Numbers 7–8 complete the earlier events. In each case, the earlier story seems to represent

78. The application of the people as a third set of ritual performers disturbs the usual assumptions on the story as a combination of two traditions which refer to Moses (vv. 6-7a, 8b-10a, 12b, 13-14, 15b) and Aaron (vv. 11, 21). Thus, Moses as the main subject in the divine instructions and Aaron as performer in the story on implementation (v. 21) is comparable to the relationship of Exod. 25–31 to 36–39. The former chapters are mainly addressed to Moses as the tent-builder, while the latter refer to the named craftsmen as well as the people as the builders.

the fundamental framework, repeated by the later story dedicated to certain aspects of the basic phenomena. It must be important that the categories of locality and material objects of the building account are central also to the Numbers story. The making of the tent and its implements represents the fundamental event, supplemented and perfected by the later events centred around the different orders of human actors, each related to some locality within the comprehensive locus of theophanic manifestation. Both the function of the priests (Exod. 40.31-32) and the sanctification of the Levites (32.25-29) are referred to in Exodus 19–40. Accordingly, this story seems to present the fundamental chord of the Sinai stories, repeated by a second and complementary chord in Leviticus 1–10, both repeated and completed by the third version in Numbers 7–8.

Also in the third case, the completing function of the repetition is connected with more subtle effects. The perfect 'purification'[79] of the Levites in Numbers 8 has the story of the 'sanctification' of the Levites in Exod. 32.25-29 as its counterpart. In the latter text the transition of the Levites into sacred service is expressed by the motif 'filling of hands', referring to categories of priestly sanctification. The Exodus terminology is usually contrasted with the categories of 'purification' in Numbers 8. 'Hand-filling' is seen to reflect some old tradition which ascribes priestly status to the Levites, while 'purification' reflects the concerns of a younger tradition anxious to underline the subordinate character of the Levites.[80]

To the aspect of purification is added the concept of 'wave-offering', the Levites dedicated by the rite of *t^e^nûpâ*.[81] Traditionally understood as a special type of sacrifice, the term refers to a rite of dedication according to Milgrom, applicable for different types of sacrifice.[82] But also in the latter case, sacrificial categories are referred to. This is underlined by the 'stemming of hands' by the people, corresponding to the treatment of the animal sacrifices by the Levites (v. 12). And finally, the conceptual implications of the event are even extended by

79. Levine, *Numbers 1–20*, pp. 273-74.

80. E.g. de Vaulx, *Les Nombres*, pp. 118-20; Budd, *Numbers*, p. 92. On the other hand, see Milgrom, *Leviticus 1–16*, p. 539, on the 'hand-filling' of Exod. 32.29 as referring to spoils.

81. Verses 11a, 13b, while the two concepts are put together in vv. 15b and 21.

82. Milgrom, *Leviticus 1–16*, p. 473; cf. Levine, *Numbers 1–20*, p. 276.

categories of substitution and the Passover events (vv. 16-19).[83] After the divine smiting of the first-born in Egypt, all first-born in Israel belong to YHWH. But 'instead of' the first-born, the Levites have been 'taken' (vv. 16, 18).

The complexity of these categories—confounded by the problems of the sacrificial language[84]—makes any exact understanding difficult for modern readers. But at the very least, the contrasting relationship with the parallel story of Levitical sanctification in Exodus 32 must indicate a frame of reading. The Levites sacrificing the people in Exodus 32 is contrasted with a new story about the people sacrificing the Levites in Numbers 8. The counterpoint effect of the two modes of Levitical sanctification underlines the category of sacrifice, and a rather bloody one at that. The significance of this category is added to by the motifs of substitution and Passover in Numbers 8. The relationship of the smiting of Egypt's firstborn and the dedication of the Levites instead of Israel's firstborn indicates a close connection of parallel events. The Passover event is repeated and continued by a corresponding application to Israel. However figurative, the sacrifice of Israel's firstborn implies an imagery of bloody character, the Levites not only being purified, but ritually killed as the substitutes for Israel's children.

This effect is enhanced when the terminology of 'hand-filling' in Exodus 32 (related to the blood of kin and neighbours) is compared to the human 'wave-offering' in Numbers 8. The two terms refer to specialized sacrificial language.[85] But as parallel expressions of figurative language that are related to the same situation of Levitical sanctification, the imagery of the two situations corresponds. The 'hand-filling' related to the blood of kin and the 'elevation' of human sacrifices

83. E.g. Martin Noth, *Das vierte Buch Moses: Numeri* (ATD, 7; Göttingen; Vandenhoeck & Ruprecht, 1966), pp. 62-63, on vv. 16b-19 as 'späterer Zusatz' ('a later addition'), and further de Vaulx, *Les Nombres*, p. 119, on the diverse traditions combined in the theological justification of vv. 15b-19. According to Budd, *Numbers*, pp. 91-92, vv. 14-19 represent the author's further comment on the rite of purification.

84. E.g. de Vaulx, *Les Nombres*, p. 122, on the Levites as the people's sin-offering, and Kiuchi, *The Purification Offering*, pp. 111-19, on the imposition of hands as basically an expression of substitution, the offerer 'indicating that the animal is taking his place in the ritual' (p. 118). According to Milgrom, *Leviticus 1–16*, pp. 150-53, the rite simply denotes ownership.

85. Milgrom, *Leviticus 1–16*, pp. 461-73, on the 'wave-offering', and pp. 538-40 on 'hand-filling'.

substituting for the people's firstborn represent corresponding sets of imagery. This is underlined by the parallel set of animal sacrifices in Num. 8.10, 12), the figurative 'elevation' of the Levites connected with a seemingly concrete sacrificial situation of bloody animal parts elevated before YHWH.

The connection between the two sets of imagery is reflected by the mirror effect of the two scenes. The Levites sanctifying themselves by the sacrifices of the next of kin corresponds to the Levites being sanctified as the people's sacrifice in Numbers 8. The effects of juxtaposition is also indicated by the family categories. The blood of 'his son and his brother' of Exodus 32 corresponds to the Levites as the substitutes for the firstborn, the people ritually sacrificing their sons (vv. 16-18).

In this way, the scene of vv. 5-26 continues the preceding scenes of Num. 7–8 in harmonizing the effects of tension and conflict left by the parallel stories. The now acceptable initiative of the people's leaders in Num. 7 contrasts with the people's wilfulness in Exodus 32 and indicates a new situation of acceptable doing. The location of Moses in the inner sanctum mitigates his peculiar exclusion in Exodus 40 and also reconciles the contrasts of the latter and the tent scene of ch. 34. The references to Aaron as the perfect maker of the golden lamp mitigates his function as the perverted metal-worker in Exodus 32. This is concluded by the story about the purification of the Levites related to their sanctification in the aftermath of the Golden Calf episode. The bloodiness of the latter is transformed by the new scene. The actors are set in juxtaposed roles of sacrificer and sacrificed, and this time happily concluded by the 'waved' sacrifices taking up their service in the Tent of Meeting. The perception of conflict and unresolved tensions in the earlier stories is put to rest by the impression of a totally perfect situation, the narrative figures set together in a harmonious hierarchical relationship of perfect action.

Numbers 9.1-14

The introductory v. 1 both separates from and links the account of the Passover celebration to the preceding stories. The reference to the locality as well as the dating indicate the special significance of the new episode. On the other hand, the introduction 'YHWH spoke to Moses' concluded by the element 'saying' makes v. 1 an extended version of the introductory Num. 8.1, 5, 23, as well as Num. 9.9. Accordingly, the Passover celebration is presented as a successive and climactic episode in continuation of the former events, all referring to the encounter situation of Num. 7.89.

Such a function corresponds to the formal character of the passage. The account of the Passover celebration in vv. 1-5 is continued by vv. 6-14 given to problems of proper celebration which are concluded by divine instructions in vv. 9-14.[86] Formally, vv. 1-5 reflect the same structure as the episodes in ch. 8. The divine instructions (vv. 1-3) are mediated by Moses (v. 4) and implemented by the people (v. 5). The episode is told without any narrative detail, representing the bare skeleton of the event structure.[87] This corresponds to the starkness of Num. 8.1-4. In both cases, the story of implementation is formed from the language of the formula of compliance. This corresponds to the preceding stories of implementation in Num. 8.3-4, 20-22. In all cases, the formula is applied in extended forms. The version of Num. 9.5 corresponds especially to the construction of Num. 8.20, while vv. 3, 4b and 22b represent different applications of the same elements of extension. While the verb *'āśâ* connected with *pesaḥ* also represents a usual construction ('do Passover'),[88] the parallel dependence on the language of the compliance formula indicates the connection between the episodes of Numbers 8–9.[89] They are related both as successive and interlinked expressions for a situation of perfect doing.

Seen for itself, the formal structure of 9.6-14 could be described as 'casuistic'.[90] A concrete problem is brought before Moses and Aaron (vv. 6-7), the divine decision is sought (v. 8) and declared (vv. 9-14). But the motifs of vv. 6-7 indicate the close connection between vv. 1-5 and 6-14. Not able to 'do Passover on this day' (v. 6a) as the others 'do Passover' (v. 5), they go to Moses and Aaron 'on this day', the significance of the day being prepared for by the repeated temporal references of the preceding episode. Accordingly, vv. 6-14 continue the story of

86. Verses 6-14 are usually seen as reflecting late problems of proper celebration which have been added to the established legislation: e.g. Budd, *Numbers*, pp. 98-99; de Vaulx, *Les Nombres*, pp. 123-24. For Olson, *Death of the Old*, pp. 96-97, the passage has a function of clarification, reflecting the legal material's flexibility and openness to new circumstances.

87. Characterized as 'banale' as well as 'maladroite' by de Vaulx (*Les Nombres*, p. 123), the latter due to the peculiar dating of v. 1.

88. E.g. Deut. 16.1; 2 Kgs 23.21.

89. Cf. also the constructions of vv. 12b and 14ab.

90. Comparable to, e.g., Num. 15.32-36, according to de Vaulx, *Les Nombres*, p. 124.

implementation. The perfect character of the people's doing is illustrated by a story on some who were not able to contribute their part and hurry on 'that very day' to Moses and Aaron to put their problem right.

The connotational references of the story are added to by the special terms used in vv. 7 and 13 for the special action. The proper Passover celebration consists in the people 'presenting offering' (*hiqrîb qorbān*).[91] This refers to the preceding episodes of chs. 7–8. The terms are applied throughout the story of ch. 7, their conceptual significance being enhanced by the corresponding gift motifs of Exodus 35–36 and Leviticus 1–7. Also, *hiqrîb* is used in the preceding story in connection with the Levites 'offered' as the people's sacrificial gifts. The men of Num. 9.6-7 are depicted not only according to the categories of sacred doing, but also continue the generous magnanimity of the people's leaders in ch. 7 and the people's dedication in ch. 8.

In this way, Num. 9.6-14 function as a continuation of the preceding story of implementation, the eagerness of the unclean to participate being a concrete illustration of the perfect action of the celebrants. This corresponds to the location of vv. 6-14. Set after the extended formula of compliance in v. 5, the episode continues the story of how the children of Israel 'did' just as YHWH had commanded with a problem not covered by the divine instructions. Such a function would also correspond to the formal character of vv. 1-5. Providing the mere skeleton of a proper story, it is fleshed out by the narrative details of the concrete episode.

As a whole, vv. 1-14 continue the episodes of perfect action in chs. 7–8. The Passover celebration also represents an example of the dedicated people bringing their gifts and even complaining when unable to do so. Moreover, the category of 'gifts' also prepares for the seemingly sudden return to 'the day of erecting' in v. 15. Comparable to the connection of theophanic manifestation and the people's gifts in Exodus 35–36 and Leviticus 1–9, the Passover celebration as an episode of 'gifts' also refers to the conceptual connection of sacred action and theophanic manifestation.

Such a connection is also reflected by the development of the people as actors in the stories of Numbers 7–9. The people are gradually introduced as the subjects of sacred action. Apart from the people's

91. The application of this special term in vv. 7 and 13 also reflects the connection between the narrative vv. 6-7 and the regulations in vv. 8-14. Moreover, the special constructions of vv. 12b and 14ab link with the formulaic language of v. 5.

leaders in the first episode, the people are active—with Moses and Aaron as the central actors—in the Levites' episode. This is continued by the Passover episode in which the people alone are the actors,[92] apart from the mediating function of Moses (in v. 6 together with Aaron). The development is concluded by vv. 15-23, in which the people are the central actors. Beside the final reference to Moses in v. 23, the people are here depicted not only as the subjects of perfect obedience, but also directly related to the manifestation of the divine will.

The significance of this development is underlined by the references to categories of hierarchy and locus. The movement from Moses in the inner sanctum to Aaron in the outer sanctum to the Levites serving in the Tent of Meeting to the people of Passover—without any explicit locus aside from the reference to journey in vv. 10 and 13—could indicate a movement from high to low. But while the harmonious hierarchical relationship of perfect actors must be important, all 'doing' exactly what was divinely commanded, the conclusion of Num. 9.15-23 indicates that the composition is orientated towards a climax centred around the journeying people as actors. The perfect obedience of the people set in the theophanic relationship, which is related to the locus of the travelling sanctuary, represents the central event of the Sinai story as a whole.

The movement towards vv. 15-23 as the climax is illustrated by the journey motifs of vv. 10 and 13. The concrete situation of vv. 6-8 refers to the problem of impurity, so problematical that it has to be put before YHWH. But the answer connects the problem of impurity with the problems of travellers on 'a distant way' (v. 10). Followed by the journey motifs of vv. 16-23, the 'way' motifs of vv. 10 and 13 link the events of Passover and post-Sinai journey.

Passover and 'the Day of Erecting'

That Num. 9.1-14 and vv. 15-23 are interlinked, in spite of the distance indicated by the dating notes, is underlined by the connection between vv. 1-5 and the preceding stories. The formal character of vv. 1-5 relates the Passover episode to the preceding episodes of perfect action. This is emphasized by the conceptual linkage between the Passover celebration and the purification of the Levites in Numbers 8. The Levites as the

92. The significance of which illustrated by Ezra 6.16-26 and 2 Chron. 30.1-3, where the status of the priests and the Levites is important for proper celebration.

substitutes for the people's firstborn in Num. 8.16-19 refers to the first Passover. All the firstborn belong to YHWH due to his smiting the Egyptian firstborn, and this relationship is actualized by the purification of the Levites. The original smiting of the firstborn is repeated by the Levites presented as the people's wave-offering instead of the people's firstborn. According to these categories, the celebration of the Passover makes a natural continuation of the ritual killing of the Levites. Conceptually, the events of Numbers 8 and 9 are identical as parallel expressions for the same events. If the 12 days for the dedication of the leaders' gifts in Numbers 7, followed by the Aaron episode and the purification of the Levites, left little room for the proper celebration of Passover on the fourteenth day, any effects of overlapping would correspond to the connotational references of the two stories.

This must be important when we consider the reference to 'the day of erecting' in Num. 9.15-23 and thus the return to this day as the pivotal event for Numbers 7–9 as a whole. The introduction of the Passover into this context must indicate the interest in adding this theme to the connotational impact. This is underlined by the jarring note struck by the relationship of the datings in vv. 1 and 15. Due to the special character of vv. 15-23 as an echo of Exod. 40.36-38, the effect of jarring is somewhat mitigated. A rather loosely 'impressionistic' application is to be expected from a passage with a function as some narrative refrain. But even so, the transition from the fourteenth day to the first within a narrative framework of linear relationships must reflect the author's interest in presenting the Passover celebration as the last event of Sinai in addition to the erection of the sanctuary as the pivotal event. This is also reflected by the meticulous elaboration of vv. 1-14 within the context of Numbers 7–9.

Such an interest is also indicated by the character of Num. 9.1-23 seen as a whole. The passage reflects a structure of Passover celebration centred around divine instructions and implementation extended by a new set of Passover instructions, and concluded by a description of the theophanic manifestation related to the people's journey. Such a structure is comparable to the composition of Exodus 12–13 concluded by the description of the theophanic manifestation in Exod. 13.20-22. Also this passage is centred around the divine instructions on the celebration (Exod. 12.1-20, 43-49; 13.1-16). The mediation by Moses (Exod. 12.21-27a) corresponds to the situation of the Passover according to Numbers 9. The first two sets of instructions are followed by stories of implementation (Exod. 12.27b-28, 50). In both cases, the implementation is shortly referred to by extended versions of the formula of compliance, the people doing 'just as YHWH had commanded Moses and Aaron'. This corresponds to the structure of instruction, mediation and implementation by the extended compliance formula in Num. 9.1-5.[93]

Moreover, in both cases the people's implementation is followed by motifs of divine manifestation (Exod. 12.29, 51). This is comparable to the present connection of Passover celebration in Num. 9.1-14 followed by the theophanic motifs of vv. 15-23. Corresponding to the journey motifs of the latter, the divine manifestation of Exod. 12.51 also refers to the people's journey, while the smiting of the firstborn in v. 29 is followed by the description of the people's departure in vv. 30-41.

This is added to by the connection between the imagery of Num. 9.15-23 and Exod. 13.20-22. The cloud and fire related to the change of day and night are common to both texts. The application of the fire motif especially must be an important indication of the connection between the texts, as Numbers 9, as well as Exod. 40.36-38, elaborate only the cloud motif as the signal to the people, while the fire motif is retained for the impression of the tent during the night. Moreover, the theophanic manifestation is in both cases related to the situation of journey. The combination of itinerary elements with 'breaking camp' and 'settling' in Exod. 13.20 and the theophanic description in vv. 21-22 is also basic for the composition of Num. 9.15-23. The connection between the texts is emphasized by Num. 10.11-13, which reflect both the special elaboration of 9.15-23 and the combination of itinerary and motifs of theophanic guidance in Exod. 13.20-22.[94]

The elaboration of Numbers 9–10 must reflect an interest in presenting the departure from Sinai as parallel to and somehow repeating the departure from Egypt.[95] But it must be important that the references to Exodus 12–13 do not present the departure from Sinai as a copy of the Exodus, but are elaborated within a literary frame given to the central events of Sinai. Numbers 7–9 represent the third version of the events

93. Cf. also Levine, *Numbers 1–20*, p. 293, on Num. 9.1-14 bearing close affinity to Exod. 12.

94. Cf. also the departing people as 'hosts' in Exod. 12.41, 51 and as a key word in Num. 10.14-28.

95. Cf. Budd, *Numbers*, p. 97. The connection between the texts is also illustrated by the usual understanding of the Numbers version as a result of a Priestly author adapting older traditions: e.g. de Vaulx, *Les Nombres*, p. 127.

presented in Exodus 35–40. While the second version of Leviticus 8–9 is also important to the Numbers story, the echo effect of Exod. 40.36-38 and Num. 9.15-23 points to the special relationship between the first and third versions. The two versions of the narrative refrain highlight 'the day of erecting' as the climactic event of Sinai, the effects of which extended into a permanent journey situation. Without disturbing this presentation, the connotations of Passover are added to the significance of this climactic day. Presented as the last of the Sinai events,[96] the celebration of the Passover, concluded by the theophanic manifestation and followed by the events of departure from Sinai, repeats the first Passover as a new Exodus. Set within the framework of 'the day of erecting' and thus reflecting the events of Sinai, the new Exodus has a new character compared to the first. This is underlined by the sacrifice of the Levites as the event which introduces the Numbers Passover.

The Smiting of the Firstborn

The significance of the Passover passage as well as the references to the first Exodus in Numbers 10 is underlined by the Passover motifs of Numbers 8. The original connection of the Passover celebration and the divine smiting of the Egyptian firstborn is repeated by a corresponding set of events, the new Passover initiated by a new scene of the firstborn 'smitten'. However figurative, the description of the sacrifice of Israel's firstborn implies an imagery of bloody character, the 'waved' Levites ritually killed as the substitutes of Israel's children.

On the other hand, the effects of parallelism could also indicate the special character of the new Passover, as well as intimating the character of the new Exodus. In contrast to the divine smiting of the Egyptian firstborn, the people represent the subjects in the second episode. While Moses and Aaron are the ritual actors, the formula of compliance in Num. 8.20 presents the people as the perfect actors of sacred action, corresponding to the rite of v. 10 and the Levites as the people's 'given' (v. 16). The significance of the people as the central actors of this sacrifice is underlined by the parallel story of Levitical sanctification in Exodus 32, with a counterpoint relationship of sacrificers and sacrificed.

The contrast of the Passover accounts in Exodus 12–13 and Numbers 8 implies the transition from the divine actor to the people as the subjects of the decisive act, and a corresponding transition from the

96. The making of the trumpets in Num. 10.1-10 is related to the departure.

Egyptians to the people as the victims. Instead of a situation of Israel related to the Egyptians as the enemy, the divine actor with a *deus ex machina* function, the corresponding situation is transferred to groups within the people. The imagery implies an aspect of 'internalization', the basic conflict indicated by the contrast of Egyptians and people transferred to a corresponding constellation within the people. That this process has retained the aspects of conflict is indicated by the terrible imagery of the contrast story in Exodus 32. However peaceful the story of Numbers 8 and however cheerfully the 'waved' Levites entered their service according to Num. 8.22, the tensions implied are underlined by the bloody 'hand-filling' in the parallel story.

That such subtle perceptions could be implied by the imagery of Numbers 8 is indicated by the comparable transformation of the 'plundering' motif in Exod. 33.6. The motif refers to the 'plundering' of the Egyptians in Exod. 12.35-36. Related to the building of Moses' Tent of Meeting in Exodus 33, the people's 'self-plundering' represents their passive contribution to the erection of the first Tent of Meeting. Moreover, the significance of this motif is underlined by the qualification 'after Horeb', the people depicted in a permanent situation of 'self-plundering'.

The two sets of imagery are strangely parallel. In both cases, the transformation of the motifs reflects a subtle process of internalization. The outer conflict of suppressor and suppressed are transferred into an inner process which implies aspects of conflict. The latter is indicated by the terminology. The 'self-plundering' of Exod. 33.6, as well as the sacrifical terms of Numbers 8—the latter enhanced by the contrast story of Exodus 32—refer to connotational categories of a rather bloody character.

The parallelism of the two sets of imagery is also suggested by their referential contexts. Exodus 33.6 is part of the aftermath of the Golden Calf episode. By the contrast story of Levitical sanctification in Exodus 32, Numbers 8 refers to the same context. As has been seen, the contrast relationship to the Golden Calf episode is important to Numbers 7–8 as a whole. Moreover, both Exod. 33.6 as well as Numbers 8 display the connotational significance of the Tent of Meeting. The former prepares for the building of the contrasting Tent of Meeting built by Moses 'for himself', while the latter forms part of the third version of the events of the day when the grand Tent of Meeting was erected. Corresponding to the 'self-plundering' in Exod. 33.6 as the expression for the people's contribution to the first tent building, the dedication of the Levites in Numbers 8 refers to the theme of 'gifts'.

Thus, the parallel transformation of the two sets of motif could even reflect some subtle connection of referential relationship. This is also indicated by their connection in the Passover story. In Exodus 12 the smiting of the firstborn (vv. 29-33) and the plundering of the Egyptians (vv. 35-36) are closely related as events of the departure (vv. 34 and 37). The compositional interest in this relationship is underlined by its narrative incongruence. As a description of successive events, vv. 35-36 are rather badly set after v. 33!

The connection of the smiting of the firstborn and the people plundering the Egyptians during the first Passover corresponds to the internalized versions of these events in the Sinai stories. The people 'after Horeb' are depicted in a permanent state of self-plundering. Comparably, the new Passover connected with the departure from Sinai is introduced by the people ritually killing their firstborn by 'waving' the Levites. The parallel transfer of central Passover motifs from a situation of Egyptian enemies to some internal contrast related to the people must be important for the situation 'after Horeb' as a new Exodus in a new mode.

4. *Conclusions*

Compared to Exodus 35–40 and Leviticus 8–10, the third version of 'the day of erecting' seems above all to have a function of completion and harmonization. Impressions of tensions and conflict are put to rest and the loose strands of the parallel versions joined to the weft. Everything is accomplished just as divinely ordained. Apart from Joshua, left in Exod. 33.11 as the servant in Moses' Tent of Meeting, the main actors of the preceding stories appear again, all perfectly attuned to the divine will and to each other, all set set in their proper station according to the circumambulation of the new locus. The harmony of the third version is not disturbed by any contrasting situation, comparable to the Golden Calf episode as the shadow of the building story of Exodus and the priestly usurpation marring the climax of Leviticus 9. Numbers 7–9 present an idyll of perfect observation.

On the other hand, this idyll sets the stage for a new series of contradiction and conflict. The narrative refrain of Num. 9.15-23 concludes the Sinai stories, and also extends the situation referred to as a permanent situation of the journey as a whole. Every station on the way implies the theophanic relationship of the day when the sanctuary was erected, the people meticulously observing the divine guidance. This is contrasted with the perception of the people's journey according to the story cycle introduced in Numbers 11. Every station on the way represents a new situation of intolerable weakness and wilfulness. Thus, while Numbers 7–9 seem to reconcile the contradictions and tensions of the earlier stories, this harmonized version of the Sinai events prepares for a new series of contradictions.

Corresponding to Exodus 35–40 and Leviticus 8–9, the composition of Numbers 7–9 presents 'the day of erecting' as the climactic event of Sinai. Implicitly, this points to the significance of the events of Exodus 19–40. This is underlined by the parallelism of Exod. 40.36-38 and Num. 9.15-23. The echo effect of the two conclusions—the latter concluding the Sinai events as a whole—seems to indicate that Exodus 19–40 represents the basic version of what happened at Sinai, somehow repeated by Lev. 1.1–Num. 9.23 as a second version. The divine movement from the sacred mountain to the new locus, with a corresponding emphasis on material categories connected to human activity and related to the people as the performers of sacred action, represent the central aspect of the post-Sinai reality. This aspect is extended by the combination of theophany and journey in Exod. 40.36-38 and Num. 9.15-23, and by the introduction of Passover and Exodus in Numbers 8–10.

The way in which this perception of the post-Sinai reality is presented indicates that the single stories form part of a rather open-ended system of function. Related to the linear frame of successive events, Numbers 7–8 can simply be read as stories different from those of Exodus 35–40 and Leviticus 8–10, presenting events that started somewhat later in the day and which completed the earlier events. The tent set up and furnished is continued by a story on sanctified priests, who performed the sacrifices, while Numbers 7–8 add new aspects necessary for the transport and upkeep of the sanctuary. The relationship of Numbers 8 and the Passover passage of Num. 9.1-14 points to the purification of the Levites as a central event for the third version, thus nicely rounding off the story of Leviticus 8–9.

The aspects of harmony and reconciliation can also, to a certain degree, be related to the linear frame. The now acceptable initiative of the people's leaders in Numbers 7 contrasts with their earlier wilfulness in Exodus 32. The location of Moses in the inner sanctum in Num. 7.89

completes his peculiar exclusion in Exodus 40 followed by the encounter scene of Lev. 1.1, and thus also reflects the elevated position of Moses in the first Tent of Meeting.[97] The references to Aaron as acting perfectly in Num. 8.1-4 mitigates his earlier efforts as metal-worker in Exodus 32. Similarly, the bloodiness of Levitical sanctification is transformed by the second story. The new sanctification is happily concluded by the 'waved' sacrifices taking up their service in the Tent of Meeting. The perception of conflict and unsolved tensions in the earlier stories is put to rest by the impression of a totally perfect situation in the later stories.

But at the same time, the special effects of parallelism and repetition also give the impression that a linear development towards a climactic end is disturbed, the surface effect of the narrative added to by hints of depth and cross-currents. The earlier events are not nullified by the later events, but seem to be supplemented by the connotational effects of a parallel version. This is illustrated by the narrative refrain of Exod. 40.36-38 and Num. 9.15-23. Separated by a great series of successive events, the parallelism of the refrain reflects the parallelism of the events. Effects of juxtaposition and contrast seem to be characteristic of the compositional mode of repetition. The narrative figures are presented in different modes, the actor of the one episode mirrored by his contrast function in a different story. This effect is highlighted by the concluding contrast of the journeying people according to Num. 9.15-23 and Num. 11.

Concretely, the importance of repetition and parallelism, as well as contradictions, is illustrated by the established scholarly readings, for which such effects have represented the basis for the identification of parallel sources and traditions. Recently, effects of repetition and parallelism have been related to a new emphasis on the final shape of the materials.[98] The combination of the different categories of analysis,

97. Exod. 33.8-11; 34.34-35.

98. E.g. Utzschneider's 'Makrostrukturen' ('macrostructure'), the Priestly retelling of an original story understood as reflecting an abstracted structure of 'Makropropositionen' ('macro-concepts') (*Das Heiligtum*, pp. 134-44). Dozemann, *God on the Mountain*, pp. 145-55, turns to 'repetition' as a key term for the conceptual coherency of the materials, centred around the relationship of 'Zion', 'Sinai' and 'Horeb' as three different expressions for an ongoing reflection about divine cultic presence, now brought together and connected in the canonical Sinai complex. The application of the mountain setting reflects two types of 'repetition'.

tradition and redaction historical observations perceived as the basic set of data and related to modern 'literary' models of reading, is not unproblematical. To me, it is obvious that the final shape must represent the basic entity for analysis. As effects of repetition seem to represent a typical compositional mode, so the problems of different strands within the final composition are best addressed if postponed until the reader has obtained some basic idea of what the effects of parallelism really imply.

The complex character of the phenomena involved warns us against any expectations of models of interpretation that comprehend everything. With regard to function, it is difficult to go beyond the formal characteristics of repetition and parallelism connected to some referential function. These effects are applied within a narrative frame of linear character. Each episode is set in a system of successive events, the people from Egypt arriving at Sinai to undergo a series of events that are ended by departure and a new series of events. But with a basic function within such a narrative framework, certain episodes have a special sub-function with regard to other episodes, indicated by effects of repetition and parallelism.

This makes the question of context rather open-ended. The linear relationship to preceding and following events must be basic. But this is supplemented by the referential relationship to episodes, which according to categories of linear development, are too separate for any intimate connection. And when certain key episodes, for example the Golden Calf, seem to have a referential relationship to many episodes of rather different character, the fluidity of contextual and connotational relationships could have rather free-flowing ramifications.

At the very least, these effects invite us to a process of 'referential reading'. The single episode does not stand alone, but should be read together with other episodes. Moreover, the single episodes are not

According to 'repetition as mimesis', the Priestly and Deuteronomistic redactions present copies of the archetypical 'Mountain of God' tradition which has the concept of Zion for theological centre (p. 151). According to 'repetition as ungrounded doubling', the Priestly Sinai and the Deuteronomistic Horeb are brought together as a single symbol by a Priestly 'canon conscious redaction' (p. 153), the meaning of which is not dependent on one or the other but on 'the echoing of two dissimilar things' (p. 149). Both for Utzschneider and Dozemann, models of contemporary literary interpretation have been combined with the established results of traditio-historical research.

equal in this respect, but are set within a connotational system that points to certain 'key' or 'nucleus' episodes as particularly central. The significance of Exodus 40 for Lev. 1.1–Num. 9.23 indicates 'the day of erecting the dwelling' as the obvious example of such a nucleus episode. In addition, the composition of Numbers 8–10 relates this episode to the Exodus as another nucleus episode. The first Passover and the departure from Egypt are repeated in a new mode by the final events of Sinai and the new departure.

But when the significance of nucleus episodes could indicate an overarching design for the organization of the Sinai stories—in addition to the basic linear relationship—it seems to be criss-crossed by other references of a structural character. Thus, the juxtaposition of Exodus 35–40 to the Golden Calf episode, followed by the making of Moses' Tent of Meeting in chs. 32–34, is important to the function of Exodus 19–40 as the basic version of the Sinai stories. As a loop within the loop, this juxtaposition must be significant in its own right. But when added to by the parallels of Leviticus 8–10 and Numbers 7–9, the significance of the juxtaposition within Exodus 19–40 is subtly altered.

Each episode seems to represent a treasure-house of connotations which are displayed by their relationship to other episodes. The Golden Calf story is perceived differently when related to Exod. 33.6-11 or to 34.29-35, to Exodus 35–40, to Leviticus 10, and especially to Numbers 7–8. In the same way, the perception of the Passover night as described in Exodus 12–13 is changed when related to the repeated smiting of the firstborn in Numbers 8 or to the 'self-plundering' of Exod. 33.6. A story of triumph and vindication is subtly changed. Repeated in an internalized way, the nucleus event is transformed, and perhaps even 'completed' when its 'real' implications are actualized by the later event. This impression is supplemented by the parallelism of the Levitical sanctification according to Numbers 8 and Exodus 32. When the reader turns from these stories to Exodus 12, the perception of the first Passover night has been changed, its gruesome aspects of divine brutality underlined by the juxtaposition of the two episodes of Levitical sanctification.

Such differences could even indicate that the key episode does not represent any definite set of connotational effects, but serves as a formal shape of potential meanings, its impact dependent on the story to which it is related. Ultimately, this must imply that the compositional mode presupposes the contribution of the reader. The fluid character of the referential relationships implies that each reading could represent a new arrangement of related stories.[99]

In this way, the effects of repetition and parallelism seem to reflect a complex system of referential relationships. The three versions of 'the day of erecting', as well as the contrasted Tents of Meeting in Exodus 33 and 40, represent rather explicit expressions for such a system. But the references to the Golden Calf episode in Numbers 7–8 represent expressions which put heavier demands on the attention of the reader. Finally, the transformation of the Passover motifs of 'the plundering of the Egyptians' and 'the smiting of the firstborn' illustrates that the compositional mode can also manifest rather subtle effects. The fluid character of the impressions, the reading of one story constantly enriched and correspondingly disturbed by the flow of new sets of connotations from related stories, dissolves *the* meaning of the single story into fragments for ever-changing combinations. In such a situation, the effects of repetition and parallelism are ultimately akin to the effects of the poetic *parallellismus membrorum.*

More practically, the compositional mode indicates that the meaning of the texts should not be identified too directly with what to a modern reader is perceived to be their subject matter. This can be illustrated by the two stories about the sanctification of the Levites in Exodus 32 and Numbers 8. The sacrificial language of the latter clearly has a figurative function.[100] The substitute sacrifice of the people's firstborn is concluded by the 'waved' sacrifices entering their service at the Tent of Meeting. The language of the parallel story in Exodus 32 could be perceived as more 'direct' and 'realistic'. Regarded as an ancient tradition on the origin of the Levitical institution, this story would be read in what is conventionally regarded as the literal sense. But even such a reading is disturbed by the motifs of 'hand-filling'. Related to human sacrifices, the motifs must reflect a transferred usage of the ritual language of priestly sanctification. And when the two stories are set over against each other as counterpoints, they transcend the confines of what

99. I hope that this effort to perceive the implications of the compositional mode can be distanced from the many current versions of 'reader's response' interpretations. However illusory the idea of a reader objectively registering textual impressions, the basic perception of the text as an attractive 'other'—the reading a disciplined effort to open to this 'otherness'—represents to me a heritage of the scholarly past not to be squandered.

100. Levine, *Numbers 1–20*, p. 276, on the 'waving' rite.

is experienced as 'realistic' language. The interest in combining such stories seems far removed from their assumed subject matter as, for example, legends on the origin of the Levitical institution.

This corresponds to the presentation of the priests. The divine instructions on the priesthood related to the building of the Tent of Meeting in Exodus 28–29 is contrasted with Aaron's function in Exodus 32. The impact of this contrast is emphasized when the episode with Aaron as metal-worker is followed by the scenes of the Levites as priests and Joshua, according to Exod. 33.11, permanently serving in the Tent of Meeting. A comparable contrast of priestly roles is set up by Nadab and Abihu related to the extraordinary manifestation of the divine presence according to Exod. 24.1, 9-11 and Lev. 10.1-2. Concluded by the perfect actions of Aaron as metal-worker and the harmonious constellation of priests and Levites in Numbers 8, the counterpoint effect of the composition is sadly misrepresented when transcribed into, for example, pro- and anti-Aaron legends. The materials probably represent traditional topics and themes, comparable to the literary tradition represented by the building account of Exodus 35–40. But the concrete elaboration of the stories reflects other and much more subtle considerations.

The effects of repetition and parallelism connected with a figurative language also imply the limitation of one's competence as a reader. The categories of scholarly analysis represent a rather large-meshed net for what the composition seems to indicate as the worthwhile catch. But it must be important that the narrative framework invites us to a process of structured reading. Certain referential relationships are presented as significant. Also in this respect, the linear development combined with nucleus episodes indicates the direction of the narrative flow, inviting the reader's attention to follow special channels. The linear development of Exodus 19–40 heads towards a climax of theophanic manifestation, underlined by the new versions of 'the day of erecting' in Leviticus 1–10 and Numbers 7–9. Above all, the significance of linear development is important when related to narrative stages. The composition represents an arrangement of stories related to Egypt, the journey before Sinai, the Sinai events, and the journey after Sinai. In this case, the composition represents the confluence of the aspects of linearity and parallelism, the key episodes repeated in a different mode (cf. Chapter 5 Sections 2 and 4).

Finally, the linear development seems to be connected with overarching phenomena of thematic and conceptual character. For the main story of Exodus 19–40 the categories of encounter seem to represent the central concept. Elaborated by the theme of divine movement from the sacred mountain into the world below, the categories of encounter link the diverse materials into a coherent whole. The corresponding elaboration of Moses and people as narrative figures is part of this thematic development. The emphasis on the locus of encounter indicates that temple concepts related to the idea of extraordinary encounter are basic to the narrative development. The conceptual implications are expressed by the juxtaposition of divine mountain and huhuman-made tent, connected with the idea of divine and human movement relative to the encounter. With the events of Exodus 40, repeated and completed by Leviticus 8–9 and Numbers 7–9, the divine movement into the world below—related to the people as the theophanic actors—seems to represent the central expression of what Sinai was all about.

With the inclusion of the journey motifs in Exod. 40.36-38 and Num. 9.15-23, the key episode of Exodus 40 is extended by another set of connotations. The itinerary motifs refer to the cycle of stories centred around the journeying people. Two sets of important connotations are combined, the theophanic encounter of Exodus 40 being presented as a permanent situation repeated throughout the journey. The implications of this combination are indicated by the development of the encounter situation within Exodus 19–40,[101] as well as the transformation of both the concepts of locus and theophanic manifestation. The locus in the shape of a travelling sanctuary corresponds to the theophanic manifestation transformed into a signal for departure, just as the observation of the theophanic signals for movement or settlement represents the people's perfect Torah obedience.

Finally, Numbers 8–10 add the nucleus situation of Passover and Exodus to the connotational impact of the events on the day when the sanctuary was erected. The state of permanent theophanic relationship presented as the permanent journey situation in Num. 9.15-23 and followed by the departure from Sinai in Numbers 10, also implies the categories of Passover and Exodus.

The contraction of the key episodes could even indicate that the complex shape of the composition is carried by a rather simple skeleton of

101. The elaboration of the ascent motifs in Exod. 33 is of special importance for the concluding combination of theophanic encounter and divinely guided journey in Exod. 40.36-38 and Num. 9.15-23.

conceptual character. This could balance the impression of the stories as rather open-ended with regard to meaning. Linked by a basic conceptual background, the richness of connotational reverberations could primarily reflect the implications of the central concepts. This is also indicated by the character of the concepts. Centred around the idea of locus as a place of intimate encounter for the divine and human actors, the intricate interplay of potential meanings due to the effects of repetition and parallelism could primarily reflect that they are addressed to readers equally centred in a basic perception of what is referred to.

Chapter 5

THE CYCLICAL CHARACTER OF THE SACRED EVENTS

1. *Exodus 18*

The central position of Jethro the Midianite[1] makes Exodus 18 stand out in its context.[2] It has provided the basis for complicated historical and traditio-historical models both with regard to the origins of Yahwism and the covenant-oriented judicial system of Israel.[3] Its special character is also reflected by a history of reception unusual for an Exodus text. The chapter has been accepted as a coherent expression for a literary unit,[4] often ascribed to the E-source.[5] The scholarly evaluation

1. Cassuto, *Exodus*, pp. 211-12, points to the contrast with the Amalek story in Exod. 17.8-16. For Durham, *Exodus*, pp. 240-43, Exod. 18 is theologically a most important expression of the unification of the family of Abraham, Jethro the symbol for the line of Cain/Keturah/Ishmael/Esau, while Aaron and the elders represent the line of Seth/Sarah/Isaac/Jacob (p. 242). For Blum, *Studien zur Komposition*, pp. 159-60, the chapter represents 'the story on Jethro's conversion', related to the serious problems caused by the non-Israelite family connections of Moses. The presence of Aaron the priest and the elders of the people in v. 12 marks the official recognition of Jethro as accepted in the fold (p. 161).

2. A special Midianite tradition for Coats, *Moses*, pp. 54-55; an 'Einschaltung' ('insertion') with regard both to the D- and P-compositions for Blum, *Studien zur Komposition*, p. 155.

3. Cf. the review of Childs, *Book of Exodus*, pp. 321-26.

4. With a 'literary and thematic unity virtually unparalleled' in Exodus, according to Durham, *Exodus*, p. 241.

5. For Van Seters, *The Life of Moses*, p. 209, a Yahwist composition, the latter part of which is a midrash on Deut. 1.9-18 (pp. 218-19). For Blum, *Studien zur Komposition*, pp. 155-58, ch. 18 reflects a complicated traditio-historical process based on a separate and ancient Moses tradition thoroughly reshaped in vv. 1-12 (pp. 158-59), while vv. 13-27 and Deut. 1.9-18 represent two parallel versions of an ancient pre-Deuteronomic tradition. Num. 11 is seen as a later and rather free elaboration of the Deuteronomic version (pp. 156-57).

corresponds with any reader's immediate delight in this story as very well told, full of attractive details and with vividly profiled situations.[6]

The 'sharing of the burdens' theme (Exod. 18.13-26) is common to a number of texts. Traditionally related to institutional categories as a reference to the origin of Israel's legal system, the theme is elaborated in Num. 11.4-34, usually attributed to the Yahwist, and in a Deuteronomic version in Deut. 1.9-17.[7] The thematic connection between Exodus 18 and Numbers 11 is underlined by their function within the composition. The former represents the last episode of the pre-Sinai journey, while the latter refers to the first concrete episode of the post-Sinai journey.[8] Some basic connection between the narrative environs which surround the Sinai stories is also suggested by the Midianite motifs. Jethro is a central figure in Exodus 18, while Num. 10.29-32 presents a comparable family situation as part of the people's departure. The connotational impact of Midianites mixed into the sacredness of Sinai is rather peculiar and must reflect the significance of these motifs framing the Sinai story.[9]

The Thanksgiving: Exodus 18.1-12

The character of the first scene in vv. 1-12 corresponds to the setting of the story as the last episode before the Sinai events. Exodus and journey are looked back upon as past events. Alluding to the form of Thanksgiving,[10] the references to 'all which Yahweh had done' in Egypt and

6. The general impression of literary unity is also illustrated by R. Knierim, 'Exodus 18 und die Neuordnung der mosaischen Gerichtsbarheit', *ZAW* 73 (1961), pp. 146-71, p. 148. Chapter 18 as a whole reflects a special event structure of ritual character, consisting of narration of the divine acts of salvation (v. 8), praise ('Doxologie') in vv. 9-11, sacrifice and cultic meals (v. 12) concluded the following day by the judicial events ('Rechtsprechung') in vv. 13-27.

7. E.g. Van Seters, *The Life of Moses*, pp. 208-209.

8. Cf. Chapter 5.2 on Num. 1.1-3 and Exod. 15.22-26 as parallel introductions to two sets of journey stories.

9. According to Blum, *Studien zur Komposition*, p. 163, the Sinai stories are enclosed by a bracket of Midian traditions. The two bracket stories have no direct connection. The present location of Exod. 18 is due to its late insertion into a finished composition. With the shape of the Sinai stories already established and the end of the Sinai stories already occupied by Num. 11 and 10.29-32, the location before the Sinai stories was the only possibility left (p. 157).

10. Cf. Childs, *Book of Exodus*, pp. 323-24, on the confession in v. 11 as climax, following the pattern of Ps. 135.

Yahweh's deliverance 'on the way' comprise the preceding events. The story concluded by Exodus 17 are looked back upon as one series of events which belong to the past. Preceded by the confession of Jethro, the meal of v. 12 has the character of joyful thanksgiving.

The retrospective character of vv. 1-12 is comparable to the 'Song of the Sea' in 15.1-21. Both passages belong to scenes centred around the human actors responding to the divine deeds. Also their contextual settings are comparable. Exodus 18 is set between the story cycles of journey and Sinai, ch. 15 between the Egypt and the journey stories. Both are followed by itinerary forms (15.22-23 and 19.1-2). Both stand out in their contexts, interrupting the narrative flow by their retrospective character, looking back and commenting upon the preceding events.[11]

It has been difficult to find a precise label for the literary character of 15.2-18.[12] But introduced by vv. 1b-2 and centred around narrative forms, the unit has important elements in common with the references to a situation of thanksgiving in 18.1-12. The function of the two passages is connected with their retrospective character. According to the narrative frame in 14.30-31 and 15.19, together with the refrain of 15.1 and 21, the Song of the Sea celebrates the salvation from the Egyptians. Correspondingly, the parallel forms of 18.8a and b refer to the preceding events of miraculous intervention. This corresponds to the setting of Exodus 18 after the events of journey concluded by the victory over Amalek.

The character of the two passages underlines the significance of their contextual setting. The flow of successive events is interrupted by the retrospective intermissions which separate sets of events. The Egyptian events are related to each other as expression of one series of events, followed by the events of the pre-Sinai journey as another series. The

11. The parallelism of the two passages could also be reflected by the character of the central actors. The role of Jethro the Midianite as the officiating priest of the sacred meal at the sacred mountain is remarkable. The role of Miriam the woman, who according to 15.20-21 leads the dancing women in a scene of thanksgiving parallel to the proper scene of Moses and the men in v. 1, could be related to the role of women in Ps. 68.12. But within the context of Exodus, her role is as peculiar as that of Jethro. On the other hand, the connotational collusion of such people allocated strange roles corresponds to the character of the Moses substitutes in Exod. 18.

12. F. Crüsemann, *Studien zur Formgeschichte von Hymnus und Danklied in Israel* (WMANT, 32; Neukirchen–Vluyn: Neukirchener Verlag, 1969), pp. 191-93.

organization of the materials reflects a sacred story of different stages. Moreover, the contraction of the preceding events in 18.1-12 indicates that the stages of Egypt and journey are closely related. Compared to these events, the next story cycle of Sinai must introduce a special stage of the sacred story. In this respect, it is important that Exodus 15 and 18 indicate the special character of the Egyptian and journey events. Reflected by confession and thanksgiving, the pre-Sinai story represents a story of divine intervention.

The retrospective character of Exod. 18.1-12 as well as the transition into a new set of events is underlined by the rest of the chapter which is orientated towards the future events. The intolerable burdens are shared and Moses is set free for the higher duties of mediation. This corresponds to the function of Moses in the following Sinai stories.

The development of the story as a conclusion to the journey events and an introduction to the Sinai events corresponds to the itinerary notes in Exod. 17.1, 19.1-2.[13] Set in this framework, the events of ch. 18 form part of the events of Rephidim, the hostility of Amalek being balanced by the arrival of the Midianite,[14] and to be read as the very last episode of the journey stories which sets the stage for the Sinai events. This is also suggested by the way the story is begun in 18.1. The introductory *wayyišma‘* indicates the connection with the events of ch. 17. While the nominal qualifications of Jethro signal the arrival of a new actor, the verb continues the narrative of the preceding chapter, presenting a series of successive events concluded by the departure of Jethro followed by the next scene in 19.1-2 when the people break camp and settle in front of the mountain.

But the neatness of this linear relationship is disturbed by the reference of v. 5, the significance of which is underlined by the reference to Horeb in 17.6. The events of Exodus 18 are located at the divine mountain. With Jethro functioning as a central figure and concluded by his departure, ch. 18 is rounded off as an independent story. Accordingly, ch. 18 presents a set of events somehow parallel to those of the following chapters, which also have the divine mountain for reference. The emphasis on the mountain location in 18.5, and the corresponding problems of reconciling this observation to 19.1-2, seems to be

13. On the significance of the itinerary note 19.1-3a within chs. 19–24, see Dozemann, *God on the Mountain*, p. 13.

14. The contrast relationship is stressed by Cassuto, *Exodus*, p. 212.

deliberate.[15] The words and sentence elements of 18.5b and 19.2aβ,b, suggest a connection of mutual reference.[16] Given the different interests of the two descriptions, expressed by the dating in 19.1a and the presentation of Jethro and his flock in 18.5a, the echo effect of the two descriptions of the arrival at the divine mountain points to their connection.

The reader is presented with what seems to be a deliberate ambiguity. The immediate transition from the events of ch. 17 to the Jethro episode of ch. 18, as well as the itinerary note of 19.1-2, separate the Sinai stories proper and the events connected with Rephidim. The elaborate character of 19.1-2 obviously signals that the events of chs. 19–40 are something apart. On the other hand, the reference of 18.5, added to by the formal connection with 19.2, subtly links the Jethro episode to the context of the divine mountain, presented as somehow parallel to the following Sinai events.[17]

On the other hand, it has already been seen that this type of ambiguity[18] represents a normal expression for the compositional mode. Compared to the composition of chs. 19–40 and the repeated versions of 'the day of erecting the sanctuary', the contextual setting of ch. 18 seems to represent a new expression of the normal mode. In all cases the composition implies the ambiguity of stories with a function as part of the linear development combined with a subtle double-effect of parallelism. This corresponds to the contexual function of Exodus 18.

15. On the other hand, Blum (*Studien zur Komposition*, pp. 155-58) asserts that the relationship of 17.1 and 19.1-2 reflects the editorial problems when ch. 18 should be inserted into a proper location.

16. The common *bô* is connected to a structure of *midbār–šām* related to *ḥānâ* with an emphasized subject which is concluded by the climactic *hāhār / har hā'ᵉlōhîm*.

17. It is possible that such an interest also could be relevant for the preceding journey stories. The issue is raised by the important observations of Blum (*Studien zur Komposition*, pp. 162-63) on the local reference in Exod. 17.6a related to 15.25b-26 and 16.4-5, 28-29. The identification of the localities of the journey with the mountain of Torah-proclamation suggests that categories of 'zeitlich/räumliche *Abfolge*' ('temporal and spatial order') could have been abolished.

18. A comparable ambiguity is also reflected by the contextual setting of 15.1-21. Together with ch. 14, the passage could be related both to the cycle of Egypt stories and to journey stories: e.g. Dennis J. McCarthy, 'Plagues and Sea of Reeds. Exodus 5–14' *JBL* 85 (1966), pp. 137-58.

The formal signals indicate that the story has a prime function as a conclusion to the pre-Sinai journey stories. But in addition, the reference in v. 5 subtly changes this impression, inviting a second reading. The Jethro episode also represents a relatively independent mountain story which presents a completed series of events taking place at the divine mountain. The parallel 'sharing of the burdens theme' in Exodus 18 and Numbers 11 underlines the significance of the events set in motion by Jethro. This is also indicated by the Midianite references in Num. 10.29-32, related to the departure from Sinai.

As two sets of divine mountain stories, Exodus 18 and chs. 19–40 seem peculiarly symmetrical however different in size. Chapter 18 read as a parallel version of the Sinai events would correspond to the function of chs. 19–40 as a special cycle of Sinai stories, repeated and added to by the next cycle ended by Numbers 9. Set in such a pattern, ch. 18 could represent a version of the following stories *in nuce*. As a first version it could intimate the basic aspects of the Sinai events, preparing for the richer versions of the following stories.

The Substitution of Moses: Exodus 18.13-27

Due to the retrospective character of vv. 1-12, it is primarily vv. 13-27 which reflect the parallelism of the Jethro episode and the events of Sinai. The story of the second day presents how parts of the Moses function were transferred to representatives of the people. This is comparable to the main story line in Exodus 19–40. Concluded by the people as the new theophanic figures, the substitution of Moses by a new set of actors is presented as the climax of the Sinai events. The appointment of 'lesser judges' in Exodus 18 could represent a special version of the theme of substitution.[19]

Such a connection is indicated by the character of the candidates for the high office of Moses. In Exodus 19–40, the people represent highly unsuitable figures for the sacred role of the encounter. The substitute judges in ch. 18 could represent a corresponding collusion of 'high' and 'low'. The description of their function is ambiguous, related both to oracular and judicial as well as military categories. According to vv. 22

19. Cf. also the corresponding relationship between Lev. 8 and 9, the former centred around Moses as the officiating priest, while the latter presents Aaron and his sons as the priests. This represents a priestly version of the subtitution theme, parallel to Exod. 18 on the judicial function.

and 26, which relate to the description of the Moses function in vv. 13-14 and 16, judicial categories are important.[20] This is supplemented by the qualification of 'the leaders' in vv. 21 and 25, which refer to military categories.[21] And finally, the oracular function represents a comprehensive category for the new officials. According to v. 15, the functions of Moses refer to the people's need to 'enquire' of God.

The description of the new office entails too many tensions when read as a story that provides information on the origins of Israel's judicial system. The relationship of judicial and military categories in particular has caused much discussion.[22] At the very least, it must be important that the Moses-function is related to offices of secular connotations. 'Secular' is a rather problematical term[23] with regard to war and judicial practice. But in contrast to the part of the original function retained for Moses himself as, for example, 'God's opposite' (*mûl hā'ᵉlōhîm*) in v. 19, the sharing of duties implies the separation between an extraordinary relationship of encounter and more mundane offices. Compared to the function of Moses, the function of the substitutes is 'lesser'. This is added to by the military references of vv. 21 and 25.[24] Comparable to a modern list of 'generals, colonels, captains and sergeants', the qualification of the officials seems to refer to rather mundane categories of practical reality.

But at the same time, the duties of these mundane officials represent parts of the original Moses functions which respond to the people's need for oracular intercession (v. 15b). With v. 16 as the concrete

20. Cf. also the category of *rîb* in Deut. 1.12b expanded by the admonishing address to the judges in vv. 16-17. Also in this case, the judicial categories are added to by the references to administrative and military functions in v. 15.

21. E.g. Knierim, 'Exodus 18'.

22. Cf. the preceding note, while Van Seters, *The Life of Moses*, pp. 212-99, finds the assumed collapse of the Deuteronomic distinction between officers and officials in Exod. 18 so peculiar that it could reflect the diaspora situation, when the military offices had become meaningless.

23. The contrasts of 'sakral' ('sacral') and 'bürgerlich' ('civic') describe the two types of judicial practice in Exod. 18 according to M. Noth, *Das zweite Buch Moses*, p. 120; further Knierim, 'Exodus 18', pp. 163-67. Such a separation is strongly rejected by Durham, *Exodus*, p. 251.

24. The significance of the military terms is underlined by the preceding Amalek episode. According to Cassuto, *Exodus*, p. 212, the portrayal of Moses as exhausted is important for both episodes (17.11-12), while the choosing of substitutes in 18.25 corresponds to the choosing of the men in 17.9.

explication of this need, the lesser duties of the military officials are also contained within this definition. Their performance represents an oracular function. Accordingly, the officials, however mundane, are part of a new hierarchical order of mediation. The character of this order is indicated by the peculiar combination of sacral and mundane connotations, the ancient colonels and captains and sergeants sharing the extraordinary function of the oracular medium when serving as judges.[25]

The connotational clash of this description corresponds to the elaboration of the people as the Moses substitutes in Exodus 19–40. The choice of the military categories for the qualification of the role of 'lesser judges' corresponds to the people as the unlikely theophanic actors in ch. 40. In both cases, the connotational effects make the terms of 'secularization' and 'sanctification' equally apt for a description of what has taken place. The juxtaposition of ordinary humanity and the transference of sacred functions imply the basic movement from 'high' to 'low' with its emphasis on human reality as the locus of divine manifestation.

Also in ch. 18, the change has repercussions for the position of Moses. The appointment of lesser judges means that Moses is set free for the higher aspects of mediation. The new situation is visualized by the opening scene of the Sinai stories in 19.2-3. While the people settle down, Moses is free for an immediate ascent on his own.[26] The elevation of Moses-substitutes combined with the idea of Moses set free for higher things is comparable to the aspects of Moses substituted by the people in ch. 40 and Moses elevated into a semi-divine figure in ch. 34. Taken together, the two versions of the common theme of substitution indicates the 'upward mobility' of the human actors. The movement from 'high' to 'low' results in the expansion of the human reality by ordinary people allocated sacred roles, while the hierarchically higher human is high indeed. It is even possible that the ambiguous term *mûl hā'ᵉlōhîm* in Exod. 18.19 could refer to categories that correspond to the apotheosis of Moses in ch. 34. With 'God's front' a possible

25. The deliberate character of this collusion is underlined by the comparable combination of prophetic categories and administrative duties in Num. 11.

26. The implications of such a scene are illustrated by Exod. 24.14, reflecting both the necessity of the judiciary as well as the need for Moses to be set free to meet higher objectives.

translation,[27] the term could imply an understanding of Moses' position comparable to the (also ambiguous) elaboration of the *pānîm* motifs in 34.29-34.

The significance of Moses in the new phase of the story is given remarkable expression by the formal organization of the materials in Exodus 18. The introduction to the second scene in vv. 13-26 alludes to the introduction of the first scene in vv. 1-12. Jethro's seeing 'all that he was doing for the people' (v. 14a), is juxtaposed to his hearing 'all that God had done for Moses and for Israel his people' (v. 1a).[28] Related to Jethro as the central figure, the parallelism of the sentences connects the two sets of events. The first day is dedicated to the divine actions in relation to the people and to Moses, which have beeen 'heard' by Jethro. The second day is dedicated to the actions of Moses in relation to the people, which is 'seen' by Jethro. The connection of the two events is also indicated by the juxtaposition of the scenes in vv. 12 and 13-14. Two groups of different actors in two types of ritual proceedings are set against each other, the one the joyous celebration of divine actions, the other the expression for the intolerable character of Moses' actions.

The parallelism of the two sets of events introduced in vv. 1 and 14 is underlined by the formulaic language. The first version of the construction *'et kol 'ašer 'āśâ* with a divine subject is repeated in vv. 8a and 9a and continued by dependent (vv. 8b, 9b) and parallel (v. 10a, b) constructions. Also for the second part, 'do' is an important term (vv. 14b, 17b, 18b, 23aa, 24b) and now with Moses as subject. Given the formulaic character of language when the motif is related to the divine subject, the constructions of vv. 14a, b and 17b must refer to the corresponding sentences on the divine actions. In addition to the connection of vv. 1 and 14, both introducing two successive scenes related to Jethro's 'hearing' and 'seeing', the formulaic language presents YHWH's and Moses' acts as somehow parallel. The parallelism is underlined by the qualification of 'goodness' added to the stereotyped language in vv. 9 and 17. The acts of YHWH are juxtaposed to the acts

27. The usual application of *mûl* suggests the function of preposition 'opposite, in front of' God. But it is difficult to separate between usages of *mûl* with function as a preposition and as a noun 'front, foremost side'. The expression could as well be rendered 'God's front', implying Moses as God's representative 'to the people'. Extended with *hāyâ l^e* in v. 19bα, the construction is comparable to 4.16b.

28. Cassuto, *Exodus*, p. 218.

of Moses, the one set belonging to the past and 'good', the other to the present 'non-good action' and to the future.

The strange parallelism between divine and human actions is the more peculiar given the grandeur of the divine acts. We would naturally expect that such a relationship between vv. 1 and 14a should be reflected by motifs which extol Moses the religious hero. But on the contrary,[29] the grand connotations of the formulaic style are contrasted by the pathetic image of Moses in his daily chores, set in a hopeless situation and even rather stupid in the way he solves his problems (vv. 13-14). The formulaic language underlines this contrast. Applied as a question in v. 14 and as a demotion in v. 17, it functions as a pun, the 'no-goodness' of Moses' actions contrasting with the divine 'goodness'. But with Jethro proposing a better action (v. 23) and the story ending with Moses 'doing all that he had said' (v. 24), the episode has resulted in a better practice for the future.

The relationship of the two scenes in vv. 1-12 and 13-27 implies a remarkable qualification of the sacred story. The narrative reality is separated between the actions of God and Moses. 'All that God has done' belongs to a past epoch, solemnly celebrated in vv. 1-12. 'All that Moses was doing' refers to the present and future epoch in the people's life. The significance of this separation is underlined by the contextual setting of Exodus 18, concluding the pre-Sinai journey and introducing the cycle of Sinai stories.

The details of Exodus 18 adds to the perception of the new situation. In contrast to the congregation of thanksgiving in v. 12, related to a past of miraculous events, the congregation of v. 13, related to Moses' actions, represent the never-ending problems of a man and his 'neighbour', resulting in Moses' being stuck in the human reality of never-ending conflicts. But at the same time the ironic twists of the formulaic language and the indirect description of Moses as quite stupid in his dealings with the burdensome aspects of human reality profoundly assert the sacred character of his action. Comparable to the colonels, captains and sergeants performing oracular duties, the relationship of vv. 14a and 18b retains the significance of 'all that Moses was doing'. With substitutes appointed to fulfil the lesser aspects, it is possible for Moses to fulfil the higher aspects.

29. This is illustrated by Coats, *Moses*, pp. 54-55, to whom the character of Moses as 'heroic man' is important. The Moses of Exod. 18 is found to be sadly non-heroic and as such separated from both J and E as a Midianite tradition.

The significance of human action is asserted and added to by the separation of the actions of Moses and of his substitutes. The mundane character of the officials taking over Moses' burdens underlines the human character of the new phase of the sacred story. Moses and his substitutes represent a hierarchy of human action, the people related to successive layers of actors performing their parts. Moreover, the people are also to be set in this hierarchical order of sacred doing. If Moses is set free, he will be able to make known to the people 'the doing that they shall do' (v. 20bb).[30]

This also indicates that ultimately the people's action represents the central reference of Moses' action. The parallelism of vv. 1 and 14, the present efforts of Moses juxtaposed to the divine acts of the sacred story, indicate the elevated position of Moses in the new era. But even so, his function as 'God's front' is to make possible the people's right action. Also 'God' is related to this aspect. Compared to the miraculous character of the sacred story, now past, the divine activity in the new phase of the sacred story is related to 'laws' and 'teachings' in vv. 16b, 20, 'God' manifesting himself through the mediator as the initiator of proper human action.[31]

The emphasis placed upon ordinary human reality—the ordinariness reflected both by the description of the overburdened Moses, the people engaged in neighbourly quarrels, and the lesser oracular functions put in the hands of 'colonels, captains and sergeants'—is added to by the central position of Jethro. The crisis of the new situation is solved by ordinary common sense, the character of which is stressed by the connotational effects of Jethro as a Midianite. His significance in Exodus 18 is underlined by the parallel story in Numbers 11. Here the perception of an intolerable situation leads to the miserable complaint of Moses (vv. 11-15), and the problem is solved by divine intervention. In Exodus 18 both roles are allocated to Jethro, 'seeing' the problem and shrewdly suggesting its solution.[32]

30. The formulaic character of the language is added to by the connection of human 'doing' and divine 'commanding' in v. 23a, corresponding to the formula of compliance (e.g. Exod. 39.32, 42-43; 40,16).

31. The relationship is comparable to the imagery of Exod. 34.34-35, with the divine actor confined to the tent, while the illuminated Moses leaves the tent to mediate the divine sayings to the people.

32. Cf. the comparable juxtaposition in Num. 10.31 and 33, both the divine

In this way, the character of the events presented in vv. 13-27 corresponds to subtle mountain references of v. 5. The elaboration of the episode indicates events, the implications of which are strangely parallel to those of chs. 19–40. At the same time, the linear setting of successive episodes separates ch. 18 from the following Sinai stories. The solemnity of the mountain imagery related to the divine and human interaction in the first scenes of Exodus 19 is not disturbed by the absurdity of the scenes in the parallel story. Conversely, the formal separation makes it possible to present ch. 18 as a bold and rather humorous commentary on the implications of the Sinai events. The implications of the divine movement from the mountain to the world below and the corresponding changes of the world below is illustrated[33] by the utterly human scenes of ch. 18, absurdly related to influences from above.

The sacred story consists of different stages, moreover stages of a quite different character. The Egyptian and journey stories represent the first stages, characterized by miraculous divine acts of salvation which are now concluded. Sinai represents a new stage in the story development, dedicated to ordinary human reality as the locus of sacred action performed by human subjects.

2. *Numbers 11 and Exodus 18*

The Contextual Setting of Numbers 11.4-34

After the description of the departure from Sinai in Numbers 10, the next chapter presents the reader with a clash of contrasts. Read according to categories of different literary origin, Numbers 9 and the main part of Numbers 10 have been related to Priestly traditions and Priestly redaction,[34] while Numbers 11 is seen as an expression of older

cloud and the Midianite being attributed the function of guide through the wilderness.

33. But certainly not explicated: the peculiar parallelism of YHWH's actions of the past and Moses' actions of the next stage leaves the reader in the same state of wonder as the apotheosis of Moses in Exod. 34. Added to by the theophanic manifestation as a signalling device in Exod. 40, these illustrations of the implications of the divine movement into the world below seem to veil as much as convey what the story is really all about.

34. The Hobab incident is often seen as the first expression of Yahwistic material; cf. Noth, *Das vierte Buch Moses*, p. 69; de Vaulx, *Les Nombres*, pp. 144-45; Budd, *Numbers*, pp. 113-14. The transition from Num. 10 to 11 can be related

materials. Whatever the original character of the materials in the two chapters, their present shape represents a marked effect of juxtaposition.[35] Numbers 7–9 extol a situation of perfect action, fittingly continued by the description of the solemn departure from Sinai in Numbers 10. This is suddenly interrupted in Num. 11.1 by a story of revolt and punishment. The contrast is stressed by Num. 9.15-23, which extends the climactic event of Sinai into the journey as a whole. The 'day of

to categories of theme. According to Noth, *Das vierte Buch Moses*, pp. 67 and 74-75, Num. 9.15–10.36 represent the Priestly conclusion on the theme 'Gottesoffenbarung am Sinai' ('God's revelation at Sinai') which began in Exod. 19, while the following stories are dedicated to the theme 'Führung in der Wüste' ('guidance in the desert'), the main characteristics of which are the misery and complaints of the people. According to Budd, *Numbers*, p. 111, the section Num. 9.15–10.28 represents an *haggadic* interpretation of the Yahwistic material in Num. 10.29-36, the original motif of obedience being contrasted with the motif of disobedience.

35. To Wilcoxen, 'Some Anthropocentric Aspects', this reflects a main compositional interest. The difference between the wilderness stories before and after Sinai points to stages of religious development. In connection with traditio-historical categories, similar issues are also raised by Coats (*Moses*, p. 143) with regard to the relationship of the parallel wilderness stories in Exodus and in Numbers as an expression of some compositional development. He suggests that for the final redaction of the narrative the Sinai traditions serve a distinctive structural role. Before Sinai the rebellion meets no particular punishment, while after Sinai it provokes the divine wrath. Indications of such a pattern can also be traced in the older materials. A similar pattern, but limited to the book of Numbers, is recognized by Olson (*Death of the Old*, pp. 121-23). Num. 11 marks the transition to a situation of disobedience and divine punishment, connected with the break between Num. 10.36 and 11.1. Num. 1.1–10.36 is given over to a positive picture, while 11.1–25.18 is dominated by a series of rebellions and plagues. The book as a whole reflects a 'two-generation structure' with Num. 1.1–25.18 as the first part. Due to the contrasts of obedience in Num. 10 and complaints and revolts in Num. 11, 11.1 is seen as introducing the second part of Num. 1.1–25.18. This is divided into two sections, 11.1–20.29 and 21.1–25.19, with 21.1 understood to strike a positive tone for the first time. The frame of reference for this structure is strictly limited to the book of Numbers, the traditional understanding of chs. 1–10 as part of the Sinai stories being refused in favour of what is asserted as the present redactional markers. Also Budd, *Numbers*, p. 111, finds a 'changing pattern of obedience/disobedience' in the journey stories. According to V. Fritz (*Israel in der Wüste: Traditionsgeschichtliche Untersuchung der Wüstenüberlieferung des Jahwisten* [MTS, 7; Marburg: N.G. Elwert Verlag, 1970], p. 70), a corresponding development of 'before and after' is related to the Deuteronomistic pattern in the book of Judges.

erecting the dwelling' represents the permanent situation of journey, the people 'always' set in a situation of *visio Dei* and perfect observation. With Numbers 11 as the first expression of what really happened on the journey, the reader is confronted by what seems to present two radically different journeys.

The clash seems to reflect a deliberate effect of composition. This is indicated by the introductory episode in vv. 1-3. Formally, it is presented as an independent episode related to a special camp site (v. 3). But the schematic character of the story and its lack of details are underlined by the following episode in vv. 4-34. It might be regarded as an independent ad hoc expression of a theological concern[36] or as rudiments of an older tradition preserved as a separate story.[37] In any case, it states without any embellishment the basic character of the new reality after Sinai. Given the detailed character of the following story, vv. 1-3 seem to serve an an introductory presentation of the new situation, mediating between Numbers 10 and 11.4-34.[38]

Both the literary character and the function of these verses correspond to Exod. 15.22-26. A comparable structure of stark facts, this passage also represents the bare bones of a certain type of wilderness story.[39] In Num. 11.1-3, the murmuring leads to divine punishment, in

36. A 'narratives Beispielsstück' ('narrative paradigm') comparable to Judg. 3.7-11 and related to Deuteronomistic influence; cf. Fritz, *Israel in der Wüste*, pp. 68-70; Aurelius, *Der Fürbitter Israels*, pp. 144-46; further Budd, *Numbers*, p. 118; Coats, *Moses*, p. 115; Van Seters, *The Life of Moses*, p. 223.

37. A basic expression of the theme of revolt and punishment, the passage has been separated from the following story due to the influence of Deut. 9.22, according to de Vaulx, *Les Nombres*, p. 149.

38. Cf. also the parallel introductions *wayᵉhî* in Num. 10.11, 35 and 11.1. The formal connection can be related to the motif development. Corresponding to the parallelism of cloud and nightly fire in Num. 9.15-16, the description of the departure is related to the cloud (Num. 10.11-12, 34), while Num. 11.1-3 refers to the nightly manifestation of fire. This continues the final *ḥānâ*-scene of Num. 10.36—the character of the divine return to his people made concrete by the terrible scene of Num. 11.1-3. Such an ironic twist of the conventional theme corresponds to the character of the miraculous meal in vv. 4-34. In this way, the juxtaposition of idyll and conflict could be reflected by the contrasts of day and night, related to the people on the journey and in the camp.

39. Set in what is assumed to represent the special 'Pattern I' of the murmuring tradition and without any basis in an original local tale, according to Childs, *Book of Exodus*, p. 268; for Durham (*Exodus*, pp. 211-12), the text represents a composite of motifs and source material; for Van Seters (*The Life of Moses*, pp. 176-77),

Exod. 15.22-26 to the miraculous solution of the crisis. In both cases, the short version is followed by a detailed wilderness story of a character that corresponds to the introductory episode (Exod. 16 and Num. 11.4-34). The relationship of two skeleton stories fleshed out by the following detailed story is underlined by their contextual setting. The two short stories introduce two parallel sets of journey stories, stating the basic character of the people's journey before Sinai and after Sinai. Their relationship is also reflected by the concrete materials of the following stories, both centred around food and manna motifs. The relationship of the introductions and the thematic parallelism of the following episodes underline these stories as important expressions for the organization of the materials.

The referential relationship between Exodus 16 and Numbers 11 is added to by the connection between Numbers 11 and Exodus 18. They are linked by their function as expressions of episodes which frame the cycle of Sinai stories. Also in this case the relationship is reflected by the concrete materials, most directly by the subtitution of Moses theme. The double relationship to two stories corresponds to the complex character of Numbers 11. But the connection with Exodus 18, concluding the pre-Sinai journey stories, underlines the significance of Numbers 11 as the first post-Sinai story.

The organization of the materials separates different story cycles. The parallelism of the two sets of journey stories, with its seemingly monotonous repetition of the same events, seems to indicate that these stories refer to stages in the narrative development. The difference is indicated by the character of the two sets of journey stories.[40] In the first cycle given over to the pre-Sinai situation, the complaint of the people is answered by the miraculous divine intervention which solves the

the text represents a reflection of the form of prophetic *legenda* adapted by the Yahwist to conform to the murmuring/intercession pattern.

40. The difference is illustrated by the traditio-historical arrangement of the murmuring stories by Coats, *Moses*, p. 109. The perception of crisis and divine intervention of help reflects the original pattern. The change to a negative evaluation of the complaint expressed by the divine reaction of punishment is typical of the later reworkings of the murmuring traditions. On the other hand, Childs (*Book of Exodus*, pp. 258-64) finds two original types of structure for the murmuring stories: Pattern I is initiated by a crisis, followed by the people's complaint and the divine intervention, while Pattern II is initiated by the people's complaint, followed by the divine punishment.

crisis. In the second, the people's complaint, connected to crises comparable to those of the first cycle, leads to the divine anger and punishment.[41]

The 'Thanksgiving'

The effects of repetition and parallelism are pronounced in Num. 11.4-34. Related to source- and traditio-critical categories, they have been understood as expressions of a highly composite 'secondary' composition. The artificial compilation of different themes—of complaint, miraculous response and punishment typical for the journey stories[42] related to the motifs of burden-sharing—is assumed to reflect the disunity of the story in its present shape.[43] On the other hand, it has proved difficult to differentiate between significant layers within the story.[44]

The complex character of the story can be related to the subtleties of referential relationships. The connection with Exodus 18 is reflected by the main structure. The two stories combine the themes of sacred meal and substitution of Moses, related to the events of two days. The combination of meal and substitution is underlined in Numbers 11 by being stated twice, both in the divine instructions in vv. 16-20 and when presented as events in vv. 25-33. But compared with Exodus 18, the order of meal and substitution is changed. The miraculous provision of meat represents the climactic event. Corresponding to the order of the divine instructions in vv. 16-17 on the elders and vv. 18-20 on the meal preparations, the story is concluded in vv. 31-33 by the divine miracle, when the gathering of the food is concluded by the meal interrupted by the divine wrath.[45]

41. The consequences of ignoring this simple organization of the materials, recognized as early as 1968 by Wilcoxen, 'Some Anthropocentric Aspects', is illustrated by the difficulty of relating the narrative mode to categories of literary origin; see also Van Seters, *The Life of Moses*, pp. 167-75, on the problems of the narrative patterns proposed by Childs, *Book of Exodus*, pp. 258-64, or Aurelius, *Der Fürbitter Israels*, pp. 205-207, on the murmuring stories as reflecting Exod. 32 which represents the original expression of Moses as intercessor.

42. Childs, *Book of Exodus*, pp. 258-64; Coats, *Moses*, pp. 109-24.

43. E.g. Van Seters, *The Life of Moses*, pp. 227-28; Aurelius, *Der Fürbitter Israels*, pp. 176-78; Coats, *Moses*, pp. 119-20.

44. Ascribed to one author who has interwoven different traditional material into one narrative by Van Seters, *The Life of Moses*, p. 229; correspondingly also Aurelius, *Der Fürbitter Israels*, p. 178.

45. This order reflects the connection to Exod. 16.

The parallelism of the two meals in Exodus 18 and Numbers 11 is subtly elaborated. Both are related to the Egypt events. In Numbers 11 the people long to eat meat, and the longing is immediately related to the past meals of Egypt (vv. 4-5). This could be seen as a given stereotype of these stories.[46] But the connection of Egyptian motifs and ritual categories adds a special flavour to the meal. Corresponding to the celebration of the Egyptian events by confession and meal in Exodus 18, the food motif is connected to the people's 'remembering' of the past Egyptian events (vv. 4-5, 18, 20). The remembering is accompanied by the people's weeping. In v. 20, this is qualified as 'weeping before YHWH'[47]—the significance of is which added to by the element 'who is in your midst'. The outpourings are related to the ritual categories of complaint and prayer.

This presents a situation of 'remembrance' which starkly contrasts with the meal 'before God' in Exod. 18.12. In both cases, the ritual connotations of 'before' is added to by the idea of a special divine presence. In Exodus 18 this is indicated by the categories of divine mountain, while the implications of YHWH in the people's 'midst' in Numbers 11 are prepared for by the events of Sinai. By means of the divine movement from mountain to camp the shameless weeping is directly related to the divine 'ears' (v. 18) and 'face' (v. 20). With a parallel orientation towards the Egyptian events, the meal of thanksgiving has been changed into a situation of complaint, the confession perverted into the plaintive question: 'Why indeed did we go out from Egypt!' (vv. 18, 20). In the Golden Calf episode, the positive significance of the Egyptian events is adhered to, while the character of divine presence is perverted. In Numbers 11, the weeping of the people implies the wish to have the Egyptian events reversed, linked to the wish for a change of food.

So far Numbers 11 presents a story parallel to Exod. 18.1-12. Certain basic components are common to the two stories, while the effects of repetition and parallelism have a function of juxtaposition. The Numbers version represents a distortion of the Jethro celebration, the thanksgiving changed into perverted remembering. This effect is underlined by the parallelism of 'the rabble' and Jethro the Midianite. The juxtaposed events are set in motion by 'foreigners'.

46. E.g. Van Seters, *The Life of Moses*, p. 230 on a popular J theme in v. 5.

47. E.g. Judg. 20.23; 2 Chron. 34.27; while 1 Sam. 8.21 suggests similar categories for the weeping 'in the ears of YHWH' in v. 18.

Manna and Meat

The perversion of the sacred story is expressed by the meat motifs. The 'desire' of the 'rabble' taken up by Israel is transformed into the cry for meat (v. 4). The anti-meal connected to meat is important for the narrative development (vv. 4, 18, 21-22, 31-33). The significance of this connection is elaborated in a special way. Manna is introduced as the sub-motif which contrasts with the meat (vv. 6-9). To the meat-hungry, their 'soul is drying' with nothing to look at but manna (v. 6). The significance of manna is underlined by the digressive presentation of its appearance and collection in vv. 7-9, which is juxtaposed later by the extended presentation of the quails in vv. 31-32.

The contrast of meat and manna implies that the allusions to the thanksgiving of Exodus 18 are supplemented by the reference to Exodus 16.[48] Corresponding to the desire for meat in Num. 11.4, the crisis of Exodus 16 is initiated by the people's hunger. The introduction in v. 3ab suggests a parallel relationship between 'meat' and 'bread'. Both are desired by the people and both divinely provided by the double miracle (vv. 8, 12-14). But the development of the story clearly emphasizes the significance of 'bread'. In the following events, only the manna motifs are elaborated. The double miracle of meat and bread[49] seems to be presented as an initial demonstration of the divine power (vv. 6-8, 12), while the repeated provision of manna gives the people the bread on the journey. This corresponds to the introduction to the story. The utterance of the people in v. 3 is juxtaposed to the divine utterance of vv. 4-5,[50] the people's longing for meat and bread being set

48. Usually Exod. 16 and Num. 11.4-34 have been separated from each other as parallel expressions of the same traditions, the former dominated by P-materials, the latter belonging to J; e.g. Coats, *Moses*, pp. 119-20; Blum, *Studien zur Komposition*, pp. 146-48. Aurelius, *Der Fürbitter Israels*, p. 179, refuses any connection between the two texts. The dependence of Num. 11 on Exod. 16 is stressed by Van Seters, *The Life of Moses*, p. 182. The Yahwist story requires a pre-P account of the provision of manna, and accordingly, Exod. 16.1a, 2-3*, 4-7, 13b-15, 21, 27-31, 35a, are attributed to the Yahwist (p. 187).

49. The seemingly illogical character of the combination is illustrated by Childs (*Book of Exodus*, pp. 277-79) and Durham (*Exodus*, pp. 216-17, 223-24). At the very least, the combination serves to prepare the composition of Num. 11.

50. Verses 4-5 are usually found as a disturbing insertion influenced by Deuteronomy, e.g. Aurelius, *Der Fürbitter Israels*, p. 171; contrast Van Seters, *The Life of Moses*, p. 186.

against the divine rain of heavenly bread which, moreover, is given to test the people's observation of the Torah.

In this way, the contrasting of meat and manna in Numbers 11 is prepared for by the Exodus contrasting of meat and manna/bread.[51] The desire for meat and the rejection of manna means the rejection of the divine provision of fare presented in Exodus 16. Corresponding to the connection of the temporary quails and the permanent manna in Exodus 16, the contempt for the permanent manna makes YHWH reverse the original order of events. In grossly enlarged form (vv. 19-20, 31), the first part of the double food miracle is repeated. And in this case the meat divinely provided is turned into a deadly meal. The perversion of the miraculous meal corresponds to the people's perverted 'remembering'. Just as the people changed the sacred story into a complaint, so the miraculous feeding is changed into a scene of divine killing.

The description of the punishment in v. 33 could even suggest that not only the food miracle but also the more central events of the sacred story have somehow been reversed. Related to the narrative frame of repeated Passover and Exodus in Numbers 8–10, the divine 'smiting' (*hikkâ*[52]) implies that the people are treated like the Egyptians. The people's repetition of 'the smiting of the firstborn' in Num. 8.17 is repeated by a new divine 'smiting', now directed towards the people. Such a reversal would correspond to the perversion of the people's 'remembering' and of the miraculous meal, as well as to the implications of the 'rabble in the people's midst'.

Introduced by vv. 1-3, which in their turn are juxtaposed to the parallel introduction in Exod. 15.22-26, the referential allusions of the meal motifs in vv. 4-34 underline the character of the post-Sinai situation. Before Sinai, the people's complaint, also in this case connected to the perverse 'remembering' of Egypt, resulted *deus ex machina* in a

51. The motif elaboration could also be related to the vegetarian 'eating of bread' in Exod. 18.12. The formal separation of v. 12a and b by the initial verb of b indicates the separation of two events. Jethro first performed the sacrifices, upon which 'they' came and 'ate bread'. A similar distinction between sacrifices and meal is made in Exod. 24.5-11, while 32.6 more directly relates the sacrifice and the eating.

52. See Exod. 3.20 and especially the formulaic language of Exod. 12.12, 29, Num. 8.17. The referential significance of the term is underlined by the '600,000 men on foot' in Num. 11.21. The special qualification of 'men on foot' reflects the description of the people in Exod. 12.37; cf. Van Seters, *The Life of Moses*, p. 229.

manifestation of miraculous feeding. After Sinai a comparable event results in a new food miracle, but now of a mortal character. The effect of the juxtaposition is underlined by the parallel location of Exodus 16 and Num. 11.4-34 as the first episodes of the two stages of journey. Between the two different divine modes are located the Sinai stories. According to Exodus 19–40 the significance of Sinai is visualized by the final scene of 40.34-38 given over to the Tent of Meeting as the new locus of divine manifestation. Within this context, Numbers 11 presents the implications of the divine movement from mountain to tent. While Exod. 40.34-38, elaborated by Num. 9.15-23, extols the wondrous character of the climactic encounter of God and people, Numbers 11 is dedicated to the other aspect of intimate togetherness. Climaxed by a miraculous meal of divine 'smiting', the character of the episode corresponds to the divine worries of Exod. 33.1-5.[53] The Numbers story illustrates the mortal dangers implied by the divine co-walking 'in the people's midst'. Concluded in Numbers 10, the story so far has extolled the wonders of intimate theophanic relationship. Numbers 11 presents the other aspects of this situation. This is underlined by the sharp contrast with the pre-Sinai journey. What was tolerated in the first cycle of journey stories has become intolerable in the post-Sinai stories. The story of miraculous salvation and guidance extolled in Exodus 18 has been turned into a story of harsh retribution.

The Substitution of Moses

The relationship of Num. 11.4-34 to Exodus 18 also underlines the positive aspects of the new situation. As a version of the Sinai events, Exod. 18.13-27 is dedicated to a new reality centred around the concept of 'human action'. Moses, the oracular soldiers, and the people are parts of a new hierarchical order of sacred action. The significance of this order is indicated by the parallelism of 'all that YHWH had done' and 'all that Moses was doing'. The past events of miraculous intervention are concluded, while the present and future is dedicated to the deeds of Moses.

Compared to the presentation of the sacred story in Exodus 18, Numbers 11 marks a return to miraculous categories, but in a perverted form corresponding to the perverted remembrance. But a corresponding

53. Cf. also the intimations of Lev. 9.23–10.2, the parallelism of the two manifestations of 'consuming fire' as an expression for two aspects of the divine presence.

parallelism between YHWH and Moses is reflected also in this episode. The combination of the miraculous meal and the substitution of Moses is twice expressed, both as intimated in vv. 16-20 and as actualized in vv. 24-33. The repetitions underline the significance of the parallelism of the *rûaḥ* motifs in vv. 25 and 31. The installation of 70 elders as prophets is effected by YHWH taking 'from the *rûaḥ* which (was) over' Moses (cf. also the similar construction in v. 17). In the same way the food miracle is effected by the *rûaḥ* setting out 'from YHWH'. As part of the compositional effort to present the connection between the two events, the parallelism must be important. The spirit taken from Moses and related to his helpers results in prophecy. The spirit from YHWH results in the food miracle.

The parallelism between God and Moses is stressed by the connotational impact of the spirit motif. Connected to an event of prophetic inspiration and in a context that refers to the divine spirit, one would expect that the prophetic inspiration was also related to the manifestation of the divine spirit. This is illustrated by the wish of Moses in v. 29 which applies the conventional language of prophetic inspiration. But instead of some construction corresponding to 'YHWH setting his spirit over them', the peculiar parallelism of vv. 25 and 31 separates between the manifestations of the divine 'spirit' related to the food miracle and of the 'personal'[54] spirit of Moses related to the prophetic inspiration of the elders. This is added to by the character of both spirit manifestations, which are equally forceful. Parallel to the impressive strength of the spirit from YHWH, the spirit from Moses sends 70 persons into ecstasy, even the two left in the camp.

However subtly, the description indicates some important parallelism between Moses and the divine actor. Corresponding to Exodus 18, YHWH is related to acts of miraculous intervention, while Moses is related to the duties of journey (vv. 11-14). In both cases the significance of the miraculous categories is reduced. In Exodus 18 they belong to the past, while the present and future are dedicated to what Moses was 'doing'. In Numbers 11, the miraculous intervention refers to the

54. The significance of these motifs in Num. 11.17, 25 and 1 Kgs 2.9, 15 is stressed by Z. Weisman, 'The Personal Spirit as Imparting Authority', *ZAW* 93 (1981), pp. 225-34. The concept of the personal spirit of Moses and Elijah demonstrates their special status and authority (p. 234). The description is comparable to Num. 27.20, the personal 'spirit' of Joshua being enhanced by the 'majesty' taken from Moses.

terrible acts of retribution, while the burdens of the concrete journey situation are related to Moses and his substitutes. Underlined by the differences of the two stories, the parallelism of the divine and human actors and the corresponding emphasis on Moses as the actor in the post-Sinai reality must be important.

The elaboration seems to suggest some subtle transition from a past situation characterized by divine action and passively receptive people to a new situation centred around human action related to divine demands, with a corresponding emphasis on concrete human reality as the locus of manifestation. This is also reflected by the peculiar combination of sacred and rather mundane categories in the description of the Moses substitutes. In Exodus 18 the 'lesser' part of the mediator's duties is transferred to a set of officials qualified by military titles, the ordinariness of a list of 'colonels and majors and captains and sergeants' clashing with the loftiness of the oracular functions. A corresponding collision of connotational effects is presented in Numbers 11 by the elders of Israel sent into prophetic ecstacy. Here the character of the tasks is not indicated, apart from from their special function as 'co-carriers' of the people (v. 17). With the ecstatic manifestation of Moses' spirit confined to the investiture, the only indication of function is implied by the titles of 'elders', in v. 16 added to by the parallel 'scribes',[55] referring to administrative categories.

The extraordinary mixture of the sacred and mundane in these descriptions obviously does not refer to socio-political categories of institutional reality. The ideas of oracular colonels and ecstatic scribes can hardly reflect the application of 'realistic' language, but seem to reflect—and rather funnily at that!—a common interest in imbuing ordinary human reality with a sacred character. Such an interest would continue the narrative line of Exodus 19–40 given over to the divine movement from mountain to tent and the substitution of Moses by the people as theophanic figures, the latter also being presented as an absurd situation.[56]

If the label of 'secularization' catches some aspects of this development, the process reflected is of a profoundly sacred character, resulting

55. Levine, *Numbers 1–20*, pp. 323-24.

56. A corresponding tendency is expressed by the last expression of the substitution theme in Num. 27.15-23. Moses' 'majesty' is transferred to Joshua, whose function on the other hand is related to military categories and dependent on the oracular powers of the priest.

in the expansion of human reality as the new locus. In the Sinai stories this aspect is above all reflected by the parallel story concluded by the apotheosis of Moses in Exodus 34. The parallelism of God's and Moses' actions—as well as the implications of Moses as 'God's opposite'—in Exodus 18 and the comparable parallelism of the two actors in Numbers 11, relate Moses to comparable categories of extraordinary function. The elevation of the people as theophanic actors as well as the oracular officers and the ecstatic scribes is accompanied by the elevation of Moses into some semi-divine position. This aspect seems also to be reflected by the following episode of Miriam's and Aaron's revolt in Numbers 12.

Numbers 12

The prophetic categories link the two stories of Numbers 11 and 12.[57] In both cases these categories are related to unlikely characters, with Miriam and Aaron being depicted as prophets comparable to the ecstatic elders of Numbers 11. The parallel tent scenes related to the divine confirmation of prophetic position also indicate the connection between Numbers 11 and 12.[58]

The ecstatic administrators imbued with Moses' spirit seem to reflect a theme of profound secularization/sanctification. This is added to by Numbers 12. The new type of prophecy is related to a hierarchical order of ordinary prophets represented by Aaron and Miriam climaxed by Moses as the extraordinary prophet.[59] Comparable to the relationship of

57. The relationship of Num. 11 and 12 as juxtaposed stories giving a theological valuation of prophecy is important to Blum, *Studien zur Komposition*, pp. 79-80, 194-95, but refused by Van Seters, *The Life of Moses*, p. 236.

58. Cf. also the mixture of the themes of contention in Num. 12.1-2, which refer both to prophecy and to the Cushite woman, the significance of the latter being stressed by the repetition in v. 1. The peculiar combination of a mixed marriage and categories of prophecy is comparable to the combination of 'rabble' and the investiture of prophets in the preceding story. 'The children of Israel' are related both to 'rabble' and prophetic representatives' in their midst, parallel to Moses, the extraordinary prophet, married to a representative of the 'rabble'. On the other hand, Van Seters (*The Life of Moses*, pp. 238-39) explains the mixture of prophecy and interracial marriage by referring to Amos 9.7, seen as an expression of a debate on inter-racial marriage within prophetic circles.

59. The function of such an 'addition' to the story of Num. 11 could be illustrated by Num. 16.3. The claim of general 'holiness' represents a logical but improper application of the new situation. Comparable to the relationship of Exod. 34

Moses, the lesser judges, and the people in Exodus 18, the prophetical order of Moses, Aaron and Miriam, and the elders—in this case extended to the people as a wish (Num. 11.29)—presents a parallel hierarchy of sacred function.

Ultimately, the expansion of human reality implied by Exodus 18 and Numbers 11–12 can be related to the development of Exodus 19–40 with the parallel conclusions of Exodus 34 and 40. The main storyline concluded by the people taking the place of Moses as theophanic figures is juxtaposed to the description of Moses as imbued with divine qualities. The 'upward mobility' of all the human actors, which is indicated by the juxtaposed images of Exodus 34 and 40, is more directly expressed in Exodus 18 and Numbers 11–12. Compared to the peculiar juxtaposition of the two Exodus scenes, Exodus 18 combines the two aspects within the development of one story, while in Numbers 11–12 they are set out in successive episodes. The oracular colonels set Moses free for the higher functions. The burdens of Moses are shared by the once ecstatic scribes, who in their turn are related to a hierarchical order of ordinary and extraordinary prophets.

For the story of Exodus 19–40 the categories of extraordinary encounter and *visio Dei* are important for the qualification of the new situation. For Exodus 18 and Numbers 11–12 the oracular and prophetic categories seem to function as parallel expressions for the expansion of the human reality after Sinai. They are added to by the priestly version of the substitution theme in Leviticus 8–9. Completed by Numbers 8, the sanctification of priests and Levites—both groups separated 'from among' the people[60]—reflects a corresponding stratification of sacred functions.

The Rabble

The indications of 'upward mobility' for the human actors, in a world expanded by sacred qualities and functions, are in Numbers 11 combined with a corresponding movement of 'downward mobility'. This is expressed by the introduction of a new narrative figure, the 'rabble'. According to v. 4 the appointment of prophetic scribes is the result of a set of events set in motion by the 'rabble'. For the first time,[61] the

and 40, Num. 11 continued by ch. 12, stating the hierarchical significance of Moses as prophet, would disturb such an application.

60. E.g. Exod. 28.1; Num. 3.12.

61. Cf. the earlier juxtaposition of men related to women, sons and daughters

people presented in the negative mode are separated into two groups.[62] The 'rabble in their midst had insatiable appetites'[63] and 'also' the children of Israel began to complain. The separation of the two groups is underlined by the qualification of the rabble with the element 'in their midst'. This corresponds to the parallel qualification of YHWH in v. 20.[64] The referential relationship of the two qualifications is also indicated by their connection with motifs of weeping. The divine presence in the camp is mirrored by the presence of the rabble, now suddenly activated as the instigators of the revolt.

Inciting the children of Israel to weep for meat and 'remember' the past (vv. 4-5), the rabble's function is strangely parallel to the function of Jethro the Midianite in Exodus 18. While each story develops the components in different narrative contexts, the intiative of outsiders in both cases leads to a parallel set of events, the 'remembering' of the sacred story followed by sacred meal and the substitution of Moses. Whatever the implications of such a theme of 'foreign influence'—stressed by the foreign wife of Moses in Num. 12.1—the composition of the two stories presents Jethro the Midianite and the rabble as contrasting figures.

Related to the narrative context, the only possible reference to the presence of 'rabble' in the people's midst can be found in the short note of Exod. 12.38.[65] When the people left Egypt, a special group went 'with them'. While the translation of the noun which describes this group is as uncertain as that of the 'rabble' in Num. 11.4,[66] the qualification 'with them' obviously separates 'the children of Israel' (v. 37) from a special group lumped with the cattle as co-ascenders. The

in Exod. 32.2 followed by the juxtaposition of the Levites and the rest of the people in v. 26. Also Lev. 10.1-2, related to 9.24, reflects actors separated from a larger group and with a negative function.

62. Cf. also the position of Miriam in the succeeding story. The female form of the introductory verb in Num. 12.1 and the punishment directed only towards Miriam indicates a relationship between Miriam and Aaron in Num. 12 which is comparable to the juxtaposition of rabble and people in ch. 11.

63. Levine, *Numbers 1–20*, p. 321.

64. Van Seters, *The Life of Moses*, p. 229.

65. In support of this connection Van Seters (*The Life of Moses*, p. 229) points to v. 21 as a parallel reference to Exod. 12.37. In addition, the divine 'smiting' of v. 33 corresponds to the Egyptian connotations. This effect is also prepared for by the Passover and Exodus allusions in Num. 8–10.

66. E.g. Levine, *Numbers 1–20*, pp. 320-21.

subtlety of such a referential connection is comparable with the application of the 'plundering of the Egyptians' motif in Exod. 33.6, with rather substantial repercussions for the understanding of the gold motifs in the Golden Calf episode as well as the dedication of the gifts in the building account. Both Exod. 12.35-36 and 38a,[67] rather incongruously set in the Exodus story, seem to prepare for the application in later stories.

While obviously important, the delicacy of the literary effects makes any rendering of meaning rather tentative. Connected by some aspect of 'foreign influence',[68] the presence of the rabble in the people's midst as well as the Egyptian ornaments leads to perversion. The YHWH of the Egyptian events is transformed into the Golden Calf in the Exodus story. In Lev. 10.1-2, the 'strange fire' substitutes for the fire of divine manifestation. Comparably, the 'rabble' incites to the perverse 'remembering' in Numbers 11, resulting in the change from heavenly bread to deadly meat.

But also, the perception of 'foreign influences' connected with perverted substitution is turned upside down by contrast stories. When related to Jethro the Midianite and to the people's raw materials transformed into the Tent of Meeting, 'foreign influence' is necessary for the happy ending of the stories. In Numbers 11 the rabble has a pronounced negative function. But also in this case, the double outcome of the story mitigates the impression of negativity. The influence of the rabble leads not only to the mortal meal, but also to the enrichment of the human reality by the inspired administrators. Moreover, corresponding to Jethro the Midianite as a family member, the marriage of Moses to a representative of the rabble (Num. 12.1) has no negative repercussions for his position as the intimate of YHWH.

The Internalization of the Story

The parallel stories underline the significance of emotionality in Numbers 11. While the people are bitterly complaining in Exod. 16.2,

67. Cf. also the corresponding reference to Exod. 12.37 in Num. 14.

68. Cf. also the 'strange' fire in Lev. 10.1-2 with a negative function comparable to the Golden Calf episode. The theme could even be alluded to by the element *zārā'* (with aleph) in Num. 11.20; cf. Levine, *Numbers 1–20*, p. 324. The wished-for meat as loathsome/foreign contrasts with the rabble's contempt for the divinely provided manna.

Numbers 11 presents the first occasion of 'weeping',[69] emphasized by the repetitions of vv. 4, 10, 13, 18 and 20.[70] In the next grand episode of Numbers 13–14, this is continued by a new scene of weeping (14.1)—the impression of *bākâ* added to by an initial 'screaming' and even presented as taking place all through 'this night'. And the story is concluded by the people's 'much sorrowing' (v. 39), followed by their desperate attempt to make good their sins (v. 40). Given the scarcity of emotional references in these stories, the weeping of the introductory post-Sinai episodes must signal that a critical phase has started.

The intensification of the people's reaction is matched by the parallel emotional state of Moses according to vv. 11-15. Compared to earlier expressions of Moses in a negative mood,[71] the emotional intensity of Numbers 11 introduces a new state of violent protest.[72] This is underlined by Exodus 18. Here, the intolerable character of Moses' situation and its solution is related to the 'seeing' and wisdom of Jethro, while Moses is presented as rather mutely accepting his duties (vv. 15-16).

The two sets of emotional reactions in Numbers 11 point to the harshness of the post-Sinai conditions. And while the burdens of Moses are lightened, the weeping of the people is not mitigated by any helpful intervention. However difficult the initial situation, the divine reaction is particularly harsh, the people's tears underlining YHWH's burning anger and his 'smiting a truly abundant smiting' (v. 33). The human situation has been profoundly changed after Sinai. The divine movement into the world below and the corresponding expansion of the human reality imply new demands. The weakness of the people is no longer tolerated, but provokes a divine response comparable to the terrors of the Passover night.

The emotional categories seem to be connected with the new character of the crisis. Compared to the hunger of Exodus 16, the scorn of manna and the lust for meat and other Egyptian delicacies represent a new orientation towards more internalized categories of psychical

69. Apart from the ritual weeping of Lev. 10.6.

70. The localization of the weeping at the tent door in v. 10 could refer to the imagery of Exod. 33.8-10—the former obeisance contrasting with the new situation.

71. Cf. Moses protesting his vocation in Exod. 3–4, complaining on behalf of the people in Exod. 5.22-23, and crying for help in a personal crisis in Exod. 17.4.

72. The significance of such aspects is underlined by the Elijah story, this case too being connected with the theme of substitution.

character. This is underlined by the subtle description of the people's failings. Compared to the material categories of the Golden Calf and the 'strange fire' of Lev. 10.1-2, the qualification of the people's weeping as a perverted 'remembering' of the sacred story reflects a refined transcription of ritual language related to psychical categories. Moreover, this tendency is continued by the following stories. The events of Numbers 12 are set in motion by envy and attempted usurpation of Moses' position by Miriam and Aaron. In Numbers 14 the crisis is caused by the people's imaginary fear, juxtaposed to a concluding scene of desperate but stupid bravery caused by the people's sorrow (vv. 39-45). The events of Numbers 16 are started by the claim of collective 'holiness' turned against the positions of Moses and Aaron (v. 3).[73]

The direction towards 'inner' categories of psychical and emotional character is underlined by the repetitive character of the journey crises. The basic food and enemy motifs of Numbers 11–14 refer to the pre-Sinai situation represented by Exodus 16–17. But turned into lust for different food and imaginary fear, the crises of the post-Sinai situation have been subtly transferred from an outer, material reality to the 'inner' life of the pilgrims. The shift of emphasis could even be reflected by the description of the investiture of the elders. Compared to the factual appointment of oracular officers in Exodus 18, the ecstatic state of the new officials caused by the infusion of spirit refers to remarkable categories for the qualification of the people's admininistrators. While the ecstatic state is confined to the one event of investiture, it did take place, the people's reality being enriched by scribes who themselves once had such an extraordinary experience.

Summary

Framing the Sinai stories proper, Exodus 18 and Numbers 11–12 unfold the implications of the divine movement from mountain to camp and the corresponding substitution of Moses by the people. The resulting expansion of the reality 'below the mountain' is illustrated by the

73. Cf. also the effort of Budd, *Numbers*, p. 281 to find some chiastic pattern for the Yahwist's arrangement of these stories for the second phase of Israel's journey. The pattern is introduced and concluded by episodes of apostasy (Exod. 32 and Num. 25), to which are related juxtaposed episodes of discontent (Num. 11 and 21), insubordination by individuals (Num. 12 and 16), and insubordination by Israel (Num. 14).

substitution theme in the two stories. With a special emphasis on human reality and human action, the functions of Moses are shared out among representatives of the people. The combination of mundane normality and sacred qualities implies a process for which secularization and sanctification are equally valid terms. The divine movement from above to below results in a process in which the human reality, emphatically defined as burdensome and rather sordid, is profoundly sanctified. This is underlined by the diversification of the human roles, implying a hierarchical order starting with Moses and ending with the people. Corresponding to the apotheosis of Moses in Exodus 34, both Exodus 18 and Numbers 11 reflect the location of Moses on the hierarchical ladder as high indeed. But the bottom layer of human reality has also been diversified by the separation of 'the children of Israel' and the 'rabble'.[74] While Jethro leaves the people, according to Exod. 18.27, and Num. 10.29-32 leaves the reader in uncertainty whether the Midianite family member really accepts the invitation to join the pilgrimage, the rabble are permanently in the people's midst and even united in marriage with Moses. Accompanied by outbursts of emotion and with crises internalized, the post-Sinai reality is highly tense, the tensions being caused by the new intimacy of divine and human co-habitation, and relieved by the people's weeping and the frightful discharges of divine anger.

Secondly, the relationship of Exodus 18 and Numbers 11 is important for our perception of the function of these stories. The effects of repetition and parallelism in the Sinai stories suggest the 'unrealistic' character of the language. This impression is underlined by Exodus 18 and Numbers 11. Based on categories of traditional social reality and

74. Cf. Olson, *Death of the Old*, pp. 122-23, who stresses the negative aspects of the first post-Sinai stories, finding a transition to a positive tone first in the story in Num. 21.1. Equal importance must also be given to the fact that the villains in the seemingly negative stories have contrast-figures. In Num. 11 the 'rabble' is juxtaposed by the ecstatic elders, as well as by Jethro in Exod. 18. In Num. 12 Miriam and Aaron represent the negative roles, with even this constellation split with Miriam as the chief villain. Num. 14 separates two heroes contrasted with the rest (vv. 6-10, 24, 30, 36-38) and even introduces a new separation between 'you' and 'your children' (vv. 29-33). Num. 16.1-2 introduces a new set of villains, from which the rest will separate (vv. 6-10). This corresponds with the bloody contrast of Levites and their relatives in Exod. 32. The indications of the human reality as profoundly dual in character is also reflected by the two contrasting descriptions of the journey in Num. 9–10 and 11.

utilizing the connotational value of the concepts, the two stories obviously reflect language of a 'transferred' character. The presentation of oracular officers and ecstatic elders in Exodus 18 and Numbers 11 does not describe institutional reality with specific socio-religious implications, but makes use of the established connotations to indicate the character of the new situation. This is underlined by the qualification of Aaron and Miriam as prophets in Numbers 12. Compared with the conventional language of Ps. 105.15, for example, which extends the *nābî* title to the patriarchs, the concrete character of Num. 12.6 attributes the characteristics of the prophetic function to Aaron and Miriam. This heightens the connotational impact of the language. Aaron the priest and Miriam his sister suddenly fighting for prophetic authority in opposition to the supremacy of Moses would be meaningless as expressions of institutional reality but reflect some transferred usage of the motifs. This is underlined by the function of this story as the continuation of the preceding episode given over to the investiture of ecstatic scribes. In both cases, the impact of the story results from the connotational effects of 'prophecy' being related to persons who represent non-prophetic offices. Facing a situation from the past—meticulously elaborated as a story from the past but with details which signal that these events should not be read literally as a story from the past—the reader is provoked to a deeper pondering of what the story is all about.

Finally, the relationship of Numbers 11 to Exodus 16 and 18 is important for the understanding of repetition and parallelism as a compositional mode. These effects are connected with the materials organized as story cycles. Events of a certain character are related to each other as parts of a cycle, the cycles in their turn being related to each other according to the character of the events they present. The cycles of pre-Sinai journey stories, Sinai stories and post-Sinai journey stories, represent the significance of the events as successive, each series marking a new stage or level of development in a comprehensive story.[75] The organization of the materials mirrors the special perception of the relationship of the events. Not only the scenery, but also the character of the actors, including the divine actor, and their relationship change from stage to stage.

This development represents a basic aspect of the compositional

75. The potential significance of such a connection between the compositional arrangement and sets of events perceived as successive stages is illustrated by Wilcoxen, 'Some Anthropocentric Aspects', pp. 347-50.

mode, with effects of repetition and parallelism as its prime expression. Within the single cycle, a certain type of situation is repeated over and over again, for example, the encounter episode in Exodus 19–40 or the stereotyped expressions for some crisis in the journey stories. Based on the same narrative components monotonously repeated, the 'sameness' of the episodes underlines the character of each story cycle and the stage of development represented by each cycle. The latter aspect is underlined when events are repeated not only within the one cycle, but also from cycle to cycle. The 'sameness' of situation repeated on a new stage of narrative development sets off the new situation, of a profoundly different character yet somehow 'repeating' certain aspects of the preceding stage.

The relationship of Exodus 16 and 18 and Numbers 11 illustrates that this effect of repetition is especially important for the juxtaposed stories which refer to the pre- and post-Sinai journey. This juxtaposition in its turn reflects the significance of the Sinai events for the narrative development. After the Sinai events, the people's complaint represents a completely new phenomenon and, correspondingly, the divine response is new. The effect of repetition underlines the character of the new situation—the people's complaint after Sinai echoes the earlier complaint and yet provokes such a terribly different divine reaction.

This organization of the materials also underlines the significance of the linear movement of the stories. The linear relationship does not reflect an outer arrangement of the materials as a narrative framework for the Sinai event, for example, as a grossly swollen expression for Torah propagation, which resulted in a clumsy arrangement of identical journey stories set before and after Sinai. The monotonous repetition of the 'same' events reflects their significance. The same actors move from stage to stage, each stage being represented by a new cycle of stories which indicate the character of the new situation.

But while this seems to represent the grand compositional movement, it is criss-crossed by other effects of referential relationships which are also connected with effects of repetition and parallelism. This is illustrated by Exodus 18. Within the linear development, the chapter is important as the conclusion of the pre-Sinai journey, the function of vv. 1-12 being comparable to Exod. 15.1-21 as the conclusion of the Egyptian stories. Correspondingly, the chapter also prepares for the following story cycles. Moses being set free for the higher aspects of his function makes possible his function in the Sinai stories. And the appointment of the 'lesser' judges introduces the substitution theme so important for the Sinai stories, which is also continued by the investiture of the scribes in Numbers 11 and the appointment of Joshua in Numbers 27. But in addition, Exodus 18 seems to represent an expression *in nuce* of the Sinai events as a whole. As a fundamental first chord of the Sinai events, the story reflects the *parallellismus membrorum* effects that are most easily perceived in their 'synthetical' mode by the three versions of 'the day of erecting the dwelling' or in the 'antithetical' mode by Exodus 34 and 40.

The 'rabble' of Numbers 11 illustrates the presence of other much more subtle types of referential relationships. Introduced by what seems a casual note in Exod. 12.38, the presence of the rabble is of no consequence for the following story cycles, until the post-Sinai journey represents a situation ripe for their contribution. But juxtaposed to Jethro the Midianite and meticulously combined with themes established by the other stories, their entering the stage in Numbers 11 has been carefully prepared.

3. *Numbers 13–14*

The Relationship to Numbers 11–12

Generally assumed to reflect a complicated redactional process,[76] the present shape of Numbers 13–14 can also be regarded as well configured to the context.[77] Compared to the motifs of meal and prophecy

76. According to Levine, *Numbers 1–20*, pp. 347-49, it presents a fusion of materials drawn from JE, P, and perhaps even other independent sources, the fabric of the text at some points being unravelled easily, at others being the result of a complete Priestly rewriting of the original JE narrative. Van Seters, *The Life of Moses*, pp. 366-70, finds a basic J story in Num. 13.3, 17-20, 22-24, 26-28, 30-31; 14.1-4, 11-25, 39-45, which has been extended by Priestly clarifications. The scouts' mission has been related to the whole of the Promised Land, Joshua the scout added to Caleb, and the definition of who are to die in the wilderness has been added to; cf. also Olson, *Death of the Old*, pp. 129-38; de Vaulx, *Les Nombres*, pp. 164-79.

77. Cf. esp. Olson, *Death of the Old*, pp. 138-52, for whom these chapters have a crucial role for the literary and theological structure of Numbers. As an explanation of how it came to pass that the first generation had to die in the wilderness while the promises of land were transferred to the next generation, the scouts' story is a key episode, related to the census lists of Num. 1 and 26 and referred to in Num. 32 and 34.

in Numbers 11–12, the new revolt episode is centred around motifs of war. Apart from the basic common situation of 'murmuring' connected with some crisis, the 'murmuring' intenified to 'weeping' (Num. 14.1) corresponds to Numbers 11.[78] The comparison underlines the intensification of the crisis in Numbers 14. The revolt of the people is extended into two scenes, the latter unfolding the emotional reaction implied in the first (Num. 13.30). Without any narrative intermission, the scouts' report ended in Num. 13.33 is immediately responded to by a howl of anguish from the people (14.1). The motif of weeping is added to both by the 'conflation'[79] of v. 1a which must indicate that the weeping was loud indeed, and by v. 1b, according to which the miserable screaming persisted all night. Attributed to men who worry for their wives and children according to v. 3, the weeping scene makes the people cut an absurdly sorry figure.

The elaboration of the scene continues and heightens the contrasting effect of Numbers 11 and 10, the absurdity of the post-Sinai scenes being juxtaposed to the image of the sonorous march from Sinai by Israel's hosts, all colours flying. The intensification of the emotional categories in Numbers 14[80] is also reflected by the revolt's being turned into violence (v. 10) and the people's sorrow leading to a new tragedy (vv. 39-45).

This development is underlined by the corresponding emphasis on the revolt as being connected with 'inner' categories of psychological and mental character. Compared to the people's hunger in Exodus 16, the revolt of Numbers 11 is connected with the jaded appetites of the people, tired of manna and lusting for meat. The implications of what seems a rather childish reaction is supplemented profoundly by the qualification of the foodstuffs. The food divinely provided stands in contrast to the Egyptian delicacies. The rejection of the former and the longing for the latter implies the rejection of the sacred story. These intimations are elaborated by the scouts' episode. In contrast to the fear-situation of Exodus 14, for example, the people of the Numbers story do not themselves see the terrible might of the enemies. Theirs is a fear of imagination, ignoring the report of the positive scouts and accepting

78. The significance of this is stressed by Coats, *Moses*, pp. 121-22.

79. Levine, *Numbers 1–20*, p. 362.

80. Continued by the following episode in Num. 16–17, and concluded by the lament of Num. 17.27-28, the effect of which is prepared for by the 'Greek chorus' of Num. 16.34b and 17.6b.

what the negative scouts say. The emphasis on mental and psychological categories is continued in the next revolt of Numbers 16–17, during which representatives of the people seek to usurp the functions of Moses and Aaron.

The serious implications of the revolt are added to by the scouts' episode. Continuing the perverted 'remembering' in Numbers 11, which professes Egypt as the good place, the reference to the divine acts of guidance is preceded by a wish for death and introduced by the plaintive 'why?' (Num. 14.2-3). Turned into a lament, the sacred story is perverted to a story of divinely caused woes. Moreover, YHWH is presented as the subject of the Exodus in v. 3a. In the earlier revolts, Moses or Moses and Aaron have been presented as the leaders responsible for the crisis.[81] Now, the lament presents the divine actor as the author. The sacrilege is even added to by the desire to return[82] to Egypt (v. 4).[83]

In addition the role allocation continues the situation of Num. 11.4-34, the significance of which is underlined by the new motifs of scouts and military conquest. In the meal episode, the people in revolt are split for the first time into two negative groups, when the 'sons of Israel' are influenced by the 'rabble'. A corresponding constellation is represented in the next episode. The people's revolt is influenced by the negative scouts (Num. 13.26-29, 31-33). Also in this case, the situation of 'murmuring' is represented by the people being turned against Moses. This situation is retained in both revolt scenes (Num. 13.30; 14.1-4) and is also reflected at the end of the episode (v. 39, continued by vv. 40-45). The adherence to the basic role allocation related to Moses and people underlines the significance of the new set of sub-figures.

In Numbers 11 the influence of the 'rabble' is balanced by the appointment of the prophetic elders. Two groups of figures which represent negative and positive roles are added to the constellation of people and Moses. This development is continued in Numbers 13–14,

81. Exod. 14.11-12; 16.3; 17.3; also 32.1.

82. The ambiguous first verb of v. 4b is related to Neh. 9.17 and translated as 'head back' by Levine, *Numbers 1–20*, p. 363.

83. On the other hand, the serious character of the challenge is weakened when addressed to one's 'brother', in contrast to the complaint of vv. 2-3 which is addressed to Moses and Aaron. In this respect, the revolt of 16.3 marks a new step of intensification, the leadership of Moses and Aaron being directly challenged by a group of usurpers.

and more directly related to the narrative development. The influence of the negative scouts is countered by the positive scouts. In both scenes of revolt, the positive group speaks for Moses. Usually not lacking in words in such situations, Moses this time, in both scenes, does not confront the people. The implied negativity against Moses (Num. 13.30) and against Moses and Aaron (14.2) is responded to by the positive scouts acting as spokesmen.

The implications of these changes are indicated by the parallelism of the acts of the two positive sets of actors in the second and climactic scene. Moses and Aaron fall 'upon their faces in front of the whole congregation' (v. 5), followed by the 'tearing of the clothes' by Joshua and Caleb in v. 6. The prostration and tearing of clothes are part of the same imagery as expressions for the emotional reaction, usually deep sorrow, when a terrible calamity has to be faced.[84] The imagery both indicates the parallel reactions of the two groups and underlines Joshua and Caleb as the active spokespeople.[85] This effect is enhanced by the referential function of the speach, the language of the salvation oracle allocating the role of Moses to the scouts in Exod. 14.13-14.

The elaboration of the scenes indicates that the positive scouts are set in a relationship to Moses that is comparable to the transfer of the Moses function to the officers of Exodus 18 and the elders of Numbers 11. The elaborate parallellism between Moses and the two positive scouts represents a new expression for the 'substitution of Moses' theme. And also in this case, the motifs reflect a peculiar collusion of extraordinary and mundane categories. The role of Moses is taken by two scouts of good social standing (Num. 13.2),[86] comparable to the

84. The reaction of Moses and Aaron is ususally seen as an expression of a movement of intercession (e.g. Budd, *Numbers*, p. 156), while Levine (*Numbers 1–20*, p. 363) refers to the grief situation of Josh. 7.6. To de Vaulx (*Les Nombres*, p. 175), v. 5, like the other Priestly contributions (in Num. 16.4, 22; 17.10; 20.6), implies that Moses and Aaron are under threat of death, corresponding to the confrontation in Exod. 17.4. The prostration 'in front of the people' makes it improbable that the movement in this case primarily refers to intercession. A number of texts (2 Sam. 1.2; 13.31; Job 1.20; Josh. 7.6; cf. also earth upon the head as a related expression for self-abascment, e.g. 1 Sam. 4.12; 2 Sam. 15.32; Job 2.12-13) illustrate the connection between the two acts of prostration and tearing asunder of the clothes and thus the connection between the acts of Num. 14.5-6.

85. Cf. a corresponding development of the imagery in the scene of 2 Sam. 13.31-33.

86. Related to traditio-historical categories, the change of name in Num. 13.16b

oracular officers of Exodus 18 and the ecstatic scribes of Numbers 11.

The diversification of roles is underlined by the elaboration of the episode. In the first revolt scene, Moses alone is supported by Caleb alone as the positive sub-figure (Num. 13.30). This is changed in the next scene. The witness of Caleb is met by a new negative report (vv. 31-33), followed by the people's howl and a scene of confrontation which is now related to Moses and Aaron (Num. 14.2, 5). Corresponding to Moses and Caleb as the positive actors of the first scene, Moses and Aaron[87] in the second scene is supported by Joshua and Caleb (vv. 6-10). The role allocation of the two scenes is also reflected by the divine statements in vv. 20-35. The first (vv. 20-25) is addressed to Moses and refers to Caleb, while the second addressed to Moses and Aaron refers to Caleb and Joshua.[88] The development reflects the narrative movement towards a climax. Compared to the earlier revolt scenes, the tension of the situation is greatly heightened by the drama of Num. 14.1-10. The impact of this scene is prepared for by the first scene of revolt (Num. 13.30). In the same way, the intimations in the first divine statement on the men 'not seeing the Promised Land' (vv. 22-23) are unfolded by the second statement in vv. 26-35.

The meticulous shaping of the materials points to the significance of the role allocation in these stories. The basic constellation of Moses and

could reflect a wish to identify the Hosea of the list (Deut. 32.44) with Joshua son of Nun; cf. Levine, *Numbers 1–20*, p. 352. But comparable to Judg. 6.32, 34 and also 13.24-25, the new name could prepare the transition from ordinary to extraordinary, corresponding to the transfer of the spirit of Moses in Num. 11 and of the 'majesty' of Moses in ch. 27.

87. Related to the narrative development, Aaron added to Moses bridges the situations of Num. 12 with Aaron as a negative sub-figure related to prophetic categories, and Num. 16–17 with Aaron as a positive sub-figure related to priestly categories.

88. The elaboration of the revolt into two scenes could be continued by the complex organization of three scenes in the next revolt in Num. 16–17. To the main narrative thread of revolt (Num. 16.1-11, 16-19) and ordeal (vv. 20-22, 35) are added sub-scenes related to special actors in revolt (vv. 12-15) and punished in a special ordeal situation (vv. 24-33). The two negative scenes are continued by a new episode of ordeal which designates Aaron as the priest in Num. 17.16-28. The connection between the three ordeal scenes is reflected by the people's reaction in Num. 16.34b; 17.6b, 27-28. While it is natural to relate the compositions to a background of different traditions, the impact of their present shape is distorted when a redactional process of cutting and pasting is perceived as the basic compositional effort.

people is added to by new sets of sub-figures of special character. Moreover, it must be important for the perception of the revolt that the Moses-function is shared out to representatives of the people. Compared to Exodus 18, the post-Sinai episodes of Numbers 11–12, 13–14 and 16–17 elaborate the 'substitution of Moses' theme as part of the revolt situation. The issues of the conflict are subtly shifted from the juxtaposition of Moses and people as the embodiments of 'high' and 'low' to the juxtaposition of negative and positive representatives of the people. The elaboration of the conflict, greatly intensified and connected to sub-figures who represent voices within the people, must be important for the perception of these stories.

The Scouts and the People

The comparison to Numbers 11 underlines the connection between the two episodes as well as the complex character of the scouts' story as a further elaboration of established themes. Instigating the revolt, the 'rabble' of Numbers 11 and the negative scouts have comparable roles as sub-figures. But the role of the former is confined to the start of the story and is continued by the people's craving for meat. Similarly, while the ecstatic elders as 'co-carriers' have a function comparable to the positive scouts as Moses substitutes, their investiture is rather loosely attached to the main story. In comparison, the juxtaposition of the positive and negative scouts is important to the narrative development in Numbers 13–14. Moreover, the scouts as the object of special interest is also indicated by the two ordeals of Num. 14.10, 36-37, which leave the negative scouts dead and the positive ones alive.

This development is supplemented by the subtle manner in which the sub-figures are related to the people. In the divine statements in Num. 14.20-35, the positive scouts are not juxtaposed to the negative scouts, but to the people as the negative contrast figures (vv. 24, 30). The positive fate of relationship to the land is contrasted by the people's non-relationship and death. The juxtaposition of positive scouts and people implies the identification of the negative sub-figures and the people, and thus a connection comparable to the relationship of 'rabble' and people in Numbers 11. But the scouts' episode presents a more elaborate version. The story returns to the negative scouts as individual figures in Num. 14.36-37. Also the juxtaposition of positive scouts and the people in the divine statements is prepared for by the second revolt scene. Caleb and Joshua address the people (Num. 14.7) and are responded to by the community preparing to stone them but stopped from doing so by the divine intervention (v. 10).

Moreover, the juxtaposition of positive scouts and negative people is added to by a new set of figures. The second divine statement in vv. 26-35 introduces a new type of separation within the people. To Joshua and Caleb is added the children as the future possessors of the land, and they are also juxtaposed to the 'sons of Israel' given to death in the wilderness (vv. 31-34).[89] Related to the grand story devoted to the people's movement towards the land, the separation between the men and the children must be vitally important. This is also reflected by the meticulous elaboration of the two scenes of revolt followed by two divine statements. Moreover, it is prepared for by the intercession scene in vv. 11-19, which mitigates the divine plans to destroy the people. Also the concluding tragedy of vv. 39-45, set in motion by the people's sorrow over the harsh message, points to the second divine statement as the climax of the episode.

But however complex the elaboration of the sub-figures in the scouts' episode compared to Numbers 11, the basic connection between the two episodes is indicated by the roles of the scouts. The positive scouts are extended by the small children. Similarly, the juxtaposition of positive scouts and negative people in the divine statements implies that the role of the negative scouts has been transferred to the people. This is underlined by v. 34, which explicitly identifies the people with the negative scouts. 'You' are addressed as the scouts inspecting the land for 40 days, the identity of 'you' on the other hand being defined by the introductory address to the grown-up 'sons of Israel' in vv. 27-28aα.[90]

89. A comparable extension is also found in Num. 16. Here, Aaron and Moses represent the role of positive protagonist, set against the usurpers in an ordeal scene corresponding to Num. 14.10, 37. In addition, a second set of positive sub-figures related to a separation within the people is represented by the challenge to the people to 'ascend' from the negative sub-group (vv. 23-27). The connection between the two sets of positive figures is reflected by the parallelism of v. 21 and vv. 23-27, the former being addressed to Moses and Aaron.

90. The significance of this identification is illustrated by Noth, *Das vierte Buch Moses*, p. 89. Verse 34 is enclosed in brackets as an isolated conjecture within the P story, which rather badly connects the motif of 40 years to the 40 days of scouting (p. 98). Whatever redactional layer is represented by v. 34, it must be important that the conclusion of the next revolt episode in Num. 17.27-28 represents a corresponding (though differently expressed) identification of the people and the main actors of the episode.

The positive scouts extended by the children and the negative scouts identified with the grown-up men point to the people as the 'real' actors of the story. Formally, the scouts present independent figures important for the narrative development. But they have a representative function and ultimately personify the attitudes of the people. This corresponds to and also adds to the role of the 'rabble' in Numbers 11, who on the one hand represent a separate group 'in the midst' of the people, and on the other have a limited function as some personification of the evil influence which takes possession of the whole people.

The blurring of the identities of the actors, as well as the significance of the sub-figures in Numbers 13–14, is also reflected by the concluding scenes. Verses 36-38 return to the theme of the positive and negative scouts, the one negative group being killed instantly 'before YHWH', and the positive spared. The final scene in vv. 39-45 continues the story stopped in v. 35. The divine statements of vv. 28-35 mediated by Moses result in the sorrowful reaction of the people, which in its turn leads to a terrible defeat (vv. 40-45). The double tragedy mirrors the connection of the scouts and the people as negative actors.

In continuation of Numbers 11–12, the scouts' episode seems to reflect the diversification of the human reality after Sinai. The basic roles of Moses and people are elaborated by the contrasting subfigures of negative and positive scouts. This contrast combines the two themes of revolt and substitution of Moses and also prepares for the fateful contrast of men and children. The aspects of conflict within the people are stressed by the scene of violent confrontation between the people and the positive sub-figures, stopped by the divine intervention (v. 10). The violence of the revolt as well as the new character of the divine intervention represent something new in these stories. Corresponding to the separation of the people into juxtaposed groups, the divine intervention has now become partial, in favour of a positive group and against the negative group. Apart from the different fates of men and children, the divine partiality is reflected by the allusions to ordeal scenes in Num. 14.10, 36-38. Moreover, it is continued in the next episode by the two negative ordeals in Num. 16.26-34, 35, which are concluded by the positive ordeal of 17.16-28. Compared to the blind divine violence directed towards the people as a whole in ch. 11 and 17.6-15, the new type of confrontation corresponds to the ordeal situation in the Individual Psalms, the divine intervention choosing sides between actors in the conflict.

The aspects of divine partiality is prepared for by Numbers 12. Although formally an independent episode, this story is linked to 11.4-34 by the common theme of prophecy. The confrontation of Aaron and Miriam results in the vindication of Moses and the punishment of Miriam. Numbers 14 as well as 16–17 continue and elaborate these aspects in connection with the development of the roles of the sub-figures. Also the formal manner in which these aspects are expressed corresponds and thus indicates the consistency of the stories introduced by Numbers 11. In all cases the revolt of the people is extended by loosely added scenes. The basic constellation of Moses and people is added to by new figures, while the 'murmuring' against Moses becomes mirrored by an internalized conflict between representatives of the people, responded to by a divine intervention of a partial character.

The Relationship of Numbers 13–14 to Numbers 16–17

The scouts' episode reflects the fact that the revolt situation has become the focal point for important thematic lines as the expression both for the diversification of the human role in the post-Sinai reality as well as its implications of heightened tension and inner conflict. The basic situation of revolt is supplemented and enriched, and according to modern notions of logic, rather blurred, by new sets of protagonists. Important aspects of this development are continued by the elaboration of the next revolt episode in Numbers 16–17. The main thread of this story relates the conflict to categories of priestly 'nearness', with Aaron as the central positive protagonist contrasted with a set of negative sub-figures. The gradual emphasis on the sub-figures as the formally central actors is continued in this episode. The narrative development is dominated by two ordeal scenes related to the negative figures (Num. 16.16-19, 35 and vv. 23-33) and the concluding ordeal which presents Aaron as the truly chosen priest (17.16-26). Also in this story the people are the actors in a scene of general revolt followed by divine retribution (17.6-15). But now the people's revolt has a subordinate function. The people revolt because the ordeals result in too harsh a fate for the losers (v. 6). This continues the elaboration of the revolt in Num. 14.2-10 when the people, influenced by the negative report, turn against the positive scouts.

Also in the priestly revolt the actor who presents the contrast to the negative sub-figures is closely aligned with Moses. The initial revolt is, according to Num. 16.3, directed towards Moses and Aaron and concerns their common 'self-exaltation over' the holy people. Correspondingly, v. 18 sets Moses together with Aaron as participating in the ordeal, while vv. 16-17 only refer to Aaron as the positive protagonist. The parallelism of Moses and Aaron is also reflected by what seems a hopeless blurring of what the contention is all about. The added scene of revolt (16.12-15, stressed by vv. 28-30) presents the supremacy of Moses as the contended issue, in contrast to the dominating theme of priestly 'nearness'.[91] Such effects are comparable to the parallelism of Moses and positive scouts in Numbers 14 and could be seen as a new expression for the 'substitution of Moses' theme. The transfer of functions from Moses to representatives of the people implies the blurring of issues as well as of roles.

But compared to the other expressions of the subtitution theme, the priestly categories could have a special function. The people as visionaries in Exodus 19–40, the oracular officers of Exodus 18, the ecstatic scribes of Numbers 11, the preaching scouts of Numbers 14 and the majesty of Joshua the warrior of Numbers 27 indicate a profound process of ordinary reality infused by sacred character. The priestly categories of Numbers 16–17, especially when concluded by the wondrous ordeal in Num. 17.16-26, could refer to different aspects. Thus, the story of Numbers 11 seems to be complemented by the emphasis on Moses as the sublime prophet in Numbers 12. Corresponding to the separation of lesser and higher duties in Exodus 18, the 'secular' implications of the substitution theme in Numbers 11 are balanced by the reference to higher functions in Numbers 12. Accordingly, the 'secular' substitutes of Moses could represent one part of some layered reality of sacred functions, while the higher aspects of these functions are reflected by Moses, the extraordinary prophet set over Miriam and Aaron as normal prophets. Aaron the chosen priest, in contrast to the rivals, who in spite of sharing a common character of 'holiness' (Num. 16.3) are usurper priests, could have a corresponding function. Just as the elders, truly inspired by Moses' spirit, are complemented by higher prophets, so the people as truly holy represent only one rung of a grand hierarchical ladder of sacred functions.

But even as a reference to some hierarchical order, the priestly

91. See, for example, Levine (*Numbers 1–20*, pp. 405-406) on the episode as composed from the two sources of JE and P, the former rewritten or extended by P and other priestly insertions; contrast the efforts of Hauge (*Between Sheol and Temple*, pp. 197-206) to identify some basic structure for the final shape of the story.

protagonists in Numbers 16–17 should not be confined to categories of institutional reality. This is already suggested by the preceding episodes. The ecstatic scribes set together with Aaron, the priest, and Miriam, his sister, as contenders for prophetic supremacy, followed by scouts spouting the sacred formulas of the salvation oracle, must present a deliberate blurring of institutional concepts. The 'substitution of Moses' refers to a reality beyond the categories of religio-sociological character, while utilizing the conventional connotations of the concepts.

More directly, some transferred usage of conventional concepts is indicated by the conclusion of the story in Num. 17.27-28. Impressed by the events concluded by the wondrous ordeal which designates Aaron as the truly chosen priest, the people exclaim:

> Behold! We expire, we perish all of us, we perish!
> Everyone who comes near, who comes near
> the dwelling of YHWH, shall die.
> Do we have to complete the expiring? (Num. 17.27-28)

The repeated death motifs within so simple a frame make these verses a moving expression of the people's anguish. Their impact is emphasized by the terrible scenes of death just witnessed. As an isolated exclamation, 'we die!' might have a rhetorical effect, referring to an intolerable situation of physical or emotional character.[92] But in this case the death motifs continue the preceding imagery of people being swallowed by the earth and consumed by fire and destroyed by divine smiting. The relationship to the preceding scenes is underlined by the connection of death and 'nearness' in v. 28. Related to the divine dwelling, the 'nearness' resulting in death corresponds to the preceding story of priestly 'nearness' and terrible death for the unworthy, concluded by the miraculous election of Aaron in Num. 17.16-26.[93]

Some connection with the preceding scenes is obviously basic for the function of the complaint. But by its formally loose relationship to the context the character of this connection is not immediately seen. Set after the story on Aaron's rod, the people's cry of anguish at first hand seems a peculiar ending to such a wonderful scene. Formally, the death motifs could refer to the divine statement in v. 25, when YHWH directs Moses to place the rod of Aaron in front of the ark to remind the people

92. E.g. Gen. 30.1 or Judg. 15.18.

93. Cf. the repeated *haqqārēb* in v. 28 corresponding to the applications of the root *qrb* in Num. 16.5, 9, 10, 17, 35; 17.3, 4.

'so they shall not die'. On the other hand, this does not express any threat, but a command which, if implemented, will protect the people against the fate of dying. And as Moses truly implemented the order (v. 26), there should be no reason for such a miserable lament.

If not seen as misplaced in the context,[94] the lament is often related to the following divine instructions in Numbers 18.[95] Addressed to Aaron and referring to priestly duties and prerogatives protected by the threat of death (18.3, 5, 7), the instructions are obviously connected thematically with the preceding story. On the other hand, the anguish of the people in Num. 17.27-28 is better related to the preceding episode than to the divine instructions which follow.

Moreover, the function of Num. 17.27-28 as a scene which concludes the episode of chs. 16–17, could be related to the scouts' story. Also this episode is concluded by a scene centred around the people in a comparable situation of distress (14.39-45). The significance of 17.27-28 and 14.39-45 as parallel conclusions is underlined by their formal character of loosely added scenes. In both episodes the dramatic scenes in which the contenders play an important part are followed by the divine response to the people's revolt (14.11-35; 17.6-15). In both cases the transition from sub-figures to people has been caused by the people actively taking sides in the struggle, turning against the positive scouts and protesting the fate of the priestly usurpers (14.10, 17.6). And after the harsh divine response, both stories return to the sub-figures as the central actors in a scene of negative (14.36-38) and positive (17.16-26) ordeal. Then both stories return to a concluding scene which present the strong emotional reaction of the people to what has taken place (14.39-45; 17.27-28). The rather artificial arrangement of the scenes adds to the significance of the common dramatic structure.

In the priestly story, the connection of the concluding scene with the preceding events is also indicated by Num. 16.34b and 17.6b, which present similar expressions for the people's reaction. The first reflects

94. According to de Vaulx, *Les Nombres*, p. 203, the lament is more suitable as concluding, for example, 16.29-35 or 17.12.

95. E.g. Budd, *Numbers*, p. 193. On the other hand, Levine (*Numbers 1–20*, p. 432) reads Num. 17.28 as an allusion to the prohibitions of access associated with the Levitical functions (e.g. Num. 1.51; 3.10, 38; 18.7), the people expressing their fear of trespassing. Also Noth (*Das vierte Buch Moses*, p. 118) suggests such a solution, but rather reluctantly, as the preceding episode has not related the people, but other protagonists, to such categories.

the panic after the first ordeal. The people run away from the scene of the disaster, exclaiming 'the earth could swallow us!' The second is set after the divine intervention by fire, and is addressed to Moses and Aaron: 'You have killed the people of YHWH!' The death motifs link the three sets of reaction. Due to the emphasis on the sub-figures as the central actors in this episode, the three stylized references to the people as actors must be important. This is added to by the location of the three reactions, each concluding a scene of ordeal. Acting like a Greek chorus, the people underline the significance of what has taken place. Concluded by the miserable wail of 17.27-28, the three reactions gradually heighten the tension as well as the emotional contents of the story. The fate of dying is directed towards the people themselves from the initial fear of death to the murder of 'YHWH's people' to 'we are dying'. Also the positive story of Aaron's rod is part of this development, the trebly miraculous rod indicating the extraordinary character of a 'nearness' which does not result in death.

In the main scenes of the episode, the negative and positive aspects of priestly 'nearness' are expressed by Aaron and the usurpers as main protagonists. This story, concluded in v. 26, leaves the usurpers dead and Aaron wonderfully chosen. The continuation of the story in vv. 27-28, with its sudden transition from the protagonists to the 'we' of the people, indicates that the fate of death connected with ritual 'nearness' is transferred to the people as the real embodiments of the priestly function. Related to 'the dwelling of YHWH', the 'coming near' corresponds to the ritual categories of the contest. By dying, the people present the fate of the usurpers. But set out as a lament, the deathly 'nearness' is not presented as an act of voluntary usurpation, but as a fact of necessity. Doomed to 'nearness', the people are related both to the fate of the villains and the function of Aaron. And when the extraordinary character of this function has been demonstrated by the wonderful rod, the people have every reason to fear the future trials.

This final twist of the story corresponds to its beginning. According to Num. 16.3 the revolt concerns the 'self-exaltation' of Moses and Aaron, against which is professed the 'holiness' of the people. Set into such a context the ordeal that follows will decide this issue, the stand of the usurpers being the concrete expression of the claim of general 'holiness'. This is also reflected by the definition of 'holiness' in vv. 5-7 and also 17.2-3, which relates the concept to ritual 'nearness'. On the other hand, the general character of the challenge in Num. 16.3 invites the reader to expect that the people should be more directly involved than merely witnessing what elite figures do on their behalf. This is borne out by the concluding lament. Numbers 17.27-28 marks the return to the initial issue of the people as holy and links the episode as a whole to this issue. The story is actually centred around the people's holiness. They are the real actors of the story, while the usurpers and Aaron serve as illustrations of the people's situation as doomed to 'nearness'.

Such categories correspond to the qualification of the people's future in the very first divine message from the mountain in Exod. 19.4-6. The people as a 'kingdom of priests and a holy people' (v. 6) is a condensed expression of the categories that are set out as a story of priestly 'nearness' in Numbers 16–17. Moreover, the context of Exod. 19.6 reflects a corresponding application of the ritual categories. While the people will 'make themselves holy' (vv. 10, 14), the following scenes are centred around the improper ascent under threat of death. And comparable to Numbers 16–17, the story of Exodus 19–20, dominated by YHWH and Moses as the central actors, is also concluded by a scene given to the people's reaction of fear, when 'we' are related to death due to dangerous 'nearness' (cf. Chapter 1.3 on Exod. 20.18-21).[96]

Given over to a conceptual cluster of priestly function, holiness defined by spatial categories of 'nearness' and related to different actors of accepted and negated status, and death—the whole being related to the people as the ultimate priestly actors—the two texts are parallel expressions of some transferred application of the priestly concepts. The difference between the two elaborations can be referred to their different place in the compositional development. The intimations of Exod. 19.4-6 are turned into an episode which illustrates the absurdity of the divine project and thus provides the tense introduction to the events which are happily concluded in Exodus 40. Set after Sinai, the story has reached a stage where the people are facing the reality of their priestly state, the implications of which are demonstrated negatively and positively by the priestly protagonists of Numbers 16–17.

96. The intimations of the people in the priestly role in Exod. 19 could also be reflected by the ambiguous references to the ascent by the undefined 'they' in v. 13b and to a group of (as yet non-existent) priests separated from Moses and Aaron in vv. 22a and 24b. The enigmatic character of these references and the formal looseness of scenes added to scenes is comparable to the formal character of Num. 16–17 and also to the subtlety of the final application on the people in 17.27-28.

The connection to Exodus 19 underlines the character of the priestly categories in Numbers 16–17. Related to a context of priestly sanctification as it is set out in Leviticus 8–10, the struggle of Aaron and the priestly usurpers refers to a connotational background of institutional priesthood. Limited to this context, the transfer to concepts of popular priesthood in Numbers 16–17 seems a rather radical application of such categories. This is underlined by the following stories which do not return to the idea of the people as priests, but relate the priestly function to Aaron and his sons. But the connection between Numbers 16–17 and Exodus 19 extends the contextual references for a story on popular priesthood. Exodus 19.4-6 introduces a story on the people as actors in the extraordinary encounter, concluded in Exodus 40 by the people being permanently related to the theophanic manifestation. The significance of this conclusion is underlined by its repetition in Numbers 9. Accordingly, the Sinai story as a whole is centred around the people as the new theophanic figures. In this way, the connection between Exodus 19 and Numbers 16–17 refers the latter to the grand issues of the Sinai story. The post-Sinai people is set in a situation of permanent *visio Dei*. This qualification is added to by the categories of priestly holiness. Corresponding to the elite function of Moses transferred to the people, the categories of priestly function are also used for the qualification of the people's new reality.

Moreover, the priestly qualification represents an immediate extension of the categories of encounter. The concepts of ascent into sacred space and intimate 'nearness' connected with death for the unworthy, correspond to the connection of priestly 'nearness' and death in Numbers 16–17.[97] The parallelism of these concepts must imply the possibility of cross-application and transferred usages. This is underlined by the Tent of Meeting as the new locus of sacred space, common to both expressions of extraordinary 'nearness'. Especially when added to by the parallel versions of 'the day of erecting' in Leviticus 8–10 and Numbers 7–8, the connotations of institutional ritualism form part of the new perception of theophanic encounter which is developed in Exodus 19–40.

97. Cf. Chapter 2.2 for the comparable reapplication of the concept of ascent in Exod. 33, transferred from the categories of divine mountain to the idea of journey and a divine co-ascender.

The Representative Function of the Sub-Figures

The implications of Num. 17.27-28 make it necessary to return to the relationship of the people and the sub-figures. In Exodus 18 and Numbers 11 the officers and the scribes are portrayed as separate figures with a function related to the people. The transfer of the Moses-functions to a new set of actors seems to represent the enhancement of human reality, enriched and diversified by a hierarchy of sacred functions transferred to certain groups within the people.

The development of the post-Sinai revolts adds to this impression. In the priestly episode the sub-figures have become the central actors. The role of the people is correspondingly reduced. But at the same time the separate identity of people and sub-figures is blurred. While the people are present in the story as actors, witnessing the acts of the protagonists and even influencing what takes place, the peculiar conclusion implies the people are the 'real' actors also for the roles that have been enacted by the sub-figures. The subtle transition is prepared for by the scouts' story. Here the connection of people and sub-figures is effected partly by the extension of the roles of the sub-figures, partly by a process of identification. The small children are added to the positive scouts, while the grown-ups are identified with the negative scouts (Num. 14.28-34). In particular the divine address in v. 34—'you' on the one hand being identified with the scouts, on the other with the people—corresponds to the transition between the levels of identity in Numbers 16–17. But in the scouts' story, the following scene in 14.36-38 returns to the separate identity of the sub-figures. The relationship of the actors in Numbers 16–17 is both more subtle and more consistent. By the loosely added scene in 17.27-28, the lament of the people seems to reflect a mental process of identification. The people see their own reality represented by the events, as if the main protagonists suddenly were unmasked and the people see themselves.

Accordingly, the sub-figures have a rather complex and subtle function. On one hand, they are the central figures of the drama, with roles separate from the people. This aspect is underlined by the context. The roles of Joshua and Aaron are preceded by their presence in earlier episodes and continued by their roles as separate figures in the following episodes. But their solidity as separate figures is dissolved in the scouts' and priests' episodes. Ultimately, they are unmasked as ephemeral figures that embody the potentialities of the human situation after Sinai. The subtleties of personification and identification seem to imply a double process of 'unmasking'. In Numbers 14 the identification of the people as scouts is performed by the divine actor in an address to 'you'. In the following story the people on their own perform the unmasking of 'they' as 'we'. In both cases, the process implies a corresponding unmasking of the people. Having performed as actors in the drama, taking sides against the positive scouts and for the priestly usurpers and thereby influencing the course of the drama, the people have their character revealed. Just as they identified with the negative roles in the ephemeral story, their future roles in the 'real' story seem doomed in advance. So the people have good reason for their anguish.

The reader is also left with some disturbing questions. The two episodes indicate the gradual development of the sub-figures as personifications of the people. Due to the connection of these stories with the earlier episodes, the reader has to face the possibility that the actors of the other stories could also have a corresponding representative function for some 'real' story. This question is emphasized by the connection between Numbers 16–17 and Exodus 19. Returning to the concept of popular priesthood intimated by Exodus 19, the special conclusion in Num. 17.27-28 could have repercussions not only for the preceding story of priestly 'nearness', but also for the reading of Leviticus 8–10 and Numbers 7–8. The connection between Exodus 19 and Numbers 17 could present the conceptual framework also for the stories in between, to be read as illustrations of some 'real' story in which the gradual development of the priestly character of the people is the central issue. What then is the 'real' story?[98] Implicitly, the divine speech of Num. 14.28-34 identifies the story of the people as negative scouts—doomed to walk until they all are dead—with the narrative of the following chapters. Similarly, Exod. 40.36-38, complemented by Num. 9.15-23, refers the story of the people as permanent visionaries to the following journey. But with regard to any story dedicated to the people's priesthood, no indications are given apart from the evocative intimations of Exodus 19 and Numbers 17.

These questions are supplemented by the subtle elaboration of the people as narrative figures in the priestly episode. The double role of the people, who perform both as actors and as spectators identifying

98. This question is emphasized by the parallel enigmas raised by the apotheosis of Moses in Exod. 34, related to the substitution of Moses by the people in Exod. 40, and by the contrasting qualifications of the post-Sinai journey in Num. 9.15-23 and ch. 11.

with the *dramatis personae*, represents a sophisticated arrangement. The story refers at least to two levels of narrative reality, which are related as simultaneously 'real'. The people take part in a story concluded by the election of Aaron as the true priest. The 'realistic' character of such a story is illustrated when, as a matter of course, it is referred by readers modern and ancient to the ritual institutions of Israel or post-exilic Judaism.[99] To describe the intended function of such a story by the labels of 'simile' or 'allegory', for example, would ignore the narrative assertion that the people are actively involved as participants, and that the separate identity of Aaron the priest is retained in the episodes that follow. But the seemingly solid foundation of narrative realism is subtly undermined by the conclusion when 'they' are unmasked as 'we'. This turns the events of the story into some theatrical performance watched by the people as a separate audience, witnessing the character of their reality as 'we' illustrated by the ephemeral figures of the drama.

Thus, for the function of a story concluded in Num. 17.26 by the transition to 'we' in vv. 27-28, 'simile' and even 'allegory' seem apt labels. But when 17.27-28 refers to the exclamations of 16.34b and 17.6b, and thus represents an integrated part of the preceding story, the reader has to conclude that 'simile' and 'realistic language' reflect equally valid aspects of the narrative. Moreover, the author seems at pains to present these aspects as valid only when held together. Numbers 17.27-28 hints at a 'real' story in which the people are candidates for priesthood. The significance of such a 'real' story of popular priesthood is underlined by the beginning of the Sinai stories in Exodus 19. But while the transition from 'they' to 'we' reduces the preceding events to a function of ephemeral illustration, the ramifications of this 'real' story are not found outside the narrative.[100]

Such effects could ultimately be related to the role of the reader. The role of the people as it is set out in Numbers 16–17 is remarkably

99. Similarly, the oracular officers of Exod. 18 have been set in a context of legal institutions. In the same way, the description of the ecstatic scribes of Num. 11 refers to the institution of 'elders', Num. 12 to prophecy, and Num. 27.15-23 to categories of military leadership.

100. Confronting parallel problems for the reading of the Song of Songs, Lacocque (*Romance She Wrote*, pp. 12-15) claims that Midrashic tradition is an alternative to the dichotomy of 'naturalistic' and 'allegorical' readings.

similar to what takes place in the reader's mind when influenced by these stories. Comparable to the chorus of Greek tragedies mediating the reactions of the audience, the voices of the people set words to the reactions of the reader. Sharing the role of spectator, watching from outside and gradually drawn into the drama, the reader is also engaged in a process of identification, ultimately sharing in the anguish of the addressed 'you' in 14.34 and the lamenting 'we' in 17.27-28. It must be possible to surmise that the portrait of the people in these stories is also designed for such a function.

4. *Numbers 13–14 and Exodus 14*

The Two Modes of 'Fear Not!'

Framed by Numbers 11–12 and 16–17, the scouts' story has an important function as part of the compositional development. For this part of the story, the people's death—presented as a process of 40 years for the grown-ups and as impending death for 'we' doomed to 'nearness'—represents a central theme. The impact of the story in such a setting is profoundly supplemented by the relationship to Exodus 14.

In both texts the people's revolt is linked to a situation of war. The stories also reflect a basic common structure, which is the more remarkable as the formal character of both texts has invited to heavy traditio- and redactio-critical operations. Thus, both stories are set in motion by the divine initiative. This is typical for the Egypt and Sinai stories, while journey episodes are initiated by the human actors.[101] Accordingly, the introductions of Exod. 14.1 and Num. 13.1[102] function as a signal to the reader that stories of some special significance are to be expected.

For both stories, the events set in motion by the divine initiative lead to confrontation with the enemies—real in the first case, imagined in

101. This is illustrated by the relationship of Exod. 14 to the Passover and wilderness traditions as a classical traditio-historical puzzle. E.g. McCarthy, 'Plagues and Sea of Reeds', pp. 137-58; G.W. Coats, 'The Traditio-Historical Character of the Reed Sea Motif', *VT* 17 (1967), pp. 253-65; *idem*, *Moses*, pp. 81-108, 116-18; B.S. Childs, 'A Traditio-Historical Study of the Reed Sea Tradition', *VT* 20 (1970), pp. 406-18; *idem*, *Book of Exodus*, pp. 221-24.

102. Underlined by Deut. 1.22-23 which attribute the mission of the scouts to the people's initiative. In Exod. 14.1-4 the divine initiative is stressed by the people having to 'return' (v. 2) to a crisis which is set up by the divine author (v. 4).

the other. The people's perception of the enemies' might represents the central feature of the introductory events (Num. 13.27-29, 31-33; Exod. 14.5-10a). This leads to the revolt (Num. 13.30; 14.1-4; Exod. 14.10b-13). In both cases, the people's complaint is confronted by an admonishing address in the formulaic language of the salvation oracle (Num. 14.8-9; Exod. 14.13-14).[103] The next events follow different courses, due to the different cast of the stories. But in both cases the address of admonishment is followed by a divine statement on what is going to happen. Also, the outcome of the episodes is peculiarly symmetrical. The death of the Egyptian army in the sea corresponds to the men of Israel, perceived as fighting men facing death in the desert.

Thus, the two episodes have in common a number of quite significant features compared to other revolt stories. They are added to when we turn to the details of the stories, for which the language of the salvation oracle is of special importance. This is illustrated by 2 Chron. 20.1-29, which has a similar structure related to a corresponding motif cluster. In this story the perception of the enemy (vv. 1-2) is followed by the fear reaction of the victims (vv. 3-13), here with fasting and prayer taking the place of the revolt. These scenes are followed by the proclamation of a salvation oracle (vv. 14-17, repeated by the king's admonishment in v. 20). The structure of events correspond to the introductory events in Exodus 14 and Numbers 14. Compared to these texts, the salvation oracle represents the sole divine statement in 2 Chronicles. But the rest of the story is set out remarkably close to Exodus 14. After the divine intervention (vv. 22-23; cf. Exod. 14.19-29) follows the impression of the destruction of the enemy (vv. 24-25; cf. Exod. 14.30) concluded by thanksgiving (vv. 26-28; cf. Exod. 14.31,[104] followed by 15.1-21).

The parallel structure of events and central motifs, underlined by the individual character of the single story, indicates the close relationship of the Exodus and 2 Chronicles' stories as expressions of the same

103. Cf. E.W. Conrad, 'The "Fear Not" Oracles in Second Isaiah', *VT 34* (1984), pp. 129-52. The two versions represent freely-shaped applications of the traditional forms. This is illustrated by Deut. 1.29-31 as a third version. Verses 29-30 especially reflect a closer relationship to the motifs of Exod. 14.13-14. The impact of the formulaic language is also reflected by the motif of 'firmness' (*ḥzq*) in the exhortation of Num. 13.20 and especially in the enemy descriptions of vv. 18 and 31 and Exod. 14.4, 8, 17.

104. Cf. also the concluding fear motifs 2 Chron. 20.29 and Exod. 14.31.

literary tradition.[105] With Numbers 14 for a third expression of this tradition, the parallelism of this text and Exodus 14 could simply reflect the influence of the common language represented by the salvation oracle. On the other hand, such a relationship also implies the connotational impact of the stereotyped language and thus the implicit connection when two stories centred around the salvation oracle are set within one narrative context.

Such a connection is indicated by the concrete elaboration of the common elements. In both texts the implementation of the divine instruction leads to a situation in which the people have to confront the enemy. The character of this confrontation is expressed by an introductory description of the enemy's might related to the people, concluded by the people's perception of mortal threat. In Exodus 14 this is effected by the artful building up of tension when the repeated references to the approach of the mighty Egyptian army are juxtaposed to references to the people (vv. 5-9). The two situations of approaching enemies and encamped people are brought together in v. 10. The impact of this scene is intensified by the extended motif of 'seeing': 'The children of Israel lifted their eyes and see!', and this prepares for the final description of the enemy and the people's reaction of fear.

The people's 'seeing' represents the central motif of this description. This motif is repeatedly applied in the rest of the story, and could reflect the influence of the salvation oracle.[106] The divine salvation is 'seen', and this is juxtaposed to the 'seeing' of the Egyptians (v. 13). Also the dead Egyptians are 'seen' (v. 30), as well as the divine hand (v. 31). The latter application is added to by the parallel fear motif, in which 'seeing the divine hand' and 'fearing YHWH' is connected with the people's trust in YHWH and Moses. This represents the positive counterpart to the people's 'seeing' and 'fear' related to the enemy in v. 10.[107]

The motif of 'seeing' is also important in Numbers 13, primarily attributed to the scouts. While the scouts are sent to 'see the land' (vv. 18-20) and make the people 'see the fruit of the land' (v. 26), the

105. Cf. DeVries, *1 and 2 Chronicles*, p. 328, who sees the Chronicles story as a 'quasi-holy-war story', reflecting the Exodus account 'as in a Doré etching'.

106. Deut. 20.1 illustrates that the motif 'seeing the enemy's might' is a traditional part of the salvation oracle.

107. This connection between vv. 10 and 31 is stressed by Childs, *Book of Exodus*, p. 227.

concrete report only applies the motif in the negative sense as 'seeing the enemy's might'. The introductory report on the bountiful country (v. 27) is overshadowed[108] by the description of the enemy (vv. 28-29). This is continued by the second report (vv. 31-33) which solely refers to the land in negative terms to underline the impression of the enemy's might. The motif of 'seeing' is used for special effect. The element 'we saw' is applied three times as some narrative refrain, concluding both reports. It is related to the 'descendents of Anak' (v. 28bβ), to the extraordinary size of everyone (v. 32bβ), and to the 'sons of Anak' (v. 33). In the third and climactic version of the element in v. 33 its shape is altered to 'there we saw', and further extended by the juxtaposed 'in our eyes' and 'in their eyes'. The climactic effect is supplemented by 'the sons of Anak' extended by the repeated reference to the mythical Nephilim. The heavily loaded conclusion indicates that the two reports are formed as a rhetorical whole, building towards v. 33 as the climax.

While the introductory scenes of Exodus 14 and Numbers 13–14 are different both with regard to imagery and rhetorical effects, they both prepare for the climactic moment of terror when the impression of the enemy as 'seen' is taken in by the people. Their parallel function is reflected by the parallelism of Num. 13.33 (followed by 14.1) compared with Exod. 14.10. In both cases the extension of the motif 'seeing the enemy' is related to a corresponding lingering on the people's reaction of terror. Comparable to the double reaction of 'fear' and 'crying' in the Exodus story, the pleonastic style of Num. 14.1a makes the people's weeping loud indeed. In both cases this scene prepares a scene of revolt.

In Exodus 14 the people's 'seeing' and 'fear' with regard to the enemies is juxtaposed to a parallel application of these motifs. Related to the divine miracle, the 'seeing' is connected to 'fear of YHWH' and 'trust in' YHWH and Moses (Exod. 14.31). A corresponding application of the motif cluster is also reflected in Numbers 14. But corresponding to the different orientation of the two stories, the positive aspects are not elaborated in the event structure in the Numbers story, but serve as a negative description of the people. The people who have 'seen' the former miraculous manifestations (Num. 14.22, and

108. Underlined by Deut. 1.25-26, where the favourable report of the scouts is juxtaposed to the recalcitrance of the people. The negative aspects of the report are connected to the people's revolt (vv. 27-28), while the conflict of the scouts is alluded to in v. 36.

implicitly also v. 11), will not 'see' the Promised Land (repeated v. 23a and b). And instead of the response of 'trust' in the Exodus story, the people have 'discarded' and 'not trusted' YHWH (Num. 14.11, to which is added 'tempted' and 'not listened to' in vv. 22-23).[109]

The common motif structure connects the experience of the crisis and the corresponding reaction of fear to a parallel experience of the divine intervention and the corresponding response of confession. This is expounded positively in Exodus 14 and negatively in Numbers 14. In the latter, the development of the proper line of events is halted by the people stuck in the situation of 'seeing' and 'fearing the enemy'. What in Exodus 14 introduces a story of miraculous intervention and jubilant response is in Numbers 14 perverted into a contrasting story of retribution and sorrow. Also the latter is oriented towards a climactic event of divine intervention. But differently channeled by the people stuck in their reaction of fear, the divine intervention is now turned against the people.

The perversion of the proper events in the Numbers version is also reflected by the special conclusion in 14.39-45. Moved by their sorrow over the divine condemnation, the people march against the enemy, that is the response which, according to 2 Chron. 20.20-21, should have taken place after the admonishing address in Num. 14.6-9. But it is too late to make a new beginning. Their bravery does not represent the proper expression of non-fear, but is against the divine 'mouth' (v. 41). Now YHWH is not 'in your midst' and not 'with you' (vv. 42-43). The references to the salvation oracle could also be echoed by the challenge 'Do not ascend! for YHWH is not in your midst' in v. 42. The construction reflects effects of alliteration.[110] The allusions to the formulaic language underline the mock character of the events, setting out the people's bravery as a pathetically self-made effort to undo the initial scene of fear and revolt, in the vain hope of introducing an alternative story of miraculous intervention.

The contrasting effect of the two stories underlines the parallelism of the two introductory descriptions concluded by the people's reaction of fear. However different with regard to circumstances and rhetorical

109. Cf. also the formulaic references to the divine name and glory connected with the miraculous intervention in Exod. 14.4, 17-18 and Num. 14.21-22.

110. Followed by a *kî*-sentence composed of nominal statements, *'al ta'*^{a}*lû* ('do not ascend!') takes the place of the stereotypical command *'al tîr*^{e}*'û* ('do not fear!') of v. 9.

effects, both clearly are shaped to present two scenes of frightening intensity. In both cases, the terror of the people is the natural reaction to an impossible situation. Moreover, there are no indications that the people of Exodus 14 in any way were 'better' than the people of Numbers 14. The parallelism of the introductory events—the threat of the enemies, followed by the people's reaction of terror, followed by the address of salvation oracle—presents identical situations as far as the people's heroism is concerned. Even if imaginary, the threat of the enemies 'seen' by the scouts, all outstanding representatives of the community, is as real for the people as what they 'see' in Exodus 14. The two revolts are of the same character. Apart from aspects of intensification and the diversification of roles which characterize the Numbers version, the relationship of the two stories does not explain why the people are miraculously helped in the one situation and punished so bitterly in the other. The wish to stone the positive guides (v. 10) is obviously very bad. But prepared for by Numbers 13, a reaction of despair is most understandable, especially by men concerned about the fate of their wives and children. It is primarily the heavy divine condemnation which informs the reader that the people behave very badly in the Numbers story. Related to the parallel revolt in Exodus 14, the reason why the people are treated so differently in Numbers 14 is as obscure as in the case of Moses and Aaron in Numbers 20, who also happen to arrive in a situation where they are condemned for their lack of 'trust' (v. 12).

The different location in the narrative development seems the only explanation of why the people are so differently treated. Corresponding to the contrasting relationship of Exodus 16 and Numbers 11, the two stories are set before and after Sinai. Before Sinai the *deus ex machina* enters the situation of terror and provides the miracle which produces the result of 'trust'. After Sinai the people are obviously expected to produce the trust on their own. This corresponds to the difference of the divine response when facing the people's hunger in Exodus 16 and the wish for meat in Numbers 11.

The absence of the *deus ex machina* is underlined by the change of actors when the people's terror is responded to. In Exodus 14 the revolt is confronted by the address of Moses, followed by divine promises. According to v. 4, Moses has even been informed beforehand of what is going to happen. In the parallel situation in Numbers 14, Moses is silent, while the admonishing address is delivered by Joshua and Caleb.

The divine actor does not intrude upon the scene until the admonishers are in danger (v. 10). The parallelism of the two stories underlines the consistency of the changes in Numbers 14. The absence of the divine miracle-producer corresponds to the passivity of Moses. And while the salvation oracle is common to the two stories, its effect as oracular address is spoiled when it is overwhelmed by the negative plurality of ten scouts, all with a social background as respectable as that of Joshua and Caleb.

In Exodus 14 the miraculous categories bridge the two situations of 'fear' and 'trust'. The separation between the two situations and the transition from the one to the other is even reflected by the local categories. The people 'see' the Egyptians from the two opposite shores (vv. 9 and 30), the miraculous crossing of the sea being the link between the opposites of human disposition. After Sinai the people are expected to move on their own from terror to 'trust' (v. 11). And when they are unable to produce such a miracle, the divine intervention takes the form of cruel retribution.

The Men and the Little Children

To some degree the parallelism of the two stories can be explained as being due to a common dependence on the formulaic language of the salvation oracle. But the common points are so many and so consistently elaborated that they can only be seen as effects of deliberate juxtaposition. This impression is increased by a special type of reference which links the two stories, the most direct of which[111] is presented in the people's complaint in Num. 14.2b-3 and by the qualification of the people as grown-ups and 'little children' (*ṭap*) vv. 28-35.

The people's complaint consists of three elements. In the first, a rhetorical wish for death is related to the localities of Egypt[112] and the

111. Cf. also the strange order in 14.25 to 'turn and journey into the desert by the way of the Reed Sea'. A similar order to return and camp 'on the sea' is presented in Exod. 14.2. This is prepared for by the itinerary references of Exod. 13.17-18, which also present a special detour by way of the Reed Sea to avoid dangerous enemies, comparable to Num. 14.25. Too vague for any exact description, the itinerary notes seem to indicate a parallel movement relative to the Reed Sea, leading to the place of divine retribution.

112. Cf. a comparable element in Exod. 16.3aα and also Num. 20.3b, and further the motif connection between graves in Egypt and death in the wilderness in Exod. 14.11.

wilderness. The next element refers to the sacred story of Exodus, but is posed as a complaining question and thus presents the Exodus as a negative movement to a place of death (v. 3b).[113] This idea is central for the people's complaint in the revolt stories.[114] So far, the complaint of Numbers 14 represents a staple of the other complaints, echoing the perverted presentation of the Exodus as a movement into a place of death. The main difference is that Numbers 14 has added the wilderness to Egypt as the preferred locality of death, in this way retaining the motifs of the earlier complaints and added 'this land' as a third place of death (v. 3).

But the third element in v. 3b is more specific. In the form of a question this element introduces the idea of a return to Egypt as 'good for us'. The significance of the element is added to by v. 4 which repeats the idea of return to Egypt. This underlines the correspondence of v. 3b to the similar element in the complaint in Exod. 14.12, when the people assert the slavery of Egypt as 'good for us'. The constructions are so unusual and the connotational implications of 'return' to Egypt and 'slave for' Egypt are so important to these stories, that the echo-effect of the two complaints must point to the special relationship of the two stories.

This underlines the significance of Num. 14.4, where the idea of return to Egypt is shifted from rhetorical function to practical reality. When the people call upon each other to return, the revolt of this story represents a climax compared to Exodus 14 as well as to the other revolts.[115] The people take practical steps to undo the miraculous story of salvation. This corresponds to and continues the perverted 'remembering' of Numbers 11, which resulted in the divine perversion of the original food miracle presented in Exodus 16. Corresponding to the relationship of the food miracles when presented in the pre- and post-

113. See, for example, Coats (*Moses*, p. 109) on this element as part of a pattern which includes the account of some crisis and the reaction of the people qualified as a challenge to the validity of Mosaic leadership, often together with an account of the response of Moses and also God.

114. Cf. the short form of the *lāmâ*-question in Exod. 17.3b; Num. 11.20bγ; 20.4; 21.5, while Exod. 16.3 and Num. 16.13a refer to the Exodus in the form of accusation. In addition, the rhetorical question in Exod. 14.11 alludes to this connection of Exodus and death.

115. This effect is stressed by Coats, *Moses*, pp. 122-24, and Olson, *Death of the Old*, pp. 144-45.

Sinai modes, Numbers 13–14 takes the story one step further back to the events of the Sea. Exodus 14 is repeated in a new mode. The people's wish to undo the sacred story by the return to Egypt as the better place is mirrored by the divine force, directed not against the 'outer' enemy of Egyptians or the 'children of Anak' but against Israel.

In Exodus 14 the people about to die in the desert (vv. 11-12) are spared by the miraculous journey through the waters, while the pursuing Egyptians die. Also in Numbers 14, the people confronting 'the sons of Anak' designate themselves as doomed to death (vv. 2-3). But the juxtaposition of two opposed groups is altered in this story. According to the second divine statement in vv. 28-35, the intervention is internalized to the men and their children as two opposed groups. The shift refers to the complaint of v. 3, where the men about to die worry over the fate of their wives and children.[116] Accordingly, the men will die in the desert, while the children will be brought to the land.

But when the story moves from the outer enemies to a separation within the people, aspects of the basic situation are also retained. The reversal of fates, related to two sets of juxtaposed figures, is common to both stories. However different when turned outwardly against the Egyptians and inwardly against the men of Israel, the divine intervention is of a partial character and also reverses the fates. The actors who embody physical might are condemned to death, while those initially perceived as victims are spared.

The reversal of fates is directly reflected by the contrasts of Egyptians and people in Exodus 14, but more circumstantially in the Numbers story due to the shift from outer enemies to a contrast within the people. The men who according to Num. 14.3 expect to die, duly do so. But also in this story, those condemned to death are qualified by military categories. Comparable to Pharaoh and his army, the narrative figure 'the people' is represented in Numbers 14 by the 'men', perceived moreover as fighting men. This is indicated by v. 3 which underlines the male character of the people weeping and lamenting throughout the night. And according to v. 29, the men are 'mustered' and 'numbered'.[117] In comparison to the revolting people presented as fighting

116. To Olson, *Death of the Old*, p. 147, this reflects an effect of irony, with vv. 28-29 and 32-33, 35 presenting the retribution as the divine fulfilment of the men's wish. Cf. also Van Seters, *The Life of Moses*, p. 379.

117. The military categories of this qualification is stressed by Levine, *Numbers 1–20*, p. 369.

men, the women and children of Num. 14.3 represent the weaker part, and are accordingly the object of the men's special concern. But by the divine intervention, the children perceived as the fatherless victims of the 'sons of Anak' are to be spared. And when their fathers all are dead (vv. 31-33), they are destined to 'see' the land and thus also implicitly the terrible 'sons of Anak'.

Thus, in both stories the divine retribution is directed towards soldiers doomed to die. The imagery of an army dying in the sea is contrasted with an army dying in the desert, in both cases juxtaposed to a positive group surviving the journey through the sea and the desert. The strange effect of distorted mirrors can also be related to the qualification of the two armies. According to Num. 14.3 and 31, the doomed are depicted as fathers about to die, in contrast to their children who will survive. Conversely, the context of Exodus 14 implies that Pharaoh and his army represent fathers who have experienced the death of their firstborn (Exod. 12.29-30).[118] Some basic components of the original story are transferred to a new actualization, located to the post-Sinai reality and 'internalized' to a separation within the people.

Such a connection between the two stories is also indicated by the special constellation of men and 'little children' in vv. 3 and 31 of Num. 14. The worry of the men is related to the fate of their wives and children qualified as 'little children' by the special term *ṭāp*.[119] 'Women and little children' as objects of the men's worry reflect the connotational impact of the words. Alone or together with other possessions, 'women and little children' are the proverbial victims, given to plunder[120] or to special violence.[121] Correspondingly, 'little children' are the objects of their fathers' special care and protection.[122]

But while women and children together are well-suited as an expression for the men's worry, the significance of the special term for children is underlined when the divine statement of v. 31 returns to the

118. The significance of these motifs for the composition is illustrated by the story about the Levitical sanctification followed by the Passover celebration and journey in Num. 8–9.

119. The use of this word is profiled by the parallel *b^{e}nêkem* in v. 33 and the parallelism of *ṭāp* and *bānîm* in Deut. 1.39.

120. E.g. Gen. 34.29; Num. 31.9, 17-18; Deut. 20.14.

121. E.g. Deut. 2.34; 3.6; Judg. 21.10; Ezek. 9.6.

122. E.g. Gen. 43.8; Num. 32.16-17; Deut. 3.19; and, further, Gen. 50.8; Judg. 18.21; 2 Sam. 15.22.

complaint. The women are ignored and the people as a whole are described by the juxtaposition of men and their 'little children'.[123]

The significance of this juxtaposition is indicated by the special description of the people departing from Egypt in Exod. 12.37. The 'children of Israel' are grouped as 600,000 *g^e^bārîm* 'on foot' [124] and 'little children.'

The participation of *ṭāp* in a column of *g^e^bārîm* represents an unusual situation.[125] In the Exodus account, it is prepared for by the bargaining between Moses and Pharaoh in Exod. 10.8-11, 24-29. In the first, Moses asks for all the people and all their animals to leave. Pharaoh interprets this to mean the *g^e^bārîm* together with the 'little children' and refuses; only the men can leave. In the second, Pharaoh allows that 'you' and 'also the little children' can leave (v. 24). But Moses insists that 'also' (v. 26) the cattle must be permitted to leave.

Accordingly, the description of those departing in Exod. 12.37-38 reflects the successful bargaining of Moses in Exodus 10. The men and the little children and a great number of cattle are the expression of a perfect exodus. But this effect is increased and subtly altered by the insertion of 'the mixed multitude' as a new group of travellers. Followed by a full sentence, the introductory 'also' (*w^e^gam*) of v. 38 separates two main groupings. The children of Israel consisted of 600,000 foot soldiers apart from the little children. As a second group, separate from the proper representatives of the people, a huge crowd 'went with them' along with much cattle.

In view of the other effects of parallelism it seems rather obvious that the special qualification of the people departing from Egypt as foot

123. This word is retained in the following episode in Num. 16.27, where the usurpers are left alone together with their 'women and their children and their little children'. Aside from the obvious emotive effects of the word when children are related to the terrible doom about to take place, the pleonasm could reflect the use of the word in the preceding episode.

124. The significance of Exod. 12.37 is also illustrated by the reference in Num. 11.21. The reference to the men as 'mustered' and 'numbered' in Num. 14.29 could reflect the connection to the numbered foot soldiers of Exod. 12.37.

125. In addition to Num. 32 and Gen. 50.8, cf. 2 Sam. 15.22, where the inclusion of the children among the professional soldiers witnesses the total commitment of Ittai the mercenary. Judg. 18.21 is of special significance for the situations found in Exod. 12 and Num. 14, set in a context of military conquest initiated by a scout episode. The vulnerability of the children, parallel to 'cattle' and 'riches', is expressed by their being placed in front of the train, away from the pursuers.

soldiers and 'little children' and the constellation of fighting men and 'little children' in Numbers 14 refer to each other. Both the military qualification of the people as well as the application of *ṭap* are too special to be accidental. Moreover, the significance of the children as actors in both stories is reflected by the special preparation for their presence in Exodus 10 and Num. 14.3. It seems reasonable to conclude that the description of the train in Exod. 12.37 prepares the juxtaposition of the men and their children in Numbers 14, the initial grouping an intimation of what is to be unfolded in the latter story.

Such a conclusion is supported by the 'rabble' in Numbers 11. As an allusion to the 'mixed multitude' of Exod. 12.38, the application of the 'rabble' represents a comparable type of reference. Also in this case, a seemingly casual element of the description of the people departing from Egypt is elaborated by the post-Sinai story, when the fatal implications of the initial 'mixed multitude' are unfolded by 'the rabble' in the people's midst. Also the 'plundering of the Egyptians' in Exod. 12.35-36 can be seen as an expression for this subtle but important type of reference. Formally awkward in its context, the reference is elaborated into a central theme by the people's 'self-plundering' in Exod. 33.6 related to the 'gift' motifs of 32.1-6 and chs. 35–39. Also the 'waving' of the Levites in Numbers 8, as the substitutes for the firstborn of Israel represents a similar connection, repeating in a new mode the bloody events of the first Passover.

The delicate character of these effects makes it difficult to describe their implications. At the very least they have repercussions for our understanding of the effects of parallelism and repetition. The relationship of Exodus 14 and Numbers 13–14 indicates a basic function of contrasting effects, the latter repeating the former in a new mode. The subtle system of reference expressed by the 'little children', the 'rabble' and the 'Egyptian riches', adds to the perception of such effects. The events of the sacred story are profoundly linked. One story is essentially contained within the other. Certain elements of one story are carried over into the next, their hidden implications being unfolded in events to come.

It must be important that the most direct examples of such compositional effects refer to 'internalized' categories. Some process of profound 'internalization', as it is expressed by the episodes of Numbers 8 and 11–17, can be related to at least two aspects. The situation of outer crisis related to Egypt has been transferred to conflicts within the people, reflected by the constellation of the sub-figures in Numbers 11–17 and the partial character of the divine intervention. Similarly, the crisis is related to 'inner' categories of psychic-mental character. The hunger is turned to lust for Egyptian delicacies and the fear of the enemy is turned to an inner struggle between fear and trust. This development is accompanied by the heightened emotional character of the revolts, which are climaxed by the howl of anguish in Num. 17.27-28. And perhaps with an even greater emotional impact, the reader is profoundly touched by the image of doomed fathers and their dependent children set in the wilderness for 40 years.

5. *Conclusions*

The referential richness of the story contained within Numbers 13–14 makes it impossible to contract the reading into a definite description of what the story is all about. What seems at the outset to present a rather simple narrative plot, enacted by a series of starkly drawn figures, gradually evolves into a complex drama of highly emotional character and of ever-widening connotational ramifications. But at the very least, the relationship to the context of Numbers 11–12 and 16–17, on the other hand to Exodus 14, strengthens the impression of story cycles as vitally important for the composition. The scouts' episode is part of the cycle of post-Sinai stories, the character of which is set out by their relationship to Exodus 14. But conversely, the difference of the two cycles of journey stories underlines the significance of YHWH, Moses and the people as the central actors in all these episodes. However different, the cycles are related as parts of one story. Thus, the attributes that are ascribed to these three actors could serve as a condensed expression for the narrative development.

The Divine Actor

The YHWH of the scouts' episode strikes a cruelly harsh stand. Within a book obviously intended for a positive function as some sort of religious address, the allocation of such stark and brutal harshness to 'God' is remarkable. This evaluation is of course rather suspect as the natural reaction of modern readers weaned into a religious tradition of softer character. But a corresponding reaction must have been shared by the ancient readers. The author seems at pains to create such an impression. This can be illustrated by the repeated application of *peger* (Num. 14.29, 32, 33). Apart from the general associations of the uncleanliness of dead bodies, the word is commonly used as an especially harsh expression for 'corpses', connected with nightmare visions of death and destruction[126] and evoking feelings of disgust.[127] In Numbers 14 the negative connotations of the word are evoked three times, even made intolerably direct as 'your corpses'.[128] The three applications of 'your corpses' in Numbers 14 must represent a most brutal form of address.

The contrast to the pre-Sinai stories underlines both the consistency of the divine image in the post-Sinai stories as well as the deliberate character of its drawing. The people of the two sets of journey stories present such closely related manifestations of human nature that the corresponding divine responses could also be expected to have the same character in the two story sets. But confronting what is essentially the same human manifestations, the pre-Sinai YHWH stands forth as a benevolent *deus ex machina* who solves human problems by wondrous acts, while the post-Sinai YHWH is a frightening figure of destructive brutality. In its present shape, the composition juxtaposes two images of 'God' which set together would present a Janus-headed figure of elaborate contrasts.

But other aspects would also have to be included in such a composite. The YHWH of Sinai evokes the stereotyped aspects of a third figure, comparable to Shamash delivering the heavenly laws to the royal mediator. But also the passivity of the divine actor in Egypt, listening to the cry of the people for 430 years, must be represented in the composite image. It could of course be referred to categories of rhetorical function, the people's pain setting out the glories of Exodus. But figures like Job and Qoheleth, as well as the I-figures of the Psalms of Lament, would protest that a God sitting on his hands for 430 years implies too much suffering to be reduced to literary effects. The bare bones of the events of Exodus 1–14, when human suffering and divine passivity are followed by glorious acts of salvation, are remarkably parallel to the event pattern in the Psalms of Lament and Thanksgiving.[129] The

126. E.g. 2 Kgs 19.35; 2 Chron. 20.24-25; Isa. 34.3; 66.24; Jer. 33.5; Amos 8.3; Nah. 3.3.

127. Jer. 31.40; Ezek. 6.5; 43.7, 9.

128. Apart from these examples, the construction with suffix in the second person is found only in Lev. 26.30, in a context which presents a nightmarish vision of a future for 'you' to be avoided at all costs.

129. This connection is underlined by the situations of thanksgiving in Exod. 15.1-21 and 18.1-12.

YHWH of Egypt, Passover and the first journey could be identified as a narrative version of the psalmodic 'My God'. But when the image of the post-Sinai YHWH overlays this type of divine figure, the incongruence becomes rather obvious. This can be illustrated by the book of Job. Facing a plot which involves comparable difficulties, the author solves the problem by attributing the dirtier deeds to Satan, the divine assistant.

Held together as the manifestations of one deity, the images of YHWH in the sacred story represent an astounding collection. It is natural that such a being should represent a secondary collage to modern readers, compiled by fragmented images which reflect the theological development of many hundreds of years, and whose more palatable features legitimately could be reconstructed into a 'God of salvation' or 'liberation', of 'covenantal Torah proclamation' or of some mystical sacramental presence. But by those responsible for the present shape of the composition, these very different, at times revolting, aspects are set together as the manifestations of the one divine actor of the sacred story.[130] While ascribed to 'YHWH' as a narrative persona, the divine manifestations cannot reflect any interest in presenting a general and comprehensive image of this being YHWH, especially not an image which could function as theologically or emotionally attractive to the readers. Just as the divine 'face' was inaccessible to Moses according to Exodus 33, so the divine essence is hidden behind the narrative persona whose very different manifestations correspond to the requirements of the sacred story. The divine actor has a different countenance within each phase. The different aspects must reflect the character of the events set out in the story.

The Sinai events represent the pivotal point for the change of divine behaviour. The divine descent into the world below, the loftiness of the sacred mountain exchanged by a flimsy tent made by human hands, while the theophanic manifestation is given the function of signalling device, marks an astounding change in the divine and human condition. While the people seem to be unaware of the new conditions, the intercession scenes of Exodus 33 have warned the reader that the story is

130. The deliberate character of the composite can also be referred to the two theophanic manifestations of Lev. 9.23–10.2. The meticulous parallelism of the two scenes reflects *in nuce* the contrasts of the pre- and post-Sinai YHWH, just as the contrasting human responses of jubilation and weeping correspond to the emotional colouring of the two journeys.

about to enter a completely new phase. YHWH as 'co-ascender' implies that he will have to destroy the people (vv. 3 and 5). However bitter, the post-Sinai journey presents what the people have to pay for the privilege of divine presence in their midst.

Moses

Compared to the versatility of the divine actor, Moses presents a more staid figure. He is the mediator, set as a channel between the two levels of reality represented by YHWH and the people, faithfully climbing the divine mountain and implementing the divine instructions in the world below. Presented with a rather one-dimensional portrait, the reader is only occasionally permitted a glimpse into the implications of his role. His function as the channel between heaven and earth is profoundly deepened by his remarkably active role in the Golden Calf crisis of Exodus 32–34. When the story has come to a dead end, Moses is both able to control the people and undo what they have done, and skilfully influences the divine actor to continue what he has set in motion. Also more human aspects of his role can be alluded to. The shrill protest of Num. 11.11-15 illustrates the terrible burdens placed upon his shoulders and the tragic dimension of his fate.

His 'revolt' in this episode and the elaboration of his protest in Exodus 3–4 reflect the theme of the 'negative hero'. Parallel to the people, Moses also embodies the human reality when he ascends to the sacred encounter. The parallelism of Moses and people is illustrated by the enigmatic story of revolt in Num. 20.1-13. Both Moses and Aaron are portrayed in revolt, and this is taken to its bitter end by the emotive descriptions of their fates as dying outside the Promised Land, sharing the fate of the revolting people.

But while presented as an embodiment of the human hero of the sacred encounter and thus assigned the same role as the people, Moses mainly reflects the positive aspects of this role. The aspects of negativity, and so also conflict and miraculous change, are primarily embodied by the people. Compared to the Elijah figure, the role of the human hero of the sacred encounter has been shared between two actors, each assigned differing aspects.

The relationship between Moses as the traditional hero of encounter, set against the people as the improbable candidate for the sacred role, is developed by the theme of substitution. His labours serve to have himself substituted by other actors. The theme is intimated from the start of the Moses biography when, according to Exodus 4, Aaron is appointed as his spokesman. But above all, the theme is central for the Sinai and post-Sinai episodes. The story of Exodus 19–40 describes how Moses is substituted by the people set in his place as the new theophanic figure. In addition, the officers of Exodus 18, Aaron the priest, the scribes of Numbers 11, the scouts of Numbers 13–14, until Joshua the warrior is endowed with his 'majesty' in Numbers 27, mark the transfer of functions. According to Exodus 18 this process implies that Moses is set free from his labours to fulfil the higher functions of mediation. On the other hand, the fact that Moses is excluded from the theophanic relationship in Exodus 40 suggests that the substitution also implies aspects other than liberation from ordinary duties. The transfer of Moses' 'spirit' in Numbers 11 and his 'majesty' in Numbers 27 indicates a process of depletion, related not only to duties, but also to personal endowments and ultimately to categories of identity.

This development also adds to the perception of his function as the mediator. The substitution of Moses indicates a process remarkably parallel to the changes taking place on the divine level. The divine descent from the mountain to the world below is mirrored by the transfer of Moses' functions to substitutes who markedly represent human ordinariness. In both cases the process implies a strange movement from 'high' to 'low', when aspects of profoundly sacred character are taken from a corresponding setting and transferred to the baseness of human reality. The fate of the mediator is not only parallel to the fate of the people, but also seems to reflect the changes in the divine reality.

The story does not indicate what it means to the divine actor to be confined to the tent as a signalling device. But in the case of Moses, subtle episodes indicate that his depletion marks the elevation into godlike stature.[131] The apotheosis in Exodus 34 and his godlike role in ch. 39 is juxtaposed to his exclusion from the theophanic experience in ch. 40. The transfer of Moses' spirit to the 70 scribes in Numbers 11 is balanced by his stature as the unique prophet according to Numbers 12. The parallelism of the 'action' of YHWH and Moses in Exodus 18 and of YHWH's and Moses' 'spirits' in Numbers 11 must imply that he has been assigned a new role which transcends the level of a human being.

131. The parallelism of Moses and people as figures of elevation and transformation is above all reflected in Exod. 33–34. Conversely, the theme of substitution is also applied to the people when the men of Num. 14 are substituted by their children.

The enigmatic character of these hints reflects that the elevation of Moses does not represent the central aspects of the sacred story. But for the reader, they provide tantalizing glimpses into the perception of reality which underlies these stories. The imagery of sacred mountain and the impossibility of any direct contact between YHWH of the summit and the people of the world below indicates the immense distance between the two levels of being. But it does not present any absolute barrier. The people are elevated into the intimate relationship of permanent *visio Dei.* Moses seems to be brought beyond the border that separates the divine and human. He can be presented as the substitute of the divine actor, while the emanations of 'horned light' even suggest that he shares in the divine essence.

Thus, for Moses the Sinai events also represent the pivot for two phases of the story. The theme of substitution is continued in the post-Sinai stories when aspects of the Moses function is transferred to new actors. The consistency of this development is illustrated by Exodus 18. On the one hand a short version of the Sinai events, on the other closely related to Numbers 11, the story links the two cycles of Sinai and post-Sinai stories. But while the changes in the Moses biography seem less dramatic than the fates of YHWH and people, his fate also represents a riddle. Above all, this is suggested by what seems a deliberate juxtaposition of Exodus 34 and 40. The godlike stature of Moses as the man inside the Tent of Meeting, whose glory is seen by the people of the outside, is juxtaposed to the counter-image of Moses excluded from the Tent of Meeting while the people are set in a situation of permanent *visio Dei.*

The People

The people present a role as versatile as that of YHWH. In their case, however, the phases of the story are not reflected by what they do, but by what is done to them. The people represent the epitome of passivity, while the active force of the story is represented by the divine actor.[132]

132. The interplay of actors representing forces of 'active' and 'passive' character, with Moses as the 'middle' force of reconciliation, should induce profound musing to anyone adept at Hegelianism. The Egypt stories are centred around the divine initiative, with the people correspondingly passive. In the journey stories, the events are initiated by the people, while the divine actor has to react. But in this case too the manifestation of revolt depicts a people basically passive, however outwardly active. The relationship of Egypt and journey stories is repeated by the

The manifestations of the pre- and post-Sinai people reflect the monotonous repetition of the same inclinations. Left to themselves, this set of heroes would gravitate towards Egypt. Revolting already at the start (Exod. 5.13-23), the people remain essentially the same throughout the story. In spite of the differences when the revolts of the pre- and post-Sinai stories are described, the common reference to aspects of thirst and hunger and enemy crises underlines the monotonous sameness of the people.

Designated to become participants in the situation of encounter, the people are allocated a sacred role. But they present primarily its negative aspects and act as the buffoons of the story, in contrast to Moses who embodies the proper response by a human participant in a sacred endeavour. The composition of Exodus 19–40 is centred around the dilemma of how such actors may take their intended part. Their character as buffoons and their divinely intended role as the heroes of the extraordinary encounter present an absurd clash of contrasts. Only the intercession of Moses and the divine condescension make possible a harmonious outcome.

Only at certain important points is the absurdity of the role allocation added to by other aspects, when the people transcend their normal mode. However distorted, the divine intention to dwell among the people (Exodus 25–31) is mirrored by the people's wish to have gods who can go in front of them. And when YHWH announces that he can not ascend himself, but will send a divine substitute to go in front of the people, they respond with sorrow (Exod. 33.1-6). This is out of character for a set of buffoons and suggests actors who are well aware of what is at stake. And in the building story Exodus 35–39 (cf. also Num. 7–9) the 'heart-driven' people manifests itself in a mode which corresponds to the occasion.

Above all, the positive aspects of the people are indicated by Exod. 40.36-38 and Num. 9.15-23. Permanently related to the theophanic manifestation, the people of the post-Sinai journey are perfectly attuned to the divine will. The impact of these contracted qualifications of the journeying people is prepared for by the positive descriptions of the people in the building story in Exodus 35–39 and the parallel version of

active YHWH of Sinai stories followed by the active–reactive people of the new journey. Exod. 32–34 present an intricate interplay of the people as active and later utterly passive, while Moses in his dealings with the people and especially YHWH is presented in a peculiarly active mode.

Numbers 7–8, concluded by the Passover celebration in Num. 9.1-14. This underlines the effect of stark contrasts when Exod. 40.36-38 and Num. 9.15-23 are followed by the journey stories. The image of the perfect journey by observant visionaries is set against the image of the journey as a series of permanent revolts.

In this way the third actor is also depicted in the shape of a Janus-headed being. Comparable to the contrasts of the pre- and post-Sinai YHWH and of Moses depleted and elevated, the people present the contrasts of perfect and ludicrous embodiments of the sacred role. The formal character of the contrast is especially similar to the manner in which Moses is described. The elevation of Moses represents a subordinate theme, while the theme of substitution is a consistent aspect of his biography. Similarly, the journey as a story of revolt is the central theme for the description of the people. In the Moses biography, Exodus 34 implies a second version of the main story concluded in ch. 40. In the same way, Exod. 40.36-38 and Num. 9.15-23 intimate a version of the journey different from the main story detailed by the revolts. While the reader's attention is drawn to the main story, both versions are set out as equally valid and presented in such a manner that the one does not fundamentally disturb the impression of the other. Left with both sets of impressions, the reader has to ponder the possibility that the miserable journey of permanent revolt 'really' represents the perfect actualization of the divine will, just as the exclusion of Moses 'really' could imply his elevation. At the very least, some connection between a perfect journey of theophanic relationship and a mock version of constant revolt is suggested by the discussion on YHWH himself as co-ascender in Exodus 33. YHWH as co-ascender implies his presence as the people's destroyer. According to these categories, the terrible manifestations of YHWH in the post-Sinai story demonstrate that he is truly present among the people.

But apart from such hints of a formally multi-levelled but internally consistent story, the greater part of the narrative is given over to the negative aspects of the people as a set of Sancho Pancha's destined for the noble role. This also implies that their fate has a tragic dimension. The separation of men and children in Numbers 14 is a condensed expression of such aspects. Reflecting the substitution theme traditionally related to figures of Moses' and Elijah's stature, the emotional force of the situation—doomed fathers and their dependent children walking together for 40 years—is remarkable.[133] The aspects of tragedy are also suggested by the character of the story as a whole. The sacred story is a series of crises. Repeated again and again within each story cycle, the one type of crisis, happily overcome, results in a new type of crisis. The people's suffering in Egypt is followed by the journey crises of water, food and enemies. The miraculous solution of these crises results in the problem of the Sinai stories, when the people of the world below will be brought near to YHWH of the above. The happy ending of this story leads to the crises of the new journey which, moreover, presents a journey of inexorable movement into death. Prepared for by the terrors of divine brutality when YHWH suddenly turns the tables and smites the people, the miserable wail of Num. 17.27-28 represents the natural reaction of a people doomed to embody a sacred role.

These aspects are underlined by the elaboration of the people's revolt in the post-Sinai stories. The imagery of YHWH on the mountain, separated from the people below the mountain, while Moses represents the bridge between high and low, is basic for the story of Exodus 19–40. This imagery implies some perception of the dual character of reality. The divine movement from mountain to camp must suggest that this basic duality between 'high' and 'low' has been overcome. But at the same time the aspects of duality seem to have been transferred to the world below. Now the people reflect different aspects of a new reality profoundly split between 'yes' and 'no'. The perfectly observant people set in a situation of permanent *visio Dei* in Num. 9.15-23 is juxtaposed to a people depicted in permanent revolt. And the character of the revolt has been subtly changed. In the post-Sinai phase the revolt is connected to sub-roles of protagonists that represent the contrasts of 'yes' and 'no'. Numbers 11 introduces a set of stories characterized by internal opposition between clashing tendencies, the violence of which gradually intensifies. Some profound process of 'internalization' is also indicated by the psychological and mental categories of the new type of revolts, which correspond to their heightened emotional character. This development is stressed by the absence of the *deus ex machina* in the post-Sinai stories. Of particular importance for the revolt of Numbers 14, the contrast to Exodus 14 underlines the new demands put on the people. On their own the people are expected to manage the passage from terror to trust.

133. This is underlined by the inverted parallelism of this scene compared to the description of Abraham and his son in Gen. 22.

Above all, the aspects of some profound duality connected to a process of internalization is illustrated by the theme of 'Egyptianism'. The destructive force of YHWH related to an outer conflict with Egypt has been turned against the people. Correspondingly, the plunder of the Egyptians has been turned inwardly into an act of 'self-plundering' according to Exod. 33.6, while the murder of the Egyptian firstborn in Numbers 8 is represented by the Levites as Israel's firstborn. This is supplemented by the internalization of 'Egypt' as the place of attraction, concluded by the wish to return to Egypt. The post-Sinai people are a people in profound inner conflict, the tragic aspects of which is stressed by their character as doomed to failure and the presence of a divine actor who cannot tolerate failures.

On the other hand, the impression of the people's fate as tragic is too easily coloured by the individualistic mind-set of a modern reader.[134] It must be important that 'the people' remains the narrative persona throughout the stories. The significance of this role allocation is illustrated when the people's short-comings result in the divine wish to make a new start by a new set of human actors (Exod. 32.9-14; Num. 14.11-20). When Moses makes YHWH change his mind, the divine condescension means that 'the people' are retained as the persona in the stories that follow. The substitution of the men by the their children in Numbers 14 obviously refers to bitter changes. But however bitter, the story of the people is continued by the children as the embodiment of the narrative persona. Each story cycle presents a different phase of the one movement from Egypt to the Promised Land by the one actor, 'the people'. Each story cycle presents a new set of conditions for the human participants. Just as 'God' manifests himself differently from cycle to cycle, so the people are brought from one level of being to a new level.

Viewed from this perspective, the terrible retributions could as well be perceived as expressions of a process of purification and inner change. The death motifs could even be related to categories of death and rebirth. While extended into a process of 40 years, the relationship of men and children in Numbers 14 implies a process of death and rebirth for the people as the narrative persona. Thus, what are perceived as brutally harsh manifestations on the part of the divine actor could veil much more attractive aspects. This is indicated by the emphasis on

134. Cf. the title of Olson's study: *The Death of the Old and the Birth of the New*.

YHWH as 'merciful' in Exod. 33.19 and 34.6-7. The contextual setting refers this qualification to the post-Sinai reality of co-ascent and terrible death. On the other hand, this context also suggests that the idea of divine 'mercy' should not be translated into too conventional theological stereotypes. Above all, the special character—and some special theological interest—of the narrative seems to be expressed by the choice of the people as the human heroes. The sacred story shaped around such a cast represents a remarkable undertaking. The choice of actors corresponds to the equally remarkable shift of locus from the mountain to the world below, as well as the transfer of the Moses function to figures who present stereotypes of ordinary human reality. Held together, these changes both endow the buffoons of the story with aspects of truly heroic proportions and imply that the qualities of the world above are infused into the reality below.

The emphasis on suffering and death could reflect such aspects. When Moses, the proper hero for a sacred story, was elevated to a singular experience of *visio Dei*, his human nature limited the experience to the 'backside' of the divine reality. The description of the people could refer to similar limitations of perception. However elevated, the people are bound to the dark aspects of a fate truly glorious. The acknowledgment of Egypt as the better fate is a natural expression for how divine 'mercy' must be perceived by a people very much on the way.

The Story

Exodus 19–40, as well as the texts which gradually emerge as relevant for these chapters, indicate a highly complex and subtle system of referential relationships. But while the ramifications of the stories invite the reader into a never-ending pursuit of meaning, the stories begun in Numbers 11 point to the organization of the materials into story cycles as the basic pattern for the composition. Egypt and Exodus, the journey to Sinai, the Sinai event, and the post-Sinai journey present the sacred story as a set of successive phases. Each cycle is centred around some basic situation gradually developed by the monotonous repetition of similar episodes. The transition from cycle to cycle marks the change into a new situation.

Second, the cycles are related to each other in a special order. The retrospective character of Exodus 15 points to the Egyptian events concluded by Exodus and the crossing of the sea as the first cycle. But according to the new event of retrospection in Exod. 18.1-12, the events of Egypt and the pre-Sinai journey are combined into a miraculous story of divine 'actions' which is concluded and can be solemnly celebrated.[135] Verses 13-27 introduce a new set of events, dedicated to the 'actions' of Moses, his substitutes and the people.[136] When the journey is ended by the people brought 'to me' (19.4), the story has entered a new phase. Corresponding to the linkage of Egypt and journey stories, Exod. 40.36-38 and Num. 9.15-23 link the two cycles of Sinai and post-Sinai stories. These passages extend the theophanic relationship of 'the day of erecting the dwelling' into the journey as a whole. The Sinai stories are concluded by the Tent of Meeting set up and filled by the divine presence. But the climactic event of *visio Dei* also represents the permanent situation of the whole post-Sinai journey.

Such a separation between two sets of story cycles, in which Sinai both marks the end of one series of events and a new beginning of a new series, is also reflected by the narrative development. The main actors are the same as before Sinai. But the Sinai events have dramatically changed their relationship. The separation can also be related to the special character of the events presented in Exodus 1–18. The people in movement from Egypt to the sacred mountain—the latter implying a special relationship to its divine inhabitant—presents a series of events which is comparable to the motif structure reflected by the Individual Psalms.[137] Parallel to the Elijah story of 1 Kings 19, Exodus 1–18, including the encounter situation of the following chapters, could be seen as a greatly expanded narrative version of an established hagiographic pattern.[138]

Such a background would profile the special character of the Sinai events in the composition. According to the traditional pattern, the arrival at Sinai should mark the happy conclusion of the preceding events, when the salvation from death and the movement towards the

135. Cf. also the corresponding references in Exod. 19.4 and Num. 14.22 to a sacred story of miraculous intervention.

136. Implicitly, Num. 14 indicates a corresponding separation of the post-Sinai journey concluded by the death of the 'fathers' and new phase of conquest dedicated to 'the children'.

137. Hauge, *Between Sheol and Temple*.

138. Cf. also Smith, *The Pilgrimage Pattern*, pp. 190-91 on 'pilgrimage' as a basic pattern for the Priestly redaction of Exodus.

sacred abode is climaxed by the extraordinary experience of God.[139] But in this version, the people brought 'to me' marks the beginning of a new set of stories. With the people as actors, the climactic event of intimate encounter represents a critical problem, the solution of which makes necessary a protracted series of dramatic events. And when happily solved on 'the day of erecting', the situation of intimate encounter is extended as the central situation of the post-Sinai journey.

In this way, the present organization of the two sets of story cycles also reflects a basic connection with the traditional pattern of events. The story of Exodus 1–18 is continued. The people's movement from Egypt as the negative locality is concluded by the people being brought to the divine 'me', the relationship to 'me' being extended into the two following cycles. But the traditional motifs of the encounter are transformed. Compared to the descriptions of the ideal person 'who' in Psalms 15 and 24 as well as Isa. 33.14-16 is fit to ascend and dwell on the holy mountain, the Sinai stories are dedicated to the question of 'how' the sacred role can be actualized when the people are cast as the 'who'. The traditional concepts of ascent and locus are transferred from the mountain imagery to the idea of a travelling sanctuary and the people's journey together with a divine co-ascender.

The radical character of this transformation is underlined by the way the second set of story cycles is elaborated as a parallel to the first set. On the one hand, the Sinai encounter marks the climax of the story of salvation from Egypt and journey towards the divine 'me'. But also, the Sinai events mark a return to the beginning of the story. Above all, such a return is indicated by the elaboration of the pre- and post-Sinai journey stories. But more subtly, the elaboration of the 'plundering of the Egyptians' theme in the tent stories in Exodus 32–40, the sacrifice of the Levites in Numbers 8, and the parallelism of the Exodus from Egypt and the departure from Sinai, reflect this connection. The key episodes of the first set of story cycles are repeated in the second set and in a way which subtly changes their implications. A story of successive crises has been internalized to situations of conflict within the people, and the outcome of miraculous intervention and wonderful salvation is changed to failure and divine retribution. While the first set of cycles remain important as the basic story, its significance is gradually and subtly unfolded when repeated on a new level in the second set.

139. Cf. Ps. 42 concluded by Ps. 43.3-4 as an expression of the traditional event structure; see also Hauge, *Between Sheol and Temple*, pp. 75-118.

The character of the Passover and journey events as somehow repeatable could reflect a narrative reality of 'circular' character.[140] The neat order of successive events is changed into certain basic phenomena which have to be faced again in a new mode. This could also be related to the other effects of parallelism. Each story cycle is characterized by a key situation monotonusly repeated. Also, more special effects could reflect the 'circularity' of the sacred events. Exodus 35–40, Leviticus 9–10 and Numbers 7–8 present three versions of 'the day of erecting'. In addition, the parallelism of the conclusions in Exod. 40.36-38 and Num. 9.15-23 seems to present the Sinai events as organized into two parallel story sets. Similarly, Exodus 18 has a double function. It concludes the first set of journey stories, but also presents a version of what the Sinai events were all about. Important in this respect are also parallel phenomena elaborated with effects of juxtaposition. The stories of Exodus 32–40 contrast two Tents of Meeting, the first concluded by the apotheosis of Moses and the second by the elevation of the people. Similarly, Exodus 32 and Numbers 8 present two contrasting versions of Levitical sanctification. Held together, such effects must reflect the special character of the sacred story. Somehow, certain episodes have implications that can be perceived only when 'repeated' in different modes.

But while this leaves the impression of rather free-flowing referential effects, the story cycles imply a basic order for the perception of these stories. Set in a framework of narrative linearity, the relationship of the events indicates a series of phases, each story cycle standing on its own as an expression of a special phase of development and followed by a new phase. It is natural to assume that this order must also have repercussions for the perception of the parallel stories within each cycle. Some 'spiral' character of the sacred story—an essential 'something' repeated but differently embodied in a new set of conditions—can be illustrated by the parallelism of the Egyptian army juxtaposed to the children of Israel in Exodus 14 and the grown-ups juxtaposed to the children in Numbers 14. The latter juxtaposition does not completely mirror the former as the 'real' expression of what Exodus 14 was all about. Similarly, the repetition of the Passover murder of the firstborn

140. The basic connection between seemingly different types of events could also be reflected by the tendency to transfer the Sinai categories to the episodes of the pre-Sinai journey, pointed out by Blum (*Studien zur Komposition*, pp. 162-63) as a suggestion that the temporal character of successive events has been 'aufgehoben' ('suspended').

in Numbers 8 does not invalidate the first night of Passover. The basic components of the events are repeated on a new level of development, 'development' referring both to the narrative stage as well as to the disposition of the narrative figures.

The references of Exod. 12.35-38 could illustrate such a connection between the events. Rather loosely set into the story, this passage presents aspects of the departure from Egypt. Both the plundering of the Egyptians and the description of the train composed of men and children have been prepared in the preceding stories and thus are part of the Egyptian crisis happily concluded. But in addition to such a function, the references are important for the Sinai and post-Sinai stories. Some aspects of the primordial events are carried along, their real significance hidden until the story has reached a new phase. The implications of the Egyptian plunder, the 'rabble', and the juxtaposition of soldiers and 'little children', are contained in embryo all the way from Egypt. Somehow, the solution of one crisis implies a new tension of opposed tendencies. Some seeds of a new duality on a different level are brought along and matured by the events to come into a new crisis brought closer to the core of the people's being. In this way, the narrative development seems to present the unfolding of lawful events. And when the references of Exod. 12.35-38 prepare for the revolts of the post-Sinai journey, these episodes too—which in a sacred story should represent the very epitomes of impropriety—are presented as equally lawful. The situation of permanent revolt is also part of what has to be in a story of ordinary people brought to the divine 'me'.

Postscript: The Reader as Whore and Potential Saint

The shape of the composition must also have repercussions for the type of reader who was envisaged by the authors. Basically, the shape seems configured to an active type of reading. The effects of parallelism and repetition together with the subtle system of allusions imply that the perception of meaning is a function of the referential connections. What at the beginning seems to represent a rather simple organization of stories turns into an ever-growing web of referential relationships. While 'context' must primarily refer to the successive order of the stories which indicates the basic order of how the materials are to be read, other types of 'contextual' relationships gradually emerge as important. Moreover, the subtlety of these references—the examples observed above probably being the most salient expressions for the compositional mode—makes the question of meaning a function of the reader's ability of perception. The compositional mode seems to imply that ultimately any perception of the sense of the stories has to be of a subjective character, dependent on what echoes of which stories are called forth in the process of reading.

The radical character of this open-endedness is illustrated by the development of what must represent central ideas in the composition. The idea of the divine movement from above to below is underlined by the corresponding development of the substitution of Moses by actors very much of the world below. To a modern reader such a qualification of ordinary human reality as the locus of sacred manifestation would be as applicable to some massively hierarchical ritualism as to some offshoot of the 'God is dead' movement. To the ancient readers, the implications of the idea probably represented comparably different theological postures.[1] The ambiguity of the central concepts seems to presuppose that, sooner or later, the reader will have to enter into some dialogue with the text. Corresponding to the fundamental character of

1. Cf. Chapter 5.3 on Num. 16.3.

the questions raised, the dialogue must imply the reader's stand on what life is all about. The open-ended character of the composition as well as of the central concepts suggest that the texts can relate to many types of projected meaning. Generously encompassing very different mental projections, the composition seems shaped to return them strangely blurred and profoundly enriched.

The special elaboration of the central concepts could even indicate that the disturbance of established ideas represents the main thrust of the authors' efforts. The sacred story, both as a literary exposition of conventional themes and as a theological treatise on the relationship of 'God and man', must have touched upon religious stereotypes of fundamental character. The elaboration of these stereotypes seems intended to inspire a process of pondering, to disturb as well as provoke, the subtle echoes caused by the referential effects leading to ever new questions on the significance of what is read. Thus, whatever the stand of the reader, the stories are badly read if they do not invite some form of departure.

Due to our ignorance of the contemporary religious conditions which more sharply could underline the concerns of the authors, such vague suppositions must represent the basic conclusion on the function of the stories. But on one point it is necessary to venture a bit further. The sophisticated mode of the literary address, together with its ambitious scope and sheer size, as well as its history of reception, must point to some established setting both for its production as well as for its reception. The sacred story in its present shape presupposes some established milieu both for its origin and its reception, characterized by the preoccupation with certain traditions as well as by the potential capacity to respond to a new and rather radical reinterpretation of fundamental concepts.

A concrete setting of such a character was suggested by Wilcoxen in 1968.[2] According to his ideas, the present shape of the Pentateuchal traditions presupposes the 'patterning activity' of 'redactors' which reflects the fact that the traditions have been used by many generations for the religious education of the young. The educational function gradually influenced the narrative structure, resulting in an 'analogical structure' when the educators used 'the imaginative power of the traditions to speak to their sons and help them grasp the interior meaning of

2. Wilcoxen, 'Some Anthropocentric Aspects'.

"growing up Israelite"'. While the contents of the stories are highly theocentric, 'the structure and function may be just as anthropocentric'.[3]

Concretely, the influence of the educational setting, expressed through the principles of 'analogical structure', resulted in the sacred history as a description of how Israel 'the man' was made. The five themes of the Pentateuchal narratives which present the making of Israel, correspond to five stages in the development of a man.[4] After the birth of exodus, Sinai represents the initiation of the people as the *bar mitzvah*, at which point moral responsibility begins. Accordingly, the lenient treatment of Israel before Sinai reflects the pre-adolescent childhood, while the trials after Sinai correspond to the period from adolescence to adulthood. The latter is connected with categories of social integration, with a divinely sanctioned order for the people's communal life related to juvenile revolt or adult acceptance.[5]

This process of 'patterning' is primarily due to the function of the sacred story in the religious education. The traditions were 'in some measure deliberately shaped', while it is 'improbable...that any group of Israelites ever consciously decided to artificially shape their sacred history according to the stages of development of a man's life'.[6]

Although his argument is rather loosely related to textual data, Wilcoxen's emphasis on function as significant for the composition also in its final shape is worthy of attention. Moreover, his ideas on background and function seem remarkably well suited to the formal shape of the composition, and could well explain why the story is as it is. The contrast of the journey stories before and after Sinai is emphasized as vital for our understanding of the composition. Related to categories of religious education and experience, the formal organization of the materials implies 'development' and 'stages of development' as key concepts.

This corresponds to the findings offered in the present study. For the function of 'the people', retained as the narrative figure throughout the different story cycles, 'stages of development' must be a relevant description. According to the transition from one cycle to the next, the people pass from one set of experiences to another. Not only is the

3. Wilcoxen, 'Some Anthropocentric Aspects', p. 350.
4. Wilcoxen, 'Some Anthropocentric Aspects', p. 347.
5. Wilcoxen, 'Some Anthropocentric Aspects', pp. 347-50.
6. Wilcoxen, 'Some Anthropocentric Aspects', p. 350.

identity of the narrative figure retained, but also, through the effects of repetition and parallelism, certain key phenomena are returned to in new versions and presented as relevant for the people on a new stage. Further, the categories of 'development' imply that the biographical—or, rather, hagiographical—data related to Israel as the narrative persona have a special function as references to the religious biography of the reader. This implies a process of 'identification' as the basic mode of reading. The actors of the sacred story represent paradigmatic figures for later generations.

Implicitly or explicitly, such a reading has represented the traditional scholarly model when questions of function have been pondered.[7] This is especially true for certain central motifs which, read in the literal sense, have seemed easily transferable to historical situations perceived as particularly important.[8] When such insights are related not just to

7. Most directly illustrated by the perception of later redactional layers as expressions for a new theological interest projected into the older traditions. Such a process implies that the literary figures are seen as the negative and positive mirrors of the redactors' contemporary situation. Thus, for Budd (*Numbers*, p. 163), the Yahwist ponders the lessons of 721 BCE; for Utzschneider (*Das Heiligtum*) the Priestly story on the sanctuary reflects the problems of the post-exilic community on how to integrate the traditional temple cult with Torah piety. The process has been given a particularly clear expression by Olson (*Death of the Old*), for whom the concern of the book of Numbers is to establish a model or paradigm which will invite every generation to put itself in the place of the new generation (p. 183). The present location of Deuteronomy as well as the whole Pentateuch also reflects this concern, retaining the perspective of the new generation as a hermeneutical paradigm for all succeeding generations (p. 188).

8. The land motifs have been of special significance in this respect, their paradigmatic application connected with a historical situation of Exile or national crisis. Given the established character of such readings, it is remarkable that Olson (*Death of the Old*, pp. 185-86) cautiously suggests other types of hermeneutical reference. Also for Olson, the early layer of the Priestly tradition which established the structure of Numbers reflects the problems of Exile and the post-exilic period. But the later Priestly additions and redactions were not confined to the interests of this period. The experience of the Exile with the people awaiting a return to the land corresponds to the portrait of the new generation in Numbers. But as 'every generation of God's people' has a corresponding experience of 'living between promise and fulfillment', 'the stance of the new generation on the verge of entering the long-awaited land of promise has continued to be the definitive portrait of the community of God's people throughout its history' (p. 186). However vaguely, this must indicate that the older traditions were read metaphorically by the authors represented in the latest layers.

certain layers or to isolated parts of the sacred story, the central aspects of Wilcoxen's ideas seem well configured to the compositional mode. But to me, one particularly important supposition stands out as questionable. Wilcoxen's emphasis on a setting of religious education related to young people identifies juvenile experiences with the fate of the people. This cannot be reconciled to the character of the stories. Such a setting could hardly have 'patterned' the sacred story into its present shape, with its frightening implications of human suffering and divine harshness. Transcribed by Wilcoxen, the post-Sinai stories are 'trials' and 'tests' which present the alternatives of juvenile revolt or adult acceptance.[9] This description would conform rather nicely to some general educational programme of uplifting character, but badly to the bloody categories of the actual stories.[10] If educational, the programme of this composition refers to a post-graduate course of advanced character and with teachers correspondingly qualified. Only jaded students can be invited to identify with a hagiographical pattern of slavery in Egypt contrasted with a much more dangerous relationship with YHWH on a journey which leads to death and rebirth, followed by a new movement towards a land peopled by the 'children of Anak'.[11]

This impression is stressed by the sophisticated character of the literary effects and the corresponding demands put on the reader. The mental agility demanded by the compositional mode of parallelism and repetition indicates a milieu of rather elite character. Both with regard to religious experiences and to their literary manifestations, the character of the composition must reflect some community of correspondingly advanced character.

Such a setting could also, at least to a certain degree, indicate the background for the special elaboration of the central concepts. The shift

9. Wilcoxen, 'Some Anthropocentric Aspects', pp. 347-50.

10. Such aspects are better reflected by Olson (*Death of the Old*), when stressing the significance of the death motifs in Num. 13–14. But in this case too the impact of the stories is only partially transmitted and thus implicitly changed into the stereotypes of a modern and more palatable religiosity: the old generation have a negative function of warning, while the new generation represents the figure of identification for 'God's people' (pp. 183-88).

11. This argument seems to be negated by the modern use of these stories for the religious education of the very young. But there is a marked difference between the impact of stories freshly perceived and a perception dulled by centuries of conventional applications and apologetic omissions. Such a process seems the unhappy lot of any 'canonized' text.

of locus from above to below and the corresponding shift from Moses to people as theophanic figures represents an astounding reinterpretation of religious stereotypes. Within a religious grouping of elite character, such a rendering of the sacred story must have had quite a strong impact.

An impact of such a character—with corresponding effects of reinterpretation and a new religious practice—could also be related to the Torah theme of the stories. The significance of ordinary human reality as the locus of theophanic presence corresponds to the special elaboration of the extraordinary encounter as an event of Torah instruction. The arrival at the divine mountain marks the conclusion of one phase of the sacred story and the introduction of a new phase when the sacred story has to start all over again in a new mode. The character of the new mode is indicated by the categories of human 'action', embodied by instructions which prescribe the details of ordinary human life as the way to holiness. In this way, the shape of the story could present a concrete illustration of what the hagiographical pattern means when related to the categories of Torah.

1. *The Reader According to Numbers 15.37-41*

If the stories can be regarded as paradigms, with a function related to the religious practice of the readers, it is necessary to probe the relationship between the two levels of reality represented by the literary figures and the addressed readers. The established models of paradigmatic reading presuppose a rather direct relationship between the two levels. This is demonstrated by the motifs of 'land' and 'temple' which traditionally have served as a *tertium comparationis* when the text should be linked to the level of application. The relationship to the Promised Land is important in the Pentateuch. This concept is seen as the vehicle for later theological interests when the relationship to the 'land' as a sociopolitical entity was of special importance. Such a reading presupposes a direct relationship between theological interest and literary expression. The concept of 'land' in the Pentateuchal stories is identified with its assumed significance for later generations in a special historical situation.

Such a reading could represent a rather limited perspective for the perception of the land motifs in the Pentateuch.[12] This is illustrated by

12. The implications of the traditional reading are illustrated by the discussion

the corresponding limitation of the number of the historical periods that can be regarded as suitable for the production of the texts. The Pentateuchal layers are traditionally related to certain periods in Israel's history which are recognized as periods of political success or—usually—crisis. In the earlier phase of historical investigation, the offer of possibilities for theologically important situations was quite varied. But the reductionism of modern historians with regard to what parts of Israel's past can be legitimately presented as 'historical' has increasingly led to the Exile and lately, more and more monotonously, the post-exilic period as the only possible setting for the theological reflection presented in the Pentateuch.[13]

The idea that the texts reflect a process in which contemporary political and religio-sosiological problems were solved in the disguise of Pentateuchal figures may of course be relevant. At the very least, passages like Leviticus 26 and Deuteronomy 4 illustrate some basic connection between the Pentateuchal application of the land motifs and Israel's experience of Exile. But even so, the traditional scholarly reading is problematical in its presupposition that the relationship to the 'land' as a political entity, as well as the existence of 'Israel' as a political or social entity, represents the central interest of 'Old Testament religion'. In its turn, this presupposition results from a rather simplistic hermeneutical model. As a matter of course the Pentateuchal land motifs are equated to what the 'land' is assumed to represent in historical situations of a special character. The attraction of 'the land' as a socio-political entity, reflecting those aspects of the texts which are meaningful to a modern reader as data for a religio-historical reconstruction, has excluded other types of linkage between literary expressions and theological interest.

Similarly, motifs that refer to connotations of temple and ritual practice have formed an important medium of linkage between the literary

of the dating of the Pentateuch offered by N.P. Lemche, *Die Vorgeschichte Israels: Von den Anfängen bis zum Ausgang des 13. Jahrhunderts v. Chr.* (Biblische Enzyklopädie, 1; Stuttgart: W. Kohlhammer, 1996), pp. 213-18.

13. For example, the Yahwist of von Rad, reflecting early and even premonarchical attitudes to the land as a divine gift. In contrast, the Yahwist is related to the crisis of 721 BCE by Budd (*Numbers*, p. 163), to a Deuteronomistic frame by Van Seters (*The Life of Moses*) while Lemche (*Die Vorgeschichte Israels*, p. 217) suggests that the Pentateuch should be regarded as 'Diasporaliteratur' (the literature of the Diaspora).

situation and the assumed historical setting for the theological message of the texts. Also in this case, the linkage is assumed to be of a direct character. Further, the connotational impact of the motifs is related to the down-to-earth categories of institutional reality. The textual references to ritual categories are equated with the authors' or their contemporaries' assumed relationship with the temple institution. The presentation of the Tent of Meeting reflects what took place or should have taken place in the contemporary cult, primarily related to the Jerusalem temple, whether rebuilt or in ruins. And when the Priestly layers are added to the older layers, the result of the redactional process is perceived as a mechanical fusion. The concerns of the different layers are not organically connected, but the Yahwist's concerns about the people's relationship to the land are supplemented by the Priestly interest in the institutional cultic practices and how they can be related to the Moses tradition.

Just as the passages of Leviticus 26 or Deuteronomy 4 illustrate the significance of the categories of Exile as an actual mode of reading, it would be presumptuous to refuse any connection between the ritual references of the stories and the concrete cultic practices of Israel. What I perceive as positively wrong, and fatally so, is the attraction of a certain type of phenomenon as essential for the perception of what the texts are really all about, leading to the exclusion of other phenomena. The traditional reading of land and temple motifs presupposes a direct relationship between the textual reality and the reality of the addressed reader. The two levels are linked by certain phenomena of conceptual character, assumed to be common to both levels and of equal significance. When the common concepts are reduced to categories of a religio-sociological or political character, recognizable as 'real' for a modern reader, the perception of the texts is rather constricted.

However traditional for the scholarly reading, such a simple hermeneutical model hardly corresponds to the subtleties of the texts. The effects of parallelism and repetition imply modes of reading that transcend the categories of a literal type of linkage. Apart from the observations discussed above, Num. 15.37-41 permits a unique glimpse into how the narrative reality can be related to the reality of the readers.

The relationship between Numbers 14 and 15 has posed a special problem.[14] The central parts of the scouts' story have usually been

14. Illustrated by the efforts to find some relationship to the narrative context in Olson, *Death of the Old*, pp. 170-74.

related to the Yahwist, while ch. 15 is connected to Priestly traditions.[15] Formally, ch. 15 continues the preceding chapter, presenting an episode of divine instruction which follows upon the scouts' episode. According to this setting, the addressed 'you' of ch. 15 are identical with the people of the preceding chapter. At the same time, some distance is indicated by the introductions of vv. 2 and 18 which refer to a situation when 'you' are settled in the land. And according to v. 38, the addressees include the coming generations.

The application of the 'scout' (*tûr*) motif in v. 39 is important as a reference to the preceding story.[16] The people shall put tassels on their clothes 'so you can see it so you can remember all the commandments of YHWH so you can do them and not go 'scouting after' your heart and after your eyes, as you are whoring after them' (v. 39). Apart from the sense 'scout after', indicated by the relationship with the preceding episode, *tûr* can also refer to mental categories.[17] But set in the formulaic language of vv. 39b-41,[18] the application of *tûr* stands out. Given the significance of the motif for the story of Numbers 13–14, it is natural to conclude that it connects the instructions to the story of the scouts.

This is stressed by the comparable connection between *zānâ* in Num. 15.39 and *z*ᵉ*nût* in Num. 14.33. The application of this term in the latter text is as peculiar[19] as that of *tûr* in Num. 15.39. The parallel use of such special terms in the two texts must have a referential function, signalling the connection of the two texts. Accordingly, the relationship

15. For example, as a repository of late ritual law (Levine, *Numbers 1–20*, p. 386). But according to Budd (*Numbers*, pp. 155, 177), the Priestly author of Num. 15 has left an important mark on the shape of the scouts' story.

16. Wenham, *Numbers*, p. 126, Budd, *Numbers*, p. 178.

17. Used with *dāraš* in Eccl. 1.13, and with *da'at* and 'seek after wisdom' in 7.25. In both cases, the activity referred to is connected with the 'heart', which sets the direction for the mental 'exploration'. This is comparable to the application in Num. 15.39 where the 'scouting after heart and eyes' together with a parallel 'whoring after them' identifies the heart and eyes as organs of inclinations and wishes. For Levine, *Numbers 1–20*, p. 401, the verb extended with 'after' indicates a passive meaning 'to be led about'.

18. Reflecting the style of the Holiness Code according to de Vaulx (*Les Nombres*, p. 187), while for Budd (*Numbers*, p. 177) the linguistic connections both with the Holiness Code and Deuteronomy indicate a Priestly author familiar with these traditions.

19. Illustrated by Budd, *Numbers*, p. 153, who sees v. 33 as part of an 'emphatic gloss', having a strong affinity to Ezek. 23.35.

to the tassels is presented as the antidote to the attitude illustrated by Numbers 13–14.

Such a connection is also reflected by the motifs of seeing. Juxtaposed to the wrong 'scouting after heart and eyes', 'seeing the tassels' represents the positive attitude. This corresponds to the significance of the motif of seeing in Numbers 13–14 and Exodus 14. Underlined by the formulaic language, 'seeing' is related both to the perception of the enemies' might and of the divine manifestation, the contrasts of perception connected with the contrasts of fear and trust. This corresponds to the contrasts of Num. 15.39-40 with a comparable connection between experience and emotional-mental categories. 'Scouting after heart and eyes' is contrasted with 'seeing the tassels' which leads to the remembrance of the divine instructions and to the state of holiness. The significance of the address is underlined by the concluding 'I am YHWH'-formulas of v. 41 (cf. Exod. 14.4, 17-18; Num. 14.21-22).

In this way, the instructions on the tassels in Numbers 15 link the address to 'you' to the story of the scouts in Numbers 14. The linkage indicates some form of identity between the narrative level and the level of applicatory address. This is primarily expressed by the parallelism of the two sets of figures, which present both 'they' and 'you' in a situation of 'scouting' and 'whoring' related to two contrasted modes of 'seeing'. The parallelism is added to by the formulaic language of v. 4, asserting that 'you' also are brought from Egypt by YHWH. 'They' and 'you' are essentially identical, having the sacred story in common. This relationship is stressed by the contextual relationship which formally identifies the addressed 'you' in Numbers 15 with the people of Numbers 14.

But at the same time, the shift to the land as the place of implementation (Num. 15.2, 18) and the extension to the coming generations (v. 38) separate the two situations of 'scouting'. The group of 'you' is extended to include figures not actually present in the preceding episode. The address of 'you' must even primarily refer to the reader as part of the extended people. More importantly, the levels of narrative and application are separated by the different situations that are implied. Numbers 14 refers to a concrete crisis, Numbers 15 to a permanent situation of general 'scouting'. A singular episode when the people failed to take possession of the land is related to a general situation of religious practice qualified by the contrasts of 'whoring' and 'holiness'.

The difference between the narrative episode and a situation of religious practice is also reflected by the qualification of the two sets of actors. The narrative figures are separated into the juxtaposed groups of positive and negative scouts related to the people as children and grown-ups. The addressees of Numbers 15 represent scouts who can turn from negative scouting to positive seeing, and who thus embody the being of whores as well as of potential saints. The whore can be deflected from the ways of the wandering eyes and heart when the eyes are firmly set upon the tassels.

In this way, the relationship of the two texts reflects the shift from narrative to the level of application. The formal connection between the two groups of actors and the use of certain terms and concepts state the basic identity of the two groups. At the same time, the shift of situation and the imperceptible shift of actors reflect the difference between narrative and application. The reader is both present in the story and at the same time is its observer. The story presents the character of 'scouting' and its consequences are related to actors bound to experience the death of the army. In contrast, the reader is both participating and observing, on the one hand suffering the agony of fathers and children, on the other hand free of the chains of the narrative, and thus able to learn from the story to change the ways of 'scouting'.

The significance of such a transition from narrative figures to participating observers is underlined by a comparable shift from 'they' to 'we' in Num. 17.27-28. The shift concludes the dramatic story on priestly 'nearness' in Numbers 16–17. In this case, the transition from narrative to application is not formally marked, compared to the change from narrative to divine instructions in Numbers 15. 'We', identified as the people in Num. 17.27, are part of the story, witnessing and commenting upon the three ordeals of Num. 16.34, 17.6 and finally 17.27-28. As narrative figures, the people are separated from the main protagonists, observing the struggle for the priestly 'nearness' by Aaron and the usurpers. But with the concluding cry of anguish, the main theme of 'coming near' as well as the fate of death is suddenly related to the people. 'We' are the real actors of the story, and the usurpers and Aaron serve as illustrations of what priestly holiness implies.

The type of application represented by Num. 17.27-28 is comparable to 15.37-41. In both cases, the relationship of narrative figures and the figures of application is indicated by the parallelism of central motifs, 'scouting' and 'whoring' corresponding to the use of 'death' and 'nearness' motifs. It must also be important that in both cases the change from story to application expressed by the shift of actors is rather fluid. 'We' the people participate in the story of Numbers 16–17, while the setting of ch. 15 after 14 identifies 'you' with the people of the scouts' story. But while formally imperceptible, the implications of the shift are important. 'Nearness' is transferred from institutional categories of priesthood to the people, while the 'scouting' of the addressees in Numbers 15 is set in a situation of general religious practice.

The narrative presents concrete events centred around certain figures, the main issue of the events being transferred to a new group both separate from and yet essentially identical with the narrative figures. Both as scouts and as priestly candidates, the narrative protagonists have a representative function. The story is not told for its own sake as, for example, the expression of an interest in sacred figures or important events of the past, but is intended for the level of application.

The two texts also indicate the character of the application and thus the point when the meaning of the story is unfolded. The critical point in the transition from narrative to application is reached by a process of identification, when the narrative figures are perceived as embodiments of some aspect of being which is vital to the addressee. Without the recognition that 'they' are 'we', the instructions on the tassels obviously will not be observed. Having been identified as 'scout' and thus equipped with 'scouting eyes', the need to fix eyes on the tassels will have meaning.

In this way the narrative figures seem to have a function of truly paradigmatic character, representing the observers to the point that 'they' become 'we'. On the other hand, it is important that the narrative situation does not have any direct or literal relationship to the situation of application. Compared with the traditional assumptions on a direct relationship between the levels of narrative and application, which are illustrated by the use of the land and temple motifs, Numbers 13–15 and 16–17 indicate a much more distant and indirect relationship. The process of identification requires a subtle mental transfer from one level to the other until 'they' become 'we'. The wandering eye and the fate of lethal holiness are in common and represent the points of identification. In this respect, the relationship reflects an essential identity between the two sets of actors. But what to scholarly analysis represent highly important subject-matters—on one hand the failed conquest of the land and on the other the legitimacy of the priestly institution—are of subordinate significance, except as an illustration of what constitutes 'scouting' and 'holiness' on the level of application. This does not imply that the subject-matters are unimportant. The connotational impact of the central concepts must demonstrate what really is at stake. The people of the wandering eye witness the potentialities of their disposition dramatized by the scouts' story, while the people destined for priesthood face the implications of their fate by the extraordinary ordeals of Numbers 16–17. Presenting paradigms, the narratives are important as descriptions of religious reality, influencing the reader's perception of what a life related to YHWH is all about. But the relationship of 'they' and 'you/we' indicates what type of interest has been decisive for the shaping of the stories.

In both texts, the application of the stories refers to religious experience and practice. Equally important, categories of individual religiosity are referred to. This is obvious in the case of the tassels. But the impression of individual categories is underlined by the character of the two applications. The tension of the stories is connected with the people split between the interaction of sub-figures which is concluded by the contrasts of losers and victors. On the level of application, these constellations are transferred to the inner reality of the religious practitioner. When 'you' as the 'scouting whore' are prescribed the tassels as the way to holiness, the interaction of the narrative figures is internalized. The relationship of negative and positive figures is transferred to categories of mental and psychic character, connected with the religious practice of a 'you' who, moreover, embodies the scouting whore and a potential saint. Similarly, the contrasts of usurpers and the truly chosen priest of Numbers 16–17 are transferred to the spectators doomed to 'nearness'.

By such a linkage, the interaction of the narrative figures represents the interaction of the reader's inclinations and dispositions. The essential aspects of the reader's inner reality are enlarged and underlined by the narrative figures. This makes it possible to experience the real significance of what takes place in the inner world. The addressees share the depths and the heights represented by the narrative figures. For 'you' both the state of whoring and of holiness are equally relevant, the former the natural state of being, while holiness is presented as the result of religious practice.

This must also have repercussions for the type of religiosity practised by the addressees as composites of sharply contrasted and conflicting inclinations and possibilities. 'You' as whore and potential saint represents a dual being. Moreover, the duality is not related to some kind of permanent co-existence of the two beings. The religious practice is directed against the inclinations of the whore and aims at the state of holiness. This implies the category of struggle. Mental and emotional aspects connected with an internal struggle between conflicting inclinations must have been essential to the religious practice of such a 'you'.

Such aspects can be related to the conflicts of the post-Sinai stories. Moreover, they can also be mirrored by the sacred story as a whole, each story cycle presenting the people stuck in some critical situation, which, when happily solved, is followed by a new type of crisis. The people enslaved in Egypt are saved by the Exodus which entails the crises of food and water, followed by the duality of 'high' and 'low' in the Sinai stories. When these aspects are united by the divine descent from the mountain and a corresponding shift from Moses to people as theophanic figures, a new set of contrasts is introduced by the post-Sinai stories in which representatives of the people embody the struggle of opposed tendencies.

The sharp contrasts of the stories seem to reflect a perception of reality as basically dual in character, the duality representing an intolerable state which must be overcome by the interaction of divine and human actors. This also implies that categories of development and change are part of this religiosity of struggle. The addressees of Numbers 15 as whores and potential saints represent an apt contraction of such aspects, suggesting a religiosity of radical inner change connected with some form of transformation of being. With the eyes of a whore, 'you' are a candidate for sainthood when the eyes are firmly fixed upon the tassels. This also means that to the adressees, the events of the story have not yet come to pass. With the instructions implemented, the sacred journey of 'you' can proceed. And having been brought from Egypt[20], the reality of 'you' is not confined to the categories of the scouts' episode but encompasses, potentially, the whole sacred story in all its aspects. This must also include the miraculous categories of the first story-cycles as well as the divine intervention of

20. The qualification of 'you' as brought from Egypt indicates that at some special points, the narrative reality is directly identified with the situation of the addressees. This differs from the distant and indirect type of relationship indicated by the two types of 'scouting' in Num. 14 and 15. Such a difference could be related to the significance of certain key episodes which represent the basic categories for the composition as well as for the practical religiosity involved.

the latter cycles. Saved from Egypt and brought to Sinai, the post-Sinai 'you' have obviously reached a state of being for which human 'action', in obedience to the divine demands, is essential for the sacred story to continue.

Also, it must be important for this type of religiosity that the aspects of inner duality and struggle are not coloured by moralistic indignation or blunt exhortation. Limited to the narrative context, the contrasts of Numbers 14 are usually perceived as expressions of an exhortatory interest, the positive and negative scouts together with the men and children understood as negative and positive paradigms to be rejected and imitated by the reader.[21] But the religiosity represented by the application in Numbers 15 reflects a much more complex and subtle understanding of the human condition, even if the latter is obviously negatively valued. Depicted in a permanent situation of negative scouting and whoring, 'you' as a matter of course embody the reality of the negative figures doomed to death. Related to this situation, the tassels provide some concrete anchorage for the drifting eye, making possible the transformation of the whore. Compared with the atmosphere of doom and tragedy in the story, the application in Numbers 15 suggests a religiosity of practical and rather cheerful character. The state of sainthood is truly attainable by the natural whore. Obviously, this process is characterized by inner conflict and struggle, the serious character of which is underlined by the tragic dimension of the narratives. But the linear development of the composition, connected with the imagery of Exodus and journey, emphatically presents the potentiality of the human condition. That this understanding also includes aspects of tolerant acceptance and humour—of a rather earthy kind—is suggested by the repeated revolt scenes. As projections of the practitioners' inner reality, these images must reflect the rich and subtly varied character of the religiosity involved.

This richness also puts a corresponding demand upon the reader's organs of perception. The mental agility required is illustrated by the applications in Num. 15.37-41 and 17.27-28. Compared to the solidity of land and temple motifs when read as antedated projections of late political and cult-institutional crises, the leap from the narrative drama to tassels, or to the wondrous rod of Aaron as relevant for 'we', requires mental operations of a rather lofty character. A kind of reader is

21. E.g. Olson, *Death of the Old*, p. 183.

addressed whose abilities of creative imagination are on a par with the standards of the authors. Moreover, such a reading corresponds to the general impression of the character of the narrative materials. The referential effects connected with repetition and parallelism invite one to a process of dialogue between text and reader, the active contribution of the latter providing a necessary part of what comes out as the 'message'. If such categories seem to refer to mental processes of a rather lofty and subjective character, the religiosity of Numbers 15 indicates that they are firmly rooted in practical reality.

The application of the narrative in Num. 15.37-41, underlined by 17.27-28, also implies a practical mode of reading. The meaning of the story is connected with a discipline of 'participatory reading' characterized by a process of identification. When one is able to find oneself represented by the narrative figures and the significance of one's own reality is recognized by what is played out on the textual scene, the story has a meaning. And corresponding to the making of tassels and the wandering eye firmly fixed, the recognition of oneself in the story also must include some practical measure. Ultimately, the meaning of the story emerges when it is actualized by its real hero, the reader.

BIBLIOGRAPHY

Allen, L.C., *Ezekiel 20–48* (WBC, 29; Dallas: Word Books, 1990).

Alter, R., *The Art of Biblical Narrative* (New York: Basic Books, 1981).

Aurelius, E., *Der Fürbitter Israels: Eine Studie zum Mosebild im Alten Testament* (CBOTS, 27; Stockholm: Almquist & Wiksell, 1988).

Barstad, H.M., *A Way in the Wilderness: The 'Second Exodus' in the Message of Second Isaiah* (JSSM, 12; Manchester: Manchester University Press, 1989).

—*The Myth of the Empty Land: A Study in the History and Archeology of Judah During the 'Exilic' Period* (Symbolae Osloenses, Fasc. Suppl. 28; Oslo: Scandinavian University Press, 1996).

—'History and the Hebrew Bible', in L.L. Grabbe (ed.), *Can a 'History of Israel' be Written?* (JSOTSup, 245; Sheffield: Sheffield Academic Press, 1997), pp. 37-64.

Barton, J., *Reading the Old Testament: Method in Biblical Study* (London: Darton, Longman & Todd, 2nd edn, 1996).

Berge, K., *Die Zeit des Jahwisten: Ein Beitrag zur Datierung jahwistischer Vätertexte* (BZAW, 186; Berlin: W. de Gruyter, 1990).

—*Reading Sources in a Text: Coherence and Literary Criticism in The Call of Moses: Models—Methods—Micro-Analysis* (Arbeiten zu Text und Sprache im Alten Testament, 54; St Ottilien: Eos Verlag, 1997).

Beyerlin, W., *Wider die Hybris des Geistes: Studien zum 131. Psalm* (SBS, 108; Stuttgart: Katholisches Bibelwerk, 1982).

—*Weisheitlich-kultische Heilsordnung: Studien zum 15. Psalm* (Biblisch-Theologische Studien, 9; Neukirchen–Vluyn: Neukirchener Verlag, 1985).

Blum, E., *Studien zur Komposition des Pentateuch* (BZAW, 189; Berlin: W. de Gruyter, 1990).

Booij, T., 'Mountain and Theophany in the Sinai Narrative', *Bib* 65 (1984), pp. 1-26.

Braun, R., 'Solomon, the Chosen Temple Builder: The Significance of 1 Chronicles 22, 28, and 29 for the Theology of Chronicles', *JBL* 95 (1976), pp. 581-90.

Brichto, H.Ch., 'The Worship of the Golden Calf: A Literary Analysis of a Fable on Idolatry', *HUCA* 54 (1983), pp. 1-44.

Brinkman, J., *The Perception of Space in the Old Testament: An Exploration of the Methodological Problems of its Investigation, Exemplified by a Study of Exodus 25–31* (Kampen: Kok Pharos, 1992).

Bronner, L., *The Stories of Elijah and Elisha as Polemics against Baal Worship* (POS, 6; Leiden: E.J. Brill, 1968).

Brueggemann, W., 'The Kerygma of the Priestly Writer', *ZAW* 84 (1972), pp. 397-414.

Budd, P.J., *Numbers* (WBC, 5; Waco: Word Books, 1984).

Cassuto, U., *A Commentary on the Book of Exodus* (trans. I. Abrahams; Jerusalem: Magnes Press, 1967).

Childs, B.S., *The Book of Exodus: A Critical, Theological Commentary* (Philadelphia: Westminster Press, 1974).

— 'A Traditio-Historical Study of the Reed Sea Tradition', *VT* 20 (1970), pp. 406-18.

Christensen, D.L., 'Narrative Poetics and the Interpretation of the Book of Jonah', in E.R. Follis (ed.), *Directions in Biblical Hebrew Poetry* (JSOTSup, 40; Sheffield: JSOT Press, 1987), pp. 29-48.

Clines, D.J.A., *The Theme of the Pentateuch* (JSOTSup, 10; Sheffield: JSOT Press, 1982).

Coats, G.W., *Rebellion in the Wilderness: The Murmuring Motif in the Wilderness Traditions of the Old Testament* (Nashville: Abingdon Press, 1968).

—*Moses: Heroic Man, Man of God* (JSOTSup, 57; Sheffield: JSOT Press, 1988).

— 'The Traditio-Historical Character of the Reed Sea Motif', *VT* 17 (1967), pp. 253-65.

Cody, A., *A History of Old Testament Priesthood* (AnBib, 35; Rome: Pontifical Biblical Institute, 1969).

Cogan, M., and H. Tadmor, *II Kings: A New Translation with Introduction and Commentary* (AB, 11; New York: Doubleday, 1988).

Conrad, E.W., 'The "Fear Not" Oracles in Second Isaiah', *VT* 34 (1984), pp. 129-52.

Crüsemann, F., *Studien zur Formgeschichte von Hymnus und Danklied in Israel* (WMANT, 32; Neukirchen–Vluyn: Neukirchener Verlag, 1969).

Davies, G.I., 'The Wilderness Itineraries and the Composition of the Pentateuch', *VT* 33 (1983), pp. 1-13.

DeVries, S.J., *1 Kings* (WBC, 12; Waco, TX: Word Books 1985).

—*1 and 2 Chronicles* (FOTL, 11; Grand Rapids: Eerdmans, 1989).

Dillard, R.B., *2 Chronicles* (WBC, 15; Waco, TX: Word Books, 1987).

Dozemann, T.B., *God on the Mountain* (SBLMS, 37; Atlanta: Scholars Press, 1989).

—*God at War: Power in the Exodus Tradition* (Oxford: Oxford University Press, 1996).

Durham, J.I., *Exodus* (WBC, 3; Waco, TX: Word Books, 1987).

Eichhorn, D., *Gott als Fels, Burg und Zuflucht: Eine Untersuchung zum Gebet des Mittlers in den Psalmen* (Europäische Hochschulschriften, 23.4; Frankfurt: Peter Lang, 1972).

Eissfeldt, O., *Hexateuch-Synopse: Die Erzählung der fünf Bücher Mose und des Buches Josua mit dem Anfange des Richterbuches in ihre vier Quellen zerlegt und in deutscher Übersetzung dargeboten samt einer in Einleitung und Anmerkungen gegebenenen Begründung* (Darmstadt: Wissenschafliche Buchgesellschaft, 1962).

Elliger, K., *Leviticus* (HAT, 4; Tübingen: J.C.B. Mohr, 1966).

Follis, E.R., (ed.), *Directions in Biblical Hebrew Poetry* (JSOTSup, 40; Sheffield: JSOT Press, 1987).

Fretheim, T.E., 'The Priestly Document: Anti-Temple?', *VT* 18 (1968), pp. 313-29.

Fritz, V., *Israel in der Wüste: Traditionsgeschichtliche Untersuchung der Wüstenüberlieferung des Jahwisten* (MTS, 7; Marburg: N.G. Elwert Verlag, 1970).

—*Tempel und Zelt: Studien zum Tempelbau in Israel und zu dem Zeltheiligtum der Priesterschrift* (WMANT, 47; Neukirchen–Vluyn: Neukirchener Verlag, 1977).

Gottwald, N.K., *The Tribes of Yahweh: A Sociology of the Religion of Liberated Israel 1250–1050 B.C.E.* (Maryknoll, NY: Orbis Books, 1979).

Grabbe, L.L. (ed.), *Can a 'History of Israel' Be Written?* (JSOTSup, 245; Sheffield: Sheffield Academic Press, 1997).

Gray, G.B., *A Critical and Exegetical Commentary on Numbers* (ICC; repr.; Edinburgh: T. & T. Clark, 1965 [1903]).

Gray, J., 'The Desert Sojourn of the Hebrews and the Sinai-Horeb Tradition', *VT* 4 (1954), pp. 148-54.

Gregory, R., 'Irony and the Unmasking of Elijah', in Gregory and Hauser, *From Carmel to Horeb*, pp. 91-169.

Gregory, R., and A.J. Hauser, *From Carmel to Horeb: Elijah in Crisis* (Bible and Literature Series, 19; Sheffield: Almond Press, 1990).

Gunneweg, A.H.J., *Leviten und Priester: Hauptlinien der Traditionsbildung und Geschichte des israelitisch-jüdischen Kultpersonals* (Göttingen: Vandenhoeck & Ruprecht, 1965).

Haran, M., 'The Shining of Moses' Face: A Case Study in Biblical and Ancient Near Eastern Iconography', in W. Boyd Barrick and John R. Spencer (eds.), *In the Shelter of Elyon: Essays on Ancient Palestinian Life and Literature in Honor of G.W. Ahlström* (JSOTSup, 31; Sheffield: JSOT Press, 1984), pp. 159-73.

—*Temples and Temple Service in Ancient Israel: An Inquiry into Biblical Cult Phenomena and the Historical Setting of the Priestly School* (Winona Lake, IN: Eisenbrauns, 1985).

Hartley, J.E., *Leviticus* (WBC, 4; Waco, TX: Word Books, 1992).

Hauge, M.R., 'On the Sacred Spot: The Concept of the Proper Localization before God', *SJOT* 1 (1990), pp. 30-60.

—*Between Sheol and Temple: Motif Structure and Function in the I-Psalms* (JSOTSup, 178; Sheffield: Sheffield Academic Press, 1995).

Hauser, A.J., 'Yahweh versus Death—The Real Struggle in 1 Kings 17–19', in Gregory and Hauser, *From Carmel to Horeb*, pp. 9-89.

Hurowitz, V., 'The Priestly Account of Building the Tabernacle', *JAOS* 105 (1985), pp. 21-30.

—*I Have Built You an Exalted House: Temple Building in the Bible in Light of Mesopotamian and Northwest Semitic Writings* (JSOTSup, 115; Sheffield: JSOT Press, 1992).

Hyatt, J.P., 'Was Yahweh Originally a Creator Deity?', *JBL 86* (1967), pp. 369-77.

—*Commentary on Exodus* (NCB; London: Oliphants, 1971).

Jacobsen, T., 'The Graven Image', in P.D. Miller Jr, P.D. Hanson and S.D. McBride (eds.), *Ancient Israelite Religion: Essays in Honor of Frank Moore Cross* (Philadelphia: Fortress Press, 1987), pp. 15-32.

Jeremias, J., *Theophanie: Die Geschichte einer alttestamentlichen Gattung* (WMANT, 10; Neukirchen–Vluyn: Neukirchener Verlag, 1965).

Johnson, A.R., *The One and the Many in the Israelite Conception of God* (Cardiff: University of Wales Press, 1961).

Jonker, L.C., *Exclusivity and Variety: Perspectives on Multidimensional Exegesis* (Contributions to Bibilical Exegesis and Theology, 19; Kampen: Kok Pharos, 1996).

Kapelrud, A.S., 'Temple Building, a Task for Gods and Kings', *Or* 32 (1963), pp. 56-62.

Kearney, P.J., 'Creation and Liturgy: The P Redaction of Ex 25–40', *ZAW* 89 (1977), pp. 375-87.

Kiuchi, N., *The Purification Offering in the Priestly Literature: Its Meaning and Function* (JSOTSup, 56; Sheffield: JSOT Press, 1987).

Knierim, R., 'Exodus 18 und die Neuordnung der mosaischen Gerichtsbarheit', *ZAW* 73 (1961), pp. 146-71.

Knight, G.A.F., *Theology as Narration: A Commentary on the Book of Exodus* (Edinburgh: Handsel Press, 1976).

Koch, K., *Die Priesterschrift von Exodus 25 bis zu Leviticus 16: Eine überlieferungsgeschichtliche und literarkritische Untersuchung* (FRLANT, 71; Göttingen: Vandenhoeck & Ruprecht, 1959).

—'Tempeleinlassliturgien und Dekaloge', in R. Rendtorff and K. Koch (eds.), *Studien zur Theologie der alttestamentlichen Überlieferungen: Gerhard von Rad zum 60. Geburtstag* (Neukirchen–Vluyn: Neukirchener Verlag, 1961), pp. 45-60.

Köckert, M., *Vätergott und Väterverheissungen* (FRLANT, 142; Göttingen: Vandenhoeck & Ruprecht, 1988).

Koopmans, W.T., *Joshua 24 as Poetic Narrative* (JSOTSup, 93; Sheffield: JSOT Press, 1990).

Lacocque, A., *Romance She Wrote: A Hermeneutical Essay on Song of Songs* (Harrisburg, PA: Trinity Press International, 1998).

Lang, B., *Wisdom and the Book of Proverbs: An Israelite Goddess Redefined* (New York: Pilgrim Press, 1986).

Lemche, N.P., *Ancient Israel: A New History of Israelite Society* (Bib. Sem., 5; Sheffield: JSOT Press, 1988).

—*Die Vorgeschichte Israels: Von den Anfängen bis zum Ausgang des 13. Jahrhunderts v. Chr.* (Biblische Enzyklopädie, 1; Stuttgart: W. Kohlhammer, 1996).

Levine, B.A., 'The Descriptive Tabernacle Texts of the Pentateuch', *JAOS* 85 (1965), pp. 307-18.

— *In the Presence of the Lord: A Study of Cult and Some Cultic Terms in Ancient Israel* (SJLA, 5; Leiden: E.J. Brill, 1974).

—*Numbers 1–20: A New Translation with Introduction and Commentary* (AB, 4A; New York: Doubleday, 1993).

Loewenstamm, S.E., 'The Making and Destruction of the Golden Calf', *Bib* 48 (1967), pp. 481-90.

McCarter Jr, P.K., *II Samuel: A New Translation with Introduction, Notes and Commentary* (AB, 9; New York: Doubleday, 1984).

McCarthy, D.J., 'Plagues and Sea of Reeds: Exodus 5–14', *JBL* 85 (1966), pp. 137-58.

—'An Installation Genre', *JBL* 90 (1971), pp. 31-41.

McKane, W., *Proverbs: A New Approach* (OTL; London: SCM Press, 1970).

Milgrom, J., 'The Cultic šegāgā and its Influence in Psalms', *JQR* 58 (1967–68), pp. 115-25.

—*Leviticus 1–16: A New Translation with Introduction and Commentary* (AB, 3; New York: Doubleday, 1991).

Miller, P.D., 'The Blessing of God: An Interpretation of Numbers 6:22-27', *Int* 29 (1975), pp. 240-51.

—'Trouble and Woe (Interpreting the Biblical Laments)', *Int* 37 (1983), pp. 32-45.

Moberly, R.W.L., *At the Mountain of God: Story and Theology in Exodus 32–34* (JSOTSup, 22; Sheffield: JSOT Press, 1983).

—*The Old Testament of the Old Testament: Patriarchal Narratives and Mosaic Yahwism* (Overtures to Biblical Theology; Minneapolis: Fortress Press, 1992).

Mowinckel, S., *Le décalogue* (Etudes d'histoire et de philosophie religieuse, 16; Paris: Alcan, 1927).

—*Salmeboken* (Skriftene 1.Del, Det gamle testamente oversatt av Michelet, Mowinckel og Messel, 4; Oslo: Aschehoug, 1955).

Möhlenbrink, K., 'Josua im Pentateuch: (Die Josuaüberlieferungen ausserhalb des Josuabuchs)', *ZAW* 59 (1942–43), pp. 14-58.

Nicholson, E.W., *Exodus and Sinai in History and Tradition* (Oxford: Basil Blackwell, 1973).

—'The Interpretation of Exodus XXIV 9-11', *VT* 24 (1974), pp. 77-97.

—'The Antiquity of the Tradition in Exodus XXIV 9-11', *VT* 25 (1975), pp. 69-75.

—'The Decalogue as the Direct Address of God', *VT* 27 (1977), pp. 422-33.

—'The Covenant Ritual in Exodus XXIV 3-8', *VT* 32 (1982), pp. 74-86.

Nordheim, E. von, 'Ein Prophet kündigt sein Amt auf (Elia am Horeb)', *Bib* 59 (1978), pp. 153-73.

Noth, M., *Exodus: A Commentary* (trans. J. Bowden; OTL; London: SCM Press, 1962).

—*Leviticus: A Commentary* (trans. J.E. Anderson; OTL; London: SCM Press, 1965).

—*Das vierte Buch Moses: Numeri* (ATD, 7; Göttingen: Vandenhoeck & Ruprecht, 1966).

—*Könige*, I (BKAT, 10.1; Neukirchen–Vluyn: Neukirchener Verlag, 1968).

Olson, D.T., *The Death of the Old and the Birth of the New: The Framework of the Book of Numbers and the Pentateuch* (BJS, 71; Chico, CA: Scholars Press, 1985).

Porter, J.R., *Leviticus: Commentary* (Cambridge Bible Commentary; Cambridge: Cambridge University Press, 1976).

Rad, G. von, 'Es is noch eine Ruhe vorhanden dem Volke Gottes (Eine biblische Begriffs-untersuchung)', in *Gesammelte Studien zum Alten Testament* (TBü, 8; Munich: Chr. Kaiser Verlag, 1965), pp. 101-108.

Rendtorff, R., *Das überlieferungsgeschichtliche Problem des Pentateuch* (BZAW, 147; Berlin: W. de Gruyter, 1977).

—*Leviticus* (BKAT, 3.1; Neukirchen–Vluyn: Neukirchener Verlag, 1985).

Rogerson, J.W., 'The Hebrew Conception of Corporate Personality: A Re-Examination', *JTS* 21 (1970), pp. 1-16.

Sæbø, M., 'Offenbarung oder Verhüllung? Bemerkungen zum Charakter des Gottesnamens in Ex 3,13-15', in J. Jeremias and L. Perlitt (eds.), *Die Botschaft und die Boten: Festschrift für Hans Walter Wolff zum 70. Geburtstag* (Neukirchen–Vluyn: Neukirchener Verlag, 1981), pp. 43-55.

Schmid, H., *Die Gestalt des Mose: Probleme alttestamentlicher Forschung unter Berücksichtigung der Pentateuchkrise* (Erträge der Forschung, 237; Darmstadt: Wissenschaftliche Buchgesellschaft, 1986).

Schmid, R., *Das Bunderopfer in Israel* (SANT, 9; Munich: Kösel, 1964).

Smith, M.S., *The Pilgrimage Pattern in Exodus* (JSOTSup, 239; Sheffield: Sheffield Academic Press, 1997).

Soggin, J.A., *Judges: A Commentary* (trans. J. Bowden; OTL; Philadelphia: Westminster Press, 1981).

Steck, O.H., *Überlieferung und Zeitgeschichte in den Elia-Erzählungen* (WMANT, 26; Neukirchen–Vluyn: Neukirchener Verlag, 1968).

Sternberg, M., *The Poetics of Biblical Narrative: Ideological Literature and the Drama of Reading* (Literary Biblical Series; Bloomington: Indiana University Press, 1985).

Stone, L., 'The Revival of Narrative: Reflections on a New Old History', *Past and Present* 85 (1979), pp. 3-24.

Tadmor, H. and M. Cogan, *II Kings: A New Translation with Introduction and Commentary* (AB, 11; New York: Doubleday, 1988).

Thompson, T.L., *The Origin Tradition of Ancient Israel*. I. *The Literary Formation of Genesis and Exodus 1–23* (JSOTSup, 55; Sheffield: JSOT Press, 1987).

Travers, P.L., *What the Bee Knows: Reflections of Myth, Symbol and Story* (London: Arkana, 1993).

Utzschneider, H., *Das Heiligtum und das Gesetz: Studien zur Bedeutung der sinaitischen Heiligtumstexte (Ex 25–40; Lev 8–9)* (OBO, 77; Freiburg: Universitätsverlag; Göttingen: Vandenhoeck & Ruprecht, 1988).

—*Gottes langer Atem: die Exoduserzählung (Ex 1-14)* (Stuttgart: Katholisches Bibelwerk, 1996).

Valentin, H., *Aaron: Eine Studie zur vor-priesterschriftlichen Aaron-Überlieferung* (OBO, 18; Göttingen: Vandenhoeck & Ruprecht, 1978).

Van Seters, J., 'The Plagues of Egypt: Ancient Tradition or Literary Invention?', *ZAW* 98 (1986), pp. 31-39.

—*The Life of Moses: The Yahwist as Historian in Exodus–Numbers* (Contributions to Biblical Exegesis and Theology, 10; Kampen: Kok Pharos, 1994).

de Vaulx, J., *Les Nombres* (SB; Paris: J. Gabalda, 1972).

Watson, W.G.E., *Classical Hebrew Poetry: A Guide to its Techniques* (JSOTSup, 26; Sheffield: JSOT Press, 1984).

Watts, J.D.W., *Isaiah 34–66* (WBC, 25; Waco, TX: Word Books, 1987).

Weisman, Z., 'The Personal Spirit as Imparting Authority', *ZAW* 93 (1981), pp. 225-34.

Wenham, G.J., *Numbers: An Introduction and Commentary* (Downers Grove, IL: InterVarsity Press, 1981).

Westermann, C., *Isaiah 40–66: A Commentary* (OTL; Philadelphia: Westminster Press, 1969).

White, H.C., *Narration and Discourse in the Book of Genesis* (Cambridge: Cambridge University Press, 1991).

Whybray, R.N., *The Making of the Pentateuch: A Methodological Study* (JSOTSup, 53; Sheffield: JSOT Press, 1987).

Wilcoxen, J.A., 'Some Anthropocentric Aspects of Israel's Sacred History', *JR* 48 (1968), pp. 333-50.

Wildberger, H., *Jesaja*. III. *Jesaja 28–39. Das Buch, der Prophet und seine Botschaft* (BKAT, 10.3; Neukirchen–Vluyn: Neukirchener Verlag, 1982).

INDEXES

INDEX OF REFERENCES

OLD TESTAMENT

Genesis
1.31–2.3 130
1–2 37
2.1-3 129
12.1 27
12–50 27
22 29, 316
22.2 27
22.4-5 28
30.1 288
34.29 305
35.1-4 77
35.1-5 29
35.2 77
35.4 76
43.8 305
50.8 305, 306

Exodus
1.10 93
1–14 309
1–18 319, 320
2.2 37
3.1 25, 27
3.1-12 179
3.6 84
3.11–4.13 179
3.12 25
3.21-22 77, 135
3.22 77, 131, 134, 135
3–4 25, 29, 33, 99, 178, 180, 181, 182, 273, 311
4 178, 312
4.13 178
4.14 179
4.14-16 178
4.16 180, 255
4.18-26 178
4.27-28 178
4.34-38 183
4.36-38 315
5.13-23 314
5.22 32
5.22-23 32, 273
5–17 32
6 32
6.1-8 32
6.9 32
6.10-12 32
6.12 32
6.28-30 32
6.30 32
10 306, 307
10.8-11 306
10.24 306
10.24-29 306
10.26 306
11.2 134
11.2-3 77, 134, 135
12 59, 235, 238, 242, 306
12.1-20 234
12.1-27 59
12.12 265
12.21 271
12.21-27 234
12.27-28 235
12.28 59
12.29 235, 265
12.29-30 305
12.29-33 238
12.29-41 59
12.30-33 135
12.30-41 235
12.33 271
12.34 238
12.35-36 77, 135, 237, 238, 272, 307
12.35-38 322
12.36 77, 131, 134, 135
12.37 238, 265, 271, 272, 306, 307
12.37-38 306
12.38 93, 271, 272, 278, 306, 307
12.41 235
12.43-49 59, 234
12.50 59, 235
12.51 59, 235
12–13 234, 235, 242
13.1-16 234
13.17-18 302
13.18 93
13.20 235

Exodus (cont.)
13.20-22 234, 235
13.21-22 32, 92, 235
14 251, 296-302, 304, 305, 307, 308, 316, 321, 332
14.1 296
14.1-4 296
14.2 296, 302
14.4 296, 297, 300, 332
14.5-9 298
14.5-10 297
14.8 297
14.9 302
14.10 298, 299
14.10-13 297
14.11 302, 303
14.11-12 280, 304
14.12 303
14.13 298
14.13-14 297
14.17 297
14.17-18 300, 332
14.19-20 32
14.25 302
14.30-31 249
14.30 297, 298, 302
14.31 297, 298, 299
15 100, 249, 250, 318
15.1-21 249, 251, 277, 297, 309
15.1-2 249
15.1 249
15.2-18 249
15.17 99
15.19 249
15.20-21 249
15.21 249
15.22-23 19, 249
15.22-26 32, 248, 251, 260, 261, 265
15.27–16.1 19
16 261, 262, 264, 265, 276, 277, 279, 301, 303
16.1 264
16.2-3 264
16.2 272
16.3 264, 280, 302, 303
16.4-34 265
16.4-7 264
16.4-5 32, 251, 264
16.6-8 264
16.8 264
16.12 264
16.12-14 264
16.13-15 264
16.19-20 265
16.21 264
16.27-31 264
16.28-29 32, 251
16.31 265
16.33 265
16.35 264
16–17 274
17 249, 250, 251
17.1 19, 250
17.3 280
17.4 273, 281
17.6 32, 250, 251
17.6-7 32
17.8-16 247
17.9 253
17.11-12 253
18 110, 181, 202, 247-52, 254, 256-58, 261-63, 266-71, 273-78, 281, 282, 287, 293, 295, 312, 313
18.1 249, 250, 255-57
18.1-12 247-50, 252, 255, 256, 263, 277, 309, 319
18.5 27, 32, 250-52, 258
18.8-11 31
18.8 248, 249, 255
18.9-11 248
18.9 255
18.10 255
18.11-14 267
18.11 248
18.12 51, 248, 249, 255, 256, 263, 265
18.13-26 32, 57, 248, 255
18.13-14 181, 253, 255, 256
18.13 256
18.13-27 247, 248, 252, 256, 258, 266, 319
18.14 255-57
18.15-16 273
18.15 253
18.16-17 253
18.16 253, 257
18.17-18 181
18.17 255, 256
18.18 255
18.19 253-55
18.20 110, 257
18.21 253
18.22 252
18.23 255-57

18.24	255, 256		59, 85,		158
18.25	253		86, 92,	19.3-15	55, 57, 61
18.26	253		93, 94,	19.3-8	36, 45,
18.27	275		99-101,		49, 60
19–Lev. 10	203, 219		104-106,	19.3-6	34
19–40	18-20, 22,		108, 109,	19.3	22, 30,
	24, 27,		115, 119,		31, 49,
	29, 32,		136, 139,		59, 62,
	34, 36,		144, 148,		73, 99,
	39, 40,		150, 157,		191
	42, 43,		250	19.4-6	30, 291,
	46, 59,	19–20	23, 291		292
	60, 61,	19	19-21, 30,	19.4	30, 319
	64, 67,		33, 34,	19.6	48, 49,
	74, 78,		36, 41,		158, 187,
	80, 85,		43, 44,		291
	87, 88,		47, 48,	19.7-8	50
	95, 100-		50, 51,	19.8-19	34
	102, 104,		55, 59,	19.8-15	34, 49, 60
	105, 108,		60, 62-64,	19.8-14	45
	109, 123,		70, 72,	19.8-13	34
	125, 129,		82, 89,	19.8	31, 49,
	137, 141,		90, 96-98,		148, 149
	148-51,		114, 120,	19.10-15	50, 77,
	153-55,		142, 151,		195
	158, 160,		184, 191,	19.10-11	60
	163, 164,		193, 195,	19.10	47, 291
	173, 174,		197, 207,	19.11	39, 49,
	178, 183,		208, 212,		110
	186-92,		222, 258,	19.12-13	33, 51,
	194, 195,		291, 292,		86, 93
	199, 205,		294	19.12	60
	207, 212,	19.1–24.19	49	19.13-15	60
	219, 223,	19.1–24.2	45, 49,	19.13	47, 48,
	228, 239,		50, 55, 97		110, 291
	242, 244,	19.1-8	34	19.14	47, 291
	245, 251,	19.1-3	250	19.16-25	34
	252, 254,	19.1-2	19, 30,	19.16-20	39, 44,
	258, 266,		249-51		51, 52, 56
	268, 270,	19.1	251	19.16-19	54, 196
	277, 287,	19.2-8	34	19.16-17	22, 60
	292, 312,	19.2-3	30, 114,	19.16	49, 56
	314, 318		254	19.17	48, 50,
19–34	30, 36,	19.2	25, 27,		51, 110
	100, 160,		192, 210,	19.18-21	38, 116
	174		222, 251	19.18-20	31
19–24	13, 21,	19.3–24.2	49, 52,	19.18	44
	24, 53,		91, 156,	19.20–20.20	34

Exodus (cont.)
19.20-25 38, 39, 41, 44, 45, 47-49, 53, 72, 91, 93
19.20-24 34
19.20 30
19.21-25 33, 118, 208
19.21-24 33, 46, 47, 94, 110, 199
19.21 38, 41
19.22 48, 291
19.23-24 51
19.23 99
19.24 44, 45, 47, 48, 51, 57, 93, 291
19.25 44, 45, 49, 158
20.1–24.8 35
20.1-17 35, 44, 49, 72, 149
20.1 44
20.5 42
20.18-32 38
20.18-21 33, 35, 38-41, 43-49, 51-54, 59, 62, 64, 65, 73, 81, 86, 91, 93, 98, 99, 111, 117, 167, 196, 291
20.18-19 46
20.18 38, 39, 44-46, 110, 118, 149
20.21–24.11 34
20.21–24.2 52
20.21 27, 35, 40, 49, 51, 110
20.22–24.2 45, 84
20.22–22.33 47
20.22 38, 44, 45
20.24 38
20.26 93
20–24 192
20–23 149
23.20-23 90
23.24 42
24–25 101, 105, 106, 109, 116
24 23, 24, 34, 36, 37, 40, 41, 47, 50, 55-57, 60, 66, 68-70, 86, 97, 98, 101, 106, 107, 110, 116, 120, 195, 197, 198, 222
24.1-11 34
24.1-2 33, 44, 47-49, 51, 53, 71, 84, 91, 93, 110, 167, 208
24.1 42, 57, 58, 62, 93, 107, 197, 198, 244
24.2 45, 50, 51, 120, 148, 149, 158
24.3–34.35 55, 156
24.3–31.18 52, 70, 97, 158
24.3-18 49, 50, 55, 59, 68, 69
24.3-11 61
24.3-8 50
24.4-18 28, 52
24.4-11 68
24.4-8 110, 195
24.4-6 51
24.4-5 22, 60
24.4 49, 50, 52
24.5-11 265
24.5-6 50
24.5 50, 51, 52, 68
24.6 68
24.7-8 68, 69
24.7 50, 51, 148, 158
24.8-11 85
24.8 50, 51, 68
24.9-18 52, 91
24.9-17 49
24.9-11 34, 51, 52, 56, 58, 62, 86, 107, 112, 167, 244
24.9 50, 51, 57, 58, 62, 107, 110, 197, 198
24.10-11 34, 38-40, 48, 51, 53
24.10 53
24.11-18 48
24.11 38, 48, 51, 53, 68, 93
24.12–32.35 34
24.12–32.29 34
24.12-18 51, 52, 111
24.12-15 66
24.12 34, 35, 40, 48, 49, 51,

	52, 66, 165, 169
24.13-18	48
24.13-15	52
24.13-14	48, 66
24.13	51, 107, 197
24.14	34, 48, 107, 197, 254
24.15–31.18	34
24.15-18	222
24.15-17	39
24.15-16	111
24.15	51
24.16-18	52
24.16	31, 50, 111, 113
24.17-18	65
24.17	38, 39-41, 43, 51, 53, 58, 62, 81, 98, 112, 116, 195
24.18	51, 66
24.26	68
24.56	202
25–40	24, 37, 53, 104, 105, 109, 115, 129, 140, 218
25–36	127
25–31	23, 24, 37, 46, 52-56, 62-66, 79, 86-88, 91, 92, 100, 101, 116, 120, 122, 127, 137, 143, 149, 153, 156, 186, 201, 208, 227, 314
25	24, 94, 95, 106, 107
25.1-9	91
25.1-8	63
25.2-8	76, 123, 124
25.2-7	125
25.2-3	217
25.2	123, 124, 146, 147
25.3	123
25.4	126
25.5	126
25.8-10	123
25.8	99
25.9	137
25.10-19	125
25.10	126
25.22	163, 218, 219, 220
25.31	150
25.40	137
27.1	126
27.20	158
27.20-21	223
28.1	227, 270
28.38	136
28–29	244
29–30	193
29	193, 194
30–32	53
30.6-8	223
30.6	218, 220
30.30–33.6	34
31	125
31.1-11	122, 125
31.1-6	67
31.1	71
31.5	71
31.12-17	129, 150
31.13-16	129
31.14-15	129
31.17	129
31.18–32.1	72
31.18	24, 52, 53, 63, 65-67, 117, 156, 157, 165, 169, 170
32–40	320, 321
32–34	19, 20, 23, 37, 47, 53, 54, 59, 63, 64, 66, 70, 72, 75, 79, 80, 83-91, 93-100, 110, 114, 117, 120, 156-61, 164, 170-73, 182, 183, 186, 190, 242, 311, 314
32–33	37, 53, 66, 85
32	35, 37, 66-68, 70, 71, 92, 118, 131, 139, 146, 157, 165, 195, 197-99, 229, 230, 236, 237, 239, 240, 242-44, 262, 274, 275, 321
32.1–34.28	37
32.1-6	54, 63, 65, 67-70, 76, 86, 91, 99, 117, 169, 188, 198, 307
32.2-4	131
32.2-3	133, 134,

Exodus (cont.)
218
32.1-2 34
32.1 46, 65, 66, 83, 90-94, 118, 142, 169, 170, 280
32.2 77, 133-35, 271
32.3 77, 90, 133, 135
32.4 67, 93, 169, 170
32.5-6 68
32.5 67, 87, 90
32.6 51, 118, 131, 162, 200, 265
32.7-19 24
32.7-14 54, 63, 65, 70, 84, 87
32.7-10 117
32.7-8 65, 93, 169, 170
32.7 65, 72, 156
32.9-14 65, 317
32.9-10 199
32.11-13 84
32.11 171
32.12-17 70
32.12 34
32.15-30 68, 69
32.15-29 68, 69
32.15-20 54
32.15-16 66, 67, 117, 165
32.15 65, 66
32.17-24 65
32.17-18 66
32.18-23 95
32.19–33.5 117
32.19-29 63, 64, 117
32.19-20 66, 67, 169
32.19 64, 162
32.21-29 85
32.21-24 70, 78, 167
32.23 93, 169, 170
32.24 67, 77, 145
32.25-30 167
32.25-29 57, 68, 70, 78, 80, 195, 228
32.25 118, 162
32.26 69
32.27-28 169
32.27 75, 169
32.28 63, 169
32.29 64, 68
32.30–34.35 167
32.30–34.28 166
32.30–33.11 78
32.30–33.6 71, 73, 78, 86
32.30–33.5 76
32.30-34 65, 84
32.30 70, 72
32.31–34.35 61
32.31–33.5 34, 83-85, 98
32.31–33.3 78, 87
32.31-35 71
32.31-34 72
32.31-32 227
32.31 68-70, 75, 83
32.33–33.5 171
32.33-34 71
32.33 71, 226
32.34–33.5 114, 164
32.34-35 159
32.34 50, 71, 90, 172
32.35 71, 136
33–34 88, 106, 109, 119, 164, 184, 189, 201, 220, 312
33 35, 132, 164, 165, 237, 243, 245, 292, 310, 315
33.1-11 174
33.1-6 45, 71, 72, 81, 107, 157-59, 314
33.1-5 70, 94, 131, 266
33.1-3 71, 77, 82
33.1 71, 72, 92, 93, 171, 226
33.2 73, 90, 71, 74, 90
33.3-5 199
33.3-4 76, 91
33.3 93, 94, 311
33.4-11 82, 130, 141
33.4-7 85, 120
33.4-6 72-74, 78, 82, 90, 218
33.4 71-73, 76, 77, 81, 82, 91, 123, 133-35, 146, 200
33.5-11 159
33.5 71, 72, 74, 78, 90, 93, 94, 99, 226, 311
33.6-11 159, 183, 188, 195, 242
33.6-10 192
33.6-7 121, 122
33.6 71-73,

	75-77, 80-82, 89, 91, 131-35, 146, 150, 160, 162, 237, 242, 272, 307, 317
33.7–34.3	35
33.7-23	98
33.7-11	35, 45, 53, 72-76, 78, 79, 81, 82, 88, 89, 111, 116, 146, 158-61, 166, 167, 183, 220
33.7-10	111
33.7-8	143
33.7	42, 72-76, 78, 81, 89, 91, 111, 133
33.8–34.3	84, 85, 87
33.8-11	40, 73, 79, 82, 86, 162, 192, 240
33.8-10	38-43, 62, 73, 78, 79, 81, 82, 85, 98, 116, 166, 273
33.8-9	79, 80, 111, 162, 170, 208, 220
33.8	78, 80, 81, 111, 221
33.9-10	89, 162
33.9	82, 110, 111, 221, 222
33.10	42, 80, 81, 111, 112, 202
33.11	40, 66, 73, 78-80, 96, 161, 238, 244
33.12–34.35	159
33.12–34.3	35, 82, 84
33.12-27	83
33.12-23	26, 40
33.12-17	82, 83, 86, 87, 95, 96, 114, 164, 165, 171
33.12	75, 78, 82-84, 88, 172, 192, 221
33.14-17	90
33.14-15	95
33.14	90
33.15	90, 91
33.16	90, 91
33.18–34.35	87
33.18–34.28	177
33.18–34.3	86, 173
33.18-23	38, 40, 83, 85, 86, 93, 96, 164-66, 171, 172, 181
33.18-21	39
33.18	38, 83, 84
33.19-23	71, 83, 86
33.19	318
33.20	38, 95
33.21–34.8	115
33.21-23	96
33.21	111
33.22-23	166
33.23	38, 95
33.34-35	42
34–40	37, 53, 66
34–35	183
34	53, 66, 67, 79, 85, 87, 88, 96, 130, 149, 158, 162, 164, 165, 167, 169, 171, 173, 174, 176, 177, 180-88, 193, 199, 201, 212, 220, 221, 230, 254, 258, 269, 270, 275, 278, 294, 312, 313, 315
34.1-35	34
34.1-3	71, 83, 84, 86, 164
34.1	75, 165, 169, 170
34.2-3	33, 93
34.2	111
34.3	85, 86, 110
34.4-28	34, 98
34.4	75, 84, 85, 87, 165, 169
34.5-28	85, 87
34.5-9	84
34.5-8	85
34.5-6	39
34.5	31, 110
34.6-7	318
34.7-11	160
34.8-9	75, 83, 87, 165
34.8	39, 42, 111
34.9	86, 90, 91, 171
34.11-26	208
34.11-16	149

Exodus (cont.)

34.14	42	35–40 (cont.)	60, 65, 66, 74, 76, 79, 89, 92, 98-100, 119-21, 124, 130, 131, 143, 146, 150, 157, 158, 160, 162, 163, 174, 176, 188, 191, 193, 195-97, 199, 201, 204, 208, 216, 217, 221, 223, 226, 227, 236, 238, 239, 242, 244, 321
34.21-26	149	35–39	55-57, 63, 67, 74-76, 116, 120, 128, 140, 141, 143, 147-49, 152, 171, 191, 194, 219, 307, 314
34.24-30	219	35–36	76, 133, 175, 218, 232
34.24	93	35	54, 64, 76, 83, 87, 88, 96, 120, 130, 131, 133, 134, 136, 137, 142, 147, 148, 156, 157, 173
34.27-28	53, 75, 165, 169, 170	35.1–40.38	97, 156, 158
34.28	149, 150, 225	35.1–40.33	55, 59, 61, 98, 121
34.29-35	47, 63, 70, 87, 157, 158, 165, 166, 183, 188, 193, 205, 242	35.1–39.43	35
34.29-34	255	35.1-19	121
34.29-33	54, 117	35.1-3	129, 150
34.29	111, 165, 167	35.1	35, 193, 221
34.30-35	87	35.2	129
34.30-32	111, 166	35.3–36.7	124
34.30-31	165	35.4–36.7	76, 77, 123, 127, 147
34.30	165, 167	35.4-19	125
34.31-35	171	35.4-9	125
34.31-32	167	35.4	147
34.32	83, 87, 149, 158	35.5–36.7	64
34.33-35	83, 87, 165, 166	35.5	123, 124, 146, 217
34.34-35	35, 36, 73, 88, 116, 157, 159, 160-62, 166, 168, 173, 174, 183, 192, 208, 220, 222, 240, 257	35.10	146
34.34	221	35.20–36.7	88
34.35	165, 167, 204	35.20-29	134
34.39	169	35.20-26	128
35–41	63	35.20-22	132
35–40	24, 47, 53-55, 56, …	35.20	123, 126
		35.21-29	133, 146
		35.21-24	126
		35.21	123, 124, 134, 147, 217
		35.22-24	144
		35.22	123, 124, 132, 147
		35.23	126, 134
		35.24	126, 217
		35.25-26	126, 132, 136
		35.25	126, 134
		35.26	123, 126, 144
		35.27-28	128, 144, 217
		35.29	123, 124, 128, 129, 132, 134
		35.30–36.8	67
		35.30–36.3	121
		35.30-35	125

35.33	129	39.42-43	75, 136, 147, 171, 173, 257	40.2-15	194
35.35	129	39.42	64, 224	40.9-16	112
36–39	127, 225, 227	39.43	60, 64, 129, 130, 205, 224	40.16	194, 224, 257
36	126	40	22, 36, 37, 39, 41, 43, 59, 62, 65, 74, 75, 79, 80, 81, 86, 92, 98, 100, 111, 112, 114, 115, 118-20, 128, 130, 141, 145, 152, 154, 160, 164, 169, 173-78, 180-87, 189-96, 200-203, 205, 209-15, 217, 219-22, 225, 230, 240, 242, 243, 245, 254, 258, 270, 278, 291, 292, 294, 312, 313, 315	40.16-33	60, 194
36.1-2	146	40.1-33	35, 57, 74, 76, 120, 121, 122, 191, 204	40.16-32	75, 173
36.1-8	129	40.1-30	55	40.17-35	194
36.1	126	40.1-15	60, 74, 75, 122	40.17-33	193
36.2	126	40.1	121, 213	40.17	194, 213
36.3-7	123			40.18-33	194
36.4	126			40.19	194, 225
36.6	132, 217			40.20	150
36.8–39.43	204			40.21	194, 225
36.8–39.31	122, 125			40.22-23	112
36.8-38	127			40.23	194, 225
36.8	126			40.25	194, 225
36.9-38	127			40.26-32	193
36.21	127			40.27-32	55
36.22	127			40.27	194, 225
37–38	127			40.29	194, 225
37.1–38.20	127			40.30-32	57, 80
37.1	127			40.31-32	57, 195, 205, 228
37.8	126			40.31	194
37.17-24	224			40.32-38	58
37.21-31	127			40.32	56, 58, 112, 113, 159, 161, 194, 220
38–40	204			40.33	60, 74, 122, 129, 130, 194, 200
39–40	129, 152, 223, 224			40.34-38	35, 37, 39, 55, 61, 79, 82, 88, 94, 98, 115, 151, 152, 161, 180, 183, 188, 191, 219, 220, 266
39	147, 312			40.34-36	201
39.1-31	127, 147			40.34-35	83, 92, 99, 111, 113, 141,
39.1	147				
39.5	147				
39.7	147				
39.21	147				
39.26	147				
39.29	147				
39.31	147				
39.32-43	60, 74, 75, 122, 127, 147, 176				
39.32-41	123				
39.32	60, 75, 127, 129, 130, 147, 200, 224, 257				
39.33-43	121				

Exodus (cont.)
194, 205, 210
40.34 112, 113, 162, 190, 191, 209, 210, 222
40.35-38 40, 57, 89, 162, 163, 173
40.35-36 161
40.35 37, 56, 58, 112, 113, 161, 162, 210, 220-22
40.36-37 113, 160, 192, 209, 210
40.36-38 37-40, 42, 43, 58, 59, 62, 64, 80, 82, 92, 100, 112-14, 117-19, 141, 148, 150, 159, 160, 162, 163, 183, 185, 188, 191-93, 202, 205, 208-16, 221, 234, 236, 239, 240, 245, 294, 314, 319, 321
40.36 113, 160, 209, 221
40.38 39, 113, 160, 190, 192, 210

Leviticus
1–11 207
1–10 98, 200, 212, 218, 219, 227, 228, 244
1–9 59, 216, 217, 232
1–7 59, 83, 154, 190, 193, 194, 201, 203, 206-208, 217, 232
1 20, 190, 197
1.1–Num. 9.23 188, 239, 242
1.1–Num. 9.14 192, 212
1.1 22, 62, 82, 88, 99, 113, 114, 163, 173, 180, 190, 191, 193-95, 212, 221, 240
1.2 217
1.14 217
4.23 217
4.28 217
7.1 190, 194
7.14 217
7.32 217
7.34 217
8–11 205
8–10 190, 196, 215, 216, 223, 238, 239, 242, 292, 294
8–9 59, 191, 193-96, 200, 201, 203, 205, 206, 214, 217, 219, 221, 222, 224, 226, 227, 236, 239, 245, 270
8 190, 194, 195, 203, 204, 225, 252
8.4 204
8.5 204
8.9 204
8.13 204
8.17 204
8.21 204
8.29 204
8.31 204, 224
8.34 204
8.35 204
8.36 204
9–10 202, 321
9 57, 191, 193, 195-97, 203, 204, 220, 222, 238, 252
9.1-22 190
9.1 190
9.2 196
9.3-4 217
9.5 196, 204, 224
9.6 204
9.7 196, 204
9.10 196, 204
9.15-23 193
9.21 196, 204, 224
9.22–10.2 80
9.22-23 203
9.22 111, 112
9.23–10.2 139, 198, 201, 206, 266, 310
9.23-24 38, 40, 43, 139, 191, 205,

	219	11.2	205	7.3-9	92
9.23	113, 190, 196, 220	11.44-47	202	7.3-4	223
		11.44	206	7.3	217
9.24–10.2	195, 198	11.45	206	7.4	218
9.24	41, 53, 112, 139, 195, 196, 198-200, 205, 271	11.47	206	7.5	226
		16.2	218	7.10-88	215, 217, 222, 226
		17.5	198		
		26	329, 330	7.10-83	219
		26.30	309	7.10-11	215
10	59, 191, 197, 199, 205, 206, 212, 242			7.10	200, 201, 214, 217, 219
		Numbers			
		1	278		
		1.1–25.18	259	7.11	217, 218
10.1-2	38, 40, 43, 58, 62, 107, 139, 191, 196, 198, 199, 218, 244, 271, 272, 274	1.1–10.36	259	7.12	217
		1.1-3	248	7.15-23	215
		1.1	213-15, 259	7.18	217
				7.19	217
		1.18	213	7.84-88	219, 226
		1.51	289	7.84	200, 201, 214, 219, 226
		1–10	213, 259		
		3.5-13	225		
10.1	58, 196, 204, 217, 224	3.10	289	7.88	200, 201, 214, 219, 226
		3.12	270		
		3.38	289		
10.2	41, 53, 139, 195, 196, 198, 199, 203	7–8	215, 216, 226-28, 230, 232, 237, 239, 242, 243, 292, 294, 321	7.89	219-23, 226, 231, 239
				7–9	214-16, 226, 232, 234, 238, 239, 242, 244, 245, 259, 314
10.3	197				
10.5	204				
10.6	196, 205, 272				
		7	123, 201, 217, 218, 220-22, 224-27, 230, 232, 234, 239		
10.7	204				
10.10	206			8–10	242, 245, 265, 271
10.11	204				
10.12-20	202			8–9	231, 305
10.13	204			8	57, 68, 70, 215, 228-34, 236-38, 242, 244, 307, 317, 321, 322
10.15	204	7.1–9.14	215		
10.16-20	202	7.1-9	217, 219, 222		
10.18	204				
10.19-20	204	7.1-2	215		
10.20	205	7.1	200, 201, 214, 215, 217, 219, 223		
11	191, 198, 202, 205-209, 212				
				8.1-4	223, 224, 231, 240
11.1-2	207, 208	7.1-88	219, 225	8.1	219, 221, 226, 230
11.1	195, 203, 205	7.2-9	214		
		7.2	215, 217	8.3-4	226, 231

Numbers (cont.)
8.3 224, 225, 231
8.4 223-26, 231
8.5-26 223, 227, 230
8.5-22 225
8.5-19 226
8.5 230
8.6-7 227
8.6 227
8.8-10 227
8.10 230, 236
8.11 227, 228
8.12 227, 228, 230
8.13-14 227
8.13 227, 228
8.14-19 229
8.14 227
8.15 226, 227, 228
8.16-19 229, 234
8.16-18 230
8.16 227, 229, 236
8.17 265
8.18 229
8.19 226, 227
8.20-22 226, 231
8.20 224, 226, 227, 231, 236
8.21 227, 228
8.22 224, 226, 231, 237
8.23 226, 230
8.24 226
8.26 226
9–10 235, 275
9 192, 211-13, 226, 230, 234, 252, 258, 292
9.1-23 234
9.1-14 216, 232-35, 239
9.1-5 213, 215, 223, 231-33, 235
9.1-3 231
9.4 231
9.5 224, 231, 232
9.6-14 231, 232
9.6-8 233
9.6-7 231, 232
9.6 231, 233
9.7 232
9.8-14 232
9.8 231
9.9-14 231
9.9 230
9.10 233
9.12 231, 232
9.13 232, 233
9.14 231, 232
9.15–10.36 259
9.15–10.28 259
9.15-23 38, 40, 43, 92, 113, 114, 141, 148-50, 163, 188, 192, 209, 210, 212-16, 221, 223, 233-36, 238-40, 245, 259, 266, 294, 314-16, 319, 321
9.15-22 211
9.15-16 260
9.15 210, 213-15, 224, 232, 234
9.16-23 210, 214, 233
9.16 213
9.17 209
9.18-20 43
9.18 113, 150, 163, 210
9.19 113, 150, 209, 210
9.20 113, 150, 163, 210
9.21 113
9.22 113
9.22 209
9.23 43, 150, 163, 210, 211, 221, 224, 233
10–11 258
10 20, 210, 212, 217, 236, 258-60, 266, 279
10.1-10 236
10.10 20
10.11-13 210, 212, 235
10.11-12 260
10.11 213-15, 260
10.13 211
10.14-28 235
10.29-36 259
10.29-32 248, 275
10.31 257
10.33 92, 257
10.34 260
10.35 260
10.36 211, 259, 260
11–17 307, 308
11–14 274
11–12 270, 274, 278, 279, 283, 285, 296, 308
11 57, 78, 135, 181, 211, 212, 239, 240, 247, 248, 252, 254,

	257-87, 293-95, 301, 307, 312, 316, 318
11.1–25.18	259
11.1–20.29	259
11.1-3	260, 265
11.1	211, 259, 260
11.3	260
11.4-34	248, 260, 261, 262, 265, 266, 280, 286
11.4-5	263, 271
11.4	264, 270, 271, 273
11.5	263
11.6-20	267
11.6-9	264
11.7-9	264
11.10	273
11.11-15	257, 273, 311
11.13	273
11.16-20	262
11.16-17	181, 262
11.16	268
11.17	267, 268
11.18	263, 264, 273
11.20	263, 271-73, 303
11.21-22	264
11.21	265
11.24-33	267
11.24-30	181
11.25-33	262
11.25	267
11.29	267, 270
11.31-33	264
11.31-32	264
11.31	267
11.33	273
12	269, 271, 274-76, 282, 286, 287, 295, 312
12.1-2	269
12.1	269, 271, 272
12.6	276
13–14	135, 209, 273, 278, 280, 283, 285, 299, 304, 307, 308, 312, 327, 331, 332, 334
13	298, 301
13.1	296
13.2	281
13.3	278
13.16	281
13.17-20	278
13.18-20	298
13.20	297
13.22-24	278
13.24-25	282
13.26-29	280
13.26-28	278
13.26	298
13.27-29	297
13.27	299
13.28-29	299
13.28	299
13.30-31	278
13.30	279-82, 297
13.31-33	280, 282, 297, 299
13.32	299
13.33	279, 299
14	78, 156, 272, 274, 275, 279, 286, 287, 294, 297-303, 305-309, 312, 315-17, 319, 321, 330, 332, 334, 336
14.1-10	282
14.1-4	278, 280, 297
14.1	273, 279, 299
14.2-10	286
14.2-3	280, 302, 304
14.2	281, 282
14.3	279, 280, 303-305, 307
14.4	280, 301, 303
14.5-6	281
14.5	281, 282
14.6-10	275, 282
14.6-9	300
14.6	281
14.7	283
14.8-9	297
14.9	300
14.10	273, 279, 283-85, 289, 301, 302
14.11-36	289
14.11-25	278
14.11-20	317
14.11-19	284
14.11	300
14.13-14	281
14.20-25	282
14.20-35	282, 283
14.21	284
14.21-22	300, 332
14.22	299, 319
14.22-23	282, 300
14.23-33	286
14.23-27	284
14.23	300
14.24	275, 283
14.25	302
14.26-35	282, 284
14.27-28	284
14.28-35	285, 302, 304

Numbers (cont.)
14.28-34 293, 294
14.28-29 304
14.29-33 275
14.29 304, 306, 308
14.30 275, 283
14.31-34 284
14.31-33 305
14.31 305
14.32-33 304
14.32 308
14.33 308, 331
14.34 284, 293, 296
14.35 285, 304
14.36-38 275, 285, 289, 293
14.36-37 283
14.37 284
14.39-45 274, 278, 279, 284, 285, 289, 300
14.39 273, 280
14.40-45 280, 285
14.40 273
14.42-43 300
14.42 300
15 330-34, 336, 337
15.2 331, 332
15.18 331, 332
15.32-36 231
15.37-41 330, 333, 337, 338
15.38-41 209
15.38 332
15.39-41 331
15.39-40 332
15.39 331
15.41 332
16 187, 274, 284
16.1-11 282
16.1-2 275
16.3 187, 274, 280, 286, 287, 290, 323
16.4 281
16.5-7 290
16.5 288
16.6-10 275
16.9 288
16.10 288
16.12-15 282, 287
16.13 303
16.16-19 282, 286
16.16-17 287
16.17 288
16.18 287
16.20-22 282
16.22 281
16.24-33 282
16.26-34 285
16.27 306
16.28-30 287
16.29-35 289
16.34 279, 282, 289, 295, 333
16.35 282, 285, 286, 288
16–17 279, 280, 282, 283, 286-89, 291-96, 308, 333-35
17 294
17.2-3 290
17.3 288
17.4 288
17.6-15 285, 286, 289
17.6 279, 282, 289, 295, 333
17.10 281
17.12 289
17.16-28 282, 285
17.16-26 287, 288, 289
17.16-23 286
17.25 288
17.26 289, 290, 295
17.27-28 279, 282, 284, 288-91, 293-96, 308, 316, 333, 337, 338
17.27 333
17.28 288, 289
18 262
18.3 289
18.5 289
18.7 289
18.31-33 262
18–20 262
19.15 192
20 301
20.1-13 311
20.3 302
20.4 303
20.6 281
20.12 301
21 274
21.1–25.19 259
21.1 259
21.5 303
25 274
26 278
27 278, 282, 287, 312
27.10-15 181
27.12-23 181
27.15-23 161, 268, 295
27.16-23 57
27.20 267
27.21-22 181
31.9 305
31.17-18 305
32 278, 306
32.16-17 305
34 278

Deuteronomy
1.9-17 248
1.9-18 247
1.12 253

1.22-23 296
1.25-26 299
1.27-28 299
1.29-31 297
1.36 299
1.39 305
1.39-30 297
2.34 305
3 124
3.6 305
3.19 305
4 329, 330
5.22-31 74
9–10 117
9.12-14 65
9.12-21 144
9.16-21 117
9.22 260
16.1 231
20.1 298
20.14 305
30.6-8 149
30.6 148
30.11-14 148
32.44 282
34 25, 29
34.1-6 25
34.1 25

Joshua
1 124
7.6 281

Judges
6.32 282
6.34 282
15.18 288
18.21 305, 306
20.23 263
21.10 305

1 Samuel
4.12 281
8.21 263

2 Samuel
1.2 281
7.6 74
13.31 281
13.31-33 281
15.22 305, 306
15.32 281

1 Kings
2.9 267
2.15 267
5.17-19 175
5.27 123
6.1-38 123
6–7 124
7.13-14 122, 123
7.40-50 123
7.46-50 123
8 123, 153
8.3-4 152, 153
8.3-11 152
8.4 152
8.5-9 152
8.10-11 152
8.11 113
8.14-21 203
8.27 104
8.54-61 203
12.26-33 67
18 176, 177, 179
19 25, 26, 28, 29, 33, 61, 99, 105, 109, 115, 119, 136-39, 172, 175-81, 183, 222, 319
19.1 176
19.3-13 90, 96
19.3-5 61
19.3 28
19.5-7 179
19.5-6 179
19.5 138
19.7 61
19.8-9 30, 61
19.8 31
19.9 27, 115, 138
19.10 177, 179
19.11-13 28, 61, 157, 177
19.11-12 138, 222
19.11 31, 61, 115, 138, 157, 177
19.12 138
19.13-18 177
19.13 115, 138
19.14 177, 179
19.15-18 177
19.15 61
19.16 177
19.19-21 177, 178

2 Kings
2 180, 181
2.1-15 179
2.9-10 179
2.10 180
2.12 180
2.15 179
5 183
19.35 309
23.21 231

1 Chronicles
22 124
22 128
22 175
22.7-9 137
22.7-13 124, 175
28–29 124, 128, 174, 180, 181
28 124, 125, 137, 175, 177
28.2-3 124, 175
28.3 137
28.9-10 176
28.12 137, 175
28.19 137, 175
28.20 176
29 124, 125,

1 Chronicles (cont.)
136, 137
29.1-19 175
29.1-5 124
29.5-8 124
29.5 124
29.6 124
29.9 124
29.14 124
29.17 124
29.18 124
29.19 124

2 Chronicles
5.14 113
7.2 113
20.1-2 297
20.1-29 297
20.14-17 297
20.20 297
20.20-21 300
20.22-23 297
20.24-25 309
20.26-28 297
20.29 297
30.1-3 233
34.27 263

Ezra
6.16-26 213, 233

Nehemiah
2.17 148
7.1-9 217
7.5 148
9.17 280

Job
1.20 281
42.1-6 84
42.1-10 84
42.7-10 84
42.10 84

Psalms
15 102, 108, 109, 320
15.1 104
24 31, 102, 104-10, 115, 117, 119, 142, 149, 153, 155, 320
24.1-2 108
24.3 31, 103-105, 108
24.3-6 102-104, 108
24.3-10 102, 103, 151
24.4-5 108
24.6 81, 105
24.7 103, 105
24.7-10 31, 81, 102-105, 108
24.9 103, 105
42 38, 320
43.3-4 320
51.12 148
68 151, 153
68.12 249
68.16-18 99, 151, 153
68.16 151
68.17 151
68.18 151-53
105.15 276
135 248

Proverbs
2.16 198
5.3 198
5.20 198

Ecclesiastes
1.13 331

Isaiah
3.16-26 77
3.18-26 77
3.18 77
3.26 77
6 38
8.1 67
24.5-13 118
28.7-08 118
33.14-16 102, 108, 109, 320
33.14 104, 107
34.3 309
60.17 67
66.24 309

Jeremiah
24.7-10 148
31.27-34 148
31.31-34 149
31.40 309
33.5 309

Ezekiel
6.5 309
9.6 305
11.17-21 148
11.19-20 149
16.15-21 118
20 117
23.35 331
36.22-32 148
36.26-27 149
43.7 309
43.7-8 146
43.7-11 146
43.9 146, 309
43.10 146
43.11 146

Amos
8.3 309
9.7 269

Nahum
3.3 309

Habakkuk
3.4 168

INDEX OF AUTHORS

Alter, R. 14, 21
Aurelius, E. 26, 66, 69, 70, 84, 260, 262, 264

Barstad, H.M. 11
Barton, J. 17
Beyerlin, W. 108
Blum, E. 13, 19, 30, 32, 36, 100, 159, 166, 168, 192, 209, 247, 248, 251, 264, 269, 321
Booji, T. 22, 23, 25
Braun, R. 124, 128, 175
Brichto, H.C. 17-19, 46, 72, 73, 82, 83, 166, 168
Bronner, L. 26
Budd, P.J. 209, 213, 216, 218, 219, 222, 223, 226, 228, 229, 231, 235, 258-60, 274, 281, 289, 326, 329, 331

Cassuto, U. 60, 71, 74, 76, 77, 113, 129, 131, 154, 190, 247, 250, 253, 255
Childs, B.S. 17, 25, 33, 44-47, 58, 63, 67, 69, 70, 73, 83, 84, 91, 113, 129, 149, 159, 167, 169, 179, 247, 248, 260-62, 264, 296, 298
Clines, D.J.A. 15, 17, 102
Coats, G.W. 26, 46, 168, 179, 211, 247, 256, 259-62, 264, 279, 296, 303
Cody, A. 68
Cogan, M. 179
Conrad, E.W. 297
Crüsemann, F. 249

DeVries, S.J. 124, 137, 138, 152, 177, 178, 298
Dozemann, T.B. 12, 13, 21-26, 31, 34, 36, 37, 59, 69, 100, 108, 131, 135, 153, 154, 240, 241, 250
Durham, J.I. 37, 47, 48, 54, 66, 72, 81-83, 93, 101, 113, 117, 131, 169, 190, 247, 253, 260, 264

Eichhorn, D. 26
Eissfeldt, O. 47
Elliger, K. 202, 203

Fretheim, T.E. 150, 153
Fritz, V. 259, 260

Gottwald, N.K. 15
Gray, G.B. 225
Gregory, R. 33, 179
Gunneweg, A.H.J. 68

Haran, M. 42, 74, 76, 81, 152, 159, 167, 218
Hauge, M.R. 11, 26, 38, 146, 155, 287, 319, 320
Hauser, A.J. 26, 33, 176, 179
Hurowitz, V. 121, 122, 124, 152, 175

Jacobsen, T. 145
Jeremias, J. 26, 39, 138
Jonker, L.C. 17

Kapelrud, A.S. 121, 136
Kearney, P.J. 37, 53, 63, 66, 74, 75, 81, 117, 129, 161
Kiuchi, N. 196, 198, 202, 229
Knierim, R. 248, 253
Koch, K. 64, 102, 123, 194, 202, 203

Lacocque, A. 15, 16, 295
Lemche, N.P. 15, 329
Levine, B. 121, 123, 125, 144, 187, 213, 216, 218, 219, 228, 235, 243, 268, 271, 272, 278-81, 287, 289, 304, 331
Loewenstamm, S.E. 145

McCarthy, D.J. 124, 128, 175, 251, 296
Milgrom, J. 113, 154, 163, 192-94, 197, 198, 202-204, 212, 228, 229
Moberly, R.W.L. 17, 19, 27, 34, 36, 37, 47, 54, 63, 67, 71-74, 76, 77, 81-83, 91, 94, 117, 118, 131, 133, 159, 165, 166, 168, 169
Mowinckel, S. 26, 103, 105

Nicholson, E.W. 25, 30, 44, 47, 100
Nordheim, E. von 33, 176, 179-81
Noth, M. 194, 203, 229, 253, 258, 259, 284, 289

Olson, D.T. 20, 211, 213, 231, 259, 275, 278, 303, 304, 317, 326, 327, 330, 337

Porter, J.R. 203

Rad, G. von 329
Rendorff, R. 11, 194

Schmid, R. 69
Smith, M.S. 12, 17-20, 24, 27, 100-102, 113, 118, 319
Steck, O.H. 176
Sternberg, M. 13, 21, 48
Stone, L. 18

Tadmor, H. 179
Thompson, T.L. 12, 24, 100
Travers, P.L. 24

Utschneider, H. 12, 24, 100-102, 123, 124, 126, 127, 133, 146-48, 150, 240, 241, 326

Van Seters, J. 12, 13, 22, 23, 25, 31, 35, 46, 65, 67-69, 71, 73, 74, 82-84, 88, 89, 117, 149, 159, 166-69, 211, 247, 248, 253, 260, 262-65, 269, 271, 278, 304, 329
Vaulx, J. de 209, 213, 216, 219, 223, 226, 228, 229, 231, 235, 258, 260,, 278, 281, 289, 331

Weisman, Z. 267
Wenham, G.J. 331
Whybray, R.N. 11, 13, 14
Wilcoxen, J.A. 14, 15, 102, 211, 259, 262, 276, 324, 325, 327

JOURNAL FOR THE STUDY OF THE OLD TESTAMENT
SUPPLEMENT SERIES

164 Lyle Eslinger, *House of God or House of David: The Rhetoric of 2 Samuel 7*
165 Martin McNamara, *The Psalms in the Early Irish Church*
166 D.R.G. Beattie and M.J. McNamara (eds.), *The Aramaic Bible: Targums in their Historical Context*
167 Raymond F. Person, Jr, *Second Zechariah and the Deuteronomic School*
168 R.N. Whybray, *The Composition of the Book of Proverbs*
169 Bert Dicou, *Edom, Israel's Brother and Antagonist: The Role of Edom in Biblical Prophecy and Story*
170 Wilfred G.E. Watson, *Traditional Techniques in Classical Hebrew Verse*
171 Henning Graf Reventlow, Yair Hoffman and Benjamin Uffenheimer (eds.), *Politics and Theopolitics in the Bible and Postbiblical Literature*
172 Volkmar Fritz, *An Introduction to Biblical Archaeology*
173 M. Patrick Graham, William P. Brown and Jeffrey K. Kuan (eds.), *History and Interpretation: Essays in Honour of John H. Hayes*
174 Joe M. Sprinkle, *'The Book of the Covenant': A Literary Approach*
175 Tamara C. Eskenazi and Kent H. Richards (eds.), *Second Temple Studies: 2 Temple and Community in the Persian Period*
176 Gershon Brin, *Studies in Biblical Law: From the Hebrew Bible to the Dead Sea Scrolls*
177 David Allan Dawson, *Text-Linguistics and Biblical Hebrew*
178 Martin Ravndal Hauge, *Between Sheol and Temple: Motif Structure and Function in the I-Psalms*
179 J.G. McConville and J.G. Millar, *Time and Place in Deuteronomy*
180 Richard L. Schultz, *The Search for Quotation: Verbal Parallels in the Prophets*
181 Bernard M. Levinson (ed.), *Theory and Method in Biblical and Cuneiform Law: Revision, Interpolation and Development*
182 Steven L. McKenzie and M. Patrick Graham (eds.), *The History of Israel's Traditions: The Heritage of Martin Noth*
183 William Robertson Smith, *Lectures on the Religion of the Semites (Second and Third Series)*
184 John C. Reeves and John Kampen (eds.), *Pursuing the Text: Studies in Honor of Ben Zion Wacholder on the Occasion of his Seventieth Birthday*
185 Seth Daniel Kunin, *The Logic of Incest: A Structuralist Analysis of Hebrew Mythology*
186 Linda Day, *Three Faces of a Queen: Characterization in the Books of Esther*
187 Charles V. Dorothy, *The Books of Esther: Structure, Genre and Textual Integrity*
188 Robert H. O'Connell, *Concentricity and Continuity: The Literary Structure of Isaiah*

189 William Johnstone (ed.), *William Robertson Smith: Essays in Reassessment*
190 Steven W. Holloway and Lowell K. Handy (eds.), *The Pitcher is Broken: Memorial Essays for Gösta W. Ahlström*
191 Magne Sæbø, *On the Way to Canon: Creative Tradition History in the Old Testament*
192 Henning Graf Reventlow and William Farmer (eds.), *Biblical Studies and the Shifting of Paradigms, 1850–1914*
193 Brooks Schramm, *The Opponents of Third Isaiah: Reconstructing the Cultic History of the Restoration*
194 Else Kragelund Holt, *Prophesying the Past: The Use of Israel's History in the Book of Hosea*
195 Jon Davies, Graham Harvey and Wilfred G.E. Watson (eds.), *Words Remembered, Texts Renewed: Essays in Honour of John F.A. Sawyer*
196 Joel S. Kaminsky, *Corporate Responsibility in the Hebrew Bible*
197 William M. Schniedewind, *The Word of God in Transition: From Prophet to Exegete in the Second Temple Period*
198 T.J. Meadowcroft, *Aramaic Daniel and Greek Daniel: A Literary Comparison*
199 J.H. Eaton, *Psalms of the Way and the Kingdom: A Conference with the Commentators*
200 M. Daniel Carroll R., David J.A. Clines and Philip R. Davies (eds.), *The Bible in Human Society: Essays in Honour of John Rogerson*
201 John W. Rogerson, *The Bible and Criticism in Victorian Britain: Profiles of F.D. Maurice and William Robertson Smith*
202 Nanette Stahl, *Law and Liminality in the Bible*
203 Jill M. Munro, *Spikenard and Saffron: The Imagery of the Song of Songs*
204 Philip R. Davies, *Whose Bible Is It Anyway?*
205 David J.A. Clines, *Interested Parties: The Ideology of Writers and Readers of the Hebrew Bible*
206 Møgens Müller, *The First Bible of the Church: A Plea for the Septuagint*
207 John W. Rogerson, Margaret Davies and M. Daniel Carroll R. (eds.), *The Bible in Ethics: The Second Sheffield Colloquium*
208 Beverly J. Stratton, *Out of Eden: Reading, Rhetoric, and Ideology in Genesis 2–3*
209 Patricia Dutcher-Walls, *Narrative Art, Political Rhetoric: The Case of Athaliah and Joash*
210 Jacques Berlinerblau, *The Vow and the 'Popular Religious Groups' of Ancient Israel: A Philological and Sociological Inquiry*
211 Brian E. Kelly, *Retribution and Eschatology in Chronicles*
212 Yvonne Sherwood, *The Prostitute and the Prophet: Hosea's Marriage in Literary-Theoretical Perspective*
213 Yair Hoffman, *A Blemished Perfection: The Book of Job in Context*
214 Roy F. Melugin and Marvin A. Sweeney (eds.), *New Visions of Isaiah*
215 J. Cheryl Exum, *Plotted, Shot and Painted: Cultural Representations of Biblical Women*

216 Judith E. McKinlay, *Gendering Wisdom the Host: Biblical Invitations to Eat and Drink*
217 Jerome F.D. Creach, *Yahweh as Refuge and the Editing of the Hebrew Psalter*
218 Harry P. Nasuti, *Defining the Sacred Songs: Genre, Tradition, and the Post-Critical Interpretation of the Psalms*
219 Gerald Morris, *Prophecy, Poetry and Hosea*
220 Raymond F. Person, Jr, *In Conversation with Jonah: Conversation Analysis, Literary Criticism, and the Book of Jonah*
221 Gillian Keys, *The Wages of Sin: A Reappraisal of the 'Succession Narrative'*
222 R.N. Whybray, *Reading the Psalms as a Book*
223 Scott B. Noegel, *Janus Parallelism in the Book of Job*
224 Paul J. Kissling, *Reliable Characters in the Primary History: Profiles of Moses, Joshua, Elijah and Elisha*
225 Richard D. Weis and David M. Carr (eds.), *A Gift of God in Due Season: Essays on Scripture and Community in Honor of James A. Sanders*
226 Lori L. Rowlett, *Joshua and the Rhetoric of Violence: A New Historicist Analysis*
227 John F.A. Sawyer (ed.), *Reading Leviticus: Responses to Mary Douglas*
228 Volkmar Fritz and Philip R. Davies (eds.), *The Origins of the Ancient Israelite States*
229 Stephen Breck Reid (ed.), *Prophets and Paradigms: Essays in Honor of Gene M. Tucker*
230 Kevin J. Cathcart and Michael Maher (eds.), *Targumic and Cognate Studies: Essays in Honour of Martin McNamara*
231 Weston W. Fields, *Sodom and Gomorrah: History and Motif in Biblical Narrative*
232 Tilde Binger, *Asherah: Goddesses in Ugarit, Israel and the Old Testament*
233 Michael D. Goulder, *The Psalms of Asaph and the Pentateuch: Studies in the Psalter, III*
234 Ken Stone, *Sex, Honor, and Power in the Deuteronomistic History*
235 James W. Watts and Paul House (eds.), *Forming Prophetic Literature: Essays on Isaiah and the Twelve in Honor of John D.W. Watts*
236 Thomas M. Bolin, *Freedom beyond Forgiveness: The Book of Jonah Re-examined*
237 Neil Asher Silberman and David B. Small (eds.), *The Archaeology of Israel: Constructing the Past, Interpreting the Present*
238 M. Patrick Graham, Kenneth G. Hoglund and Steven L. McKenzie (eds.), *The Chronicler as Historian*
239 Mark S. Smith, *The Pilgrimage Pattern in Exodus*
240 Eugene E. Carpenter (ed.), *A Biblical Itinerary: In Search of Method, Form and Content. Essays in Honor of George W. Coats*
241 Robert Karl Gnuse, *No Other Gods: Emergent Monotheism in Israel*
242 K.L. Noll, *The Faces of David*
243 Henning Graf Reventlow (ed.), *Eschatology in the Bible and in Jewish and Christian Tradition*

244 Walter E. Aufrecht, Neil A. Mirau and Steven W. Gauley (eds.), *Urbanism in Antiquity: From Mesopotamia to Crete*
245 Lester L. Grabbe (ed.), *Can a 'History of Israel' Be Written?*
246 Gillian M. Bediako, *Primal Religion and the Bible: William Robertson Smith and his Heritage*
247 Nathan Klaus, *Pivot Patterns in the Former Prophets*
248 Etienne Nodet, *A Search for the Origins of Judaism: From Joshua to the Mishnah*
249 William Paul Griffin, *The God of the Prophets: An Analysis of Divine Action*
250 Josette Elayi and Jean Sapin, *Beyond the River: New Perspectives on Transeuphratene*
251 Flemming A.J. Nielsen, *The Tragedy in History: Herodotus and the Deuteronomistic History*
252 David C. Mitchell, *The Message of the Psalter: An Eschatological Programme in the Book of Psalms*
253 William Johnstone, *1 and 2 Chronicles, Volume 1: 1 Chronicles 1–2 Chronicles 9: Israel's Place among the Nations*
254 William Johnstone, *1 and 2 Chronicles, Volume 2: 2 Chronicles 10–36: Guilt and Atonement*
255 Larry L. Lyke, *King David with the Wise Woman of Tekoa: The Resonance of Tradition in Parabolic Narrative*
256 Roland Meynet, *Rhetorical Analysis: An Introduction to Biblical Rhetoric*
257 Philip R. Davies and David J.A. Clines (eds.), *The World of Genesis: Persons, Places, Perspectives*
258 Michael D. Goulder, *The Psalms of the Return (Book V, Psalms 107–150): Studies in the Psalter, IV*
259 Allen Rosengren Petersen, *The Royal God: Enthronement Festivals in Ancient Israel and Ugarit?*
260 A.R. Pete Diamond, Kathleen M. O'Connor and Louis Stulman (eds.), *Troubling Jeremiah*
261 Othmar Keel, *Goddesses and Trees, New Moon and Yahweh: Ancient Near Eastern Art and the Hebrew Bible*
262 Victor H. Matthews, Bernard M. Levinson and Tikva Frymer-Kensky (eds.), *Gender and Law in the Hebrew Bible and the Ancient Near East*
263 M. Patrick Graham and Steven L. McKenzie, *The Chronicler as Author: Studies in Text and Texture*
264 Donald F. Murray, *Divine Prerogative and Royal Pretension: Pragmatics, Poetics, and Polemics in a Narrative Sequence about David (2 Samuel 5.17–7.29)*
265 John Day, *Yahweh and the Gods and Goddesses of Canaan*
266 J. Cheryl Exum and Stephen D. Moore (eds.), *Biblical Studies/Cultural Studies: The Third Sheffield Colloquium*
267 Patrick D. Miller, Jr, *Israelite Religion and Biblical Theology: Collected Essays*

268 Linda S. Schearing and Steven L. McKenzie (eds.), *Those Elusive Deuteronomists: 'Pandeuteronomism' and Scholarship in the Nineties*
269 David J.A. Clines and Stephen D. Moore (eds.), *Auguries: The Jubilee Volume of the Sheffield Department of Biblical Studies*
270 John Day (ed.), *King and Messiah in Israel and the Ancient Near East: Proceedings of the Oxford Old Testament Seminar*
271 Wonsuk Ma, *Until the Spirit Comes: The Spirit of God in the Book of Isaiah*
272 James Richard Linville, *Israel in the Book of Kings: The Past as a Project of Social Identity*
273 Meir Lubetski, Claire Gottlieb and Sharon Keller (eds.), *Boundaries of the Ancient Near Eastern World: A Tribute to Cyrus H. Gordon*
274 Martin J. Buss, *Biblical Form Criticism in its Context*
275 William Johnstone, *Chronicles and Exodus: An Analogy and its Application*
276 Raz Kletter, *Economic Keystones: The Weight System of the Kingdom of Judah*
277 Augustine Pagolu, *The Religion of the Patriarchs*
278 Lester L. Grabbe (ed.), *Leading Captivity Captive: 'The Exile' as History and Ideology*
279 Kari Latvus, *God, Anger and Ideology: The Anger of God in Joshua and Judges in Relation to Deuteronomy and the Priestly Writings*
280 Eric S. Christianson, *A Time to Tell: Narrative Strategies in Ecclesiastes*
281 Peter D. Miscall, *Isaiah 34–35: A Nightmare/A Dream*
282 Joan E. Cook, *Hannah's Desire, God's Design: Early Interpretations in the Story of Hannah*
283 Kelvin Friebel, *Jeremiah's and Ezekiel's Sign-Acts: Rhetorical Nonverbal Communication*
284 M. Patrick Graham, Rick R. Marrs and Steven L. McKenzie (eds.), *Worship and the Hebrew Bible: Essays in Honor of John T. Willis*
285 Paolo Sacchi, *History of the Second Temple*
286 Wesley J. Bergen, *Elisha and the End of Prophetism*
287 Anne Fitzpatrick-McKinley, *The Transformation of Torah from Scribal Advice to Law*
288 Diana Lipton, *Revisions of the Night: Politics and Promises in the Patriarchal Dreams of Genesis*
289 Jože Krašovec (ed.), *The Interpretation of the Bible: The International Symposium in Slovenia*
290 Frederick H. Cryer and Thomas L. Thompson (eds.), *Qumran between the Old and New Testaments*
291 Christine Schams, *Jewish Scribes in the Second-Temple Period*
292 David J.A. Clines, *On the Way to the Postmodern: Old Testament Essays, 1967–1998 Volume 1*
293 David J.A. Clines, *On the Way to the Postmodern: Old Testament Essays, 1967–1998 Volume 2*
294 Charles E. Carter, *The Emergence of Yehud in the Persian Period: A Social and Demographic Study*

295 Jean-Marc Heimerdinger, *Topic, Focus and Foreground in Ancient Hebrew Narratives*
296 Mark Cameron Love, *The Evasive Text: Zechariah 1–8 and the Frustrated Reader*
297 Paul S. Ash, *David, Solomon and Egypt: A Reassessment*
298 John D. Baildam, *Paradisal Love: Johann Gottfried Herder and the Song of Songs*
299 M. Daniel Carroll R., *Rethinking Contexts, Rereading Texts: Contributions from the Social Sciences to Biblical Interpretation*
300 Edward Ball (ed.), *In Search of True Wisdom: Essays in Old Testament Interpretation in Honour of Ronald E. Clements*
301 Carolyn S. Leeb, *Away from the Father's House: The Social Location of na'ar and na'arah in Ancient Israel*
302 Xuan Huong Thi Pham, *Mourning in the Ancient Near East and the Hebrew Bible*
303 Ingrid Hjelm, *The Samaritans and Early Judaism: A Literary Analysis*
304 Wolter H. Rose, *Zemah and Zerubabbel: Messianic Expectations in the Early Postexilic Period*
305 Jo Bailey Wells, *God's Holy People: A Theme in Biblical Theology*
306 Albert de Pury, Thomas Römer and Jean-Daniel Macchi (eds.), *Israel Constructs its History: Deuteronomistic Historiography in Recent Research*
307 Robert L. Cole, *The Shape and Message of Book III (Psalms 73–89)*
308 Yiu-Wing Fung, *Victim and Victimizer: Joseph's Interpretation of his Destiny*
309 George Aichele (ed.), *Culture, Entertainment and the Bible*
310 Esther Fuchs, *Sexual Politics in the Biblical Narrative: Reading the Hebrew Bible as a Woman*
311 Gregory Glazov, *The Bridling of the Tongue and the Opening of the Mouth in Biblical Prophecy*
312 Francis Landy, *Beauty and the Enigma: And Other Essays on the Hebrew Bible*
314 Bernard S. Jackson, *Studies in the Semiotics of Biblical Law*
315 Paul R. Williamson, *Abraham, Israel and the Nations: The Patriarchal Promise and its Covenantal Development in Genesis*
317 Lester L. Grabbe (ed.), *Did Moses Speak Attic? Jewish Historiography and Scripture in the Hellenistic Period*
320 Claudia V. Camp, *Wise, Strange and Holy: The Strange Woman and the Making of the Bible*
321 Varese Layzer, *Signs of Weakness: Juxtaposing Irish Tales and the Bible*
323 Martin Ravndal Hauge, *The Descent from the Mountain: Narrative Patterns in Exodus 19–40*
324 P.M. Michèle Daviau, John W. Wevers and Michael Weigl (eds.), *The World of the Aramaeans: Studies in Honour of Paul-Eugène Dion*, Volume 1
325 P.M. Michèle Daviau, John W. Wevers and Michael Weigl (eds.), *The World of the Aramaeans: Studies in Honour of Paul-Eugène Dion*, Volume 2